D0941251

Broncho Billy and the Essanay Film Company

Broncho Billy and the Essanay Film Company

and
the

David Kiehn

Farwell Books   Berkeley

Farwell Books
Box 14792
Berkeley, California 94712
farwellbks@earthlink.net

ISBN 0-9729226-5-2
Library of Congress Control Number: 2003091440

Manufactured in the United States of America

First Edition

To Helen

Acknowledgments

This book began with a visit to Niles, after all these years, still a place that fascinates and inspires. I'm indebted to the community for help and encouragement, particularly the Niles Main Street Association and Bruce Cates, whose energy and enthusiasm I continue to admire. Bruce, along with Janet Pessagno, John Mack Flanagan and Irene Vincent Perez were among the founders of the Broncho Billy Silent Film Festival in Niles, an annual event that has given me some valuable leads and friendships. I'm also grateful to Dr. Robert B. Fisher and his efforts to preserve the history of Washington Township; he saved when others threw away, and without him much would be lost. He's my hero. Another champion of history is Geoffrey Bell, author of *The Golden Gate and the Silver Screen*. His pioneering work on silent film production in the San Francisco Bay Area remains valuable, and was the first source I went to for information about Broncho Billy and Essanay. He died in 1990, but fortunately his research papers are preserved at the Bancroft Library.

I thank the Bancroft staff for its help, especially Iris Donovan and David Kessler. Ned Comstock at the University of Southern California Cinema-Television Library was always very helpful. So was Faye Thompson and Howard Prouty in Special Collections at the Academy of Motion Picture Arts and Sciences Margaret Herrick Library, as well as the general staff. Thanks to Sandi Pantages and Barbara Baxter of the Alameda County Library in Fremont, Beth Werling and John Cahoon at the Los Angeles County Museum of Natural History, Bryony Dixon and Kathleen Dickson at the British Film Institute, Patrick Loughney, Rosemary Haines and Zoran Sinobad of the Library of Congress Motion Picture, Broadcasting and Recorded Sound Division, Mary Corliss of the Museum of Modern Art Stills Archive, Rob Stone and Jere Guldin at the UCLA Film and Television Archive, Sally White, Museum/Cultural Outreach Coordinator of Morrison, Colorado, Sally West at the San Diego Historical Society, Linda Barth of the Los Angeles Parks and Recreation Department, Lucy Kortum and Mert Doss at the Petaluma Historical Museum/Library, the California State Library, the Stanford Library, the Sonoma County Library in Santa Rosa, Marin County Free Library, the Santa Monica Public Library, California State University Hayward Library, Dr. Martin Luther King, Jr. Main Library in San Jose, San Francisco State University J. Paul Leonard Library, San Francisco Public Library, the Denver Public Library, Oakland Public Library, Berkeley Public Library, San Rafael Public Library, Lionel Ashcroft and the late Bill Allen of the Marin County Historical Society, Jeff Rankin at the UCLA Special Collections University Research Library, the whole staff at the Pacific Film Archive in Berkeley, Thomas Burdett at the University of Texas at El Paso S.

L. A. Marshall Military History Collection, Kate Guyonvarch at Association Chaplin, Colorado Historical Society, Robert C. Myers and the Berrien County Historical Association, Chicago Historical Society, Chicago Public Library, Golden Public Library, the California Historical Society and Regina Dennie, Jill Singleton and Velma Valencia at the Museum of Local History in Fremont.

In particular, I want to thank the board of directors for the Museum of Local History and the Niles Essanay Silent Film Museum for their help in making this book possible, and invite readers to their websites: www.museumoflocalhistory.org and http://nilesfilmmuseum.org.

My sincere appreciation to Diana Serra Cary for her compassion and assistance. A special thanks to William Sagar and the Fairfax Historical Society. I thank Harry A. Avila for his genuine interest in the project. Kevin Brownlow generously sent pages of leads to follow, and transcripts of interviews with Francis X. Bushman and Helen Ferguson. Robert S. Birchard was extremely helpful with his knowledge of westerns and the people who made them. Samuel A. Gill was endlessly supportive, kind and generous. Les and Eleanor Thomsen provided help and kindness that was inspirational. David Shepard was invaluable. Stuart Nixon effortlessly recalled his early research on Essanay when he was publisher and editor of the *Township Register,* and gave me added insight that I couldn't have gotten elsewhere. I'm deeply appreciative to Phil Holmes for his on-going support.

So many people have helped more than they can know: Karen Cates, David Caldwell, Cameron McCauley, the late Georgia Chalmers Wagner, Larry Telles, Richard Asimus, Larry Epstein, Sprague Anderson, John Avila, Nicki Bouton, Carrie Carruthers, Dale Carpenter, Jan Doyle, Bonnie Davis, Donna Ewald, the late Bob Sanborn, Ron Fimrite, David Fleishhacker, Bob Garcia, Miles Kreuger, Don Dewey, David Minkow, Mark Vieira, Bob Thomas, Anita Garcia Stubinger, Ken Swartz of KRON-TV, Diane MacIntyre of the Silents Majority, Kathleen McKinley, Conan Knoll and Alex Rosenburg of the *Fremont Argus,* Bonnie McCourt, Laurel McCoy, Kely McKeown, Steve Pool, Nadine Fawver, Russell Merritt, Hooman Mehran, Dorothy Bradley, Irene Vincent Perez, Larry Telles, Woody Minor, Luther Hathcock, Nancy Newlin, Gary Corter, Don Stow, the late Bernard Price, Larry Nelson, Donald Parkhurst, the late Ray Hubbard, Jack Parry, Judy Peeler, Jordan Young, G. Bates Creel, Leontine Rose, Edwina Hobbs, Tony and Brenda Hall, Susan Richardson for her efforts to get me a copy of the Belvoir Hotel register, Bill Rebello, Steve Rydzewski, Cole Johnson, Joe Moore, Richard Roberts, Brent Walker, Robb Farr, Joelle Sorensen, Marilyn Salmi, Chris Snowden, Steve Levin, Jack Tillmany, Neil Bolton, Marc Wanamaker, Bill Wulf and Wendy Winsted. Thanks also to Rita Roti for her encouragement early on.

I appreciate the help and information given to me by the following people, all of them direct links to the people who made the movies at Essanay: Arthur Abrott, Jack Abrott, Julie Aragon, Joyce Azevedo, John Bishop, Lorelei Brand, Susan Brandon, Charlie Champion, Tom Champion, Laura Brown-Cupell, David and Audrey Clark, Sheri Clinchard, Camille Craddock, Richard and Ruth Crizer, Roz Danielson, Erin Dealey, Eileen Dhuyvetter, Sheri Abrott Di Salvo, Sam Eakins,

Ernest Easterday, Christina Embody, Jackie Gates, Pat Goldberg, James Griffin, Robert Harned, Betty Spoor Hyde, Joyce Ilenstine, Ken Ilenstine, Allison Inkley, Larry Laurence, Barbara Leonard, Suzie Mayer, Patricia Mercer, Theo Overacker, Lorraine Owen, Beverly Padgett, Betsy Pembroke, Todd and Joan Peters, Dorothy Rose, Milly Rubiolo, Rielle Santinelli, Nancy Sargent, Edmund M. Scott, Walter Seebach, Diane Slakey, Rodna Hildebrand Shutes, Robert David Stone, Rollin Sturgeon Jr., David Sturgeon, Gerald Swanstrom, Judith Toomajian, David Totheroh, Jack and Marion Totheroh, Steve Totheroh, Fay McKenzie Waldman, Christopher Werlin, Grace Werlin, Davis West, Gene White, Richard White, June Williams and, especially, to True Boardman, who was there.

Finally, I wish to thank Helen Caswell, who made the first contact with most of the Essanay relatives; I am forever grateful for that and so much more. This book wouldn't exist without her.

Photographs

Courtesy of the Academy of Motion Picture Arts and Sciences: 83, 117, 175 bottom, 216, 222 top.

Harry A. Avila: 134 bottom, 136 top, 138 top, 142, 160 top, 163 top, 167 top, 173, 176, 179 bottom, 181, 202 top left, 222 bottom, 267 top, 279 bottom, 287, 295, 306.

Robert S. Birchard: xii top, 169 top, 236 top.

John Bishop: 80.

Bison Archives/Marc Wanamaker: xii bottom, 16, 24 bottom, 38 bottom, 68 top, 92 bottom, 116, 151, 160 bottom, 236 bottom.

True Boardman: 97, 166, 271 bottom.

Susan Brandon: 170.

Laura Brown-Cupell: 157.

California State Library: 95.

Dave and Audrey Clark: 17, 18 bottom, 20, 21, 24 top, 27 bottom, 36, 42 bottom, 43, 48, 54, 55, 59 bottom, 62, 63, 64, 71, 75, 82 top, 90, 91, 94, 103 right, 111 middle right, 131 bottom, 139 top, 156 bottom, 164 bottom, 214, 268 bottom, 274 bottom.

Richard Crizer: 109 bottom left, 110 bottom left & top left, 111 bottom left, 120 top, 123 left, 155 top, 168, 175 top, 190, 194 left, 198 top, 213, 218, 219, 281 bottom, 291.

The family of Charles Allen Dealey: 113, 126 bottom, 137 top, 143, 174, 178 bottom, 182, 197, 201, 202 top right & bottom, 210 bottom, 211 top, 221 top, 224, 225, 226 bottom, 230, 246, 277 top, 279 top, 283 top, endsheets.

Dr. Robert Fisher collection of the Museum of Local History, Fremont: 61, 79, 86, 88, 121, 149 bottom, 164 top, 180, 192, 240, 283 bottom left.

Contents

George K. Spoor.

Gilbert M. Anderson.

Introduction
"S" and "A"

Fame is fleeting. "Broncho Billy" Anderson is proof of that. But for every movie star, forgotten or not, who made millions of people laugh, cry or cheer, there were hundreds of people in the shadows who were only known by their colleagues. The art and industry of the movies became a powerful force in the first twenty years of the twentieth century because of the men and women on both sides of the camera. They were all pioneers, and recognition is long overdue.

Who were these pioneers? They were misfits, mavericks and risk-takers, but also craftspeople with skill and energy who borrowed from the past and created something new as they went along. Their success came in collaboration, under the umbrella of a film company. It all had to start somewhere.

One company, Essanay, began in 1907 with "S" and "A" — George Spoor and Gilbert Anderson. Spoor, thirty-five, had been active in film exhibition and distribution since 1896. Anderson, only twenty-seven, had packed an amazing amount of experience into four years as an actor, writer and director.

Anderson's real name was Max Aronson, born to Henry and Esther Aronson in Little Rock, Arkansas, on March 21, 1880. His family moved to St. Louis, Missouri, in 1883, and here, in his teens, he was an office clerk like older brothers Jerome, Edward and Nathaniel. At twenty, he was a cotton-buyer with brother-in-law Louis Roth in Pine Bluff, Arkansas, but Max didn't fit into a traditional way of life.[1] Although he had a way with words like his father (a dry goods salesman), he was more of a dreamer, a restless loner, a maverick with unshakeable belief in himself — he was also stage-struck. The theater was irresistible, an environment and lifestyle that called out to Max, so he enrolled in a St. Louis acting school.

The next logical step would have been to work in one of the many local theaters in St. Louis; instead, he recklessly headed for New York City, minus any professional experience to speak of, and went to Broadway. His first job in New York (the only job he could find), was in a minstrel show, hired to fill the stage as one of the "dummies." This meant he was to be seen, not heard. The catchy music, however, inspired him to sing, even though he couldn't carry a tune, and it threw off the tenor. Max was quickly hauled off-stage and fired on the spot.[2]

Other jobs followed, but not regularly. To make ends meet he posed for *Saturday Evening Post* illustrators Howard Chandler Christy, Harrison Fisher and F. X. Leyendecker. His future in theater looked bleak. As he observed years later: "I never was much of an actor, and I don't suppose I'd ever have become much of an actor if I had stuck to it. The best I ever got was sixty a week for playing juveniles, and I wasn't worth any more."[3]

These were kind words compared to the comments of theatrical agents. He remembered one agent, John Ince, in particular: "I asked him if there was anything doing, and he said, 'There's a lot doing, but not for you.'"[4] Ince suggested Aronson try the movies, and that was an insult.

Acting was considered an indecent profession by most of the general public, but even actors had little respect for the movies, although desperate poverty could modify that view. Using a stage name was one way actors protected themselves from the stigma of working in the theater, and this method of disguise carried over into movies. Taking on a stage name appealed to Max Aronson, and he pronounced himself George M. Anderson, then walked to the Edison film studio at 41 East Twenty-first Street, asked for work and was hired for fifty cents an hour to "pose" in movies.

Film acting in the early years was called "posing," a reference to modeling for photographs and lantern slides. The term wasn't completely inaccurate, even though moving pictures implied motion, because movies often included a tableau with actors freezing in a pose to imitate a famous painting or statue.

Edison sold two types of films: Class A and Class B. Class A films included *Uncle Tom's Cabin*, fourteen scenes in eighteen minutes of stage-bound action, with each scene illustrating a vignette of the story (including a tableau at the end). Class B films were more common, cheaper, simpler and often livelier — *Maypole Dance, Throwing the 16 Pound Hammer, Seashore Frolics, Elephants at Work, The Poachers, Falling Chimney*. The titles explained their content. Some lasted a minute, others stretched to five or six.[5]

Anderson's first appearance on the screen was in a Class B film, *What Happened in the Tunnel*.[6] He's seen sitting behind a woman and her black maid in a railroad coach. As the train enters a tunnel he tries to sneak a kiss, but the woman and maid switch seats in the darkness, and he kisses the maid instead, to his embarrassment and their laughter. Although the film was a novelty, only a minute long, it led to something bigger.

In October, 1903, soon after Anderson's arrival at Edison, preparations began for *The Great Train Robbery*. Edwin S. Porter, the man in charge of making this movie, could have shot it entirely at the Edison studio (as he'd recently done with *Uncle Tom's Cabin*) and used a painted, two-dimensional cutout to represent the train. But that August, Porter had made *A Romance of the Rail* with the cooperation of the Lackawanna Railroad, and he arranged to film the real thing again, in New Jersey, knowing this would add another dimension to his latest production.

In casting roles for the film, Porter turned to Anderson, who was an imposing six-foot tall, solidly built twenty-three-year-old with a long oval face, thick tangle of dark brown hair, prominent broken nose and piercing blue eyes. Porter saw him as a train robber, and asked the young man if he could ride a horse. Anderson said yes. It was a lie; Anderson knew nothing about horses, but the truth wasn't revealed until the cast and crew were transported to New Jersey early in November to shoot their first scenes.

Horses were selected at a local livery stable and everyone rode off to the location, everyone, that is, except Anderson: "Well, I started to mount my horse, and I heard some flunky in the back say, 'Hey, bud, I'd mount that horse from the other side if I were you!'

"I said, 'What's the difference?'

"'Mount from that side, and you'll find out.'

"So I found out that if you mount a horse from the wrong side he bucks you off."[7]

Anderson's trouble with the horse delayed him, and he couldn't catch up with the rest of the company. Dejected, he returned to New York alone. Fortunately, Porter forgave him, and Anderson wound up playing three different roles in the film: a train robber on foot, a man shot in the back during the robbery itself, and a tenderfoot in a saloon tap-dancing to gunfire at his feet.

After three or four days, filming was done and Porter assembled the footage. The week before Christmas, 1903, *The Great Train Robbery* made its debut at Huber's Museum, a low-class vaudeville house on Fourteenth Street in New York City. When the film was announced to the theater's usual patrons — pickpockets, prostitutes and drifters looking for a place to sleep — the crowd was indifferent. But when the movie began the audience came alive. Anderson was there: "I've seen some receptions to plays, but I've never seen such a reception to a picture in my life. They got up and shouted and yelled, and then when it was all over they yelled, 'Run it again! Run it again!' You couldn't get them out. They sat there two or three times, and finally they put on the lights to chase them out."[8]

After this success, *The Great Train Robbery* played at several New York theatres at once; the most important was Hammerstein's Theatre at 42nd and Broadway, which catered to a more sophisticated clientele. Anderson was "a little dubious about how it was going to go to that audience" so he went up to Hammerstein's to see it. When the picture was announced "the people got up and started to walk to the exits. Then it started and they looked back to see what was going on, and finally they stopped. And as it progressed they started to come back to their seats and sit down. As the picture went on you could hear a pin drop. Of course they weren't so demonstrative as down on 14th Street in the hobo district... They didn't yell, but they were mystified at it, and after it was over they all, in one acclaim, gave it a rousing, rousing reception. And I said to myself: that's it; it's going to be the picture business for me."[9]

Anderson was energized and wanted to make more story films of this caliber, but despite the overwhelming success of *The Great Train Robbery* nothing seemed to change at the Edison Company. Porter continued to make routine one- and two-minute films, and the adventurous projects favored by Anderson came few and far between. Sometimes there was no work at all. Anderson held his impatience in check for about five months, learned all he could, then he left.

Poverty forced him back to St. Louis in 1904. The next year he was back in New York with his younger sister Leona to try out a vaudeville act. That didn't go over, but Leona got work on her own singing in musicals.

In June, 1905, a touring company of the hit play, *Raffles, the Amateur Cracksman*, was finishing a successful run across the United States after a season on Broadway. The play was adapted from E. W. Hornung's popular short stories of a gentleman burglar, and Anderson thought this would be ideal for the movies. But he didn't take his concept to Porter at Edison; he chose instead to present it to a competitor in New York City, the American Vitagraph Company.

Vitagraph was owned and operated by three partners: Albert E. Smith, William T. Rock and J. Stuart Blackton. They had produced films in the 1890s, but a run-in with Edison over patent infringements curtailed that. They did, however, have one bargaining chip with Edison, a clever framing device on their Vitagraph projector, and because of this they were able to reach an agreement of sorts to stay in business by leasing their projectors and importing films for rental. Vitagraph, however, shied away from making story films again — until Anderson paid them a visit.

Anderson presented the idea of producing *Raffles* as a full-reel, seventeen-minute story film, and his connection to *The Great Train Robbery* gave weight to the proposal. The mere mention of his involvement with that money-making movie got their attention, and Anderson played up this calling card for all it was worth, convincing them to not only produce *Raffles,* but allow him to direct it.

The three partners revived a dormant division of their organization, The Vitagraph Company of America, and released *Raffles, the Amateur Cracksman* under that banner on September 23, 1905. The movie was a smash hit, and Anderson stayed on the payroll into the next year directing more than a dozen comedies and dramas at their rooftop studio on the Morton building, 116 Nassau Street, in New York City. Smith later testified: "On the strength of the success we had with this story and a few others that followed it, we bought a small plot of ground over in Brooklyn, and we built thereon a small studio."[10] With offices, laboratory, a glass-enclosed stage, Cooper-Hewitt lights and an electric power generator, it was an up-to-date movie studio in every respect, and signified that Vitagraph was now an important film producer.

But Anderson's speedy ride toward fame and fortune stalled abruptly on April 18, 1906. The earthquake and fire in San Francisco prompted everyone with a camera (including Albert E. Smith of Vitagraph) to film that ruined city, and anxious crowds flocked to movie theaters to see these images on the screen. A movie trade magazine ran a headline, "FRISCO FILMS — THE VITAGRAPH COMPANY'S BIG SUCCESS," and printed a dispatch: "It is now the 17th [of May] and we have been selling the films about two weeks. We have had a force working night and day, a double shift at double pay for overtime, to keep up with our work, and meet the demand upon us, and, in a business way, are well satisfied with the result."[11]

Vitagraph's laboratory was tied up for more than a month printing and developing earthquake footage, while Anderson stood by, helpless, unable to make narrative films. He became restless: "I didn't seem to be advancing, only as a producer, a director, making a paltry sum of money."[12] Motivated by frustration, Anderson decided that his success at Vitagraph entitled him to a partnership. When the partners rejected that idea, he quit.

In May, 1906, Anderson turned his back on New York and headed for Pittsburgh to meet with John Harris and Harry Davis, two enterprising businessmen.

Harris and Davis began a new era in movie exhibition when they opened the Nickelodeon Theater on June 19, 1905, in a storefront building on Smithfield Street.[13] Before this, films were usually seen in vaudeville houses at the end of each program, a signal to audiences that this was the last act, and it frequently chased the crowd away, clearing the theater for the next show. The Nickelodeon, however, turned this around, making movies attractive rather than repulsive, although it wasn't the first theater, by any means, devoted exclusively to movies. The difference was in the presentation. *Moving Picture World*, a movie trade magazine, described it: "The nickel place of amusement made its appearance with no greater blare of trumpets than the noise of its phonograph horn and the throaty persuasions of its barker.... It makes little difference what time of day you go to a 5-cent theater.... Each 'performance' lasts fifteen minutes. At the end of each a sign is thrown from the cinemagraph on the canvas announcing that those who came late may stay for the next 'performance.' Often they stay for several...the young men who sing the 'illustrated songs' are the only live performers in these theaters. The rest is moving pictures; and that is the startling part of the great favor with which these theaters have been received by the public.... They are great places for the foot-sore shopper, who is not used to cement sidewalks, to rest; and it took the aforesaid foot-sore shoppers about one minute to find this out: It is much more comfortable than to take street-car rides to rest, and they don't have to pay the return nickel.... In the congested districts the 5-cent theaters are proving a source of much innocent entertainment. The mothers do not have to 'dress' to attend them, and they take the children and spend many restful hours in them at very small expense."[14]

Nickel theaters sprang up everywhere: in 1906 there were hundreds of "nickelodeons," by 1907 there were thousands. In Pittsburgh alone more than a dozen theaters opened immediately, and Harris and Davis expanded their business into a chain of theaters in several cities. This is what brought Anderson to town.

Anderson knew that many films were being imported from Europe to meet the demand, and he thought Harris and Davis could cut costs by producing films in Pittsburgh for their own theaters, plus make even more money by renting to the ever-expanding market at large. The theater men were impressed by Anderson's credentials, especially his connection to *The Great Train Robbery* (which was still the most popular film around), and he was hired. But, after beginning the operation, Harris and Davis demanded movies of local events — newsreels in effect, not story films. Anderson wanted no part this, so he packed up and continued west, to Chicago.

Chicago, the rail transportation hub of the midwest, was a perfect place to distribute rental films, and, not surprisingly, competed successfully against New York City in that regard. But there was just one film producer in Chicago: William Selig, owner of the Selig Polyscope Company.

Selig manufactured movie projectors and made scenic films. The location of his office, however, at 43 Peck Court (one of the poorest sections in town), revealed his shaky financial condition. Anderson convinced Selig that, with nickel theaters desperate for story films, modestly produced movies could bring in enormous profits and turn his business around. Selig hired him.

Anderson made ten films in six months, and each one was released with liberal advertising. Business picked up. When the Chicago winter slowed down production, Anderson talked Selig into sending him west to Denver, Colorado, where Harry Buckwalter, Selig's longtime friend, could operate the camera for another string of films. There, Anderson and Buckwalter produced twelve films in one month.[15]

Anderson made comedies and dramas in Denver, but three westerns, *The Girl From Montana*, *The Bandit King* and *Western Justice*, were filmed a few miles farther west, in Golden, Colorado. These were Anderson's first efforts at directing stories of the old west, and they were a triumph.

The Girl From Montana (taking a cue from another successful stage play, *The Girl of the Golden West*) led the pack. This movie featured a heroine riding her horse at top speed to stop a posse from hanging her sweetheart. She arrives just in time to shoot the rope in two and save him. Anderson begins the film with a rare closeup of the actress, Pansy Perry, smiling at the camera as she pats her horse. By the end of the film he's made it clear: she's not only pretty, she's talented.

The Bandit King became popular for another reason — sensationalism. It elaborated on the train robbery plot with carefully orchestrated holdups of a bank and a stagecoach. The highlight of this sixteen-minute film, however, is the hard-riding action sequence, guns blazing, in pursuit of the outlaws. The bandits are tracked down and killed, as in the Edison robbery film, but the build-up to the finish is bigger.

With a successful catalog of films to his company's credit, Selig could now agree with Anderson — there was money to be made in narrative films. Early in 1907

Selig affirmed it by starting the construction of a big studio at Western Avenue and Irving Park Road.

Anderson's ability was once again rapidly boosting the profits of the company he worked for, and, true to form, he thought he deserved a piece of the pie. When Selig disagreed, Anderson quit.

But George M. Anderson's stubborn belief in himself finally paid off when he crossed the threshold of an office at 62 North Clark Street in downtown Chicago and met the person he'd been seeking for years — George K. Spoor. What Anderson had in creativity, Spoor had in business sense.

George Kirke Spoor, born on December 18, 1871, in Highland Park, Illinois, was no stranger to partnerships. In 1894, at the age of twenty-two, he was managing the opera house in Waukegan, Illinois, with Samuel Cone. Here, one night in 1896, Edward Amet, a local inventor, showed up as Spoor counted the box-office receipts. Amet invited Spoor to his machine shop a few blocks away to see a mechanical work-in-progress, Amet's Magniscope film projector. Spoor was fascinated, and this led to a new partnership: Amet made projectors and films to show, while Spoor placed them and a projectionist in vaudeville houses.[16]

The partnership dissolved in 1898, but Spoor started again, along similar lines, this time as sole proprietor, and his new company, the Kinodrome Company, signed contracts to provide his service to vaudeville houses all over the western United States, mostly in Orpheum theaters. At the heart of the Kinodrome Company was the Kinodrome movie projector. Unlike Selig's Polyscope projector, which was notorious for ripping films apart, or Amet's primitive Magniscope, the Kinodrome projector was the best on the market, made by Spoor employees Donald Bell and Albert Howell, two men who would soon revolutionize the movie equipment business with their Bell and Howell Company.[17]

When Anderson met Spoor in the spring of 1907, Spoor was running two businesses from his office: the Kinodrome service and the National Film Renting Company. It made sense to produce films as well, but Spoor was inexperienced in that field. Anderson's pitch to provide the filmmaking talent if Spoor would furnish the money was the perfect solution for both men. Spoor grew cautious, however, and offered to contribute just $2,500 to this arrangement, clearly indicating this was the limit of his investment. Anderson had already figured that amount was all he'd need to get going, and agreed to those terms. They filed for incorporation as the Peerless Film Manufacturing Company on April 29, 1907.[18]

Spoor was astonished when Anderson's first film, a comedy called *An Awful Skate,* became a huge success. The quality of this film wasn't the only reason it found favor; Anderson made it happen by going on the road selling the movie to film renters and exchanges in the east. By July a long-term partnership between Anderson and Spoor made sense, and both men announced it that month in a letter to the editor of the *Moving Picture World:* "Dear Sir — The Essanay Film Manufacturing Company announce to dealers, renters and exhibitors of moving picture films the completion of their new film making plant in Chicago and especially request your attention to their new and original film subjects, which will be ready for the market at an early date, subsequent notice of which you will receive. Respectfully, George K. Spoor. Gilbert M. Anderson."[19]

The Essanay name was born, and so was the name of Gilbert M. Anderson. Why Anderson reinvented himself yet again is a mystery, but it wasn't because he suddenly disliked the name George. He would in fact use that name many times in his life, even in his Essanay days. If the change was due to some conflict with George Spoor, both men kept it from the public, but then neither man ever spoke at length about their relationship. It was certainly not to either man's advantage to do so at first, and, besides, they had no time for it. The hard work had just begun.

Chapter One
Going West

The Essanay production staff was about as lean as it could get in its first few months. Anderson himself wrote, directed and edited the films. Gilbert Hamilton, a movie projectionist since 1898, operated the camera and processed the film. Ben Turpin, Essanay's only full-time actor, also worked as a carpenter, scene painter, prop man and shipping clerk, but his first task each morning was to sweep out George Spoor's office. Anderson said: "I take credit for Ben. When I met him he was playing little vaudeville dates, and he came out to the studio and was a janitor. He swept the floor. And he did that so nice and good, and he was so funny-looking, that I thought he'd make a good comedian."[1]

There was no money for lights, sets or costumes and everything was shot outdoors in sunlight. If the weather was bad they didn't shoot. The streets of Chicago served as a backdrop for most of their films. The rest of the time they used an open lot behind Spoor's Kinodrome business on Clark Street, with a piece of painted canvas hanging on the back fence as scenery.

A problem with the canvas was its angle to the sun; if the angle wasn't just right, shadows were cast across it, but this was a minor annoyance compared to another problem. Anderson remembered: "There was this big area-way, and the Chicago jail was there, and when we started making pictures all these inmates would come to the windows and start yelling and yelling. The sheriff came over and wanted us to either block up the back part or not take pictures. He said it caused too much of a riot with the prisoners. They'd all yell, 'Shoot him! Kill him!' They couldn't control them. So we decided to put up a studio on Wells Street."[2]

The studio at 501 Wells Street consolidated Essanay's "operation" because the film developing laboratory was already set up there. But it was still a chewing gum and shoestring production facility at best. Ben Turpin explained quite vividly how primitive the filmmaking process was, even after more actors were hired: "They didn't use automobiles to go to locations then. They sent us out in street cars. Every actor had to carry part of the scenery. Out of gallantry we let the ladies carry the tripods of the cameras while we carried chairs and screens and office furniture. Of course we had to go in all our make-up and we used to have some strange adventures."[3]

Costuming sometimes presented its own problems. Ben recalled: "One time they needed a cop's uniform and, being the regular goat, they sent me to borrow one. You couldn't get police clothes at the costumers in those days. Well, I walks into a Chicago police station and I give them a happy smile. 'Good morning, gents,' says I. 'I want to know if one of you gents will be so kind as to lend me a police uniform.' That was as far as I got. One of the big police sergeants got up and grabbed me by the coat collar. 'You can't ridicule a policeman in Chicago,' says he. And with that I was bounced on my bean out on the sidewalk."[4]

Anderson strived to turn out two films a month for the rest of 1907. The running times of each film varied between five minutes and seventeen minutes, or 300 to 1000 feet of film, respectively. One reel of film — a "one-reeler" — was no more than 1000 feet long because most projectors in those days couldn't hold a reel of film any larger than that. Film producers who found themselves making movies 500 or 600 feet in length soon realized they could increase their profits by filling the rest of the reel with another short film (frequently an educational subject, thereby combining entertainment and culture). These "split reels," as they were called, became common, and rightly so. A one-reeler could cost anywhere from one hundred to four hundred dollars to make, but the profit — $5,000 or more — was enormous.[5]

Anderson concentrated on comedies because he had a flair for them (and they were popular), but this arrangement changed when a second director, E. Lawrence Lee, was hired to make dramatic films at the end of the year. Dramas, it turned out, often had longer, more elaborate stories, and longer films commanded those higher profits. Anderson rallied by increasing the length of his comedies, then he entered Lee's dramatic territory with an ambitious historical epic — *The James Boys in Missouri*.

This full-reel chronicle of Frank and Jesse James included scenes of Jesse's admission to Quantrell's Raiders during the Civil War, the James Gang's Chicago & Alton Railroad hold up, and Jesse's death at the hands of Bob Ford. To provide the appropriate atmosphere, Anderson hired showman Barney Pierson, owner/manager of "Idaho Bill's Cheyenne Frontier Exposition," and filmed his performers at Chicago's Riverview Park and in Scotdale, Michigan. A newspaper review reprinted in *Moving Picture World* defined the movie's appeal: "*James Boys in Missouri* is a thriller from beginning to end and cannot fail to please."[6] The film brought favorable recognition, and money, to Essanay.

Within the month, Lawrence Lee proposed a followup — *The Younger Brothers*. In May, 1908, sixteen Essanay cowboys including Harry Clifton, Jack Jesperson and the ever-present Ben Turpin descended upon Berrien Springs, Michigan, to appear in the movie.[7] The film was full of murder and mayhem, and this worked against it; some cities (like Lancaster, Pennsylvania) banned it. This adverse public reaction stalled any plans for more westerns at Essanay for nearly a year.

What ultimately led Anderson to reconsider the western was Chicago's weather. Wind, snow and even overcast skies were enemies to a filmmaker, and, with plans to release one film a week beginning in January, 1908, the company couldn't afford to fall behind schedule. Even with two directors, bad weather was a constant threat and the pressure to produce was fearsome. Lawrence Lee left and was replaced by Thomas Ricketts, an actor born in London who had performed in Shakespeare, comic opera and everything inbetween. Leaving Ricketts in Chicago to do what he could, Anderson headed for California's sunny skies in San Francisco, accompanied by Ben Turpin and a fresh young cameraman named Jess Robbins.

Jesse Jerome Robbins, born in Galion, Ohio, on April 30, 1888, played a critical role in Anderson's life. A perfectionist with a knack for technical improvisation, Robbins proved adept at turning near-catastrophe into success. As a teenager managing a nickelodeon theater in Middletown, Ohio, he was forced out of business by the competition, but he purchased a projector and some darkroom equipment at a bargain price, and decided to make movies. "I didn't have a camera," he said, "just an Edison projector. But I made a diaphragm to fit inside the lens and turned it into a light box. Then I got some film stock."

When he finished experimenting he wrote to all the movie studios, seeking employment. "They were very polite in their replies. Then the Essanay Company asked me to come to Chicago; if I could prove myself, they'd give me a job." Robbins joined the company in 1908. "I guess I knew as much about the picture business as anybody else, because this was the beginning. Nobody knew much about anything then."[8]

Anderson quickly learned to trust Robbins, and they became good friends, but their trip to San Francisco was a disaster. Said Anderson: "I heard California was a great state — sun shining — but I didn't know it was the southern part of California that had the sunshine and San Francisco had the fog and rain."[9] When they arrived it was raining, and it continued for days without a break.

Unable to wait for sunny skies, Anderson and his colleagues took a train south, and found fair weather in Los Angeles. They checked into the Hollenbeck Hotel and the hotel's assistant manager suggested Westlake Park (now MacArthur Park) as a location. Anderson liked it: "There was a lake in that Westlake Park, and I had Ben jump in the lake to get a duck. And just as he came up there was a cop there, and he arrested us for being a nuisance. We had to talk our way out of that."[10]

Anderson was prevented from filming in Los Angeles, so he and his little troupe moved to Whittier. Police stopped him there, too.

But Pasadena was different. On December 28th the *Pasadena Star* newspaper announced that moving pictures shot locally would be seen that winter in 104 theaters on the Orpheum circuit. "G. M. Anderson, head of a Chicago house, is here to make the pictures. The Mount Lowe trip will be pictured today from a special car and the Tournament [of Roses] pictures will be taken New Year's day. 'I am sure,' he says, in discussing his plans, 'that the series of views will astound and delight the easterners. The great advertising and educational value of these views cannot be over-estimated.'"[11] Anderson filmed in Pasadena, then hopped over Los Angeles, and landed in Santa Monica to shoot more pictures.

Echo Mountain, near Pasadena, California, December 28, 1908.
Ben Turpin on the railing, Jess Robbins with camera, G. M. Anderson on trunk.

12 *Chapter One*

Jess Robbins in Santa Monica.
The camera is the first one ever made by Bell & Howell.

On a brisk winter morning, one of Santa Monica's most respected residents innocently opened her front door and was about to walk outside when Anderson, busy directing Ben Turpin in a scene on her front lawn, ordered the woman back into her house. A local newspaper columnist called the filmmakers "an invasion of mad men."[12]

Anderson quickly made four comedies and a melodrama at the coastal city, then took a train back to Chicago. Faced with another bout of miserable weather, he traveled west again in January, this time to Golden, Colorado. There, and in nearby Morrison, he filmed four westerns.

The Road Agents, the first of these westerns to be released, was singled out in a review by the *New York Dramatic Mirror*: "This is one of the best pictures of any description we have seen from the Essanay Company in a long time. It is thrilling without being unreasonable, and it is acted with an appearance of reality that gives us the impression of looking at actual events. No attempt is made to incorporate a complicated love story in the hold-up and the capture of the road agents, and there is no maudlin sentiment introduced to create sympathy for the criminals. It is a straight story of two highwaymen, who follow a stagecoach, intercept it by crossing over a hill, hold up the passengers and escape with their booty. They quarrel over the spoils, and one of them mortally wounds the other. In the meantime the coach arrives at a town, and the sheriff is notified and starts with a posse to run down the robbers. They meet the dying road agent, who confesses and directs the sheriff's party where to capture the other man. Then follows a thrilling chase after the fugitive, who is overtaken and led off to a fate that we have no difficulty in imagining. If other Essanay Western thrillers are anything like as good as this one we predict a wide demand for them."[13]

Contrary to Essanay's usual practice of rushing films into distribution upon completion, the westerns demonstrated a more thoughtful approach: after *The Road Agents* release in March, *A Tale of the West* came out in April, and *A Mexican's Gratitude* and *The Indian Trailer* opened two weeks apart in May. All four films were highly praised for their acting, outstanding stories and photography. *Moving Picture World* even noted the audience response to *A Mexican's Gratitude*: "The film was heartily applauded in two theaters where it was seen the past week, and everyone who attends motion picture shows knows that applause is somewhat rare."[14] This sustained attention gave Essanay a recognition that begged to be exploited, and there was one simple way to capitalize on it — with more westerns.

Anderson was clearly ready for a change. (With recent comedies such as *A Case of Seltzer* and *A Case of Tomatoes* he wasn't breaking any new ground.) Elaborate plans were made for an extended journey west, ambitious beyond anything he'd done before, with stops in Colorado, Montana, Oregon and along the Pacific Coast, a turn inland to Yosemite, then down to Mexico for three months.

In Chicago, Thomas Ricketts would continue to make dramas and "high class" comedies. These would be released, as usual, on Wednesdays, and Anderson's westerns would fill a new spot in the schedule on Saturdays.

Essanay in Golden, Colorado.
G. M. Anderson, front and center, Ben Turpin on horseback, third from left; third from right is Chick Morrison and to his left is Shorty Cunningham.

Expansion came at a critical time for Essanay; most of their competitors were already producing two reels a week (Pathe was making three!). The main question was whether the Wells Street studio could handle the developing, printing, assembling and publicity that two productions a week would require. More staff was needed, but with just 2,400 feet of floor space, the current studio was too small, and there was no room to expand.

Spoor purchased land on the outskirts of town, at Argyle Street, and work began on a brick building with more than 72,000 square feet of floor area. Finally there'd be enough office space, an up-to-date film lab, editing rooms, prop and wardrobe departments, dressing rooms, a carpenter shop, a scene dock and a stage outfitted with the latest in artificial lighting. A young electrical engineer named Allan Dwan was responsible for the new light fixtures and Anderson directed the carpenters who built the supporting framework and the stage itself.[15]

A new company logo was even designed. The old S and A cursive scrawl was incorporated into an emblem on the shoulder of an American Indian in profile wearing a feathered headdress. It bore some resemblance to the Indian-head penny, but had the finished appearance of the Mohawk Indian on the buffalo nickel that would come into circulation in 1913. The designer was a talented artist and children's book illustrator, George Spoor's sister Mary.

Essanay's substantial investment couldn't have happened without a change in attitude by the patentowners of movie machinery. Edison had been at odds with

The Motion Picture Patents Company members on December 18, 1908.
In front, left to right: William T. Rock, George K. Spoor, Jacques A. Berst, Harry N. Marvin,
Jeremiah J. Kennedy, Thomas A. Edison, Frank L. Dyer; behind the table are Peter Webber,
Sigmund Lubin, Albert E. Smith, J. Stuart Blackton, F. Singhi, Samuel Long, William N.
Selig, George Kleine and Frank J. Marion.

other legitimate claimants for years and there was no clear winner. Finally, in 1907, negotiations began on a trust that would pool all patents by its members so licenses to produce films could be issued, thereby controlling the industry. Essanay entered into that agreement, and when contracts for the Motion Picture Patents Company were ready on December 18, 1908, George Spoor was there to sign. It was the perfect present for Spoor's thirty-seventh birthday.

While Essanay's future looked bright, Ben Turpin's prospects were dismal. In two years he had broken a hip, sprained his ankles, blackened both eyes and suffered countless bumps and bruises. As he neared his fortieth birthday, with a salary still at twenty dollars a week, his frustration was evident in a rare article he wrote, published in *Moving Picture World* (probably the first time a regularly-employed movie actor was ever identified by name). He told of his part in the Essanay comedy *A Midnight Disturbance*, playing a burglar attacked by a bulldog, and the dog was supposed to bite into the pad hidden under the seat of his pants and hang on. The dog missed the pad. Ben said: "I upset some of the scenery and we had to take it over again. On rehearsing the dog so as to catch the pad, I was bit several times, but the producer only says to me — 'Well, Ben, does it hurt?'"[16]

Ben had come to Essanay from vaudeville after touring for years in a knockabout "Happy Hooligan" act. In the fall of 1909, feeling unappreciated, he returned to vaudeville, and back to square one with the same act.

Back in Golden.
Left to right: Nancy Robbins, ?, Shorty Cunningham, Fred Church, William A. Russell, Joe Dennis, Pansy Perry?, G. M. Anderson. At the far end are Joseph Smith and Jess Robbins.

Soon after that, on September 8, 1909, Anderson left Chicago to set up headquarters in Golden, Colorado, at the Dennis and Cunningham livery stable.[17] Anderson knew Shorty Cunningham and Joe Dennis from his Selig days, and the two men were once again recruited to play cowboys in the movies.

With Anderson were Jess Robbins, Jess's wife Nancy, propman William A. Russell and actor/business manager John B. O'Brien. Pansy Perry, the Denver girl who'd starred in Anderson's *The Girl From Montana* Selig film, joined the company too. From Morrison, just ten miles south, came two brothers, Chick and Pete Morrison.[18] Rounding out the group were two young men from Denver: Joseph G. Smith, a car mechanic, and Fred Church, an actor who would become a significant member of the company.

Church was born in Ontario, Iowa, on October 17, 1889.[19] He'd been bitten by the acting bug at an early age, running away to the circus, working in theatrical stock companies and even trying movies in 1908 with Selig director Francis Boggs. Church knew how to ride and handle a rope, and despite his youth was a versatile actor. Tall, handsome, and self-confident, he got along well with Anderson, and the two men would work together for years.

The first movie Anderson made in Golden was *The Best Man Wins*. It was another hard-riding western, but this time there was a love interest and a touch of comedy. Jack O'Brien played the lead, and it soon became apparent that he was new to westerns. Rigged out in an ungainly outfit of woolly chaps, billowy scarf and

The Best Man Wins.
Shorty Cunningham is fourth from left, Chick Morrison is sixth, to his left is Pete Morrison, then Fred Church and William A. Russell. Robbins and Anderson trade places at the camera.

boots too large for him, O'Brien hobbled to his horse. Anderson directed him to mount up, while Jess Robbins rolled film.

O'Brien put his left foot in the stirrup and froze beside the beast. Anderson shouted at him to hurry up; precious film was being wasted. O'Brien, near panic, said he couldn't move. A cowboy finally spotted the problem; the horse's hoof was firmly planted on the toe of O'Brien's oversized-boot.[20]

The film turned out pretty well, according to reviews, and gave the new series a notable start, but Anderson wasn't shy about seeking more publicity to help it along. He walked into the office of the *Denver Post* and spoke to its editor.

That man was George Creel, a charismatic fellow in his own right, who would soon launch into politics, and marry a beautiful actress (Blanche Bates) besides. Until that day Creel had never heard of Anderson nor paid any attention to the movies. But, as Creel wrote in an autobiography, when Anderson hinted that Creel's skill as a writer could be useful in creating some Essanay scenarios and "went on to mention that he would be willing to pay $25 apiece for as many as I could turn out, my ears flapped forward... Anderson's offer came like a fall of manna, and my blood pressure went up as I did some swift mental arthmetic. A scenario a day for ten days would mean $250 — untold riches — and what if it all went on for twenty days? Nevertheless, common honesty forced me to admit that I had never written a scenario and had no idea how to go about it. 'There's nothing to it,' shrugged Anderson. 'We're making a picture tomorrow up at Mount Morrison. Come along and you'll see how it's done.'"[21]

Creel was introduced to the filmmaking troupe, all in their twenties or younger, on an early-morning train trip. He wasn't impressed, until they reached their destination: "We were met by a dozen or so cowpunchers, all saddled up and leading a bunch of extra bronchos. The real article, too, for all came from near-by ranches, and I recognized several as having roped and ridden at Cheyenne. Trooping up to the town's one hotel, the property man opened his trunks and handed out chaparajos, bandannas, boots, sombreros, and spurs. Soon dressed, the troupe clattered downstairs and climbed on the waiting mounts.

"Our way led along brawling Bear Creek, and after a ride of two miles we came to a small ranch house tucked away in a grove of cottonwoods. Russell, the property man, had bargained with the owner some days before, paying $25 for the rent of the home and yard for the day. In addition, he was to have the use of a bunch of cattle pasturing farther back in the hills."[22]

But before shooting started, Anderson stood in front of the group as they sat in the grass, pulled a sheet of paper from his pocket, and read to them a synopsis of the story. Creel listened carefully: "*The Heart of a Cowboy* was the title of the opus, and as he droned along, stopping now and then to make a point, I lost all doubt as to my ability to write for the silver screen."[23]

The script was indeed simple, no more than a numbered list of shots describing the action for each of nineteen scenes. In Scene One, the "Girl comes out of house, holding some kodak pictures of herself. Cowboy comes up, sees picture,

G. M. Anderson, Jess Robbins, an unknown actor and Pete Morrison in downtown Morrison for Judgement. *The bridge in the background crosses Bear Creek.*

and begs it from her. She refuses at first, but finally gives him one, writing 'To Steve' on it. He asks her to walk with him, but she refuses, and he departs." That's one of the more complex descriptions; others were as simple as Scene Sixteen: "Girl riding."[24]

Creel got some additional insight into the filmmaking process when he was invited by Anderson to take a leading role in the film. Creel declined at first, calling it a crazy idea, but protests were met by Anderson's reassuring reply, "All you've got to do is follow directions."[25]

The first ten scenes at the ranch were rehearsed and filmed with few problems before lunch. But the scenes in the hills, trying to rustle cattle, nearly did them in: "The crazy creatures bolted all over the pasture, and by the time we got a dozen bunched, stolen, and duly photographed, Smith and I were good and sorry that we had ever taken up a life of crime....With just the one camera, and only Robbins' legs for transportation, there were no long rides over hill and dale. First the vigilantes raced up and down within a narrow range, and then there was a short move to another field, where the girl dashed back and forth until Robbins had footage enough to show her furious gallop for the rescue of Honest Steve. The last shot was taken just as twilight began to fall, and it was a weary lot that rode back to Mount Morrison, hoarse from yelling and bone tired from long contact with Texas saddles."[26]

Creel returned to his job at the *Post*, while Anderson made seven more westerns around Golden and Morrison before deciding to move on, but one more Colorado film deserves to be mentioned, Anderson's acting debut in an Essanay western.

The Ranchman's Rival began like all the others, with Anderson directing from a simple story he wrote. Early in production, however, the lead actor became headstrong, ignoring Anderson's direction. When Anderson became insistent the lead said with a sneer, "Why don't you pose your own pictures if you know how to do it better than I?" Anderson decided that was a good idea, so he fired the actor, took over the part and finished the film. From then on he played most of the leading roles himself.[27]

The Ranchman's Rival survives in a beautiful, complete print, and the original actor can still be seen in the few shots that Anderson didn't bother to retake. No matter. Anderson handles the part well, is the focus of attention, and the star of the show.

Anderson's company left Colorado on November 15th for El Paso, Texas. When they arrived Anderson looked around, but wasn't satisfied. Never mind that it was a real western town. He wasn't looking for the real thing; he wanted a representation of the Old West, an image of what people imagined it to be. The company shot only one complete film, *An Outlaw's Sacrifice*, in El Paso, plus parts of three others, *The Ranch Girl's Legacy*, *The Cowboy and the Squaw* and *Broncho Billy's Redemption* (the first of Anderson's famed series). They went across the border to Juarez, filmed some horses racing around the track for *The Tout's Remembrance*, then continued south. By Christmas Eve they were in Mexico City, staying at the German-American Hotel.[28]

Anderson and his company had a grand time in Mexico but didn't make a single movie because Jose de la Cruz Porfirio Diaz, the country's president, latched onto them. Diaz, a devotee of the cinema, personally conducted them on a tour of the presidential palace, then hosted a lavish dinner for the whole cast and crew with every cabinet official present to join in the festivities.

This was fun and entertaining, but with Essanay now releasing two films a week (and Anderson responsible for one of them), the company couldn't afford to dally in Mexico, so they quietly packed up and left.[29]

As the old year of 1909 was put to bed, the train carrying Anderson and his small band of filmmakers chugged toward California. For Anderson, it would mark the beginning of fame and fortune.

G. M. Anderson plays a sympathetic Mexican in The Mexican's Faith.
In the background are Chick Morrison and Jack O'Brien.

Chapter Two
Santa Barbara

On New Year's Day, 1910, the Essanay company checked into Santa Barbara's Mascarel Hotel. They were now fourteen strong; in addition to Anderson, Russell, Church, O'Brien, Smith, Chick Morrison, Jess and Nancy Robbins, there were Neva Don Carlos (a singer/actress), Frank Murphy (a set carpenter from the Chicago studio), Earl Howell and his wife May McCaskey (a vaudeville team) and new leading lady Clara Hall, with her husband Frank.[1]

Like most women of that era who'd marry a fellow actor on tour, Clara's maiden name, Clara Williams, was used on theatrical playbills. A native of Seattle, Washington, she was only twenty-one years old, but already a veteran actor. Franklyn Hall, eight years older, was born in Oakland, California, and had done his first work at the Grand Opera House in San Francisco. They'd both be key players in Anderson's westerns for the next year.

When Anderson arrived in Santa Barbara it was raining, but he wasn't concerned. Once again he went directly to the local press and announced that their fair city had been chosen above all others on the West Coast "for its excellent situation."[2] The next day, Sunday, was a day of rest, but only because it was still raining. On Monday, he and Robbins scouted around, and even managed to shoot a few scenes. On Tuesday, most of the company started off early to work.

Anderson was hoping to find a picturesque adobe farmhouse, but the only one around was inhabited by a Chinese laundry and looked unsuitable. On a hill behind nearby Montecito, he settled for a weather-beaten house made of wood, and Jack O'Brien negotiated with the inhabitants (a poor Mexican family) for the use of the site. Dora Eckl, a reporter for the *Santa Barbara Independent*, listed the points agreed upon: "Yes, the robbers may have a saddle and they can play around in sister's back yard, they can feed the chickens if they must, and they can use the woodshed for a background."[3]

Jess Robbins lifted his camera case and tripod out of the coach while Anderson ordered the actors about: "Here you, Smith, you be mending this saddle see, and I come in and ask you for work. Keep the saddle out of sight — it's English. This is a wild west show. Now let's go through this."[4]

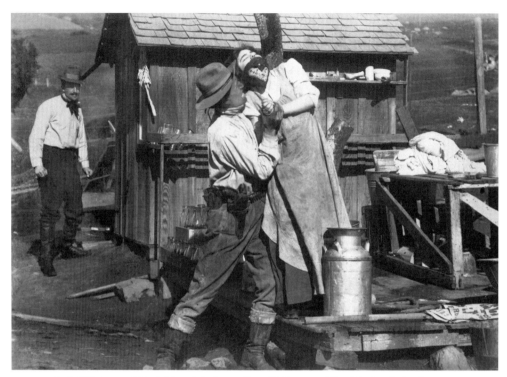

Jack O'Brien and Fred Church kidnap Clara Williams in The Mexican's Faith.

Anderson holds off William A. Russell, Jack O'Brien, Fred Ilenstine, Chick Morrison and Frank Hall (kneeling) in The Cowboy and the Squaw. *Fred Church is the bartender and Clara Williams is the squaw. Note the poster for Santa Barbara's Potter Theater on the wall.*

The film, called *The Mexican's Faith*, featured Anderson in the title role. Anderson approached Smith, who was working on the saddle, and solemnly said, "Hello, there, Cheese-box!"

Smith looked up. "Hello, Stick-in-the-Mud. How're ye coming?"

"Nix on the frijoles," said Anderson. "Do you own this cheese ranch around here?" he said in a sweeping gesture.

"Sure thing. Made it myself."

"I want some work."

"The deuce you do. What'll you take?"

"Thirty dollars."

"Too much."

"Well, anything you give me, you old tight."

After a few gestures between them Anderson stopped the scene. "That's all right. Now let's have it."[5]

The same action was repeated, this time with Robbins cranking the camera. That done, it was on to the next setup.

The weather was kind to the Western Essanay Company for the next week; it permitted Anderson to catch up to his schedule, and even gave him a chance to catch his breath. But he also had help from his partner in Chicago.

For seven weeks Essanay released a western movie each Saturday, then George Spoor thought the public might be tired of these films, so on Saturday, January 8th, a drama from the Chicago studio was released instead (even though three westerns made in Colorado and one from El Paso were probably ready to go). The next Saturday a documentary shot by Chicago Essanay cameraman Charles Kaufman (*United States Army Maneuvers at Fort Leavenworth, Kansas*) was released, followed by another drama made at the Chicago studio. By then, letters from showmen all over the country were pouring in, demanding more Essanay westerns. Spoor decided he'd made a mistake, and reinstituted the series in February.[6]

But during that first change of policy, when it looked like Anderson didn't need to hurry after all, he was able to witness a spectacular event — the first aviation meet in America. The Wright brothers historic flight at Kitty Hawk had occurred only a scant six years before (coincidently just days after the release of *The Great Train Robbery*), and now, from January 10th to the 20th, 1910, tens of thousands of people converged on the old Dominguez ranch just south of Los Angeles to see a sky filled with balloons, dirigibles and aeroplanes.

The people there that first day couldn't have felt more earthbound; heavy rains the previous week had left the ground soaking wet and automobiles were having a tough time getting through. One touring car disappeared into a mudhole and couldn't be found. Feet were caked with mud. But the grandstand was packed when the first wood-framed biplane was wheeled into view. A man in the crowd muttered, "If that darn thing can fly, I can fly myself."[7]

A mechanic worked on the plane's engine until it suddenly started with a roar. The crowd let out a gasp of surprise. Then the young, slender pilot, Glenn Curtiss, squeezed past the wires and levers to his seat and the machine slowly moved forward on tiny wheels, gaining speed as it passed the press stand. "Darn good automobile, anyhow," said the man. Suddenly the plane tipped up, and gracefully took to the skies. "Gosh," said the man. "It's a-flying."[8]

The crowd watched open-mouthed as the mechanical bird skimmed the field from fifty feet up. A *Los Angeles Times* reporter wrote: "There is a fascination about watching the flight of one of these strange things that can't be set down in cold words and black type. It is almost like the sensations of a dream. You feel an exhilaration that seems to lift you out of yourself."[9]

A man ran across the field, his coattails flapping in the breeze, and at the top of his voice he cried, "What's the matter with that band? Why doesn't the band play?" The conductor of the band stood absolutely hypnotized, his baton drooping from his fingers, as he gaped at the strange object sliding past him in mid-air. The musicians were also caught in this dream. It wasn't until the tuba player dropped his instrument that they all came back to life.

After a few hundred yards Curtiss cut the engine and his plane floated softly to the ground. Twenty thousand people drew a long breath together, then burst into furious applause.[10]

And so it went, one astonishing event after another, day after day, monoplanes and biplanes swooping and turning, balloons and dirigibles taking to the air, filling the sky with wonderful, unbelievable flying machines. The climax of the air meet came when Frenchman Louis Paulhan flew his Farman biplane to Baldwin ranch at Santa Anita and back, forty-five miles non-stop. When he landed in front of the grandstand a cheer went up, people waved handkerchiefs and the band struck up the French national anthem. A *Times* reporter claimed the response was "inane, idiotic and insufficient."[11]

There was a stampede of mechanics, photographers, reporters and mere civilians who mobbed Paulhan as he climbed out of his plane. G. M. Anderson was there in the crowd beside him, taking his hand. Paulhan shook it, but Anderson held on, directing him to where Jess Robbins was cranking his camera so Paulhan could be recorded on film at this momentus event. At that moment Paulhan appeared to trip, but, no, someone was getting underneath him, lifting him up like a football hero, and he was carried toward the clack, clack, clacking motion picture camera. Paulhan reached out and clasped Robbins by his free hand, the one that wasn't cranking the camera. Paulhan solemnly shook it, and was then reclaimed by the crowd.[12]

When Anderson was informed that his westerns were back on the schedule, he worked his people relentlessly to keep ahead of the release dates, and he rounded up the best scenery in the Santa Barbara area for his movies. Hoff Heights was a location for *The Mistaken Bandit.* Hope Drive figured in *The Cowpuncher's Ward* and *The Little Doctor of the Foothills.* The nearby town of Goleta was seen in *The Bad Man and the Preacher.* They used Mission Canyon for *The Girl and the Fugitive.* One morning, Essanay staged a holdup of a Southern Pacific train at Miramar.

The Mistaken Bandit.
Fred Ilenstine on guard while Joseph Smith and Fred Church break down the door .

A Ranchman's Wooing.
Sitting on the edge: Jack O'Brien, ?, Arthur Smith, Nancy Robbins, Clara Williams, Fred Ilenstine, Elmer Thompson, Lois Boulton, William A. Russell and Gladys Field. Fred Church plays a fiddle. Waving: Neva Don Carlos and Joseph Smith.

Anderson surrounded by bad men Jack O'Brien, Frank Murphy, Fred Church, J. Travers, Fred Ilenstine and Frank Hall in The Bad Man and the Preacher. *Note the Essanay Indianhead logo on the hitching post, there to discourage film pirates from copying the movie.*

Later, Anderson (the preacher) and O'Brien (the bad man) have a showdown. Standing by: May McCaskey (in doorway), Earl Howell (with beard), Frank Hall (wearing hat), Lois Boulton (above Hall), Joseph Smith (shaved head), Fred Church, Frank Murphy, Fred Ilenstine.

Sophie Osborn is The Cowpuncher's Ward. *Anderson is the cowpuncher, who is helped by Joseph Smith, William A. Russell, Fred Church, Fred Ilenstine, and Jack O'Brien.*

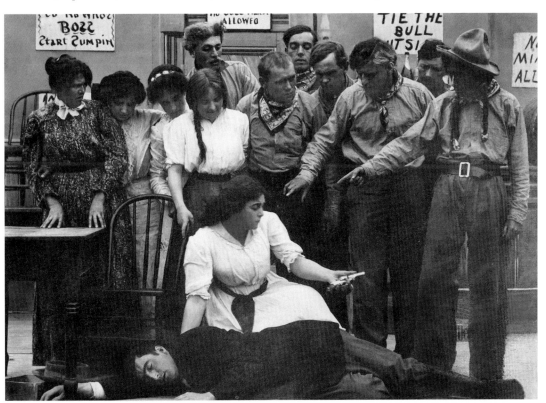

Gladys Field (holding the gun) is the ward grown up, suspected of killing Jack O'Brien. Left to right: May McCaskey, Clara Williams, Nancy Robbins, Lois Boulton, Fred Church, Joseph Smith, Elmer Thompson, Earl Howell, G. M. Anderson, Fred Ilenstine and Frank Hall.

Some of the passengers, unaware of a movie in progress, watched wide-eyed as a few actors tumbled from the train onto the ground, where a realistic, blood-curdling scene was boldly enacted.[13]

A portable shooting stage and scene flats were set up on a vacant lot next to the Santa Barbara Opera House and "interior" scenes were taken for *The Ranch Girl's Legacy*, which had been partially filmed in El Paso. The company would return to their open-air stage intermittently for three months to film other indoor scenes for their movies.

Supplementing his regular troupe, Anderson engaged several people locally to act in his films. Lois Boulton and Gladys Field came from the Elleford Stock Company, a touring company that was temporarily stranded due to the illness of its namesake. Two talented child actors, Gordon and Sophie Osborn, also came to Essanay from Elleford. When the Girton Stock Company came to town in February for an extended run at the Santa Barbara Opera House, two members, Dick Scott and Corbett Morris, worked in a few films during the day and acted on stage at night. Elmer Thompson was staying at the Mascarel Hotel when Essanay arrived; being at hand turned into a job with Essanay. Fred Ilenstine, born in nearby Santa Maria, was twenty years old, living with his family in Santa Barbara; his fascination with movies led to a job playing small parts in several films.

Amid all the activity, Anderson still took the time to please his Santa Barbara neighbors with a couple of stunts that proved so popular he repeated them elsewhere. First he invited every automobile in town to show up at the beach one Sunday afternoon, turning the Essanay camera on them and a crowd of spectators. Two showings were arranged locally at the Potter Theatre as a charity fundraiser sponsored by the Knights of Pythias, and, to complete the show, he added a live performance. It was a comedy play called *Brown's Troubles* and the Essanay cast and crew, most of them accomplished actors, filled all the parts. The dual event — pictures and play — was memorable, according to the *Santa Barbara Morning Press*: "Everyone seemed to recognize his picture. When the film of the Plaza del Mar, the band and La Monaca leading, was thrown on the screen the crowd applauded thunderously." As for the play: "Clara Williams and Earl Howell playing the leads were all that the most exacting theatergoer could ask for. G. M. Anderson and Neva Don Carlos as Mr. and Mrs. Fuller were excellent." But the greatest acclaim was not given to Anderson: "The entrance of John Brown, played by Joseph Smith, caused an intermission for fully five minutes, while the audience was recovering from its mirth. Brown's make-up was such that a sphinx would have chuckled."[14]

The success of the two benefits in February paved the way for three more shows on consecutive Sundays in March. Billed as "The S. and A. Players," the first program consisted of vaudeville acts by the Osborn children, Neva Don Carlos and the team of Howell and McCaskey, followed by a sketch called "The Arizona Kid" with Franklyn Hall, Clara Williams and Anderson. Subsequent showings presented a variation on that theme. Tickets were sold at vaudeville rates — 10,

The portable open-air stage is used for an "interior" scene in The Girl and the Fugitive. *Note the real houses and landscape through the window. Left to right: Frank Hall, Frank Murphy, Jack O'Brien, Fred Church, J. Travers (standing), Joseph Smith, Anderson, William A. Russell, Fred Ilenstine (back to back with Anderson), Dick Scott, Corbett Morris.*

A more elaborate set is used for The Ranch Girl's Legacy. *Fred Ilenstine wears a bellhop's uniform from the Mt. Morrison Hotel, indicated by the name on the cap. Anderson signs in while Frank Hall looks at the mail slots. Note the* Saturday Evening Post *tucked into one slot.*

20 or 30 cents — a bargain for the three hour program, although this time the money didn't go to charity.

Essanay's high-profile presence was unusual at the very least; most filmmakers on location kept to themselves so they could work quickly without interruption. For full-time Essanay employees to spend week after week making films, then perform on stage, too, was unheard of, especially when the films themselves weren't promoted. The fact that most of Anderson's people had come to the movies from the theatrical stage may have been the motivation for that extra effort. But even though Anderson and his company would put on plays elsewhere in their travels, it was never done as extensively as that first string of performances in Santa Barbara.

Despite Anderson's best efforts, not everyone in Santa Barbara was happy with Essanay's presence. On one remarkable occasion, scenes were being shot in front of J. M. McAvoy's San Diego Saloon on State Street when bar-owner Henry Ziegler and restaurateur Victor Clairemont rushed up from their businesses on the adjoining block. Ziegler took the crank from the camera, thereby stopping production, and Clairemont waylaid Frank Hall to browbeat him. Both angry men objected to the portrayals of Earl Howell and William Russell as bums who mooch drinks from a saloon by pretending to have epileptic fits; the premise of the film suggested a shot of whiskey stops a seizure. The *Independent* singled out Clairemont for unleashing "an international attack of language and threats," cursing Hall, who happened to be cranking the camera that day, and threatening to throw the Essanay man into the street.[15]

Anderson had both intruders arrested, but in court he dropped a petty larceny charge against Ziegler for taking the crank. Clairemont, accused of disturbing the peace, demanded a trial, and a jury found him guilty. When he was ordered to pay fifty dollars or spend fifty days in jail, his lawyer pleaded for mercy, claiming Clairemont had only been "mildly profane," but the judge held firm, giving Clairemont one hour to produce the money, and he did.[16]

According to Anderson, the incident was the result of an on-going battle between prohibitionists and "the saloon element," the latter group thinking the movie was propaganda against them. It wasn't until Anderson promised both sides he'd stay away from scenes in front of saloons that calm was restored. Neither side had reason to worry; the production in question, *Method in His Madness*, was a present-day farce-comedy and not a threat to either faction. The movie survives, and is quite entertaining. Every Essanay actor participates, and Anderson appears in the last shot as one of several people who drench William Russell with seltzer water from siphon bottles.

Anderson managed to keep the films coming until the middle of March, when it started to rain and wouldn't let up. The outlook didn't look promising, so, on March 24, 1910, the company packed up to leave for Colorado. In parting, Anderson made a statement to the *Independent*: "Since we arrived here on January 1, we have made 14 films, each about 1000 feet in length. The entire troupe including the stage carpenter, scenic artist and camera man numbers 18, so it can be seen that our stay here has been at some little expense."

Anderson claimed the company spent $26,500 in Santa Barbara, probably an inflated estimate, although production expenses had definitely increased since Essanay's creation. More likely true was his assertion that 110 prints were usually made of each western film for distribution to theaters, but *The Fence on Bar Z*, made in Santa Barbara, had received orders for 140 prints, an Essanay record. The *Independent* proudly summed up: "So satisfied is Mr. Anderson with Santa Barbara that he is planning to return here about November next and put in about three or four months of work. It is possible that he may build a studio, he says, so that he can make Santa Barbara his western headquarters."[17]

Elmer Thompson and Fred Ilenstine, went east with the company, but Essanay never returned to Santa Barbara. In Colorado, the company was able to produce eighteen movies in twelve weeks, four more than in Santa Barbara. However, Anderson gave a boost to the seaside city in an interview for *Moving Picture World*: "Santa Barbara has proven the ideal Winter resort of the moving picture man, as I believe our Western pictures have proven. Although the last two weeks of our stay in the coast town have been hampered by rather unpleasant weather, something unusual for Santa Barbara, the best part of the season has been ideal, with little rain and a great amount of sunshine."[18]

One look at Essanay's first film in Santa Barbara, *The Mexican's Faith*, with its spectacular shot of cowboys riding along the cliffs of the coastline, and it's clear that Anderson and Robbins captured the look of this community in its best possible light. Soon, other companies would take a cue from Essanay and come to Santa Barbara, making it a popular film production center for a while. But for Anderson, there were many more trails to blaze.

At the Morrison Hotel: (standing) G. M. Anderson, Frank Hall, Chick Morrison, Fred Church,
Jack O'Brien, Bob Gray, Arthur White, Jess Robbins; (middle) Clara Williams, Neva Don
Carlos, Gladys Field, Nancy Robbins; (front) Elmer Thompson, Joseph Smith, Fred Ilenstine.

At the Morrison Hotel: Jack O'Brien, Joseph Smith, Bob Gray, Clara Williams, Fred Church,
G. M. Anderson, Chick Morrison, Fred Ilenstine, Elmer Thompson.

Chapter Three
Riding the Range

The pleasant spring weather in Colorado encouraged the Western Essanay to linger in Morrison indefinitely, so in April 1910 George Spoor came from Chicago to confer with his partner on business. One day the two men were standing by the entrance to the Savoy Hotel in downtown Denver when a stranger walked up and spoke to Anderson: "Are you..."

"Yes," said Anderson, "I am the man in the pictures."

Spoor quickly realized from the tenor of this brief conversation that these casual encounters were not unique; Anderson was being recognized wherever he went.[1]

This amazed Spoor, but he already knew that Anderson's westerns were a financial windfall for Essanay, and their profits were fueling expansion. In May, Spoor sailed across the Atlantic to visit, for the first time, the London Essanay office his brother Harry had opened the year before. From there he went to Paris, investigating the market for Essanay films, and then to Berlin, where a limited agreement with a distributor was renegotiated into a full contract. Soon there'd be Essanay branches in Spain and in Australia. What every outlet wanted above all was Anderson's westerns; they were becoming a world-wide phenomenon.

While Spoor was away, Anderson and his company returned to the Chicago studio and shot interior scenes for several unfinished productions, among them a movie Anderson had begun more than six months before in El Paso. It marked the first film with Gilbert M. Anderson as Broncho Billy; he called it *Broncho Billy's Redemption*.

Redemption comes to Broncho Billy, a cattle rustler, when he discovers a young woman and her father unconscious from illness out in the prairie. He decides to take them into town for medical attention, knowing he'll be arrested by the sheriff as an outlaw. *Moving Picture World* called it: "A fascinating story of life on the plains, showing how even a bad man found his heart and developed a strain of goodness he did not know he possessed."[2]

When Anderson was asked in 1958 about the origin of the Broncho Billy name he claimed it was from a Peter B. Kyne story entitled "Broncho Billy and the

Broncho Billy's Redemption: *Jack O'Brien looks at Anderson, hands held up, as Clara Williams is removed to the doctor's office.*

Baby" published in the *Saturday Evening Post.* This was not true. *Broncho Billy and the Baby* was the name of a 1915 Anderson film, and none of Kyne's stories included "Broncho Billy" in its title. When *Broncho Billy's Redemption* was made Kyne wasn't even writing western stories; his first magazine sale, "A Little Matter of Salvage," was a sea tale printed in the September 25, 1909, issue of the *Saturday Evening Post.* And Kyne's often-filmed story "The Three Godfathers," although somewhat resembling *Broncho Billy's Redemption*, was not in print until November 23, 1912.

Anderson definitely stole some of his plot lines from popular writers (notably O. Henry), but the Broncho Billy character didn't originate there, although it's possible the source was another writer, H. Tipton Steck, who worked in the scenario department of the Chicago Essanay studio. Steck, a rapid writer, was hired by Essanay in 1908 at the age of twenty-one, and stated in 1917, while still at Essanay: "In eight months I wrote enough stuff to keep Mr. Anderson busy for two years."[3] Steck's close friend, Essanay actor Edward Arnold, said that Steck mailed so much material to Anderson on his 1909 trip through the west that Anderson telegraphed Steck to stop sending stories, he had all he could use.[4] Steck, however, never claimed credit for the Broncho Billy character.

Anderson may have heard the name somewhere; Colorado western lore mentions a couple of characters with that moniker, and there were variations of Broncho this and Broncho that, including a "Broncho Joe" in the original stage production of *The Great Train Robbery.* There was even an "Alkali Ike" in that play, a name

Anderson used in a popular comedy series he created in 1911. "I just happened to hit on the 'Alkali' name for the title," he said.[5] Perhaps Anderson, for once shy about taking credit himself (or unwilling to admit the idea came from an Essanay staff writer), chose to honor a once-popular writer — Peter B. Kyne, who died on November 25, 1957, just a few months before Anderson's statement. Most likely, the Broncho Billy name had just popped into Anderson's mind one day and it took off from there.

With Anderson back in Chicago, comedy directing once more occupied his attention, first off in a subject dear to his heart — baseball. Anderson had previously explored the topic in 1908 during a White Sox and Highlanders game at Cominsky Park, the same year he arranged, at the urging of fellow enthusiast Jess Robbins, for Essanay to film the first of three consecutive seasons of World Series games.[6] But his newest one-reeler, *Take Me Out to the Ball Game*, surpassed the earlier, episodic comedy because of a clever story line and stronger, more clearly defined characters.

It also helped that this time Anderson staged scenes between games at the park so he could concentrate on comedy bits with Augustus Carney, Neva Don Carlos, J. Warren Kerrigan and Jack, a bulldog pup, as they interacted with the Chicago White Sox team. The dog had already learned to clamp his powerful jaws onto the seat of Ben Turpin's pants, and was now unleashed on an umpire. The movie became a favorite of Anderson's, and got excellent reviews as well.

Augustus Carney, the lead in *Take Me Out to the Ball Game*, had intrigued Anderson for some time. Carney was an Irishman, approximately fifty years old, a comedian with a moody disposition who kept to himself. Carney had previously worked at the Kalem Film Company in the summer of 1907, but was primarily a stage actor. He happened to be in Chicago performing in a musical comedy, *The Goddess of Liberty*, when someone at the Essanay studio inquired if he'd like to work in their comedy films during his free time. He liked it so much he signed on with Essanay full time when the play closed in January, 1910.

Anderson saw Carney as a perfect match for a character in a new comic film series, one that was a direct ripoff of the popular "Mutt and Jeff" newspaper comic strip, except Anderson called his characters Hank and Lank.

Carney would be Hank, if only Anderson could find Lank. Months later, Anderson's vigilance paid off: "One day, quite accidentally, while walking in the street, I spied a young man who immediately appealed to my judgment as being the man I wanted. He is six feet two inches in height and weighs 122 pounds, quite a contrast with Mr. Carney, who measures a little over five feet. Victor Potel is his name, and he had no stage training whatever when I employed him."[7]

Vic Potel was born in Lafayette, Indiana, on October 12, 1889. He was rail thin, extroverted and very likable. Potel quit his window dressing job at the Marshall Field and Company department store and never looked back.

Hank and Lank were two loafers looking for a free ride, and each film centered on a simple premise: Hank discovers a scheme to get free food, shelter or money, then Lank follows Hank's lead and gets punished or caught. This one-note idea

Augustus Carney.   *Victor Potel.*

Augustus Carney, Victor Potel, Fred Ilenstine and Arthur Mackley in Hank and Lank: Sandwich Men, *standing in front of The Avenue Hotel in Golden, Colorado.*

was short-lived (only nine films were made), but served to bring Carney and Potel into Anderson's domain, positioning the actors to star in Essanay's very successful Snakeville comedy series the next year.

Essanay's filmic gold mine, however, continued to be Anderson's westerns, and their value to the company was brought forcefully home in August, 1910, as preparations began for Anderson's third trip west. At this defining moment, Essanay was rocked by a shakeup that nearly ruined the company.

The trouble came from within, involving Essanay's newest star, J. Warren Kerrigan, a Louisville, Kentucky, native who'd arrived at the Chicago studio in January, 1910. A moderately-successful stage actor born the same year as Anderson, he was also tall, black-haired and charismatic, and six months into his movie career the Essanay publicity department was touting him as their best actor, in comedy or drama.

In this interval, Essanay business manager Aubrey M. Kennedy and production supervisor Gilbert Hamilton conspired to profit from the rising demand for westerns by starting their own studio, the American Film Manufacturing Company. Its only product would be cowboy movies, and Kerrigan was chosen as American's rival to Anderson. Ironically, this company-in-the-making was to be bankrolled by John Freuler and Samuel Hutchinson, two film exchange men being pressured by the Motion Picture Patents Company to either sell their movie rental businesses to the General Film Company (the Patents Company distribution arm) at a bargain price or be forced out of business. The two exchange men fought back with a vengeance; they raided Essanay's staff for its ready-made talent and got American rolling immediately, producing films for distribution independently as one of the so-called "unlicensed" movie companies, thereby competing head-to-head against General Film and the Patents Company. But first Freuler and Hutchinson wanted to see a sample product from the renegade Essanay people, so Hamilton took Jack Kerrigan, actress Dot Farley and director Tom Ricketts to Benton Harbor, Michigan, and made a one-reeler, *Romantic Redskins*. Freuler and Hutchinson were impressed by the film, and the American Film Manufacturing Company was announced in the movie trade magazines during the first week in October.

Kerrigan, Farley and Ricketts went with Kennedy and Hamilton to American (also known as "Flying A" because of its distinctive company logo), but even more devastating was just how many of their colleagues followed them; all told, forty-seven out of sixty employees left Essanay, including comedy director Sam Morris and writer Allan Dwan. Spoor filed an injunction against American to keep the rest of his staff from being lured away with offers that literally doubled their old salaries, but the damage was already done.

Flying A, however, wasn't exactly free to do as it pleased; they were legally denied the use of any camera that incorporated the inventions of the patents holders, and Patents Company lawyers routinely sued independent film companies like Flying A to inforce the law. The upstart company avoided that particular problem by taking a cue from Anderson and leaving Chicago for parts unknown in the far

west. If the Patents Company detectives couldn't find them, Flying A couldn't be intimidated or forced to shut down.[8]

Significantly, Anderson's division remained loyal to him; his full staff (plus a few more recruits), were ready to go west immediately. This meant, however, that Spoor was left nearly alone in Chicago. It was a stressful time, and a report published in *Variety* (dated September 15th) suggested the worst: "The strained relations which have been known to exist for some time between George Spoor and his partner, Geo. M. Anderson, in the Essanay Company, are said to have reached almost to the point of open rupture. There is a report that Spoor has been compelled to negotiate for a new producer under pretext that Anderson is compelled to be away from the home plant attending to business at the Los Angeles branch. This is taken as an indication that the final break between Spoor and Anderson is at hand."[9] A statement from Spoor published two weeks later went to the other extreme, saying the strained business relationship "between G. M. Anderson and myself is absolutely untrue and the rumor has probably been circulated by discharged employees for a purpose." What's more, the departure of several employees was simply "a pruning of dead wood" and they would be replaced by new, more talented people.[10]

Spoor soon brought in a new director, Harry McRae Webster, from Philadelphia, but it took time to assemble the full staff, and therefore the Chicago studio wasn't able to release its first subject any earlier than November 1st. Anderson had to shoulder the task of producing every film on the schedule until then.

To make matters more complicated, Essanay announced a contest to find a one-word equivalent to "moving picture show," "five-cent theatre" or nickelodeon, all of which were deemed inadequate. Movies were still the ugly stepchild of live theatre, and this "canned" entertainment (as some critics snobbishly called it) was still less dignified than vaudeville or burlesque. The contest was Essanay's attempt to uplift the movie industry. Over 2,500 suggestions were received by the closing day, September 1st, and a $100 prize was awarded to Edgar Strakosch, owner of three theaters in Sacramento, California, who submitted the name "photoplay." The judges clearly explained their reason for the decision: "The word Photoplay seemed to us to have better chances of adoption by the public than combinations of more abstruse or technical terms such as kino, graph, drome, cine, etc. One may speak of 'going to the Photoplay' or 'seeing the Photoplay' as the public speaks of 'going to the opera' or 'hearing the opera,' these expressions conveying immediately an accurate idea of the character of the performance."[11] The name was appropriated for *Photoplay*, the best of the silent-era fan magazines, and used frequently in those days, but was eventually overtaken by a simpler term, "the movies."

On September 15, 1910, the Western Essanay Company, now twenty-five strong, left Chicago by train for the west. As with Anderson's previous trip, the movie trade magazines reported fanciful destinations for Essanay shooting locations: Wyoming, Montana and Washington state. This itinerary was fed to them by Anderson, but he couldn't have seriously considered that route; he didn't have time to explore the northwest, a place he'd never seen. More likely, Anderson was using the press to keep promoting Essanay as a visionary producer of westerns always on the lookout for the best scenic wonders in the country. In reality, Anderson had already directed interior scenes for several westerns in Chicago, and expected to finish them up in Colorado, an always-reliable location in the past. This was his first stop.

Rolling along with them was a railroad baggage car specially converted into a film processing lab. The car had its own electric generating plant, a movie projector to view footage, and room to store and prep cameras. The olive-green baggage car even supplied advertising: each side had a brass-mounted painting of the Indian-head trademark in a circle, with an inscription stretching across the top in bold, white letters — "Essanay Film Manufacturing Co., Negative Car." The negative car made it possible to develop and edit the film on the road, and this efficiency enabled the Chicago studio to print and release *Patricia of the Plains* a scant two weeks after it was shot in Colorado.[12]

In charge of this mobile facility was Orrin Denny, a twenty-eight-year-old still photographer born in Lewisville, Indiana. With ten years experience at his craft, he was well-suited to handle both the lab work and shoot still pictures. This meant Robbins could concentrate on cinematography while Denny set up the 5X7 view camera to take an ample assortment of scene stills and behind the scene publicity photographs (something otherwise left to chance during the fading rays of sunlight at the end of the day, a time when movie film was too insensitive to record a good

Orrin Denny.

The Essanay company in Morrison: William A. Russell and Arthur White arrange the set in the portable stage; Elmer Thompson holds the makeup mirror for Fred Church: Chick Morrison and Fred Ilenstine unload furniture. Note the Red Rocks area in the background.

Cowboys Augustus Carney, Fred Church, Joseph Smith, Harry Todd, Jack O'Brien, Bob Gray and Victor Potel are happy to take leassons from the new schoolteacher Clara Williams in The Circle C Ranch's Wedding Present, *filmed on the new portable stage.*

exposure). Like Robbins and several other Essanay employees, Denny was also allowed to bring along his wife Vera and their one-year-old daughter Vivienne.[13]

The Western Essanay's stay in Colorado was brief; only a month after their arrival they left for California. Along with them came the negative car, a boxcar full of props, and a railroad flatcar carrying a well-worn Concord stagecoach and Anderson's brand new six-thousand-dollar Thomas Flyer, an automobile purchased in Denver. But Clara and Frank Hall were not on board; they'd left for a theatrical engagement, and from there would go to the Lubin Film Company.

Anderson didn't even pause for replacements. He already had Brinsley Shaw, a thirty-four-year-old actor from New York City who'd joined Essanay in May. Shaw took over the villainous roles vacated by Frank Hall. Gladys Field, born in San Francisco and, at twenty-one, a year younger than Clara, had been with the company since Santa Barbara. She graduated to leading roles opposite Anderson.

Colorado had served Anderson well, but he felt there was still more to be found near San Francisco. The company stopped first in San Jose, then moved to the more rugged territory of Los Gatos, ten miles to the west at the foot of the Santa Cruz Mountains. Across from the Los Gatos train station was the Hotel Lyndon,

Hotel Lyndon.

Alma.

large enough to accomodate the film company, and behind the hotel was room for their new portable stage to shoot interior scenes.[14]

The company soon discovered another location a little farther up in the hills on the road to Santa Cruz, at Alma, and this became a favorite spot to film exteriors. It was a rail stop in the countryside, with only a depot, a general store and a livery stable, but it was perfect in its simplicity for Essanay's unpretentious westerns.

Jess Robbins at the camera for The Tenderfoot Messenger *in Los Gatos. G. M. Anderson directs to his left, Gus Carney stands on Fred Church's back and Victor Potel steadies him.*

Essanay in Alma for The Two Reformations. *Bob Gray is off by himself to the left. On the stagecoach: Chick Morrison at the reins, Eldon Hatch with the light scarf, Fred Church at the bottom right. On horseback: Brinsley Shaw, Victor Potel, Harry Todd, Jack O'Brien and*

Nancy Robbins. Margaret Joslin wears the white coat, Gladys Field the vest, Gus Carney stands beside her, Arthur Mackley wears the badge and G. M. Anderson stands at the edge with a polka dot tie. Most of the unidentified people are probably Los Gatos and/or Alma residents.

Arthur Mackley, Victor Potel and Matt Blair watch Fred Church handle a rope in Los Gatos.

The general store was used in *The Girl of the West* and the train depot served as a stagecoach way station in T*he Two Reformations.*

Their biggest problem, as usual, was inclement weather; it constantly tormented them. January was the worst; one four-day period brought more than sixteen inches of rain. At one point there were wash-outs along the railroad tracks, leaving Los Gatos isolated, and filming was suspended for nearly five weeks. By this time the total rainfall was a record-breaking twenty-eight inches, and a hopeless situation for filmmaking.

On February 4, 1911, the company packed up and moved south in search of fair weather, stopping forty miles east of Los Angeles in Redlands.[15] This community of citrus trees and red-clayed soil ringed by mountains looked great for westerns, but it was drizzling when they arrived. Nevertheless, the company checked in at the Hill Crest Inn, located at the corner of Orange and West Colton streets.

The weather improved enough by February 7th for the first filming to take place in nearby Santa Ana Canyon. The next day a vacant lot two blocks from Orange Street on West Lugonia Avenue was rented for Essanay's open-air stage. Anderson was heartened by this progress, but decided more cowboys were needed, and to that end he went to Los Angeles looking for seasoned professionals in the cattle stockyards.

He also visited the Selig, Biograph, Pathe and Kalem companies, all of them now in the Los Angeles area filming. Like Essanay, they were all members of the Patents Company, out west for the beautiful scenery and proverbial sunshine, if it

G. M. Anderson helps Gladys Field in Across the Plains.

could be found. Anderson and his peers were friendly rivals, willing to share information and swap tales about their many adventures. Like pioneers of the old west, this community of equals understood the hardships they all faced and was the best source of help in any emergency. They met out of respect, friendship and, sometimes, survival.

Anderson brought fifteen horses and twelve cowboys to Redlands, recruited Indians from the Banning reservation and started on *Across the Plains*, the earliest surviving film made in the vicinity. The Santa Ana River, Highland and Baseline areas were used extensively in this film. In one sequence Gladys Field drives a covered wagon at breakneck speed down the road between East Highland and the bridge over the Santa Ana River, pursued by Indians. She actually handled the reins, but the *Redlands Daily Facts*, a local newspaper, revealed she was cleverly assisted as a safety measure: "Four men lay in the bed of the wagon, each clinging to one rein, in order to stop the frightened team when the drama was over. On this occasion the wagon had several narrow escapes from overturning, going on only two wheels at times, the horses being thoroughly frightened."

This part was finished without incident, but in a shot of the rescuing posse "one of the ponies fell, throwing his cowboy rider in front of the others... The rushing horses could not be stopped, and the fallen cowboy was run over, one horse stepping on his arm and another on his hand. It was pretty tough on the actor-man, but it made a cracking good film, for the camera caught it all."[16] But that harrowing shot never made it into the film because the cowboys were supposed to be riding to the rescue, not falling all over each other. This incident led the new cowboys to ponder what they were risking their lives for, and as a result they went on strike for more money. During the standstill, the cowboys wandered the streets looking for other jobs, and eventually Anderson had to make another Los Angeles trip to find replacements.

It was during the standoff between Anderson and the cowboys that Anderson decided to prove something: maybe he didn't need them in every film. The result was a rarity, a movie with only one actor. Called *What a Woman Can Do*, the *Dramatic Mirror* praised everything about it: "This film is a distinct novelty, besides being very well acted. It is a strong, consistent life story, with only one character visible throughout the film, although others are effectively indicated. The part is played by Mr. Anderson. He is first seen as a young man receiving a letter from his sweetheart that she will marry him, and go west with him to seek their fortune. Five years later we see him as a prospector, making a successful strike. With gold now at his command, he is next seen entering his home with presents of finery for his wife, only to find a note from her that she has given up the fight and has deserted him for another. Rage causes him to burn all her belongings, and he becomes a misanthropic womanhater, refusing ten years later to go to her assistance and living on for his gold alone. He finally dies in the safe where his wealth is stored."[17] Anderson was so proud of *What a Woman Can Do* that he made it the basis for his first six-reel feature, *Humanity*, nearly five years later.

Another Redlands film had a more immediate effect on his future; it was a comedy western, *"Alkali" Ike's Auto*, with Augustus Carney in the title role as an ornery cowboy facing rival Mustang Pete for the hand of Betty Brown.

Pete and Betty were played by real-life husband and wife Harry Todd and Margaret Joslin Todd. Harry had been acting since he was a teenager, but Margaret saw herself as a homemaker and mother to their young daughter Marguerite. Margaret was only corraled into acting because she was available, but it turned out she had a natural gift for comedy. When Anderson first talked to her about playing the role, Margaret was doubtful: "I remarked to him that I was afraid I was too serious for comedy. He replied that it was my very serious aspect that made him consider me for the part."[18]

It was Margaret's calming influence, firmly stationed between the two scenery-chewing veterans, that made it all work. Her character became the object of desire for both men, and their attempts at one-upping each other brought forth a stream of delightfully comic situations.

"Alkali" Ike's Auto became a tremendous hit, but even before it was released G. M. Anderson felt inspired to produce a follow-up, *The Infant at Snakeville*. In it he re-introduced his soon-to-be-famous cowboy, but this time called him Broncho Bill, an indication this character was still in its formative stage.

The Infant at Snakeville was made after moving to Santa Monica. Anderson had barely kept to schedule in Redlands, producing only twelve films in two months (once again, the weather doing him in), and it looked like a return to Santa Monica might solve his problems. Jack O'Brien rented three houses on Ocean Avenue for

Augustus Carney, Margaret Joslin and Harry Todd in "Alkali" Ike's Auto.

the company, but they spent most of their time in Santa Monica Canyon.[19] *Forgiven in Death*, a story that ends with Anderson and Brinsley Shaw trapped in a cabin during an Indian attack, effectively used this desolate terrain. Anderson shot here again when he played a noble Indian, Gray Wolf, in his next film, *The Tribe's Penalty.*

It was in Santa Monica that Anderson's colleague, Arthur Mackley, began to direct. Mackley had been playing villains on the theatrical stage since the 1880s. By 1899 he was stage manager at Hopkin's Imperial Theater in St. Louis; the two men probably met there. Anderson saw Mackley again in Chicago shortly before the September trek west, and invited him and his wife Elhilda to come along. Mackley soon began writing scenarios, and the next logical step was to spin them out himself. His first directing effort was probably *The Ranchman's Son*, a story he wrote with a working title of *A Race With Death*.[20] Mackley was learning fast.

Bad weather continued to plague Essanay, but, as if that wasn't enough, when the sun finally came out Santa Monica was swarming with film companies. D. W. Griffith and his Biograph Company came to make a western, so did Frank Montgomery with the Bison Company, and Pathe director James Young Deer was already in town. Before long the Vitagraph Company, led by director Rollin Sturgeon, and Bison's Thomas H. Ince would establish studios there.

To further distract Anderson, George Spoor once again came west for a series of conferences with his partner.[21]

Essanay was releasing two movies a week, but the profit margins were shrinking, and more releases were needed to sustain the company. Spoor wanted to increase the weekly output to three films. The question was, could Anderson contribute two or three more movies each month?

Anderson believed he could, if the sun would cooperate, but the crowded terrain in Santa Monica didn't appeal to Anderson, so he ordered Jack O'Brien north to search for a better situation. O'Brien found what he was looking for in San Rafael, just north of San Francisco, in Marin County. It would be the Western Essanay's best location yet.

Chapter Four
San Rafael

There was a valley with farmland and cattle ranches. The little nearby towns of San Anselmo and Fairfax gave the area a decided western flavor. A stagecoach still ran over the mountains on a dusty road from Fairfax to Bolinas. And the mountains — Loma Alta on the north, Pine on the west and Tamalpais to the southwest — often protected the area from ocean fog and rain, spreading out the cloud cover and letting in sunshine. San Rafael, population 5000, had a lot going for it when Essanay arrived on May 31, 1911.[1]

O'Brien rented four houses near the Eastside Ballpark, while set carpenter Ben Lee and scenic artist Arthur White put up Essanay's portable stage just outside the park's right field foul line.[2] The last people to know this were those most affected, the San Rafael Colts baseball team. Their star player, Roland Totheroh, remembered: "One day we went to practice at our ballpark, and lo and behold! there was a bunch of cowboys and Indians all over the field."[3]

That situation was quickly resolved, for if anyone at Essanay sympathized with the team it was Anderson, a baseball fanatic. One of the ways he relaxed between shots was playing catch with the local kids.

Essanay's first film in San Rafael was *The Outlaw Samaritan*. It opened with outlaw Jack Mason (Anderson) robbing an express train singlehandedly, and was filmed on the route between Fairfax and San Rafael.[4]

Fairfax became one of Anderson's most frequently visited locations. The town was like a ready-made western set, and the surrounding hills made terrific backgrounds. Anderson was so grateful to the community for their support that he staged a wild west show in Fairfax Park to benefit the local fire department. The event included a stage holdup, broncho busting and an Indian attack. Tickets went for twenty-five cents, and two hundred and fifty dollars were raised.[5]

Anderson also recognized the worth of his cowboys, and increased their numbers dramatically. Chick Morrison was gone (probably a casualty of the cowboy strike in Redlands), but newcomers Tom O'Rourke, Joe Derlin, Joe Cassidy, Louis Morisette and Al Parks more than made up for Morrison's loss. Morisette, a youngster hired fresh from the Kalem Film Company, drove the stagecoach. Joe

Lined up at the Eastside Ballpark: Fred Church (wearing sombrero), Gladys Field, Joe Cassidy (on the stagecoach), Harry Todd, Victor Potel, Louis Morisette, ?, Al Parks, Richard Young.

Cassidy, an experienced wrangler, was the backup driver. Parks did most of the stunt riding, and was especially gifted; he could throw his horse down and, while still in the saddle, make the animal rise again.

Skilled horsewomen were harder to come by, but the Western Essanay did acquire Anna Little, a young lady from Northern California's Siskiyou County, when the company was based in Redlands. Her previous work in Ferris Hartman's musical comedies, on the face of it, didn't seem to qualify her for westerns, but she was an expert horserider. Anderson chose her, however, because of the way she looked; her black hair, dark eyes and slim figure struck him as a perfect type for Indian roles, although she was just as well-suited for any western part. But her own concern for appearances was less focused, according to a *San Francisco Call* reporter: "Anna Little, who plays the Indian maid to perfection, never worries about hairpins, puffs, plumes or lace shirtwaists. On or off the stage she wears her heavy black hair down over her shoulders and her arms bare to the elbows. 'I wear this blue army shirt by day,' she explained, 'and when I dress up at night I put on a brown one.'"[6] Anderson was considering her for the starring part in a one-actor movie when she decided to leave the company and go to the rival Bison Company in August. She would continue her western roles in many more movies, notably with Jack Hoxie and William S. Hart, until her retirement in the 1920s.

It was important to have these young men and women at hand, for western filming was rough and tumble, exhausting and sometimes downright dangerous.

54   *Chapter Four*

Fred Church practicing at the ball park.

One actor was kicked in the chest by a horse in a river-crossing scene and was at the point of drowning when Fred Church rescued him with a well-placed toss of his lariat. Even veteran actors who knew the risks too often took chances. Harry Todd and Brinsley Shaw rehearsed a realistic fight scene with a knife in one film, and Shaw was accidently stabbed. He had to go to the hospital.

It wasn't any safer behind the camera. Jess Robbins remembered a time when ten riders swerved past him in a typical posse ride-by as he cranked his movie camera. Jack O'Brien, trailing behind, rode straight toward Robbins: "I was looking into the finder of the camera. Jack and his horse grew larger and larger. I heard the clatter of hooves close upon me. Still I thought O'Brien would turn out. Horse and rider filled the picture. There was a crash. Things turned black. I woke up in the roadside ditch. The camera was on top of me, my hand crushed between the legs of the tripod. I saved the machine, but Jack and I wore bandages for a month."[7]

The most dangerous work of all was on the stagecoach. The first accident happened on August 2nd while making *The Stage Driver's Daughter*. Gus Carney recalled: "We had finished a scene and were going further up to make the next one. I was tired and got into the stagecoach, which carried the props. Everybody else, except the leading lady, who rode with the driver, walked." The lady was Gladys Field and the driver, Louis Morisette, guided four livery horses over the grade, but the animals, unaccustomed to the swaying vehicle, were spooked by some cowboys riding up, and bolted.

Louis Morisette holds the reins in The Stage Driver's Daughter, *although Arthur Mackley (with*

whip) is the father of Gladys Field (waving). Fred Church stands by the camera, Anderson directs.

The coach skidded and hopped down the graveled grade while Morisette struggled to control it, Gladys clung to the seat beside him, and Carney bounced around inside, battered by the props and seat cushions. As they swung around a nasty curve, the body of the coach separated from the front wheels. The wheels and horse continued ahead as the coach went over the embankment and plunged down a rocky slope.

Gladys started to jump, but Louis grabbed her by the waist and held on, knowing the rocks would certainly break her bones — or worse. Louis commanded, "Not until I tell you." The coach bucked and bounced, skidding like a sled down the hill until it came to a patch of brush. "Jump!" yelled Louis, and they both leaped off. The coach then started to tumble, and kept rolling, over and over, until it slid to a stop on its side.

Carney, still inside, pawed his way through the props and seat cushions, crawled out and stood staring, amazed to see the coach intact, except for the missing front wheels. Louis and Gladys suffered nothing more than bruises and scratches, as did Carney, but whenever the company went to the mountains after that, Carney walked.[8]

Anderson was receptive to story ideas from anywhere. Taylor Graves, a fourteen-year-old lad from San Anselmo, sold him a scenerio for $5. Anderson also took them, free, from books and magazines whenever they appealed to him, but more often he relied upon Josephine Rector.

Josephine had been on vacation when she bumped into the company in Los Gatos, and was introduced to Jack O'Brien. He discovered she had an interest in writing, encouraged her to submit stories, and bought some from her. She returned home to San Francisco, thinking nothing more about it, until she heard from Jack again months later when the company was stationed in San Rafael. She commuted across the bay by ferry, wrote scripts and received $15 a week.

Some stories came from the life Anderson led. *"Spike" Shannon's Last Fight* was inspired by his interest in boxing, and "Spike" Shannon's name was borrowed from a real-life San Rafael personality — Billy Shannon. Shannon was an old-time prizefighter from the bare-knuckle days. Those days were over, but his saloon, Billy Shannon's Villa, at the west end of Fourth Street was a rendezvous for would-be boxers and fighters with a national reputation (among them: Frankie Burns, "Harlem Tommy" Murphy and "Gunboat" Smith), who came to work out in a gymnasium Shannon built next door. It was in this atmosphere that Anderson met a promising young heavyweight boxer named "Soldier" Elder.

Willis "Soldier" Elder was making a name for himself as a scrapper who had little technical grace, but possessed a devastating knockout punch. His opponents rarely lasted six rounds, even those who appeared to outmatch him. He entered the ring in one memorable fight outweighed 245 pounds to 163. In the first round Elder was knocked out of the ring — twice. Elder got even, and then some, during the fourth round by winning with a knockout.[9] Soon, Anderson was paying all of Elder's training expenses, giving him a job with Essanay (as an actor and prop man), and betting heavily on Elder to win.

Taking a break at the watering trough: Billy Shannon in white shirt and tie between fight promoters Grant Gorman and George Sharkey. Seated are George Schrieder, Ben Smith, Bob Shand, Van Gorman, George Proctor, Frankie Burns and Frankie Smith.

Fred Church and Willis "Soldier" Elder spar, and size each other up.

Anderson inevitably translated the excitement of the ring into a story. It was about a fighter who falls in love, but the woman marries him only after he promises to give up the sport. Some time later, when his wife is ill, the one quick way to pay for the expensive operation she needs is for him to get back into the ring and win the big fight.

For the climactic fight scene, Anderson had a boxing ring built on the baseball field, and invited the town. The grandstand was packed with a crowd that included Mayor Kinsella, District Attorney Boyd, Fire Chief Schneider, Judge Magee, undertaker Charles Edsberg, and a cross-section of the community's inhabitants. A large contingent of ladies, also there, were not allowed to be in the film because "ladies didn't attend fights."

There was one departure from the script: in the second round, when Anderson is knocked down, a spectator leaped in to rescue him. It was Anderson's bulldog. The animal jumped at Anderson's opponent with jaws wide open, but the referee saved the day by whipping his towel at the dog. The bulldog sank his teeth into the towel and was steered from the ring. Robbins caught this on film, but it wasn't part of the script, so the scene was retaken while two men held the dog to prevent instant replays.[10]

In July, Essanay's stay in San Rafael was deemed so successful that the two-month leases on three of the four houses were extended indefinitely. The one on 801 Second Street was not renewed because Jack O'Brien was about to leave. He'd secretly gotten an offer to direct a feature-length film, *The Life of Buffalo Bill*, for the Buffalo Bill and Pawnee Bill Film Company, and couldn't pass it up. Pretending he needed a vacation, he went east to see if this was the break he'd been looking for. It was.[11]

With O'Brien gone, Frank J. Costello took over the managerial duties. Costello was a San Rafael resident and stage manager for the Garden Theatre, a performance space created when the local skating rink was divided in half.

Costello's connection to the venue came in handy when Anderson decided to sponsor a benefit for the San Rafael baseball team. The team was short of funds, but wanted to build a new grandstand, so Anderson paid the team back for the use of the ballfield by bringing the community together and having some fun.

The benefit was a vaudeville revue with a two-act play, *The Ensign*, thrown in. Nearly all of the Essanay company participated, but the highlight of the evening came when Anderson stepped onto the stage to recite "Casey at the Bat." The *Marin Tocsin* newspaper reported: "G. M. Anderson was easily the head of the bill and the way he was received proved beyond peradventure of doubt that he has not only endeared himself to the ball-loving fans but to the theatre going public as well, for it was some minutes before he was allowed to start his monologue so great was the applause which greeted him."[12]

Anderson must have gotten a great deal of satisfaction from these appearances because he often donated his and his company's time to entertain the local populace. In September there was an Elk's Club charity event, and, in October, a celebration of "San Rafael Days" that was spectacular, from all accounts.

Chief Lame Soldier (Willis Elder) and "Big Chief" Pat Rooney during the San Rafael Days celebration on October 24, 1911.

Gladys Field on the left and Willis Elder on the right during San Rafael Days.

Arthur Mackley and G. M. Anderson hold off a mob in The Strike at the "Little Jonny" Mine.

Anderson between takes in The Strike at the "Little Jonny" Mine.

All of these diversions might have distracted a lesser man from the task at hand — making movies — but Anderson seemed to thrive on it. His stories increased in complexity and his characters delved to a deeper emotional level. In *The Ranchman's Son*, Jake Webster (Anderson) accidentally kills a man in a struggle, the rancher's son is blamed and Webster struggles with his conscience before giving himself up. In *The Strike at the "Little Jonny" Mine*, Jim Logan (Anderson) refuses to lead his fellow mine workers against the hated superintendent when he realizes the strike is geared toward violence. He even joins the superintendent in fending off the mob, and his stand results in a better agreement for both sides. These moral tales of right and wrong made a connection with nickelodeon audiences, and encouraged Anderson to push ahead with even better stories.

Broncho Bill's Last Spree, only the second movie to headline this character (although released more than a year after *Broncho Billy's Redemption*), caught the public's attention in a special way, and brought Anderson to the front ranks of stardom. A comedy with serious undertones, *Broncho Bill's Last Spree* was adapted from an uncredited O. Henry short story, "The Reformation of Calliope."

In the movie, Broncho Bill is a no-good drunk who shoots up the town of Snakeville and gets arrested. An elderly lady then arrives by stagecoach and inquires about her son Broncho Bill. When the sheriff finds out, he does a surprising thing; he pins his badge on Bill and pretends to be Bill's prisoner. Bill sobers in the presence of his mother, and it looks like his wild days are gone forever.

A dynamic moment from Broncho Billy's Adventure: *Arthur Mackley, Edna Fisher and Anderson stand by while Pat Rooney (helped by Kite Robinson) carries Fred Church to a doctor.*

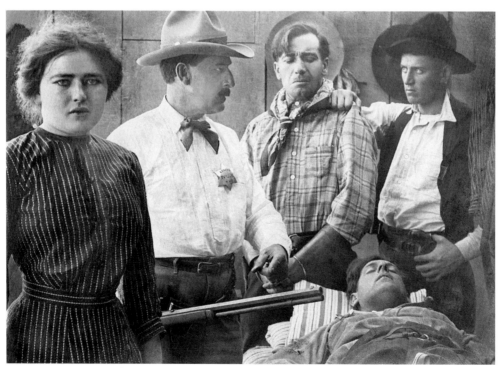

Edna Fisher, Arthur Mackley, Brinsley Shaw, Fred Church and Anderson (lying down) in The Deputy and the Girl.

While that film was still in circulation, Anderson followed it up with *Broncho Billy's Christmas Dinner* and *Broncho Billy's Adventure*, reinforcing the image. From then on, G. M. Anderson and Broncho Billy became synonymous, although he continued to make non-Broncho Billy westerns. That is, the names of his characters in the other films were different, even when their sensibilities, the stories and the settings weren't. But however he tried to make a distinction between Billy and the other cowboys, that bond became so tight he couldn't escape the connection. Indeed, many of these films would later be remade with Broncho Billy.

Edna Fisher was Anderson's leading lady in *Broncho Billy's Christmas Dinner*. She was two years younger than Gladys Field, who left Essanay for New York on August 2nd (most likely to meet Jack O'Brien, whom she would soon marry). Edna was new to films, but her youthful energy and agility more than made up for her inexperience in acting. It certainly helped when she was in the driver's seat of the old stagecoach three months after Gladys's near-tragedy with Louis Morisette.

Edna's own close call came during a rehearsal for a scene in *Broncho Billy's Christmas Dinner*. The location was the Fairfax Park Annex building at the corner of Main Street and Bolinas Road. Edna was supposed to be waiting alone in the driver's seat of the coach while the driver went inside "a saloon" to wish his friends a merry Christmas. The movie called for cowboys to fire their guns from the porch of the building and spook the stagecoach horses. The horses bolted, on cue, but two men stationed ahead to stop the animals were brushed aside as the coach raced on at full speed down the road, completely out of control. The horses swerved around a sharp turn at Deer Creek Road, the coach turned over and Edna was thrown to the ground. Early news reports claimed she'd fractured her skull and was near death; this information was repeated in the movie trade magazines. In reality she came through it with only a sprained ankle, but the incident was played up for all it was worth during the release of the film, and may have prompted those who wouldn't have otherwise seen a western to attend.[18] If so, they were in for a treat.

Broncho Billy's Christmas Dinner is among the best of Anderson's surviving work, and, in particular, the long sequence of him rescuing Edna on the runaway stagecoach is wonderfully done. There are beautiful shots taken from a distance as the coach kicks up a cloud of dirt while Anderson on horseback slowly closes the gap between them. Al Parks performs the difficult stunt (doubling for Anderson) of transferring from his galloping horse to the coach as it speeds around a curving dirt road, headed directly for the camera. And Edna is right up there on the coach herself riding it out. Following the transfer there's an effective shot taken from behind, with the camera mounted on top of the coach, as Anderson struggles at length to slowly rein in the wild horses on a dangerous mountainside road. It looks like he stops the horses just short of a precipice. Beyond that, the film is an interesting combination of comedy and drama, well-acted and solidly directed. Edna, in the role of a college student on her way home for the holidays, performs expressively and charmingly, a hint of the talent she might have fashioned into a

An Essanay location: downtown Fairfax at the corner of Broadway and Bolinas Road. At left is Henry Frustuck (owner of the building), an unknown man, the Bridges brothers and an unidentified actor.

Edna Fisher anticipates trouble from Harry Todd, Victor Potel and Kite Robinson on the porch of the Fairfax Park Annex in Broncho Billy's Christmas Dinner.

Edna introduces Broncho Billy to her parents, played by Julia and Arthur Mackley, in Broncho Billy's Christmas Dinner.

great career if she hadn't soon thereafter met Vitagraph director Rollin Sturgeon, married him and retired.

Arthur Mackley's workload as an Essanay writer and director had increased by the fall of 1911, and, naturally enough, Mackley's wife Elhilda began to regularly act in his films. Like Margaret Joslin, Elhilda was not an actress, and had initially come along just for the ride. She, too, stepped before the camera because she was handy, but she became fascinated with movies and decided to take an active part in them, using the name Julia Mackley. Arthur described his wife's technique: "She is just natural in everything she does. If in a picture she kicks you she is going to break your leg. She can't act."[17] Julia's realistic approach did not count against her, and she became a valued addition to the troupe.

On October 14th, Anderson, Fred Church and Jess Robbins went to San Francisco. Like thousands of other people, they were there to watch President William Howard Taft break ground for the 1915 Panama-Pacific International Exposition. Unlike most of them, they had a special pass to drive in and set up Essanay's camera to film the event. The camera stood by itself on a raised platform and was the best seat in the house, closer than the still-photographer section. While Robbins cranked the camera, Church and Anderson sat at the platform's edge, their feet dangling above the heads of the crowd below them.

The ceremony was held in Golden Gate Park, far from the actual site of the exposition, for the simple reason that no one knew at this early date where the real

Louis Morisette and Victor Potel are the bandits, Jess Robbins films them and Willis Elder stands tall behind Robbins on the west side of Main Street in Petaluma, December 11, 1911.

Augustus Carney stands next to Fred Church at the camera; Willis Elder is on the other side with Louis Morisette and Victor Potel holding their loot. They face west at Main and Washington.

location would be. Taft took a silver spade from *Chronicle* newspaper publisher Charles de Young, the master of ceremonies, and dug into the sandy earth. In a write-up to the film a critic quipped: "It is easily cognizable that it has been some years since the president handled a shovel, but he gets away with it effectively, if not in very fine style."[13] The earth was dumped into a small ceremonial box held by de Young, then fireworks in the shape of an American flag were set off, white and gray pigeons were released to circle overhead, and diva Lillian Nordica sang "The Star Spangled Banner." After the final, sustained note the President put on his top hat and the event was over, except for the souvenir hunters who scooped up handfuls of earth around the hole to put in their pockets, and those who stripped the red, white and blue bunting from the presidential box for keepsakes.[14]

To round out the film, Robbins shot scenes all over San Francisco — Market Street, Chinatown, the Cliff House, and a panorama from Lone Mountain. These images were contrasted with scenes of the devastating earthquake and fire only five and a half years before to illustrate the city's remarkable recovery and triumph over tragedy.

It was also a reminder to Anderson of how far he had come from his days at Vitagraph when he first witnessed the destruction of San Francisco on film. Now, like the city he loved, his future was bright.

In the last two months of 1911 the Western Essanay took one-day excursions north to Petaluma and Santa Rosa.

A crowd in Santa Rosa saw the company film a comedy scene for *The Biter Bitten* starring Gus Carney and Vic Potel. The action centered on a "stolen" horse and buggy speeding down Fourth Street, chased by an automobile, another horse with buggy and local girl Margaret Hockin on horseback. In an unexpected twist, yet another car drove toward the group as they crossed B Street. Miss Hockin had to rein in her horse, forcing the buggy behind her to ram her horse. Injuries were minor. That night the Essanay troupe performed their repertory favorite, *The Man From Mexico*, to a large, appreciative audience at the Columbia Theater.[15]

In Petaluma, the Sonoma County National Bank at the corner of Main and Washington streets was the scene of an Essanay "robbery." Five men rode up, entered the bank and "shot" cashier Arthur Mackley dead, then raced away with some loot. In the excitement of the chase, one of the bandits dropped a sack of coins and posse member Al Parks performed the stunt of scooping up the bag from the ground while riding by on his horse. It delighted hundreds of people who stood by watching. Then, as in Santa Rosa, an accident occurred, but this one was nearly tragic. Martin Poehlman, an accountant with the bank, joined in helping to capture the lead outlaw, and, unfortunately, the outlaw's revolver went off accidentally, right in Poehlman's face. Although the gun was loaded with blanks, the gunpowder was real enough, and it temporarily blinded Poehlman, who had to go to the hospital.[16] That evening the Essanay troupe again performed *The Man From Mexico*, this time at the Hill Opera House.

In December, Anderson decided not to risk riding out the winter in the Bay Area, so he sent one of his people south to find a location near San Diego.[19]

Anderson himself had to go east on business, but, before he left, a banquet at the Marin Hotel was organized by San Rafael residents to honor Anderson and his company for their many acts of kindness to the town. There were speeches, then Ethel Robinson, an extra in a few films and daughter of a local businessman, sang "several beautiful songs." Anderson stood up next, bashfully thanking the people of Marin County for their hospitality. Then Arthur Mackley, in the Scottish burr of his native land, summed up: "When we all bid fond adieu to San Rafael, I assure you that there will be a longing in the hearts of every one for San Rafael until we return again."[20] They promised to return in the spring, and it seemed likely. The company had stayed there for seven months, longer than any previous location, and had made forty-three films in the vicinity — a record for them.

Anderson left San Rafael on December 12th to attend a Motion Picture Patents Company board meeting in New York, but his main task was to find a new leading lady. He didn't want a Broadway actress; for him personality was the key to casting, not acting experience. As he said to a writer for *Photoplay* magazine: "Stage experience? Doesn't do any harm if there hasn't been too much of it! A year or so's all right — but the old timers won't do."[21]

He felt an experienced actor would be fighting his direction, which had changed since his days in Colorado. He no longer stood in front of the cast and crew reading the story aloud. It took too much time. He now preferred to explain the specific scene to the actors, and no more: "It may be the last scene or the middle scene they are playing; they don't know. I figure that their acting is not going to be affected by their not knowing and it saves a lot of time." One actor in particular, Brinsley Shaw, frequently got "sore as the deuce" during production, but when it was done and seen on the screen Shaw had to admit the method worked.[22]

Anderson was on the lookout for a spirited ideal of the young American western woman. He wanted a movie archetype, not a stereotype, of the quality that Edna Fisher embodied: she was brave, bright and adventurous, willing and wanting to try new things. When, for instance, Edna convinces the old stagecoach driver in *Broncho Billy's Christmas Dinner* to let her sit up beside him, you instantly believe she wants to be up there because this is where the action is, not that it's simply required by the story. This was part of Edna's true personality; she was adventurous, sometimes even reckless, and when the coach turned over in rehearsal it was just like her to try the scene again without hesitation. That's what Anderson was looking for, and he found it in Vedah Bertram.

Vedah was announced in the movie trade magazines in January, 1912. *Motography* magazine characterized her best: "She is a type of the healthy, out-of-door loving, athletic girl of the west, with a charm and vivaciousness in her personality which is so potent a factor in the success of picture players."[23]

When Anderson returned to San Rafael on January 8, 1912, the company was packing to move south to Lakeside, near San Diego. Anderson hurried it along. They left two days later, but a few people stayed behind. Victor Potel, now the business manager, was still settling accounts. Ben Lee's wife was ill, and they would follow when she got better. Josephine Rector refused to go.

On El Monte Ranch *with Vedah Bertram, Robert H. Gray and Fred Church at Lakeside.*

Josephine Rector.

Since Jack O'Brien's departure, Josephine had worked directly with Anderson, and they didn't get along. Anderson could be a frustrating boss for anyone seeking his guidance or opinion; preoccupied, silent and unresponsive, he gave few clues to his thoughts until one too many interruptions provoked his fury. When he finally asked her to come along with them she said: "No. I've had enough of you."[24]

The company arrived in San Diego on January 12, 1912. Their ultimate destination was the Lakeside Inn, a resort hotel famous for its race track circling Lindo Lake, where Barney Oldfield and his "Green Dragon" automobile had set a world speed record of 65 miles per hour. The community and surrounding mountains had already been used extensively by director Allan Dwan and the American Film Company for westerns with Jack Kerrigan. They moved to nearby La Mesa, so Essanay had Lakeside to itself, but the company remained in San Diego for several days because Anderson wasn't with them.

He was still in San Francisco, tending to personal business, according to a newswire report in the *San Diego Sun*: "Convinced that 'Soldier' Elder is made of championship calibre by reason of his recent defeat here of Walter Monohan, Jack Johnson's former sparring partner, G. M. Anderson, the 'White Hope's' manager, announced today that he stands ready to back his charge against either Al Panzer or Jim Flynn. Anderson is so confident of Elder's ability to trim the two fighters that he has announced his willingness to wager anywhere from $500 to $2500 on his protege."[25]

Anderson and Vedah Bertram finally came to San Diego three days later and were immediately chauffeured by Pat Rooney to Lakeside. One look at the location and Anderson liked what he saw, even though, once again, a light rain was falling.

Vedah's debut in films came as the title character in *The Ranch Girl's Mistake*, a strong story that Anderson felt was sure-fire because he'd made it two years before in his own debut, *The Ranchman's Rival*. If Anderson liked a story he never hesitated to reuse it, like anyone fond of a good yarn, and if it eliminated one of the many variables in the difficult task of producing a successful movie with a newcomer, so much the better. The next film was *A Romance of the West*, a remake of *The Fence on Bar Z*, and the following film was *The Ranch Widower's Daughters*, a variation on *A Ranchman's Wooing*. But *The Bandit's Child*, the fourth film made at Lakeside, was an original, and Anderson liked the story so much he'd use it again in later years — twice.

In March, Vedah was hurt in a horseback scene. This was a major crisis, for there was currently no one to fill in for her from within the company. Anderson, desperate to find a worthy replacement, went to D. W. Griffith in Los Angeles. Griffith, who had an exceptionally fine group of actresses working for him at Biograph, generously loaned Marguerite Marsh to Essanay while Vedah recovered.

One touchy part of the situation was not being able to reveal who this new Essanay actress was. Movie stars were commonly advertised by name now, except at one last holdout company — Biograph. Anderson, always ready to use publicity in his favor, did reveal that an actress was on loan from Biograph, but kept mum about who it was.[26] At least three films were made with Marguerite: *Broncho Billy and the Bandits*, *A Western Legacy* and *Western Hearts*. In the last one, she co-starred with Vedah, who was able to resume work by then.

Anderson narrowly escaped injury, too, but not in a movie. Taking time off for a boxing match between Soldier Elder and Jim Cameron in Los Angeles, he was driven north by chauffeur Pat Rooney. With them in the big Thomas Flyer were Elder, Elder's trainer Fred Bogan, William A. Russell, Jess Robbins, boxer Reddy Corbett and San Diego Sun reporter Jesse Puryear.

The *Los Angeles Times* sportswriter covering the fight believed Cameron was heavyweight championship material, and Elder didn't stand a chance: "Elder hardly has class enough to bring out all there is in Cameron."[27] How wrong he was. Cameron was flattened in the sixth round, and carried unconscious from the ring.

Anderson was delayed in Los Angeles and decided to take a train back. The rest of the party, and more, came home in two cars. With Rooney was Elder, Bogan, Fred Church, Kite Robinson and Joe Archer. Just north of Oceanside the Flyer went over an embankment and rolled down the hillside for 70 feet, turning over four times. Elder left the car during the first rollover, sailed twenty feet and landed on his head, but somehow managed to roll to the side as the car tumbled toward him. The others remained in the vehicle all the way down. Rooney was pinned by the steering wheel. Bogan had serious injuries. Luckily the other car was there to help and everyone was piled inside. Bogan, Rooney and Elder hobbled from the Agnew Hospital in San Diego three days later, against doctors' orders, declaring they'd had enough of hospital life.[28] They were more fortunate than the Thomas Flyer, which was a total wreck.

Essanay spent two and half months at Lakeside making twenty-two films, including three Alkali Ikes and four Broncho Billys. In one of their last, *Broncho Billy's Bible*, Anderson came closer to danger. During rehearsals for a fight with Fred Church at the edge of a rocky cliff, Anderson broke away at a dramatic moment and stepped back, but the next moment was unrehearsed; he stumbled and fell over the edge. Church gasped and peered down, expecting to see a gruesome sight. Instead, there was Anderson, a few feet below, clinging to a tree growing from a crack in the rocks. While Church got a rope, Anderson hung on until he was saved. After a short breather, the scene was completed.[29]

As the weather grew warmer, Anderson felt it was time to revisit the San Francisco area, a fortunate decision for Josephine Rector. She was encountering terrible stress at home, her marriage failing after the death of her eldest child. She separated from her husband and moved in with her parents, then decided to write to Anderson in Lakeside, asking if he wanted more scripts. At least this way she wouldn't have to work with him directly. Anderson responded to her letter immediately: "Send all the stories you have and also let me know how your account stands... I appreciate your work and realize you are a great help to us. Let me hear from you."[30]

With this acknowledgment of her worth, the tension eased between them, and when it was known the company would return to the Bay Area, arrangements were made for Josephine and her young son Jem to meet them at their destination.

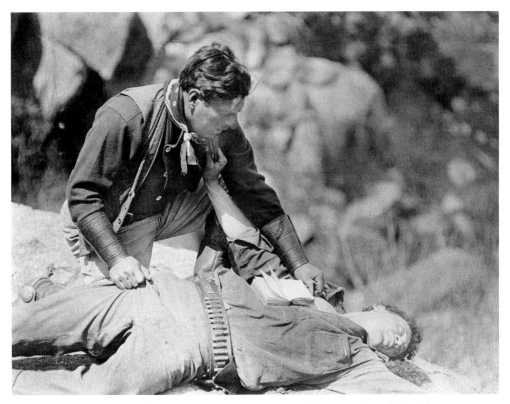

Anderson and Church at the climactic moment from Broncho Billy's Bible.

The same location from below.

But where were they going? Anderson sent Robbins north to find out, and Jess looked over a section in the East Bay that Essanay had never explored — Fruitvale, Castro Valley and Hayward. Before long, Anderson received a telegram from Robbins, and ordered the company to pack up. On Saturday, March 30, 1912, a circus-like procession of personnel and equipment left Lakeside by rail for the Southern Pacific connection north.[31] Their destination was Niles.[32]

Chapter Five
Niles and the Canyon

Niles itself was not very old in 1912. Most of its buildings had been around less than thirty years. But a few structures did date back to the 1840s, a legacy of the Spanish land grant days, when Jose de Jesus Vallejo owned the 17,000 acre *Rancho Arroyo de la Alameda*.

The first settlement was known as Vallejo Mills, named after a group of buildings at Alameda Canyon's western mouth, near the creek that provided water power for the millstones to grind the wheat from nearby fields. By 1912 the wheat fields had given way to orchards, and the old mill was in ruins. Vallejo's hold on the land was over too; he'd lost it in 1866 when a San Francisco businessman, Jonas Clark, took it all to settle Vallejo's debts.[1]

Clark sold the land. The Spring Valley Water Company bought much of it (including the Vallejo mill) to secure the Alameda Creek water rights. The Central Pacific Railroad bought property along their Transcontinental Railroad right of way (the final link of that historic route, for the Niles to Oakland section was finished after the famous golden spike event at Promontory, Utah).

The Central Pacific built a train depot just to the west of Vallejo Mills and called it Niles Station to honor one of their own, attorney Addison C. Niles, who became a California Supreme Court Justice in 1871, but it wasn't until 1884 that the railroad land, now owned by Southern Pacific, was parceled out and Vallejo Mills began to fade as Niles grew. William Snyder moved his general store from Old Town (as Vallejo Mills became known) to a new spot south of the rail tracks. John Virgil, the proprietor of Niles House (in Old Town), bought property beside Snyder. Houses went up. Two hotels. Two livery stables. Two churches. Several saloons. By the 1890s the general store had competition, and there were barber shops, meat markets, a shoe store, a harness shop — and more saloons.[2]

Alameda Canyon came to be known as Niles Canyon, but remained otherwise unchanged. The creek went through its regular cycle: lazy during the summer, raging during the winter. Similarly, the one-lane country road beside it was dusty in the summer, mud-clogged in the winter.

Niles train depot.

Niles Canyon.

The former Snyder general store on the far left was bought by Mason & Gomes after William Snyder died in 1906. This is downtown Niles in 1910.

Where Niles began, the Vallejo Mill.

The Hayward to Mission San Jose road is in the foreground.

The Belvoir Hotel, circa 1900.

Augustus Carney, Victor Potel, G. M. Anderson, Fred Church and Josephine Rector at the Belvoir. On the right is one of the tents temporarily set up on the grounds for Essanay personnel.

The Wesley Hotel.

The town of Niles was still trying to recover from the depression of 1907 when Gilbert M. Anderson and the Essanay Film Company arrived on April 1, 1912.[3] What Anderson saw was a business district barely three blocks long on Front Street. West of the Wesley Hotel there wasn't much to see: endless orchards to the 600 acre California Nursery grounds, a few scattered houses here and there, and the *Township Register* newspaper building by itself on the northwest side of town.

It would appear from the local Niles newspapers that having a big movie company in this town of 1,400 people was nothing to shout about. The April 6th headline on the front page of the *Register* — "Film Company is Located in Niles" — wasn't any larger than the one next to it — "Merchants Will Close on Sundays." None of the six headlines on the front page particularly stood out. The town's other weekly, the *Washington Press*, treated their one day scoop on the competition even more casually; their April 5th headline, "Essanay Film Company Comes to Niles," was placed on page five.[4] The news was probably downplayed because the whole town knew the story long before either paper could print it. By then the *Press* simply summed up: "As a result of the coming of the company to Niles our town already feels the impetus of its sudden increase in population."[5] The *Register* saw fit to report "nearly all available vacant rooms and two or three houses" were rented for the cast and crew.[6]

If the papers had published closer to the event it would have been a different story. For one thing, the company arrived unannounced. Marie Sharpe Bishop, at the time a schoolgirl who lived with her grandmother Emilie Chittenden at the family-run Belvoir Hotel (owned by Chittenden), remembered: "I was home for lunch, and nobody had ever heard of Essanay as far as I knew. When I came home at four o'clock the place was buzzing. They put up tents and Grandma had called everybody in town to help peel vegetables for dinner. These are the names of some of the people that arrived that day: Josephine Rector and son, Jay Hanna and daughter, Mr. and Mrs. Todd and daughter, Gus Carney, Vic Potel, and Mr. Leonard (I don't know his first name) was a director, Spider Roach, Jack Geyer and wife, Lou Morisette, Fred Church (who was a leading man and very good looking), Brinsley Shaw and his wife Hazel (she was a southern belle and, oh, he was a brute) and Bogan (he was a wrestler, Jack Geyer was a wrestler). Now these people landed in without reservations the first day and the other people were put up at the Hotel Wesley down in town."[7]

The "other people" were mostly cowboys and crew people in the habit of spending less money for a room, not that the Wesley was a bad place to stay (it had only been built four and a half years before), but the Belvoir, on a hill with its own garden and orchards, catered to summer vacationers from San Francisco. The Wesley, by contrast, was a stopover for salesmen and transients.

Local legend has it that Anderson immediately met with three enterprising townspeople — Luther Rood, editor of the *Register*, August May, president of the Bank of Alameda County, and saloon-owner Billy Moore. In the back room of Moore's saloon they discussed possible sites for Essanay's headquarters, and decided on one — an unused barn on Second Street.

The Essanay studio in 1912: the barn itself was used for storage,

the loft was a dressing room and the tent was Anderson's office.

Behind the barn: Lawrence Abrott and Ben Lee on the stage.

The west end of town: the two-story building on the far left is Billy Moore's saloon; the Township Register newspaper office is on the right. Note the "Hotel" sign (partially hidden), marking the location of the Wesley Hotel, and the orchard in the distance, where Essanay's studio will be.

Anderson's next step took him on a walk down the woodplanked sidewalks, concrete areaways and muddy paths of the business district. He was looking for a way to judge if his motion picture company would be welcomed by the community, and the way to find out, he believed, was to enter each shop and ask for money from the local merchants to pay for the barn rental. Anderson collected one hundred dollars that day.[8]

True or not, Anderson wasted no time in establishing himself; by Friday "the old Champion barn" was outfitted with the Essanay portable stage. After exactly a week in town Anderson also made a deal with barber and saloonman Joseph A. Silva to purchase Silva's bungalow at the corner of Second and F streets. He moved in, then bought land on a block between Front and Second at G Street: two lots from Frank Mortimer, three from Billy Moore and two from Alfrida Filmer.[9]

The reason for these purchases was simple; housing was scarce in Niles, and Anderson could profit from it by building and renting each unit for $25 per month to his cast and crew members.

The unimproved block was a prune orchard, but not for long; Anderson contracted for the trees to be removed and six smart bungalows packed into the space. Every available carpenter was hired to finish the project in record time, and they did. Three months later, Essanay personnel moved into the furnished homes.[10] One clever person dubbed their outpost "the reservation" and the name stuck.

It was the first home for many of them in years, and they all settled in comfortably, except for one incident caused by the fact that all the houses looked exactly alike.

Four of the first six Essanay bungalows built in Niles face Second Street and two are on G Street. Evelyn Selbie's house is the last one on the left, next door to Victor Potel's. Note the figure by the telephone pole: Broncho Billy Anderson himself.

Victor Potel and Fred Church roomed together, right next door to Evelyn Selbie and Josephine Rector. Victor said: "I remember coming home late one night and getting into a lady's bedroom by mistake. I got out in a hurry, too, but kicked her cat off the porch on entering, and the result was she wouldn't speak to me for a week. Told everybody what a mean man I was. After that I hung a green lantern on my porch so I'd know it."[11]

Essanay began filming immediately. A favorite location was at John Harding's White House Saloon, conveniently located between the mill ruins and the Canyon Road bridge at the mouth of Niles Canyon, as was the nearby Alameda Creek bed, when it was dry. If they wanted adobe buildings, there was the Vallejo adobe at the California Nursery, the Hirguera adobe further away, and structures in the Mission San Jose complex to the south. Sunol, a small town at the other end of Niles Canyon, was a popular location, too, especially along Kilkare Road. The rolling hills, many canyons and wide-open spaces around Niles were a vast movie backlot ready-made for Anderson's westerns.

Oakland-born Hal Angus, hired as an actor when the company came to Niles, recalled: "If they wanted a cemetery they'd go out to the cemetery, a real cemetery." From Angus's viewpoint, this was not just practical filmmaking, it represented Anderson's desire for authenticity. "He wanted everything as true as it could be."[12]

Six days a week the cast and crew gathered in the morning at the barn on Second Street. Cowboys saddled their horses and rigged the stagecoach for action. Jess Robbins piled his camera equipment into Anderson's Thomas Flyer and sat beside the chauffeur. Anderson sat in the back seat next to leading lady Vedah Bertram. If needed, Ben Lee and Arthur White loaded scene flats onto the bed of a dray wagon. The Flyer led this procession, everybody in costume, along Front Street past houses and businesses. The townspeople soon got used to this sight and paid little attention to it. Only visitors would stop and stare.

The Essanay company on Second Street getting ready in the morning. Willis Elder sits on the steps, Kite Robinson stands nearby, Anderson leans against the building, Harry Todd wears the tie, Fred Church holds his trusty rope. Note the shadow of the barn at the lower right corner.

Joe Cassidy holds the reins, with Lee Willard beside him.

These visitors were the ones to watch out for. At their worst they'd appear unexpectedly, caught by the eye of the camera as they peered through the bushes in the background, spoiling the scene being taken. There was nothing else to do but chase them away and retake the shot. If these people behaved themselves and stood behind the camera they were usually tolerated, but the cameraman had to be constantly on guard for their reflections in a windowpane or mirror as they stood by, staring. If their image was accidently caught on camera there was no going back for reshoots.[13]

The process of working in Niles soon became routine for Anderson, and he looked toward San Francisco for amusement. This was a city he loved passionately, so much so that he settled in at the St. Francis Hotel and commuted to Niles in his chauffeur-driven automobile. During the drive he often prepared the shooting schedule for the day in his head, and by the time the car pulled up to the Essanay barn he was ready to go. Everyone was there waiting for him to arrive, and had to be ready or face his wrath. Hal Angus remarked: "If things were going along pretty good with Anderson, then you could have some horseplay. If not, you kept your mouth shut."[14] It was typical of the man to howl at a worker who fumbled in some way, and fire him on the spot. But if the man was needed later on, Anderson would then be shouting for him to get back to work. The crew became conditioned to these moods and acted accordingly. If they wanted to keep working there was no other choice but to take it and do the best they could.

This wasn't easy; only Anderson fully understood what he had in mind to shoot that day. With him in the lead, he alone gave the word when a location suited his

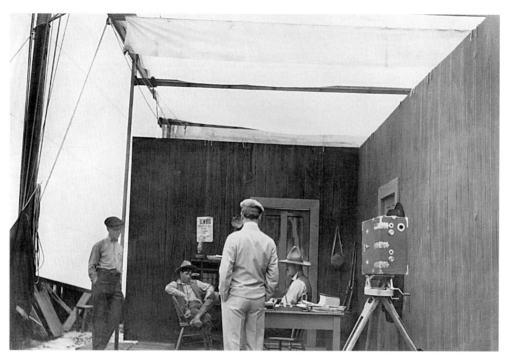

Anderson (with his back to the camera) directs Harry Todd and True Boardman at the barn in a scene from The Tenderfoot Sheriff. *Jess Robbins waits on the sidelines.*

Ben Lee, Kite Robinson (on ladder) and Lawrence Abrott constructing a set in Niles Canyon.

Hal Angus and Brinsley Shaw find a spare moment.

fancy. The procession through the canyon stopped, and it was then that he explained to everyone what was needed. If they were using the exterior of a real building, permission was received from the occupant, and Robbins set up his camera according to Anderson's instructions. But the two men didn't need to talk much. After years of working together, intutition came into play as much as words.

Elaborate sets were rare in Anderson's westerns, but if anything had to be constructed it was done very quickly and economically by Ben Lee and Arthur White. Hal Angus marveled at a process already refined by the time he came to Niles: "They'd use one set and paint it over and trim it out and take it out to the canyon."[15] Anderson was free to set up wherever he wished, putting the scene flat right next to Alameda Creek, angling it just right to catch the sunlight, and picking up a view of the picturesque hillside in the background. Little touches would be added here and there by Raymond "Kite" Robinson, a twenty-two-year-old from the Chicago studio who, on the road, had apprenticed with propman William A. Russell. He soon discovered the subtle placement of a tree branch beside a doorway could make all the difference in the world. Overhead, there were bolts of muslin cloth spread out and strung up with cord. This material diffused the sunlight (eliminating deep shadows and glaring highlights), making the fabricated "interior" look realistic. Once everything was set, and the camera properly positioned, no one in a movie theater could believe it was anything less than the real thing.

This scene from Broncho Billy and the Outlaw's Mother *shows the use of natural light through the doorway, giving believability to the set.*

More than one take was seldom necessary for each shot, and there wasn't much waiting between shots. At that pace a complete one-reeler was usually finished in two or three days, less if only a few locations were used. Anderson routinely shot 1,500 feet of film and cut it down to the final product. He claimed he never shot more than 2,000 feet of film for these productions, and that was probably true. But as the canyon's scenic variety became more understood, a cameraman went out with some cowboys to shoot "stock" footage, shots that were needed over and over: a horseman riding at full gallop along a road, the stagecoach rolling along beside Alameda Creek, a posse pursuing a fugitive. Scenes were taken up and down the canyon, developed and stored for future use. These stock shots saved time and money, and gave at least part of the company something to do if Anderson was out of town or otherwise occupied.

If Anderson knew he'd be gone for several weeks, or had to make up for lost time when he returned, he'd shoot films very quickly. One time, if Essanay publicity can be believed (and in this case it's probably true), Anderson filmed five movies in six days. That left him free to do whatever he wished for the rest of the month.[16]

There were many things besides filmmaking to occupy his time. Living in San Francisco was distraction enough, but there were also personal appearances to be made at movie theaters in Richmond, Oakland and San Francisco. One night he greeted standing-room-only crowds at theaters in two different cities.[17] Then there

Anderson stands on the running board of his Thomas Flyer in Richmond, California, during a personal appearance on May 25, 1912.

was his continuing interest in boxing; along with heavyweight Soldier Elder, Anderson began to sponsor lightweights James "Spider" Roach and Red Watson. Both men were given jobs at Essanay, but Roach proved even more valuable with his skill at baseball.

The Niles baseball team aroused Anderson's fiercely competitive instincts because it was the worst club in the Washington Township league. Anderson felt determined to change that. On June 19th, after only two and a half months in Niles, he got himself elected manager of the Niles team, and the local boys slowly dwindled in number, replaced by "ringers." Kite Robinson was already on the team as short stop, and he stayed. Watson and cowboy Al Parks were added along with Roach, but they reflected the lack of "qualified" players. Anderson had to look beyond Niles for the talent he needed to transform the club.

The first player from the outside was San Rafael Colts catcher Mervyn Breslauer, and this led to the recruitment of their star infielder, Roland H. Totheroh, who remembered: "A telegram came in from San Francisco. Broncho Billy Anderson was staying at the St. Francis Hotel — and he asked me in this telegram to join the Essanay film group, because they had a baseball team... I showed the telegram to my mother. At that time, as soon as you wore a pair of long trousers, mothers wanted you to get a job — some kind of job. It wasn't really necessary to finish up

Rollie Totheroh, actor.

school. So I thought it over. Jesus! To go to Niles! I had never heard of Niles and had never been further than Hayward... I was still dubious about leaving, but I wanted to play ball, to be a professional ball player... I didn't know I was going to be an actor." [18]

When "Rollie" Totheroh arrived in Niles he was put up at the Wesley, given a cowboy costume and assigned to be a member of the posse in an Arthur Mackley film. By now, Mackley was almost as quick at turning out a film as Anderson, and, after Anderson grabbed the people he wanted for a movie, Mackley kept the

The Rustler's Step-Daughter: *Evelyn Selbie, True Boardman and Carl Stockdale are in the foreground; cowboys Stanley Sargent, Bill Cato and Jack Wood are identifiable in the middle.*

other Essanay employees busy by directing and usually starring in another series of westerns.

Josephine Rector, the Western Essanay's one-person scenario department, made sure that Mackley and Anderson were supplied with all the scripts they needed. On this, her third go-around with the company, she was now getting $25 a week, and could increase it by acting as an movie extra for $3 a day, or play featured parts for $5. But it was writing that occupied most of her time, mainly because Anderson refused to pay for any scenario from a freelance writer if he could get them for free. Josephine remarked: "A good portion of our best scripts came from pulp magazines and the shelves of the Oakland Public Library."[19]

With a steady supply of material at hand, more actors became necessary, and Mackley immediately put to work two new arrivals — Evelyn Selbie and True Boardman. Both actors were veterans of the stage, had worked in repertory stock companies together and tried film, but were still new to it.

Selbie's first film work was in Los Angeles with the Melies Star Film Company, where her horseriding skills, learned from a childhood in Kentucky, came in handy for westerns. But her stunt riding ability was honed with the Howell Stock Company at the Central Theater in San Francisco. She described what that was like just a year after she joined Essanay: "Those were strenuous days. I don't remember how many burning houses I have had to fall out of, or how many times I've dashed on horseback over that bridge mid-stage, and fallen, horse and all, lickety splash and crash, into the great twelve foot deep tank that Mr. Howell built specially for these hair raising feats. So it's nothing terrible to take the chances we do here in Niles canyon."[20]

William True Boardman was born in 1882 to Carro True (an actress/playwright) and William Boardman (a stock trader from a prominent Oakland, California, family). True Boardman was leading-man material, strong and good looking, but just as effective in character roles. That strength made him a formidable villain too. Boardman brought along his wife, Virginia Eames, an actress he'd met and married on tour, and she joined Essanay too. Their three-year-old son, True Eames Boardman, who had already made his film debut with Selig a year earlier when his parents were in Chicago, also appeared on-camera.

Selbie and Boardman probably found work at the Niles studio through their own intitiative; actors in that era were, for the most part, their own agents, always on the lookout for steady employment in a profession known for its instability. Even the most desirable acting situation, a theatrical stock company, offered no guarantee of reliable income; an actor's worst nightmare was to be stranded on the road when a company went bankrupt, and it happened all too often. Performers learned to be adept at assessing when it was advisable to find a new job, and part of the process was using the idle hours off-stage to discuss among each other the lucky breaks or hard luck stories of mutual aquaintances, and rumors of the latest job possibilities. Trade magazines — *Variety, Billboard, New York Dramatic Mirror, New York Clipper, Motography, Moving Picture World* and others — provided information about all of the movie companies, and every seasoned actor realized this was a booming new industry for their profession in 1912. A query letter to a studio asking about employment could result in an invitation to join in, especially if a fellow actor already on salary could vouch for the performer's ability. Evelyn Selbie, hired by Essanay just weeks after True Boardman's arrival, may well have benefited from their previous work together at the Central Theater in 1907.

As the number of actors at the Niles Essanay studio increased, it became necessary to hire more crew people to build, paint and decorate the sets. Just like the actors, theater stagehands could easily adapt to this new medium, but so could other people. The carpenters who built the Essanay bungalows had skills ready-made for the movies, and it's possible Lawrence Abrott, Thomas Elliott and Alfred Griffin came aboard that way. Elliott was also a gifted blacksmith; so much the better. Earl Pearson, an Illinois native, painted realistic backgrounds. Danny Kelleher, a Niles teenager, became an assistant to propmen William A. Russell and Kite Robinson. William A. Evans, fresh from a tour of the orient shooting film for Essanay documentaries, handled the camera for Arthur Mackley.

The expansion of the company came at an opportune time; Anderson wasn't as active in Niles as he should have been. Boxing, baseball and public appearances may have distracted him, but the primary reason for his absence was the illness and subsequent death of leading lady Vedah Bertram.

Vedah Bertram.

Vedah Bertram's hospitalization was widely reported in the Bay Area newspapers, but the details have remained suspiciously vague to this day. It's known that Niles doctor Charles McKown took her to the Merritt Hospital in Oakland, supposedly for an appendix operation, and she stayed there for a month before dying on August 26, 1912. Her death certificate mentions nothing about appendicitis or any complication of it contributing to her death.[21] The Niles papers initially reported her illness, but printed nothing afterwards, either because they didn't know the true facts, or didn't wish to reveal them. The Oakland and San Francisco papers printed details they'd heard from Vedah herself: she was Adele Buck, a Boston native, a Wellesley graduate, the sister of a prominent New York attorney and daughter of a well-known Boston writer. Unfortunately, everything she revealed except her true name was false, and none of it was contradicted after her death.[22]

G. M. Anderson didn't publicly comment about her life or death to the press at that time, but privately he was terribly shaken by it. Hal Angus, then working as an actor for the Niles company, saw the devastating effect it had on the man, and said as much in 1973, but never elaborated. Anderson did mention her name many years later in various interviews as an actress who showed promise, but he would usually end up mumbling and stop talking about her in mid-sentence.[23]

Vedah Bertram had been praised for her acting ability, but that's now difficult to assess: she made twenty-two one-reel films and only six survive, hidden in archives. What can be seen shows a young, energetic, pretty woman trying her best, and at times succeeding admirably.

True Boardman and Edna Sharpe in An Indian Sunbeam.

With Vedah gone, Anderson looked for her replacement, and Edna Sharpe was the first woman he hired. Edna was a stage-struck Niles girl (another granddaughter of Belvoir Hotel-owner Emilie Chittenden), and had performed on stages up and down the West Coast, including Ye Liberty Theatre in Oakland for a year. Her first film was probably *An Indian Sunbeam*. In it she played Sunbeam, a white girl raised by Indians who falls in love with a cowboy. The cowboy was not played by Anderson; True Boardman starred — in one of his first Essanay films. Anderson is seen only briefly in a bit part as an Indian.

Anderson rarely appeared in the film releases of late September and October, the period coinciding with Vedah Bertram's illness and death. His place in the schedule was filled by three Alkali Ike comedies and two documentaries photographed by his cameramen. It wasn't until *Broncho Billy's Heart* (released on November 2, 1912) that Anderson resumed his weekly pace.

Broncho Billy's Heart was a particularly outstanding film. Arthur and Julia Mackley starred along with Anderson, but, contrary to what the title suggests, there wasn't a leading lady. Instead, Billy's heart goes out to the Mackleys and their two children, played by Audrey Hanna and True Eames Boardman. The simple yet effective story centers on Billy's sympathy for this down-on-their-luck family and how he makes a material sacrifice to keep the father from being caught as a horse thief.

Following *Broncho Billy's Heart*, Anderson once more threw himself into his work, taking advantage of any idea that came his way. One day "Fat" Rose, the youngest son of Niles liveryman Frank Rose, bought a new Indian motorcycle, and from this incident Anderson formulated *"Alkali" Ike's Motorcycle*. In a scene

Arthur Mackley, Audrey Hanna, Julia Mackley and True Eames Boardman in Broncho Billy's Heart.

At the Rose Garage. John Parry and Frank "Fat" Rose on Indian motorcycles; in the back seat of the car: Dr. Charles McKown, Joe Gomes, Frank Rose; in front: Ed Rose, George Rose and Henry Youngman.

Margaret Joslin and Augustus Carney in "Alkali" Ike's Motorcycle.

with Ike giving Sophie a ride on the motorcycle, Anderson recruited Danny Kelleher to double for Gus Carney, and Fat Rose filled in for Margaret Joslin.[24]

   Around this time another Ye Liberty actress, Bessie Sankey, began to play opposite Anderson. She had been on tour with the Marjorie Rambeau company when it unexpectedly disbanded, and returned to the Bay Area looking for work. Born in Oakland, and only twenty-one, Bessie had already acted professionally on stage for five years. Her first Essanay performance, the title role in *Broncho Billy's Mexican Wife*, was outstanding, and gave the impression she'd stick with films for awhile.

Bessie Sankey as herself and as Lolito in Broncho Billy's Mexican Wife.

In September, 1912, George Spoor came to Niles for a look at the town Anderson claimed as his choice for a western headquarters. Essanay actor Hal Angus remembered the visit: "Mr. Spoor came down and he took seven or eight of us to the Belvoir for lunch. Not Anderson." Spoor repeatedly mentioned during the meal that he couldn't understand how Anderson was able to make pictures in that old barn.[25]

This was precisely Anderson's point; with forty-six people now on the payroll, it was time to build a proper production facility. Spoor eventually met with Anderson and they discussed the future of the western division at length. The result of their conversations was announced in the *Press* on October 4th: "BIG PRODUCING PLANT FOR NILES."[26]

Spoor stayed in Niles for nearly two weeks, buying land from Bird and Frank Mortimer on the same block as Anderson's bungalows, and working out the details that would pave the way for the new studio. The movie trade magazines printed a press release shortly thereafter, with Spoor announcing: "G. M. Anderson has the finest photoplay location imaginable, situated in the very heart of a magnificent natural canyon with every convenient advantage." The article went on to claim, inaccurately, that construction was underway.[27]

But something did happen almost immediately; Kite Robinson and Niles girl Malvina Chaix were quietly married at Mission San Jose on October 7th. The bride gave up the job she'd had at Darrow's Bakery for the past two years, and the couple settled into a Niles house close to where the studio would soon be.[28] This personal commitment between Kite and Malvina seemed to confirm Spoor and Anderson's business commitment, as if to say, for better or worse, Niles and Essanay were one.

The Essanay Film Company in Niles.
Top row: Rollie Totheroh, ?, Kite Robinson, Ira Morgan, ?. Row five: ?, Frank Pementel, Tom Elliott, Stanley Sargent, Lawrence Abrott, Bill Cato, Spider Roach. Row four: Soldier Elder, ?, Joe Cassidy, Jess Robbins, Augustus Carney, Tom Crizer, Pat Rooney, Perc Pembroke?, Texas George Briggs. Row three: ?, Harry Todd, Victor Potel, Brinsley Shaw, G. M. Anderson, Fred Church, David Kirkland, ?, Row two: Malvina Chaix Robinson, Marguerite Clayton, Evelyn Selbie, Margaret Joslin, Josephine Rector, ?, ?. Front row: Marguerite Todd, Berssie Sankey, Jem Rector.

Chapter Six
A Western Town

When Anderson hired real cowboys for his westerns, these wranglers brought an authenticity to the screen that was rare for the day. The contrast was so great that audiences believed in his image of the west and other film companies were forced to follow suit. No wonder he said of moviegoers: "From the pictures, that's where they got their idea of the west."[1] Cowpunchers became commonplace in westerns, and this was good news for the cowboys; jobs on the range were getting scarce.

The big cattle drives were over and ranches didn't need the number of horsemen they once employed. As their numbers diminished, movies came along and fulfilled the dream of their lives; no longer did they have to do the worst jobs on a ranch (anything that required them to be on foot); now they could do what they loved most — riding a horse — and they got paid for it: five dollars a day, four dollars more than for ranch work.

The tradeoff was the danger involved; one misstep could be their last. The cowboys knew from years of experience how far to push themselves and their horses, which made them all the more valuable. Even still, accidents happened.

The most important cowboy in Niles with Anderson was William S. Cato. Bill Cato was born in Wyoming on April 16, 1887. He was a champion bronchobuster who spent his whole life working around horses and cattle. In late 1912 Cato became the boss cowboy for Essanay, and his concern for safety kept injuries to a minimum, but he was matter-of-fact about how easy it was to get hurt: "Changing from one horse to another, if you made a slip you'd go under. The only time I was injured was I went over a cliff with a bronc I was breaking for Anderson. I was playing a sheriff, and I think he crowded me off this new grade; it was soft, and I hit that and my horse's feet sunk in and he went over and he went down 75 feet, end over end, with me in the saddle. I wasn't even scratched, but it buggered me up. I was laid up for about three weeks on that."[2] This was exactly why Anderson valued Cato: "He was just an excellent rider. He was the double for two-reelers, the things that I couldn't do, the things that I was afraid I might get hurt. If I got hurt there'd be no more pictures made."[3]

Joe Cassidy, Louis Morisette and Al Parks had all been with Essanay longer than Cato, but only Cassidy remained in Niles past the first year, content to drive the stagecoach, care for the horses and train them to do tricks.

Jack Roberts and Bill Cato were good friends, and no wonder; like Cato, Roberts was an experienced cowpuncher, and could be trusted with dangerous work. Roberts was born in San Francisco, but roped and herded cattle for several years at various San Joaquin Valley ranches, including the Miller & Lux and Hayes outfits, and participated in the last cattle drive of the Chowchilla Ranch in 1912. He came to Niles right after that.

Stanley Sargent, the teenage son of a Monterey County superior court judge, was a championship rider who joined Essanay about the same time as Cato. Sargent suffered from a heart condition since childhood, but it didn't stop him from winning the wild horse race in 1913 at the third annual California Rodeo at Salinas.[4]

Slim Padgett, from Kansas, came to Essanay at the age of twenty-five following a "Frontier Days" show in Oakland. Some of his fellow cowboys were his brother Wallie, Hart and Hazel Hoxie, and Ed "Hoot" Gibson.[5] Slim had worked with the Kalem Film Company at Glendale in the winter of 1910-11 with Wallie, Gibson, Dell Eagles, Jessie Snow, Dick Parker and George Sourards. Kalem's studio manager, Kenean Buel, had nothing but praise for them: "They are intelligent, conscientious and obliging and I consider them the seven best riders and all around horsemen I have ever known."[6] In July, 1912 (just before his start at Essanay), Slim reaffirmed his rare abilities, in a real-life version of "the runaway coach," saving a family who was returning home from a trip to the cemetery.

Slim's seventeen-year-old wife Hazel, from Kentucky, had been with Pathé's western company in Los Angeles during the 1910-11 winter season. After her marriage to Slim in January, 1912, she performed in the Frontier Days show, too.

Thomas Crizer, born in Virginia and raised in New Mexico, rode in films throughout his Essanay years, but also learned another skill — film editing — from Anderson himself. Tom became a specialist at comedy-film editing.

Frank Pementel, a Niles kid who had worked around horses for most of his twenty years, was hired within days of Essanay's arrival, and worked there regularly until the studio closed. Sometimes Pementel doubled for Anderson, but more often he was just one of the cowboys — in hundreds of films.

Arthur Champion, another Niles youngster, rode with the cowboys until he was hurt in a fall. He was one of many Niles boys (among them: John Tyson, Dan Greenwood, Dan Baldwin, Dean Preston and Marston Dassel) who tried the movies for a short time before returning to the family business or some other profession.

Florence Perkes, born in 1892 in South Bend, Oregon, was another valued member of the team. She, too, was an exceptional rider, which may have impressed Bill Cato; he married her. She kept working for Essanay till the studio closed.

There were other cowboys: Jack Wood, Charles La Due, Henry Lilienthal. They appeared as members of the posse or actors in the Snakeville Comedies, and were otherwise unheralded. But untold numbers of riders were never mentioned by name; they just came and went.[7]

Beyond the ability to ride and handle a rope, other skills were required for westerns; the most unusual talent was shooting real bullets as a special effect. In the silent days, ricochetting bullets off rocks, shooting out windows and splintering doorframes weren't illusions; they were done with live ammunition. Texas George Briggs, a cowboy who came from the Kalem Film Company to Niles in 1912, was a rifle marksman of exceptional ability.[8] In a scene from *The Making of Broncho Billy*, Anderson draws his six-shooter and shatters a row of bottles lined up before him, then sets up a row of playing cards, draws his other gun and shoots a hole through the center of each card. Briggs did it in a continuous take while stationed off-camera, synchronizing his shots with Anderson's, and hitting the mark perfectly every time. He also rode and acted regularly, remaining with the company for nearly two years.

Opinions vary on how wild these cowboys really were, and only one harrowing incident made news in the papers. It started when Willis Elder played a prank on Al Parks, riding Parks' favorite horse without permission. Parks didn't think it was funny, and took off on another horse to get Elder. Elder returned the horse to the stable before Parks could find him, but that didn't stop Parks. He caught up with the heavyweight boxer at Ed Roderick's saloon in Irvington. The two men had a heated exchange of words, then Parks pulled out a pocket knife and slashed Elder across the forehead. Although Elder's wound was bloody but not serious, Parks didn't wait for that verdict; he fled and hid out, leaving an unpaid fifty dollar tab at the Wesley Hotel. The wound, however, did postpone a boxing match between Elder and Charlie Horn at Dreamland. Elder, nevertheless, refused to press charges against Parks and both men eventually returned to work.[9]

In later years, Niles old-timers told some tall stories about the cowboys. One tale by Fred Rogers, who worked as a bartender at the Wesley Hotel in the old days, concerned Texas George Briggs: "One afternoon in the bar a couple of cowboys made some crack he didn't like and George went for his guns. But for the first time, he'd left them upstairs. When he ran to get them, the other two guys looked at each other, got up, ran out, jumped on their horses and left town."

Rogers also claimed, "there wasn't a building in town that didn't have holes in it," presumably from all of the bullets flying around. The situation got so bad, according to Rogers, that Alameda County Sheriff Frank Barnett came to Niles and took all of the live ammunition away.[10]

Josephine Rector spoke otherwise about the cowboys: "They were all perfect gentlemen. Of course maybe they did get a little noisier on Saturday nights when there was nothing else to do."[11]

Rollie Totheroh stayed at the Wesley for awhile, and remembered his first night: "We had a piano in the front room with a bar at the side... and after we had finished dinner, we'd all go into the bar and listen to all of this commotion. That night when we were getting ready for bed, all of a sudden all holy hell broke out. This guy across from our room used to go haywire at night. He had d.t.'s or some damn thing, and he used to bang at the door and shoot off his gun. These guys used to lock his door, but he would shoot right through the door."[12]

Bill Cato, Jack Roberts and Joe Cassidy.

Gertrude Cassidy.

Jack Roberts tries out the Bell & Howell.

Florence Cato.

Cowpunchers at the Chowchilla Ranch. Jack Roberts kneels in the middle. On his left is Jack Montgomery, a Hollywood cowboy in later years, and father of future movie star Baby Peggy.

Stanley Sargent and Bill Cato.

Jack Roberts, Joe Cassidy and Carl Stockdale ready for a Hippodrome stunt. Behind them are Marguerite Clayton and Gertrude Cassidy.

Jack Roberts.

Bill Cato near Third and G streets.

Slim Padgett on Front Street. Behind him is the Southern Pacific property.

A Western Town   109

True Boardman astride a white horse. Behind him: Joe Cassidy, ?, Jack Roberts, Tom Crizer, Bill Cato, Louis Morisette, Jack Wood.

Stanley Sargent and Jack Roberts.

Jack Roberts and Bill Cato as Indians in Niles Canyon.

Texas George Briggs, Evelyn Selbie and Tom Crizer.

Bill Cato, snake charmer.

Jack Roberts sits on trick horse Kiddo.

Fred Church and Texas George Briggs in foreground.

Stanley Sargent and Jack Wood.

Tom Crizer on H Street.

Hazel Padgett.

Jack Roberts encounters a quiet moment at the Wesley Hotel bar.

Bill Cato downplayed the problems: "We'd have, probably, one drunk once in awhile, when he'd get drunk and start raising hell, but the rest of the boys would catch him before he'd done any damage, and put him to bed or muss him up a little, to quiet him down, you know." But Cato did confess to sometimes creating a disturbance at studio dances: "Well, we'd break in on that and shoot things up, but we never did hurt anybody."[13]

It's certainly true that Niles had more than its fair share of saloons. There was Easterday's Senate Bar, Silva's Corner, Cavenaugh's saloon, Harding's White House, Billy Moore's Elite, Lynch's Arcade, as well as the Wesley and Niles Hotel bar rooms. It's easy to imagine a bunch of cowboys riding into town, tying their horses to a hitching post, entering a saloon and stepping up to the bar after a hard day's work in the canyon. Following that, well, any B-western could pick it up from there.

But whatever one can imagine about the lawlessness, the truth was, Niles had law and order. Joe Roderick was the town constable when Essanay arrived, and Frank Rose got elected the next year. Neither man would have stood for too much, especially Rose, who handled other incidents with professional skill.[14] Essanay would have certainly been driven out of town if the violence had gone too far. Anyway, company employees were usually far too busy with work to engage in non-stop wild abandon, and Anderson wouldn't tolerate anyone who couldn't do their job; there were plenty of more important things for him to focus on.

As that first winter in Niles approached, Anderson was uncertain of just how much filming could be accomplished before cloudy skies and rain shut the company down. He had to work hard to make sure there were enough films to see him through rough spots in the schedule, but past experience indicated he was taking a big chance by staying in Niles. He played it safe by sending a portion of his company south to Hollywood under the leadership of Arthur Mackley.

Arthur Mackley facing the camera, about to leave Niles for Hollywood.

Mackley leased a house in Hollywood at 1425 Fleming Street which suited his needs perfectly. On the lot beside it, ready to go, was an open-air stage formerly used by the Lubin Film Company. Mackley and his troupe were able to begin work immediately.[15]

Unfortunately, Mackley's cameraman, William Evans, shot all of their footage with a defective camera. A registration problem with the camera's pulldown movement produced an unsteady image, undetected until footage for several films had been shipped to Chicago for developing and editing. By that time it became impossible for Mackley to keep up with the release schedule, and Anderson's unit in Niles had to take up the slack until Mackley could quickly remake his Hollywood films.[16]

Then Mackley faced another technical setback, static electricity on the film. This defect showed up as flashes like lightning on the image, a problem created during cold, dry weather as the film was running inside the camera. Mackley wasn't the only director tearing his hair because of this condition; it was happening to most of the other film companies in Los Angeles that winter.[17]

But not in Niles. The air was more humid in Northern California, so static wasn't as much of a problem, and Niles was more sheltered from the clouds and rain that season than in the rest of the Bay Area. Anderson had no trouble cranking out film after film without a break.

When Mackley finally got rolling again, he matched Anderson film for film, each man alternating a release.

By this time, Augustus Carney's Alkali Ike films had gone by the wayside. It wasn't that they'd failed; on the contrary, they were very successful. That was the

Augustus Carney in "Alkali" Ike's Homecoming.

irony. Gus Carney, now a rising star, created the situation himself by deciding to return to the Chicago studio, expecting more recognition for his comic talents. He got it, but not in the way he'd figured. The studio arranged for a countless string of public appearances each night at various Chicago movie theaters, and, during the day, he was shoe-horned into a variety of comic roles, whether he fit in or not. Reviews, such as the one for *Mr. Hubby's Wife*, defined the problem: "The scenario behind this picture doesn't afford any real chance for the brilliant clown acting that Carney used to give us in his western characters. It has one or two funny moments; but, for the most part, is about as flat as can be."[18] Carney was billed as "The Gibraltar of Fun" and, whatever that was, Alkali Ike suffered while Carney played in one farce-comedy after another. It was disasterous, and Carney returned to Niles to mend the damage in February, 1913.[19]

Fittingly, Carney's first new release from Niles was *"Alkali" Ike's Homecoming*. It introduced Victor Potel as Slippery Slim, settled once and for all on the name of Sophie Clutts for Margaret Joslin's character, and got the series immediately back on track.

Meanwhile, Anderson was having a problem with leading ladies. Since Vedah Bertram's death, several actresses came and went: Beth Taylor, Vera McCord, Anita Murray, Peggy Blevins. Bessie Sankey was around while most of them came through, but she wasn't always playing opposite Anderson. Perhaps they didn't get along. The solution to finding a suitable partner turned out to be as simple as placing an ad in a San Francisco newspaper. That's how Anderson found his most enduring co-star, Marguerite Clayton.[20]

Marguerite Clayton.

Marguerite Clayton (born Margaret Fitzgerald in Salt Lake City, Utah) was twenty-one, living in San Francisco with her family when she saw the ad. She had no acting experience, but her sweet disposition, fair complexion and innocent, good looks contrasted nicely with Anderson, and it won her a position with Essanay. She played small roles at first, but soon got a chance at a leading part: "Never was I so frightened. I'll never forget it. However, my part was emotional. So you see my pounding heart and trepidation was really a help rather than a hindrance. After my scene was over Mr. Anderson said, 'Your work was fine, Miss Clayton; you show that you can put feeling into it.' Feeling! I should think I did put feeling into it. If I had had to be calm and composed I never could have done it."[21] She learned quickly and became a regular not only in the Broncho Billy films, but in a variety of comic and dramatic movies.

Gathered on a set in Niles, around April, 1913. Front row: Arthur Mackley, Harry Todd, Josephine Rector, Margaret Joslin, Marguerite Clayton, Augustus Carney, Frank Dolan (seated). Second row: Bill Cato, Harry Keenan, ?, Slim Padgett, True Boardman, Tom Crizer, Carl Stockdale (wearing stiff collar), Lee Willard, Tom Elliott, Lawrence Abrott, Alfred Griffin, Frank Pementel, Kite Robinson (foot on chair). Top row: Jack Wood, Victor Potel, Fred Church.

Carl Stockdale was another important recruit at this time. He was a thirty-eight-year-old Worthington, Minnesota, native who often played the part of a much older man. His thin, haggard features made him a prime candidate for the role of a sickly old prospector or dying man. He was often cast as Marguerite's father, and the physical contrast between them worked well dramatically by emphasizing the withering effect of the harsh western environment on the old pioneer who sacrifices himself for the sake of his daughter.

In April, 1913, around the time Marguerite Clayton was hired, Arthur Mackley returned to Niles. The Hollywood Essanay company had disbanded and Mackley was ready to quit. He'd received an offer from Reliance-Majestic to make films for them, but, like Jack O'Brien had done in San Rafael, Mackley planned to switch jobs after taking a long vacation. Anderson persuaded Mackley to continue working in Niles for a month, long enough to find a replacement, then Mackley and his wife took the train east to New York, embarking for Europe on May 31st.[22]

Mackley's replacement was Lloyd Ingraham, a stock company actor for many years, who had recently worked at the Universal Film Company in Los Angeles. Ingraham kept acting at Niles for awhile, opposite Anderson in the Broncho Billy films, as he learned the skills of movie directing. Within a month he began directing.

Lloyd Ingraham, Slim Padgett, ?, G. M. Anderson, Pat Rooney, Brinsley Shaw, Stanley Sargent, Evelyn Selbie, and Fred Church in Broncho Billy's Strategy.

Anderson himself was now going at full speed, not just in movies, but in everything. In addition to a renewed interest in baseball and boxing, he piled more on his plate with the purchase of property in San Francisco. This land on O'Farrell Street was the site of the old Alcazar Theatre, destroyed in 1906. Now Anderson wanted to build a new 1,600 seat theater capable of handling musical revues and movies. The land cost $375,000, and the building was estimated to be another $150,000.[23] He called this temple of entertainment the Gaiety Theatre, and had high hopes for it: "What the Winter Garden is to New York, the Hippodrome is to London, the *Folles Marigny* is to Paris, the Metropol is to Berlin, the Gaiety will be to the city of San Francisco."[24] But an architectural drawing revealed yet another wishful affinity — Anderson's *Follies* — suggesting a West Coast equivalent to Florenz Ziegfeld's *Follies*. More prophetically, it spoke of a venture destined to be a foolish expense, something Anderson couldn't afford.

Although rumored to be a millionaire, Anderson had to give a deed of trust to the Union Trust Company for $265,000 on the property, and to build the theater he became partners with Thomas O'Day, a San Francisco building contractor. The two men had more in common than an interest in theaters: O'Day had staged a lightweight championship bout between Ad Wolgast and Battling Nelson in 1910 at Richmond, California.

Still, Anderson's income was certainly substantial. By 1910 his income was roughly $50,000 a year, and, after the success of Broncho Billy, Anderson re-negotiated with Spoor to make it $125,000 a year.[25]

By contrast, Marguerite Clayton's salary began at twenty-five dollars a week. When she became established it went up to seventy-five, very good money in those days.[26]

Movie people were well paid. Compared to clerks and factory workers, who might earn as much as ten dollars a week, the top Essanay salaries in 1909 were in the twenty to thirty dollar range. By 1914, the higher end was one hundred and fifty dollars, and averaged fifty. Brinsley Shaw made seventy-five a week. Actor/director Arthur Mackley made one hundred and twenty-five.[27] Francis X. Bushman, the matinee idol of the Chicago Essanay, got as high as three hundred and fifty. Cameramen made twenty-five in 1909, and that went up to fifty or sixty by 1914. Jess Robbins was at the top — one hundred and fifty. Directors were paid sixty a week in 1909, and that increased to one hundred and fifty at the bottom, to two hundred and twenty-five tops by 1914. Scenarios, if bought from the outside, were ten, fifteen or even twenty-five dollars in 1909. By 1914, the range was one hundred to two hundred and fifty, but, as George Spoor himself testified that year: "There is no real limit to what we have got to pay today."[28]

All of this was good news for Niles. The payroll was estimated at $1000 a week when the company came to town. By the time the studio became established, it shot up to $4000 a week.[29] This was the new gold rush.

Chapter Seven
The Studio

Nearly all of the West Coast film studios in 1912 were makeshift affairs — a house or a storefront office with an open-air stage in the backyard, or the lot next door. Los Angeles had more than a dozen of these. No wonder it was common, and perfectly correct, for actors to say they were working "on the lot."

Buildings specifically designed and constructed for movie production were rare: the first one on the West Coast, built in downtown San Francisco by the Miles Brothers, was nearly finished when the 1906 earthquake destroyed it. The Selig Polyscope Company built a glassed-in stage on their Los Angeles property in 1909, and began more construction in 1911.[1] The American Film Company finished their Santa Barbara studio in 1913, the same year as Essanay's in Niles.

The Niles studio was supposed to cost $25,000, but this estimate proved wrong. After Robbins and Anderson talked to San Jose architect George W. Page and plans were drawn up, the total climbed to $50,000. Anderson paid for additional land west of the building for a horse stable and the final cost came to $52,000.[2]

Construction was well under way by March 28, 1913, supervised by local architect and carpenter Alfred Griffin. Niles residents didn't quite know what to make of it. Having nothing else to compare it to, Chris Runckel, editor of the *Washington Press*, called the new building a "large barn."[3]

On March 31st, Jess Robbins' wife Nancy gave birth to their first child (a daughter named Jessie), which, eight days later, may have prompted an announcement from Anderson: "From this day, Jesse J. Robbins has been appointed General Manager of the western division of the Essanay Film Company. Each department will be under his personal jurisdiction and the power is vested in him to act for me in any way he may see fit."[4] It was a logical choice: Jess was organized, detail-oriented, trustworthy and knowledgable about the whole filmmaking process, better able than Anderson to devote his attention to the daily tasks and problems of the studio. Jess had been Anderson's closest collaborator for the last four years, and probably his closest friend, so it was only natural for Anderson to officially promote him to this second-in-command position.

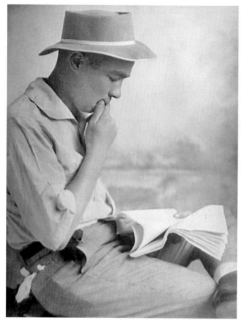

Jess Robbins.

Alfred Griffin.

Rollie Totheroh.

Ira Morgan.

The Essanay studio in Niles before the glass stage and four last bungalows were built. The Essanay barn can be seen on the left, the third building facing Second Street.

As Robbins advanced, so did Rollie Totheroh. Totheroh was unhappy with acting and wanted to quit, but Robbins heard about this and offered Rollie an alternative, the chance to become a still photographer by shooting as many pictures as he wished. Rollie agreed to give it a try, and Robbins himself taught the younger man how to work a Graflex camera and develop the film. Totheroh remembered: "I shot things right and left with this Graflex."[5] After learning the basics, Totheroh graduated to cinematography. "All the posse chases were left behind and Jess Robbins used to do them. Eventually that's how I got started as a cameraman... I'd make them very simple. I'd shoot across from left to right on one side of the road without moving the camera around alot, then I would have the posse come the other way. Stagecoaches used to knock me right off my tripod! I used to say, 'Come as close to me as you can,' and they would!"[6]

With Robbins moving into management, and Totheroh still learning the basics, the search for another cameraman began, and Ira Morgan was hired. Morgan was born on April 2, 1889, at Fort Ross, California. He graduated from Lick-Wilmerding Technical High School in San Francisco, then got a job operating an overhead crane at the Joshua Hendy Iron Foundry in Mountain View.[7] An interest in movies led him to a job with Gaumont as an installer/projectionist, and from there as a newsreel cameraman in 1911. He was married and living with his wife Georgia and her parents in Sunnyvale when he began to work for Essanay, commuting back and forth between Broncho Billy films because Georgia was pregnant. After their son Roland was born in June, 1913, they moved that September to Niles.[8]

The Niles ballteam at the old field on Harrison Mayhew's property north of town. Standing second from the left is Spider Roach, in the middle is Kite Robinson and at the end is Al Parks.

The new Sullivan ball park with the old bleachers and chickenwire screen, on October 12, 1913. The Niles Essanay team has just defeated the Southern Pacific Owls, 14 to 7. Kite Robinson leads the lineup, Spider Roach is seventh, then Mervyn Breslauer, Al Parks, Rollie Totheroh and Frank Dolan.

Frank "Fodder" Dolan.   *Eddie Fries, Frank Dolan and Perc Pembroke on an Essanay set.*

While the studio building was rising up, a new baseball field opened next to it on land owned by Niles roadmaster Thomas Sullivan. At the first pre-season game in Sullivan's Park, on Sunday, March 30th, 250 fans watched Irvington beat Niles, 12 to 2. The next week Niles lost a rematch, 6 to 5.[9]

The team's fortunes changed when a new pitcher was brought in, Frank "Fodder" Dolan, who had played with semi-pro teams up and down the Pacific Coast since his mid-teens. The young Irishman's first game in Niles was an eye-opener; Niles beat Irvington in the first game of the 1913 season, 5 to 0. The *Press* reported: "It was all Dolan. He seemed to have the entire Irvington team buffaloed. He fanned seventeen men, walked none, hit one and allowed one hit."[10] Dolan immediately found a job with the Essanay Film Company in the prop department.

Even though the large, glass-enclosed stage at the rear of the building was yet to be finished (the Trussed Concrete Steel Company in San Francisco experienced delays with their order for the steel frame and wired-glass), the new studio informally opened on June 2nd with a dance.[11] On June 11th Lloyd Ingraham directed *The Dance at Eagle Pass*, the first movie on the fifty-foot-square stage in the main building; it starred Josephine Rector (from her script), True Boardman and Brinsley Shaw. Rollie Totheroh operated the camera, his first time as principal cinematographer on a film.[12]

More than a month before, the lease on the old barn had expired; instead of renewing it, a temporary open-air stage was constructed on the flooring of what would be the new glass-enclosed studio stage. This newer space was substantially larger, enabling two "interior" scenes to be shot side by side. It gave Anderson and Ingraham, along with Jess Robbins and David Kirkland (who were also now directing), a choice of three stages. With four directors working that meant the stages could be kept constantly busy, although this often wasn't necessary.

On the Niles Essanay studio fifty-foot-square stage, Pat Rooney and Darrell Wittenmyer take a close look at a Aristo-type arc modified with an enclosure to direct its light. The lights on stands are Liliput arcs made by Kliegl Brothers.

The same stage composed as it would be for filming.

True Boardman plays the organ while Josephine Rector dances with Brinsley Shaw in The Dance at Eagle Pass. *Next to Shaw are Slim Padgett (on the left) and Jack Wood.*

Harry Keenan, Josephine Rector, Fred Church, Bill Cato, True Boardman and Brinsley Shaw inspect the evidence that convicts Shaw in The Dance at Eagle Pass.

At the new studio, set up with a temporary stage, Carl Stockdale (on the far left) observes the action. Arthur Mackley (at the camera) films Bill Cato, Spider Roach, Harry Todd, Lee Willard and Jack Roberts in The Days of the Pony Express. Lawrence Abrott leans on the stage brace. On the next set: Stanley Sargent and Frank Dolan stand next to the overhead support pole. Ira Morgan cranks the camera while Jess Robbins watches from the far right.

Another angle: Jack Roberts, Alfred Griffin?, ?, Carl Stockdale, Marguerite Clayton, Spider Roach, Lee Willard, Bill Cato, Harry Todd, and Evelyn Selbie on the same set. Note the Niles Grammar School building to the right in the distance .

Whatever the reasons for shooting on a stage set, the hills, streams and canyons around Niles continued to attract the filmmakers. Lloyd Ingraham marveled: "We could step outside the studio and shoot in any direction for our prairie scenes."[13] Anderson echoed that statement ("You walk out of the studio right into the scenery."[14]), and he continued to transport sets to the canyon. For Anderson the studio was more important as a place to keep an office, store equipment and handle technical details like developing film and cutting it. Shooting with natural light out in the open was always the quickest and easiest way for him to work, and, besides, westerns were not westerns without the great outdoors.

Nowhere else could he perform a stunt he'd pulled at other towns — the holdup of a regularly-scheduled train. Of course it was prearranged with the railroad people, but not everyone was notified. A Niles resident, A. S. Enos, remembered driving a wagon through the canyon one day when a cowboy posse burst through the brush and leaped from their horses onto a passing train: "Nobody thought to tell the passengers. You should have seen those women fainting."[15]

Niles barber Bert Silveria recalled another scene: "Here comes Anderson driving this wagon. He goes up and over this train track and on up Stoneybrook Canyon. Then a few minutes later along comes this train and they take pictures of that too. A few weeks later I see the movie in the theater here. They fixed it so it looks like the train just missed him. I've never believed anything I've seen in pictures since!"[16]

August 12, 1913, marked the first two-reel release from Niles; *"Alkali" Ike's Gal*. It was a long time in coming.

George Spoor disliked films longer than one reel, a misguided policy that probably stemmed from early disaster. In 1912 there was a rush to produce multiple-reel movies and Spoor whole-heartedly embraced the idea, but something went wrong with Essanay's first epic production, *The Fall of Montezuma*.[17] After all the publicity and build-up, this three-reel extravaganza starring Francis X. Bushman was never released. The reason is unclear, but it must have been something catastrophic — the original negative burning up or a technical problem with the film that made distribution impossible. When Essanay finally released a mere two-reeler called *The Spy's Defeat*, its first multi-reel film (on March 31, 1913), they were trailing far behind everyone else in the business.

It's important to note that Alkali Ike, not Broncho Billy, was picked to be the first two-reel subject from Niles, a strong comment on Ike's popularity. Ever since *"Alkali" Ike's Homecoming* the series was promoted heavily in Essanay advertisements. A doll was even commissioned with Alkali Ike's likeness and sold to theaters for $1.50 apiece to be given to the public as door prizes.[18]

Augustus Carney was now a star, and the Niles studio geared up to produce a greater number of films with him. The *Register* confirmed this indirectly in "Doings of the Essanay People" on September 27, 1913, reporting an incident with an overdue express train. "The delay would have been much more annoying but for the fact that Mr. Kirkland, director, and a troupe of Essanay players accompanied by a cameraman, were engaged during most of the time in taking a number of pictures for a rural comedy upon which they were working. Great interest was

Victor Potel, Harry Todd and Augustus Carney in That Pair From Thespia.

The Essanay bear and Evelyn Selbie behind the studio.

taken in the proceedings by the crowd at the station." The film in production was probably *That Pair From Thespia*. In the same column it mentioned: "Mr. Robbins is getting up a new comedy in which the Essanay bear will be featured in a number of stunts."[19] That film became *Sophie's Hero*.

Carney, who appeared in both films, was being kept busy by two directors, quite a change from the previous pace of approximately one comedy per month, and it had a telling effect on Carney's disposition. Rollie Totheroh remembered: "Carney became a pretty surly little cuss to work with."[20]

Augustus Carney's association with Essanay ended in November, 1913, nearly four years after it had begun. He left Niles for New York, where he visited all of the movie trade magazine offices he could get to before departing across the Atlantic for Paris, London and his birthplace in Ireland. When he came back he signed with Universal.

The Universal Film Company made a practice of stealing new stars from other studios by offering them twice their current salary. Universal's president, Carl Laemmle, used this tactic early on at the Independent Motion Picture Company (IMP), taking Florence Lawrence and Mary Pickford from Biograph. Universal's cost for these rising stars (who were often undervalued by their old companies) was cheap compared to the risk of developing many unknown actors from within the company in the hope that a few would become stars. Universal's method had an added advantage: the publicity was priceless.

Universal announced their acquisition of Gus Carney with a contest to give him an up-to-date name. A few of the losing entries were Augustus Bustus, Lizard Luke, Gussy Con Carney and Comic Cuss. The winning name, "Universal Ike," was not much better, nor was the first film in the series, *Universal Ike Gets a Goat*, judging by reviews.[21] Nevertheless, Universal kept him busy, under the direction of Harry Edwards, releasing one reel of film each week: *Universal Ike Has His Ups and Downs*, *Universal Ike Has One Foot in the Grave*, *Why Universal Ike Left Home*, *Universal Ike Makes a Monkey of Himself*, and more. By the thirteenth film the star and director disagreed, and Carney quit. His last film in the series, *Universal Ike Is Kept From Being an Actor*, spoke of a performer's worst fear, and signaled the end of Gus Carney's stardom. With a reputation for being "difficult" the offers for employment were no longer there, and the minor roles he received became few. He placed ads in trade papers, "Augustus Carney ('Alkali Ike') At Liberty," but like so many people who'd briefly hit the heights, there was no comeback, and Carney disappeared from the scene.[22]

Essanay reissued *"Alkali" Ike's Auto* on November 13, 1913, just weeks after Carney left the company. It was an odd decision. Re-releasing a film nearly three years old was practically unheard of in those days; most people in the business believed a film's life was over after its initial distribution cycle of six months. *"Alkali" Ike's Auto* proved the theory wrong, in this instance, by receiving a larger gross than its first run, but Essanay didn't promote Ike again, even though there were several new movies ready for release. Instead, Alkali Ike's name was written out of the main title, and their next film with him was called *Sophie's Hero*.

The Snakeville bunch in Niles Canyon. Back row: Charles La Due, Bill Cato, Al Herman; by the camera: Ira Morgan, and Stanley Sargent, Harry Todd, Victor Potel, Jack Wood, Tom Crizer, Carl Stockdale, Jerome Anderson, True Boardman, Joe Cassidy; middle: Margaret Joslin and Jess Robbins; front: Martin Killilay, Fritz Wintermeier, Rollie Totheroh, Mervyn Breslauer and Jack Roberts with an unofficial mascot.

Margaret Joslin and Augustus Carney in Sophie's New Foreman.

Emory Johnson, Joe Cassidy, Harry Todd, Stanley Sargent, Bill Cato and Jack Roberts in A Hot Time in Snakeville.

Harry Todd, Victor Potel, Fred Church and David Kirkland in The Awakening at Snakeville.

Margaret Joslin and Augustus Carney in Sophie's Hero.

Sophie's Hero survives to this day in a good print, and it reveals much about the popularity of the series. The story is simple: Ike is no match against Rawhide Bill, Mustang Pete and Slippery Slim in their bid for Sophie's hand, until he dons a bearskin and chases his rivals away. The film's appeal comes in watching each man's dignified, yet boyish, courtship of Sophie, the woman they earnestly desire. Ike is a head shorter than everyone else, but twice as determined to win Sophie, although outmatched and ganged-up on by the others. The subtle humor doesn't seem stretched, even when Ike outsmarts the others by putting on the bearskin. And, remarkably, no one is ever belittled in a mean-spirited way. In fact, every character is an individual with attributes and faults, and though they may squabble and fight, their behavior never goes completely over the top into unbelievability. Audiences can understand and sympathize with the people of Snakeville.

Sophie's Hero was followed by *Sophie's New Foreman*, then *A Snakeville Courtship*. After the last film with Carney, *The Awakening at Snakeville* (another two-reeler), the Snakeville series went into a new, even stronger phase with the remaining principal actors — Margaret Joslin, Harry Todd and Victor Potel. This trio continued to co-star in sixty-eight films.

The driving force behind the transformed Snakeville Comedies was director Roy Clements, a Sterling, Illinois native born on January 12, 1877. He'd been a stage actor for 22 years (most recently at the Alcazar Theatre in San Francisco) before joining his first film company — Essanay. Although lacking movie experience, he knew what to do with the Snakeville characters. After *Sophie Picks a Dead One*, a two-reeler, the comedies returned to one reel a week, and flourished

Rollie Totheroh and Roy Clements.

within that format. By September, 1914, far from running out of steam, they got even better; a review for *Slippery Slim and the Fortune Teller* in the *New York Dramatic Mirror* stated: "The winning combination of script and acting continue to get the laughs in these Snakeville comedies. The same cast pleases its audiences which sits in mild amusement at times and then is rocked into a frenzy of laughter."[23] The next week they made another hit with *Snakeville's Most Popular Lady*: "Sophie Clutts, Mustang Pete and Slippery Slim are at it again in one of the funniest of Snakeville releases yet shown. There is something at once so original and so out of the beaten track that it wins."[24]

Joe Cassidy, Stanley Sargent, Jack Wood, Charles La Due observe Victor Potel in a barrel in High Life Hits Slippery Slim.

Victor Potel collaborates with fortune teller Evelyn Selbie while Harry Todd and Margaret Joslin await results in Slippery Slim and the Fortune Teller.

Harry Todd, Evelyn Selbie, Margaret Joslin and Victor Potel in Snakeville's Most Popular Lady.

Clements arrived in Niles at the end of November, 1913, just as the studio's glass-enclosed stage and the last four Essanay cottages on Second Street were completed.[25] The state-of-the-art studio's main building (two hundred feet long, fifty feet deep and eighteen feet high) included in its central portion the fifty-foot-square production stage lit by artificial lights. Behind it was the glass-enclosed stage going back another seventy-five feet (and sixty feet wide). The west wing housed a carpenter shop, a scene dock for painting the backdrops, a prop room and a paint shop. A darkroom for developing film was located next to the stages. At the far west wall was a concrete film vault. Anderson's office was in the east wing, right in the corner. Hanging on the wall was a large, framed photograph of the famous scene in *The Great Train Robbery* as Anderson is shot in the back by a robber, and he loved to show off the picture to visitors. The next room down the hall was Josephine Rector's office. Jess Robbins had an office further along the hall, next to the last room, which contained the studio safes. Dressing rooms, the reception room and a small theater filled the remainder of the east wing, with the editing room attached to the projection booth. On the second floor of that wing was the wardrobe room and more dressing rooms.[26]

Behind the main building was a blacksmith shop, and storage rooms for more props and equipment. A false front on the south side of these buildings turned them into a western street set. A long, narrow horse stable, made of concrete, paralleled the blacksmith shop. Behind the stable was a corral for horses, and in the yard between the stable and studio was parking space for cars and the stagecoach.

The Studio 135

The Niles Essanay studio in December, 1913. G Street is on the left and, Second Street is just past the eight Essanay bungalows on the studio block. The three white rectangles hide roadside billboards that advertise Pinectar (a soft drink), Ingersoll watches and Acme beer. The group of buildings on the top left at Third Street is the P. C. Hanson Lumber Company, supplier of construction materials for the studio. Note the Indianhead logo on the studio building, the stagecoach and Anderson's Thomas Flyer in the yard by the horse stable on the right.

The Essanay scenario department in March, 1914: George Cantwell and his boss Josephine Rector.

The darkroom, featuring a rack amd tank film developing apparatus. The rack (shown at the upper left on its winding stand) holds two hundred feet of film. It is immersed consecutively in each of the four tanks, developer, stop bath, fixer and wash, then taken to another room for drying on a large, lath-wood drum.

The editing room, little more than a bench with rewinds. The shelf holds individual shots ready to be spliced together onto one reel. George Cleethorpe is on the left.

The two storage buildings between the studio and bungalows have false fronts (seen sticking above their rooftops) enabling them to double as old buildings on a western street set. The smaller building is a working blacksmith shop.

Frank Pementel is ready with a sledge hammer to help Thomas Elliott in the blacksmith shop.

Harry Todd reads a sign on the western street set in The Naming of the Rawhide Queen.

Rollie Totheroh took this picture of his wife Ida and son Jack on the western set.

Ben Turpin on left, George Cleethorpe second from right, on the glassed-in stage.

On a set with Robert Burroughs, Roy Clements, Warren Sawyer, Lawrence Abrott, Eddie Fries, Orlando Hicks and Danny Kelleher.

With more production capacity, more crewpeople were needed. Harris Ensign came in as a cameraman. Emory Johnson, an architecture student at U.C. Berkeley, became a camera assistant, then an actor. Mervyn Breslauer returned for good as a camera assistant and rejoined the ball team. Adolph Mayer, a projectionist who'd learned his trade in 1898, ran the projector at the studio, and also worked in the lab. George Cantwell assisted Josephine Rector in the scenerio department. Orlando Hicks became a set carpenter and his wife, Madrona, an actress. Larry Medeiros, a young carpenter in the area, built sets for Essanay. Warren Sawyer came from the Orpheum Theatre in Oakland to dress sets; his wife Eva played small parts. Earl Sudderth, a student of San Jose artist A. D. M. Cooper, applied Cooper's realistic style to scene flats, and was soon joined by another Cooper student, Leo West.[27] Adam Herman Foelker, another boxer (fighting under the name of Al Herman), came from Brooklyn to San Francisco as part of an eastern contingent to box locally and somehow ended up in Niles, joining the growing Essanay prop department.[28]

More actors made the trek to Niles, too. Henry Virtue Goerner, billing himself as Robert Henry Gray, had acted at Ye Liberty in his hometown of Oakland before coming to Essanay in San Rafael. In 1912 he went to the American Film Company in Santa Barbara, but was now back at Essanay.[29] Harry Keenan, from Indiana, began his professional career as an usher at Hooley's Theater in Chicago, started his acting career in the 1890s, and was also at Essanay for the second time.[30] Reina Valdez, a young dancer from Springfield, Massachusetts, had worked for some

Carl Stockdale, Emory Johnson and Charles Allen Dealey at the studio.

months at Lubin's Los Angeles studio. She acted mostly with Lloyd Ingraham's Essanay unit and wanted to direct a film.[31]

There had been no offical still photographer since the departure of Orrin Denny in 1912. That changed when Charles Allen Dealey arrived. Dealey had worked as a professional photographer in San Francisco since the 1890s. He took Essanay group photos and special event pictures at first. By 1914 he became manager of both the photography department and the film laboratory. In 1915 he brought in one of his sons, L. Allen Dealey to help out, and found the time to appear in a few films.[32]

The camera department was, of course, critical to the operation of the studio. Not surprisingly, cameramen didn't just operate their cameras, they knew their machines inside and out, handling care and maintenance with an eye toward improving techniques as well as preventing problems. Like everything else in the business, their job evolved. The days when a cameraman was responsible for all things photographic — still photographs and motion pictures — moved toward specialization as demands on their craft increased. Camera assistants were hired to carry equipment, lend a hand during filming and help in other ways, such as perforating film.

Ira Morgan and Harris Ensign stand on each side with Bell & Howell production cameras.
Rollie Totheroh stands in the middle with the original Bell & Howell prototype.

Camera assitants Howard West, Mervyn Breslauer and Martin Killilay sit in front.

In those days raw stock was bought unperforated because cameras were not standardized. The industry settled on 35mm film, but the sprocketed rollers inside a camera could vary between different equipment manufacturers, just as they did with projectors. In the earliest days there was chaos: Biograph's Mutograph camera punched one square perforation on each side of the film during exposure; the Lumiere camera used perforated film with one round hole on each side. Even when four perforations per image frame became the standard, the frameline could be level with a perforation hole, midway between two holes or anywhere in between. Because of this variation, a nickelodeon theater projectionist had to reframe the image on the screen every time another movie was projected. If two or more cameras were used to film a movie, producers quickly realized every camera needed to be frameline-matched beforehand, otherwise the image would move up or down when mismatched shots were cut together. (As late as 1917 this was still a problem.) What's more, the perforation size, shape and position also differed depending upon the perforator; like the camera, different manufacturers made up their own standard. Cameramen quickly learned to solve this problem with the right perforator because, chances were, without the right perforations the film wouldn't run through the camera. (The poor projectionist, faced with a similar problem, was stuck; a film that was incompatable with the projector would either show an image that jumped around on the screen or the film would rip apart in the machinery.) Standardized perforations came about after Bell & Howell manufactured a perforator in 1908 so precise, trouble-free and efficient that every film company bought them. Essanay, for instance, owned a total of ten Bell & Howell perforators by 1914. Bell & Howell perforations are still the standard for 35mm movie camera film used to this day.

The most precious items in a cameraman's care were his lenses. They had familiar names to anyone in the business: Zeiss, Cooke, Bausch & Lomb. But focal lengths were limited; 32mm was about as wide as a wide-angle lens got. The standard "normal" lens was 50mm. Focal lengths in the telephoto range, including 75mm, 100mm, 150mm and longer, were easier to design and therefore more plentiful. The drawback for all focal lengths was the f stop. A typical f stop in 1910 was 4.5. By 1915, f/3.5 was becoming more common. Either way, shooting at low light levels was difficult, and even overcast skies could lead to an underexposed negative.

The first camera Jess Robbins carried west on his 1908 trip with Anderson was a Bell & Howell prototype. After some modifications, the first production run of two cameras was made in 1909, followed by six more of that model the next year. It had state-of-the-art features: a wooden body, footage counter, hand crank, film punch, a variable shutter and interchangeable lenses. Inside, there were two, light-tight wooden magazines: the top one held two hundred feet of 35mm film, and the bottom one took up the film after exposure. On the operator's side of the camera, above the crankshaft, a viewfinder prism enabled the cameraman to compose the scene by looking through a lens mounted directly above the one used for exposing the film. This rare twin lens arrangement was designed to be raised or lower (akin to a view camera in still photography) thereby raising or

Jess Robbins shows off the prototype of Bell & Howell's first movie camera in 1908.

lowering the angle of view from the camera and conveniently bypassing the hassle of finely adjusting the height of the tripod legs. Bell & Howell's supreme innovation was the film transport mechanism: stationary pins the film was pushed onto, held for exposure, then lifted from, so the film could move to the next frame. The image was absolutely steady, an attribute that has never been surpassed.

The hand crank enabled the cameraman to vary the speed of the film through the camera, and cranking at the correct speed was one of the trickiest tasks to learn, according to cameraman Rollie Totheroh: "First breaking in, my trouble was in cranking the camera. As a rule for comedy it was 14 frames a second and sometimes you drop to 12 frames a second, for instance if somebody's running away from the camera and you wanted to speed it up." But that was just for starters; it could quickly get more complicated, as Rollie stated: "The cameraman regulated everything! We didn't have a change of focus apparatus on the camera; we'd have to reach over while still cranking and turn this apparatus we had on the mount that held the lens. Say we're on a 12-foot focus and it comes to a 6-foot focus: we'd have to reach over there while still cranking and turn to 6 feet. So both hands were really operating different things at one time. You get used to it. It comes naturally. After awhile you can get it pretty well on the nose."[33]

Eastman Kodak supplied the most popular film stock in the United States, a black and white orthochromatic negative emulsion on a nitrocellulose base, but with its slow speed (an exposure index of 18 to 24 depending up how it was developed), an insensitivity to red light and a predisposition toward high contrast, properly exposing this emulsion to bring out shadow detail in full sunlight took a formidable skill, and was an art in itself. To bring light into the shadows and reduce contrast, cameramen would mount canvas on a stretcher board, paint it white and use this as a reflector. Shooting toward the sun and exposing for the shadows was another trick, particularly effective with a posse kicking up dust behind it as the cowboys rode toward the camera. Deciding the correct exposure was based on a cameraman's experience and became second nature. Mistakes did happen, but every cameraman with a sense of pride and a desire for perfection kept foolish errors to a minimum.

Working in the studio under artificial lights took another set of skills. Several types of lighting units were available, but the three most popular were the Aristo Arcs, Cooper-Hewitt mercury vapor lamps and the Kleigl Brothers arcs. The Aristo Arc was a yellow flame fixture in a glass globe, hung overhead in a cluster, but the light wasn't easily directed. The Cooper-Hewitt light (used as early as 1904) looked like today's fluorescent lights, with long, glass tubes mounted in a row of four or eight. They could be set up in banks overhead, or to one side, giving a very even illumination, and their ultra-violet light fit perfectly into the movie film's sensitivity spectrum, although, to the observer, everyone under that light took on a ghastly, pale look. The Kliegl Brothers manufactured another style of arc, advertised as Klieglight and Liliput Arc. These open-face fixtures on stands were portable, and the light easier to direct, but the ultraviolet light they emitted irritated the eyes (making them red and itchy), a malady known as Klieg eyes.

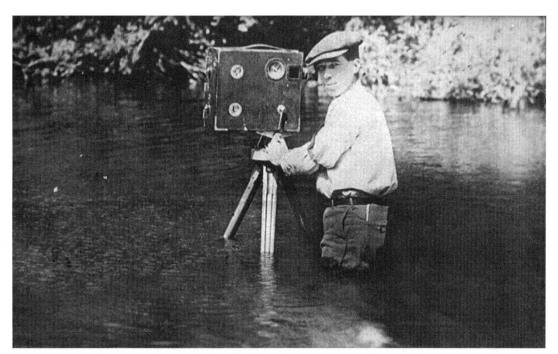

Jess Robbins and a Bell & Howell camera in Alameda Creek.

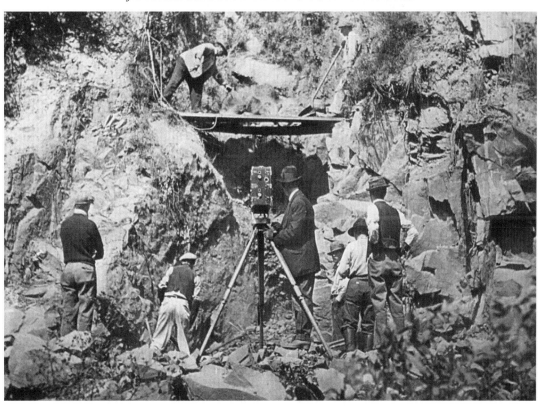

William A. Evans at the Bell & Howell in Niles Canyon. To the left: G. M. Anderson, Spider Roach; to the right: Fritz Wintermeier, Arthur Mackley, Jess Robbins; on top: Ben Lee and Lawrence Abrott.

Stepping into a studio was an assault on the senses. Arcs crackled and buzzed. The camera's wooden box amplified the grinding gears and chattering film as it advanced. The carpenter shop next door never ceased its clamor of pounding hammers and droning saws. Director shouted to be heard over everything, giving rehearsed and impromptu instructions to the actors. Francis X. Bushman remembered the first time he stepped onto Essanay's "silent" movie stage in Chicago: "There were these other companies working, and the noise was like a boiler factory."[34]

Once the film was exposed, a practiced eye was needed to process it in the darkroom. The tonal range of the film could be controlled in development; more or less time in the developer increased or decreased the contrast, as well as the exposure. The film was inspected under a ruby-red light, since the film was largely insensitive to that color, and the lab worker adjusted the time by eye. Once the density of the negative was deemed correct, the film was plunged into a stop bath, then fixed in yet another tank. The Niles studio used the rack and tank method; film was wound on a wood frame and dipped in a series of rectangular, wooden tanks lined up in the proper sequence. The Chicago studio used the drum method, moving the film on a large, open cylinder from tray to tray. Both methods worked well enough, but the rack and tank method could be done by one person, while the drum was a two-person operation that used larger amounts of solution.

The film was washed, dried on wood-framed drums, wound onto metal reels and taken to the projection room. The Niles studio didn't have a printer to make positive prints; they just looked at the original negative. If it got scratched, there was no reshooting, but damage rarely happened. After viewing the film it was edited. When that was done it went across the street to the train station for shipment to Chicago, where all publicity materials were fashioned and release prints made for distribution. It generally took two months to get a film from production into distribution, and that remained the norm throughout Essanay's life.

Despite all the technical difficulties in getting an image on film, the results could be spectacular. Even run-of-the-mill productions looked good. And prints from original negatives of the best early-era films are still stunning to see, a testament to the outstanding pictorial quality these technicians were able to achieve.

The new studio took some getting used to by Anderson and his company. For one thing, it meant settling down, setting up procedures, and working in a more methodical way. Anderson resisted at first, scouting for locations as far away as Chico, California, 150 miles to the north. But excursions around the country took up time, and in the end it was easier to shoot close to home.

On another level, working from a fixed base meant the studio had to conform to the laws and regulations of the state. The Niles studio was considered a factory because it "manufactured" movies, and it was therefore necessary to record the working hours of all employees to protect them from exploitation by the company. This meant a time clock had to be installed. This was a totally foreign concept to Anderson's way of working, and his employees weren't too thrilled either. Not surprisingly, there was trouble.

Essanay employees line up to punch the clock: Jack Wood demonstrates, behind him is Emory Johnson, ?, ?, Victor Potel (in top hat), Al Herman, Harry Todd and Mervyn Breslauer.

Legend has it that the time clock was sent from the Chicago studio, and when Anderson saw it he exploded in anger, outraged at Spoor's interference. Anderson allegedly grabbed an axe, smashed the device and sent the pieces back to Spoor.[35] The local papers don't confirm this story, but the *Register* suggested that something was going on: "A new time clock has been installed in the Essanay studio and is arousing great interest."[36] The employees had their own way of dealing with it, according to Bill Cato: "Everybody'd make a dash for that clock, you know. If I'd hit it first I'd punch for everybody, and if somebody else, they'd punch it for everybody. Sometimes we'd miss somebody. Pat Rooney came in drunk one morning and pulled out a six-shooter and shot it full of holes. We didn't have to punch it for a few days."[37] The employees eventually settled down, and their attention turned elsewhere.

One direction was west, to Sullivan's Park. The local papers only sporadically covered the progress of the Niles baseball team in previous years, mainly because the club was an embarrassment. Now, in 1913, the luck of the Niles team changed. Sullivan's Shamrocks, as they were briefly called, made an astounding comeback that season, spearheaded by the remarkable pitching of Fodder Dolan. The Newark club finished first with 14 wins and 2 losses, followed by Niles with a 13 and 3 tally. It was a close, tough race, but the Niles team took some comfort in second position by beating the Newark team in the season's last game, 4 to 2.[38] Niles continued to play other Bay Area teams into the winter, and Fodder Dolan continued to pitch admirably, for a total of 18 wins out of 22 starts. Everyone looked forward to next year.

Anderson's San Francisco theater, the Gaiety, also got off to a promising start. It opened October 18th, 1913, to high praise from all of the Bay Area newspapers. The *San Francisco Examiner* reported: "The opening show was 'The Candy Shop.' It's a show of zest and sparkle and headlong speed, and it sprang forward last night with a momentum that should carry its career far into the coming weeks. At its first act curtain the... musical comedy was greeted with an outburst that suggested a riot, and blazing color shot over the footlights until 'The Flower Shop' would have better named the piece."[39] The *San Francisco Chronicle* went down the long list of talent: "Every theater-goer knows of Rock and Fulton, the clever dancers, who have been the headliners on the biggest vaudeville time. Al Shean is an established musical comedy comedian. Tom Waters was a feature in 'The Pink Lady.' Will Philbrick has been a leading comedian with the Ziegfeld 'Follies' for years. Gene Luneska was with 'The Chocolate Soldier' for two years, and later starred in 'The Spring Maid.' Catherine Hayes is one of the best comediennes in musical comedy. Oscar Ragland's bass voice has been heard in many big successes."[40] The *San Francisco Call* headline said, simply: "'The Candy Shop' Wins Skeptical."[41]

Niles hosted its own special event the next month. A traveling show on the local Washington Township circuit had been showing movies three nights a week in the second floor auditorium of the Connors building. George MacRae, the man who ran the circuit, decided it was time for a proper movie house in Niles and built the Edison Theater, the first one in the township. The *Press* proudly stated: "The new theater will seat over 300 people. It is modern in every respect and especial attention has been given to making the theater sanitary and safe. The MacRae's building, with its modern theater, two up-to-date stores and two modern apartments, is just the kind of an improvement that Niles needs."[42]

With so much happening at the studio that year, keeping track of the departures and arrivals of everyone must have been a difficult task for Jess Robbins. But the resignation of Fred Church had to make him pause. It had been more than four years since Church started acting in westerns with Essanay in Colorado. Church was now to return there with his bride. He married Lillian Christie in Niles only weeks after she arrived from the American Film Company, and the couple decided to spend Christmas with his folks in Denver.[43]

On their return to California Fred and Lillian joined the Frontier company in Santa Paula. Church was once again making westerns under primitive conditions, if only for a brief time. Perhaps it was just an interim step on a new path, but that was life in the movie business.

Chapter Eight
Everyone Gets into the Act

On January 6, 1914, the *San Francisco Chronicle* proclaimed Gilbert M. Anderson "The King of the Movies." In an article saluting him as the shining star of the Bay Area film community, he was compared to the British Empire (on which the sun never set) saying: "At any time, some place on this earth, Bill is spurring his mustang across the screen. He never quits." The newspaper estimated 11,000,000 people watched Broncho Billy perform on-screen every day.[1]

By that time Anderson had made fifty-five Broncho Billy one-reelers and only one two-reeler, but he saw the trend toward longer films as early as December, 1911: "Film-making will develop along the line of big productions. The film of the future will cost $25,000 to produce. It will comprehend an evening's entertainment and will tell the whole story where we now give only an occasional scene. It is certain to be with the picture as it has been with the drama; the moment there is the least retrograde movement the public will begin to lose interest."[2] And yet Anderson's desire to enter the feature film market was delayed nearly three years by Spoor's failure with *The Fall of Montezuma*. What a difference it would have made in Anderson's career if he'd gone ahead with early plans for more elaborate productions.

Instead, independent studios took the lead in producing feature films. A month after Anderson's *Chronicle* article the Jesse L. Lasky Feature Play Company released *The Squaw Man*, "six reels of extraordinary dramatic action," with Dustin Farnum in the leading role.[3] This was the type of film Anderson should have already excelled at, but now he was woefully behind the competition.

Part of the problem was the Motion Picture Patents Company, the organization Essanay joined in 1908. Their distribution arm, the General Film Company, was set up to handle the constant turnover of short films. The cost of longer films to theater exhibitors required a more flexible policy, but General Film couldn't adapt. This put the producing members — Essanay, Kalem, Lubin, Edison, Melies,

Biograph, Vitagraph, Pathe Freres and Selig — at a great disadvantage. As a few of these far-sighted producers fought hard to distribute feature films in a profitable way, the industry they'd tried to control was slipping into the hands of risk-taking independent filmmakers. Ironically, as the Patents Company weakened in the marketplace, a government lawsuit charging them with monopolizing the industry made headway in the courts.[4]

This had yet to hurt Essanay financially; a whole new wing to the Chicago studio was ready for use by January. Spoor said: "Our additional studio here will be devoted to dramatic subjects exclusively. These subjects will not necessarily be all multiple reels, as I am a firm believer in the single reel features and intend to devote great effort to single reel comedies and dramatic subjects. The Snakeville Western comedies, with Margaret Jocelyn [sic], Victor Potel and Harry Todd, will continue to keep up the former and will create even the increased demand. The Anderson 'Broncho Billy' releases are holding their popularity, and Mr. Anderson is appearing regularly in his famous role."[5] Clearly, George Spoor was determined to maintain the status quo, and keep Anderson in line as well.

Anderson couldn't have been happy about this, and the frustration he felt must have been shared by at least some of his employees: director David Kirkland left in December, 1913, followed by Lloyd Ingraham in March; actors Henry Goerner, Harry Keenan, Orral Humphrey and Reina Valdez all quit within that time; publicity writer Arthur A. Penn went to New York in April. But the biggest blow to Anderson came when Jess Robbins resigned.

Robbins had learned a great deal in his six years with Essanay and wished to build on his experience by increasing the variety of films at the Niles studio. Several comedies and dramas were produced: *Love's Lottery, The Warning, The Arm of Vengeance, Single Handed, A Night On the Road* and *The Atonement*.[6] The most far afield of these productions was *Italian Love*, a dramatic comedy about an Italian mother's interference in her daughter's plan to marry an American. The Chicago studio seemed to go along with this new policy, and expressed it publicly to movie exhibitors and reporters in March through the company newspaper, *Essanay News*: "The pictures now in course of preparation at Niles will equal in scope and interest any of those made in the Eastern studios, with the added advantage that the introduction of Western scenes and effects will be an easy matter. This departure from the usual routine at Niles has brought untold satisfaction to the whole of the Western company..."[7]

It was short-lived; in the next seven months the only films released from Niles, with one exception, were the Broncho Billy and Snakeville one-reelers. The one exception was *The Good-for-Nothing*, an ambitious four-reel feature made in January that wasn't released until June, but by June Jess Robbins was long gone.

Robbins was a likable, loyal and fair-minded individual with the ability to weather disappointment, but it must have been hard for him to endure the short-sighted restraints imposed by the Chicago office.

He returned from a two-week trip back east in late March of 1914, writing several comedy scenarios on the train ride, and finishing a two-reel script in Niles

A scene from The Atonement *at the Niles jailhouse on Second Street with Jerome Anderson, Tom Crizer, Jack Wood, Reina Valdez, unknown little girl, Carl Stockdale, and Pat Rooney.*

Josephine Rector and Lee Willard, starring in The Romance of the Hills, *are married by Harry Keenan, witnessed by an unknown woman, Victor Potel and Carl Stockdale.*

Josephine Rector, Fred Church and Harry Todd in The Cast of the Die.

Harry Keenan, Tom Crizer, Harry Todd, True Boardman, Lee Scott and W. Coleman Elam in a tense moment from Greed for Gold.

The Robbins Photo Plays Company staff in Los Angeles; sitting: Alfred Griffin, Harris Ensign, Jess Robbins; standing: Emory Johnson, ?, Larry Medeiros, ?.

on the 28th; by then he'd decided to leave Essanay. The whole town celebrated his daughter's first birthday on the 31st, and it was just as much a farewell party for him. George Spoor wrote to Robbins on April 2, 1914: "Am very sorry you feel you have advanced to the limit with our company and have decided to leave us.... regret you have become impatient and have not given us an opportunity to work something out for you."[8]

Jess worked out something for himself, incorporating the Robbins Photo Plays Company on April 15th, and left Niles with Larry Medieros, Earl Sudderth, Al Griffin, Harris Ensign and Emory Johnson to open his studio in Los Angeles. Its first production was a three-reel feature film, *When a Woman Loves*.[9]

The Good-for-Nothing, Anderson's own venture into feature films, sat on the shelf for three months after an *Essanay News* announcement in March that it was finished, and no further publicity was seen until shortly before its release, although *Motion Picture* magazine (a movie-fan periodical started in 1911 with a $6000 investment from each of the Motion Picture Patents members) did present the film in story form for its June issue, which hit the newsstands in May.

The most curious aspect of *The Good-for-Nothing* was that it didn't trade upon Broncho Billy's popularity, it ignored it. By implication, Anderson wanted his feature film debut to be a success without Broncho Billy's influence, and he certainly compounded the risk by presenting a potentially unlikable personality, that of a rich, tuxedo-clad playboy spending money on good times, alcohol and women.

G. M. Anderson drinks and gambles in The Good-for-Nothing. *Behind him to the left is Frank Stockdale with a mustache; to the right is Emory Johnson.*

The Good-for-Nothing was based on a 1909 Anderson Essanay film, *The Black Sheep,* but he modified this straight drama by adding humor to the story of two sons, one bad, the other worse, who battle in a stock market showdown, the prodigal son (played by Anderson) triumphing over his greedy brother, thereby saving their parents from the poor house. That Anderson could triumph with this film by making an essentially melodramatic situation humorous was confirmed in the reviews, which were all positive. James McQuade, writing for *Moving Picture World,* called it "a strong photodrama... Many a good laugh will be raised by Mr. Anderson's impersonation of the good-for-nothing Gilbert Sterling. Through all the waywardness and consequent hard luck of the spendthrift, there is an audacious good humor and buoyant, good nature that will appeal to everyone."[10] Peter Milne of the *Motion Picture News* praised the comic aspect of the film, but pointed out "The dramatic parts are just as good as the comic parts." He also had good words to say about the production as a whole: "The photography is of a high degree throughout the entire picture and the settings are appropriate. The picture is noticable for its few subtitles. Those that do appear convey the meaning of the story perfectly."[11] Regarding public response, the *Dramatic Mirror* critic noted: "The audience applauded at intervals and at the end of this picture, in a select theater on Broadway."[12] Sime Silverman of *Variety* predicted: "With all that coin G. M. can make a serial of this one."[13]

Essanay released *The Good-for-Nothing* on June 8th, just as the Chicago studio was also about to break into the feature market through a contest in *Ladies' World* magazine. The magazine serialized "One Wonderful Night," a romantic story by Louis Tracy, and invited readers to visualize their favorite movie star in the leading role. Thousands of votes submitted by their subscribers were tabulated and Essanay's Francis X. Bushman won over competing matinee idols Maurice Costello (of Vitagraph), J. Warren Kerrigan (of Universal), Crane Wilbur (of Pathe), Carlyle Blackwell (of Kalem), King Baggot (of IMP) and Arthur Johnson (with Lubin). Bushman's win meant the Chicago studio was obligated to produce the story as a four-reel feature film.

This nudge by the magazine and the moviegoing public probably led to Essanay releasing *The Good-for-Nothing* when it did; the Anderson film would pave the way for the presentation of *One Wonderful Night* the next month. Spoor must have been pleased with the results; another tie-in with *Ladies' World* came in August.

But there wasn't any immediate relief for Anderson. Robbins had been the best-liked member of the Niles company, and his exit left a gaping hole in the Western Essanay's organization, one that Anderson couldn't fill. That April Josephine Rector also quit.

Anderson didn't follow up *The Good-for-Nothing* with a series or a sequel, nor did he immediately produce a Broncho Billy feature. Instead, he returned to the one-reel format. Beginning in July, Essanay increased their weekly releases from five to six films, and every Saturday without fail audiences could see a new Broncho Billy one-reeler.[14] With little time to delve into a story, the titles almost said it all: *Broncho Billy's Sermon, Broncho Billy's Leap, Broncho Billy's Cunning, Broncho Billy and the Mine Shark, Broncho Billy and the Sheriff, Broncho Billy and the Gambler, Broncho Billy Trapped, Broncho Billy's Fatal Joke, Broncho Billy's Double Escape, Broncho Billy's Wild Ride, Broncho Billy's Indian Romance, Broncho Billy's Mother, Broncho Billy's Dad, Broncho Billy and the Claim Jumpers.*

Broncho Billy and the Claim Jumpers is a remarkable example of what Anderson was doing at the time. Released on January 9, 1915, it was a remake of *The Stage Driver's Daughter*, a story he'd produced in San Rafael three years before, but this wasn't the result of lazy filmmaking; it was carefully put together using everything he'd learned. After hundreds of films, it was natural for him to come back to a favorite story. (Everyone in the business, including D. W. Griffith, did so.) *The Stage Driver's Daughter* had been singled out on its release and praised critically for its action and photography. *Broncho Billy and the Claim Jumpers* would have gotten equal attention if critics had cared about one-reel films in 1915.

The film survives today, and one look at it is enough to see why audiences loved these films. The acting is casual, yet to the point, and every actor does their job well. Marguerite Clayton stands out in particular because of her likable personality — cheerful, determined and daring. She's never self-conscious on screen, always in character. It's impressive to watch her actually drive the stagecoach through the canyon while Anderson, at the back of the coach, holds off the claim jumpers riding behind them.

Anderson stands off would-be lynchers Bill Cato, Fritz Wintermeier, Darrell Wittenmyer and Tom Crizer in Broncho Billy and the False Note.

True Boardman hands Anderson a pardon as fellow inmate Victor Potel looks on in Broncho Billy Gets Square.

Anderson, in handcuffs, plays cards with the sheriff, Lee Willard, in Broncho Billy's Double Escape.

Anderson and Marguerite Clayton in the decisive moment from Broncho Billy's Decision.

Everyone Gets into the Act 161

How deeply Marguerite was into her character was demonstrated at the climax of the story when she stops the coach in front of the registrar's office and jumps down to file the claim. The *Press* reported: "Miss Clayton persisted in putting a bit of personal 'pep' into the scene by jumping from the thoroughbrace to the ground." In the process she sprained her ankle and wrenched her back. Even so, she went on to finish the film without any sign of discomfort, but afterwards her injury laid her up for a week.[15]

As for the camerawork, it's perfect, exactly in the right place at all times to capture the expressions of the actors, the impressive scenery and the frequent action. There are very few explanatory or dialog title cards (a trademark of Anderson's, one he was proud of), but the plot is completely understandable. In all, the film is fresh and enjoyable.

The importance of the Broncho Billy films to Anderson's livelihood is undeniable, but the belief that he played this character exclusively while in Niles is a myth. True, there was an unbroken string of Broncho Billy films from November 9, 1912 to September 27, 1913 (beginning with *An Indian's Friendship*), but on both sides of that period Anderson played other cowboys, Indians, and men of many professions past and present. The Broncho Billy series ended at 148 films, a large number to be sure, but far less than his total acting output of at least 300 movies. The total is uncertain because he wasn't above playing small parts in films without billing; in *Snakeville's Most Popular Lady* he's hidden under makeup as an old man, and in other films he's often disguised. His fellow actors moved just as freely between lead and supporting roles, and, when not restrained by the Chicago office, they were allowed to work without his direct involvement in more than 190 films, a practice that boosted Anderson's Essanay profits.

Whether or not money was involved, plenty of people were ready to step forward if Essanay needed a crowd. Henry Youngman, a retired laborer and veteran of the Civil War, played bits in many films. Lee Scott, reduced to being an Essanay janitor after his saloon in Niles Canyon was denied a liquor license, earned extra money in films. Even Scott's wife Elizabeth joined in.[16] Ben Murphy (whose father ran the Murphy & Briscoe general store) was sometimes caught by the eye of the Essanay camera, and so was George Bonde, manager of the Niles branch of P. C. Hanson's lumber company. Ralph Richmond, a Niles Justice of the Peace, also appeared in several films.

Essanay crewpeople filled in as extras all the time, as they had done right from the beginning. This became rare in Los Angeles as skills were refined and defined, but in Niles the old ways of working continued to be the routine, and the crew seemed happy to participate. They also got paid extra for it.

Niles children were recruited for schoolhouse scenes, and if more substantial roles came along they were happy to oblige. The only brake on their enthusiasm was getting permission from their parents. Paul Donovan, son of Niles electrician George Donovan, mused in later years about how his life might have changed if his father hadn't turned down Anderson's request to give the five-year-old boy a big part in a film.[17]

Victor Potel demonstrates an electric belt while Harry Todd points to its critical component in Sophie and the Faker. *The spectators are Niles residents, except for Joe Cassidy in the striped overalls, who stands in front of Ben Murphy,. Billy Moore's saloon building is behind them..*

Josephine Rector kisses Niles schoolchildren as they go home in Broncho Billy and the Sheriff's Kid.

Marguerite Todd, fourth from right standing a head taller than Georgia Chalmers, celebrates her tenth birthday on September 18, 1913, in the Todd family Essanay bungalow.

Audrey Hanna and G. M. Anderson in Broncho Billy's Gratitude.

Donovan probably wasn't the only child who missed his chance, but there were many who succeeded: Anita Garcia, Evelyn Rose, Arnold Bellini, Tony Costa, Marston Dassel, Tony Enos, Georgia Chalmers, Gladys Rose, Pauline Alameda, Frank Rodrigues. Their pay for performing usually came from the local ice cream parlor. "They'd march us down the street and buy us each an ice cream cone. We just loved it," said Pauline Alameda.[18] Tony Costa remembered: "Occasionally we would get two or three dollars." He played his biggest role when he jumped into Alameda Creek to save a "child," but "actually it was a doll," he said.[19] Gladys Rose recalled black spots being painted on her white horse when they needed a pinto for a film, burning houses that were only false fronts and rocks made of papier-mache. "I would go to a movie, and I can remember saying, 'That's not a real rock.' As we got older, we laughed about it."[20] Georgia Chalmers remembered the racks of beautiful clothes in the wardrobe department; she would run her hand across the garments, fascinated by them.[21] Anita Garcia's mother was a seamstress, and many of her clients were Essanay people. Not surprisingly, Anita's wardrobe didn't come from the studio: "My mother made me a cute outfit. She made me a little gingham — gingham was very popular in those days, you know — she made a cute little poke bonnet and a little dress to match and in those days little girls my age, the dresses were long, had a little ruffle at the end. Darling outfit she made, and that's what I wore." She adored Broncho Billy, and thought Marguerite Clayton pretty and talented, but none of the Essanay people were ever invited to her home for dinner; even with their involvement in the community, actors weren't considered entirely respectable by the townspeople of Niles.[22]

Essanay actors often felt the sting from the public's low opinion of the profession, and were reluctant to subject their own children to that pain. Marguerite Todd had plenty of opportunities to appear in films, but when a reporter asked Margaret Joslin Todd if her daughter was destined to be an actress, she answered bluntly: "No, indeed. Not if I can help it. We are going to educate her and fit her for what she wants to do, but we hope it won't be acting. The show business is a hard life. It means struggle, struggle, all the time to get anywhere if you have it in you. And, why, even here in Niles if you just say to lots of people 'motion picture actress' it is all up with you, just the same thing as on the stage, you see."[23]

Even so, most of the major roles for children were handled by professional actors; this sometimes meant the regular Essanay actors' children, but not always. In Santa Barbara, Anderson employed Sophie Osborn, who happened to be in town performing with the Elleford Stock Company. In San Rafael, Essanay actor Thomas Kelly allowed his daughter Violet to work in Anderson's films. In 1912 Anderson used Audrey Hanna, daughter of Essanay actor Jay Hanna, and she was busy at the company for at least a year. True Boardman's son, True Eames Boardman, was appearing in a few Essanay films before he was three, but his career didn't take off until he was a year older, in 1913. At that point he seemed to be the favored actor for roles in his age group. Of the dozen or more films young True made, however, only one survives, *Broncho Billy's Heart*. In it, he and Broncho Billy play roughhouse games, and they certainly look like they're having fun. But the film that sticks in

An unknown girl, Evelyn Selbie and True Eames Boardman in Broncho Billy's Punishment.

True's memory is *Broncho Billy's Punishment*, because of a frightening scene with a double-barreled shotgun.

True and his on-screen sister were supposed to be playing cowboys and Indians, unsupervised, when True accidently shoots her with an "unloaded" shotgun. The gun, for the purposes of the plot, was actually loaded, although in reality the shells were blanks. What True didn't realize was the gun had two triggers, one for each barrel, and when he fired the gun at a tree (standing in for his off-camera sister), the recoil, as True recalled, "knocked me flat on my little keister. As the cast and crew howled with laughter my mother came running in to pick me up and railed at the director. 'What are you doing to my child?' The propman tried to explain that there were only cotton wads in the shells; and anyway, I was not supposed to shoot both barrels." The scene was done over.[24]

In 1913, Lloyd Ingraham's young daughters, Lois and Zella, acted in Essanay westerns. Lois was five and Zella was eight, but Lois seemed to work the most, according to available evidence. At the end of 1914, three-year-old Nellie Bogdon, billed under the name Bernice Sawyer, played the baby in *Broncho Billy and the Baby* and appeared in two other Anderson westerns while staying with Essanay propman Warren Sawyer and his wife. In May 1915 the McKenzie "twins," Ella and Ida Mae (they were actually cousins), began working regularly in Anderson's films and the Snakeville Comedies, often with Ida's parents Robert and Eva McKenzie. First Ella was chosen for a small part, then Ida wanted equal time. Both girls made favorable impressions and this led to long careers in the movies.

G. M. Anderson, Bernice Sawyer and Neva West in The Outlaw's Awakening.

Ella McKenzie and Ida Mae McKenzie keep occupied on the Essanay stage.

Everyone Gets into the Act   167

G. M. Anderson, Jack Totheroh and Lee Willard in The Bachelor's Baby.

Rollie Totheroh's son Jack (at eight months old) played the title role in *The Bachelor's Baby*, sharing that part with Marguerite Clayton (as the baby all grown up).

Essanay directors tried all kinds of ways to find youngsters for their films. Niles boy Sam Marshall described how he was hired: "When I was in the eighth grade the boys of the class were screen-tested. The studio needed another juvenile to work in the westerns and especially to play opposite Danny Kelleher in the Snakeville Comedy series. I got the job. Paying me seven dollars per day when I worked, it made me more affluent than my father."[25] Marshall discovered other benefits being with the company: "The two fixtures at Essanay who did me more good than any others were C. Allen Dealey, head of photographic, and Spider Roach, the coach who trained a stable of fighters for G. M. Anderson. Both took a personal interest in me. Dealey had made me an expert with the camera (still) before I was fourteen…Roach, an utterly charming wisecracker, not only polished up my boxing style (I was then a featherweight); he took me to the big fights in Dreamland Rink, San Francisco, and under his tutelage, after putting on my first pair of long pants, I got my introduction to the Barbary Coast. Always in his company I had the feeling of the Big Brother trying to help sonny learn more about life without getting hurt."[26]

Sometimes a child, any child, would do, with only one specification: that it be an infant. Lillian Scott, wife of Niles harnessmaker H. L. Scott, lived on Second Street, just across from the reservation. She remembered one day soon after the birth of her first child (named Gilbert) when a propman knocked on her door: "'We'd like to borrow your baby for a few minutes,' he said. Gilbert was about six weeks old, and I wasn't about to let them have the baby. But they pleaded and said I could come along. I guess I was curious, so I took the baby across the street to

Sam Marshall stands way in the back by the wall lamp in Snakeville's Home Guard. *Standing in front are True Boardman, Victor Potel, Bill Cato (peeking over Victor's shoulder), Carl Stockdale, Lee Willard, Margaret Joslin, Jack Wood and Joe Cassidy. Gertrude Cassidy and Madrona Hicks sit on the bench.*

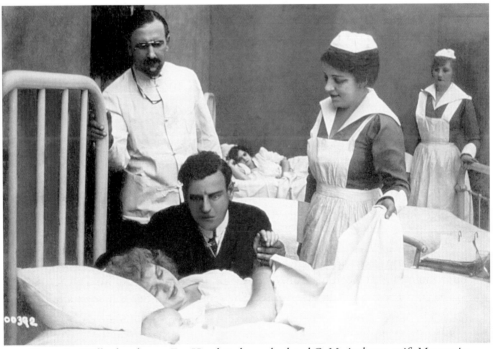

Doctor Lee Willard and nurse Eva Heazlett observe husband G. M. Anderson, wife Marguerite Clayton and baby Gilbert Scott in Her Return.

Eugenia Clinchard before her Essanay days.

the studio. One of the actresses, a beautiful girl, was in this bed they had on the stage, and they put the baby in her arms. Then, I remember Broncho Billy coming in — he was supposed to be the father, I guess — and he bugged his eyes out and looked surprised."[27]

The most remarkable child actress at Essanay was Eugenia Clinchard. Eugenia, born in Oakland on July 5, 1904, was performing on stage at the age of three. By the age of five she was in demand all over the San Francisco Bay Area, appearing in vaudeville sketches and plays. One early review gives a glimpse of her talent: "Baby Eugenia Clinchard, an adorable little fairy who sang some of the latest hits in a sweet childish treble, brought down the house on more than one occasion by her dainty gestures and fascinating baby ways. A chorus of delighted laughter greeted her every movement as, all unconscious of the impression she was creating, she flitted over the stage and danced a Spanish fandango with consummate grace."[28]

Eugenia first acted with the company in San Rafael, playing a little boy in *Papa's Letter*. It was a movie totally out of the ordinary for Anderson, a melodrama about

Eugenia Clinchard, Evelyn Selbie and Anderson in Broncho Billy and the Sheriff's Kid.

a child who dies. When Essanay came to Niles, Eugenia was there frequently, traveling by train from the family home in Alameda and staying at the Belvoir Hotel.

Essanay News issued a press release about Eugenia, a rare acknowledgment for a member of their company so young: "There is one little girl in the business who is absolutely and unconsciously clever. She is only seven years old. Eugenia Clinchard is her name, and she is another of G. M. Anderson's many 'discoveries.' Her alertness and quickness of discernment are almost uncanny in one of her tender years, except that in this child they seem so utterly natural. At rehearsal of a scene she never has to be told anything a second time, while her own little ideas are by no means to be sneezed at."[29] The article sounds like a publicity man's puff piece, but the two of her films that survive, *Broncho Billy and the Sheriff's Kid* and *A Child of the West*, strongly support these claims. In a critical scene as the sheriff's kid, she plays near the edge of a cliff, slips and falls onto some rocks, then lies unconscious. It's completely convincing. In *A Child of the West*, made in San Rafael, she pleads with a gang of vigilantes to spare the life of her father, played by Harry Todd, who stands there with a rope around his neck expecting the worst. But once little Eugenia starts addressing each cowboy individually with her request for mercy you know she'll succeed. It's a comic and touching scene, thanks to her perfect performance.

Eugenia worked at Essanay all through 1913 and into 1914. Her stage appearances continued on to at least 1917. Throughout this time her parents were either protective of her gift or in awe of it; she slept alone in the master bedroom of their home while they shared a smaller room with their young son.[30]

Anderson invited some of the most popular performers of the era to see the Niles studio. Julian Eltinge, a female impersonator in a class by himself, was the first of the "superstars" to visit. He was in San Francisco for a week-long engagement at the Columbia Theater in November, 1912, and took an afternoon off to see the Essanay company at work. Anderson invited Eltinge to play a scene in front of the camera but he declined; his theatrical contract prohibited it. However, that didn't prevent Eltinge's press agent from generating a little publicity over the offer, claiming Anderson offered to pay $100,000 for an Eltinge performance on film. *San Francisco Call* drama critic Walter Anthony wondered why Eltinge would prefer to dress like a woman and exhibit himself on stage. Eltinge replied, "Would you wear corsets for $11,000 a week?" Anthony responded, "To my confusion and shame be it recorded that I said that I most certainly would."[31]

Marie Dressler also declined to appear in an Essanay film during her visit to Niles in December, 1913, just before her musical revue, *The Merry Gambol*, was about to open at Anderson's Gaiety Theatre. It was big news for Anderson to get someone of Marie's stature into his theater; she was very popular and talented, if temperamental. The show was delayed two weeks due to the strained relationship between Marie and the Gaiety management. When the musical finally opened in February to very positive reviews, it almost immediately shut down again because of backstage conflicts. This on-again off-again battle continued until March, when Marie left for Los Angeles to make her movie debut in a feature film, *Tillie's Punctured Romance*.[32]

Al Jolson arrived in Oakland on April 26, 1914, touring the country in *The Honeymoon Express*. Anderson knew Jolson from the days when they were both struggling in New York, and probably saw Jolson's opening show at the Macdonough Theatre that Sunday. The next day they raced automobiles on the Oakland streets, and Jolson, trailing Anderson, was stopped for speeding. Some time that week Jolson went to Niles and accepted an invitation to be in an Essanay movie. That film, unfortunately, is lost.[33]

None of these visits was mentioned in the Niles papers, but one event was, partly because it involved so many people. When Marie Dressler left the Gaiety for the last time, Anderson brought back the sensational William Rock and Maud Fulton musical revue, *The Candy Shop*. In June it was replaced by another revue, *A Knight for a Day*. In July, Anderson decided to combine members from both casts, revive *The Candy Shop*, and send it on tour. He brought the company to Niles for rehearsals and thirty of the company stayed at the Belvoir for two weeks while they polished their performances on the Essanay studio stage. Niles townspeople were familiar with singers, dancers and musicians — entertainers performed regularly onstage at Connors Hall — but the local boys found it hard to ignore the chorus girls. Niles resident Fred Rogers said, "It really shook the town up."[34]

The chorus line for A Knight for a Day.

Anderson decided to capitalize on the talk around town by putting on a benefit show for the baseball team. It was an event the Press couldn't ignore: "Close to nine hundred persons came from all over to make the benefit for the Niles Essanay Indians a success, and truly they did make it a great one...The Essanay studio was turned into a real theater and long before the time for the curtain to rise seats were at a premium. Standing room was the only thing to be had when the clock struck 8:30. The show lasted two hours and thirty minutes...After the finale the floor was cleared of chairs and dancing was indulged in until the wee small hours."[35]

Injuries and accidents continued to be a part of life for the western moviemakers. Anderson stated: "In the desperate riding and driving it is a wonder that someone is not injured in every picture we take."[36] He himself took a fall that hurt his back, and, typically, wrote the incident into a story, *Broncho Billy's Wild Ride.* (Despite making light of it, the injury would haunt him in his old age.) In another film, Anderson sustained powder burns on his face when a prop exploded more violently than expected; for the next few days he was picking flakes of it out of his face. Margaret Joslin backed into some barbed wire and bore the pain of those punctures, but continued to act that day. Frank Pementel scratched his hand and got blood poisoning, a dangerous illness that could lead to death in that era; he was laid up with a fever for days. William Coleman Elam shot himself in the hand with his revolver. Slim Padgett slipped off his horse while performing a stunt and broke a foot bone.[37]

The worst accident in the Western Essanay's history occurred on November 3, 1914, during a rehearsal for *Broncho Billy's Christmas Spirit.* The coach was top-

The infamous Essanay stagecoach: Fred Church hangs on the side, Frank Pementel is at the reins, Stanley Sargent sits beside him, then True Boardman, Marguerite Clayton, Josephine Rector, Jack Roberts, Victor Potel, David Kirkland, Jack Wood, Emory Johnson and Tom Crizer in Broncho Billy's Christmas Deed.

heavy with seven people on the roof; it hit a rut in the Niles Canyon road, lost its front wheels and turned over. Lila McClemmon hit the ground face first. Florence Cato and Eva Sawyer piled on top of her. Everyone involved suffered scrapes and bruises, but Eva Sawyer also dislocated her shoulder and sprained her back. A full month passed before she was able to move around on crutches.[38] According to Nellie Bogdon's son, the incident frightened Nellie's mother so thoroughly she refused to let her child work in any other films.[39]

Whatever the hazards that faced them, the Essanay Film Company cast and crew still managed to grow in numbers and ability. It was evident they were a significant presence in Niles, and a contributor to its growth; the population had increased from 1,400 to 1,900 in two years, and Essanay's payroll of $200,000 a year made it among the most productive employers in the region.

This boost to the local economy was not unnoticed by other communities in 1914. That January Pleasanton announced the formation of the Burr-MacIntosh Company on seven acres near the business district. The California Motion Picture Corporation was building a San Rafael studio in June. A young Bay Area filmmaker named Hal Mohr opened a studio on Telegraph Avenue in Berkeley. Sadie Lindblom, wife of an Alaskan goldminer, started a studio in San Mateo at 5th Avenue and B Street in August, calling it the Liberty Film Company. Sol Lesser, who began his movie career with the Union Nickelodeum movie theater in San

Row six: Martin Killilay, Perc Pembroke, Joe Cassidy, Jack Wood, Stanley Sargent, Charles La Due, Lee Scott, Frank Pementel. Row five: Tom Crizer, Jack Roberts, Mervyn Breslauer, Al Herman, Tom Elliott, Lawrence Abrott, Orlando Hicks, Bill Cato. Row four: Spider Roach, Rollie Totheroh, Frank Dolan, Frank Stockdale, Leo West. Row three: Ira Morgan, ?, Jerome Anderson, William Stockdale, Kite Robinson, William Coleman Elam, Eddie Fries. Row two: True Boardman, Fritz Wintermeier, Carl Stockdale, Harry Todd, Gilbert M. Anderson, Lee Willard, Roy Clements, Victor Potel. Row one: Virginia Eames, Marguerite Clayton, True Eames Boardman, Margaret Joslin, Evelyn Selbie.

Row four: Joe Cassidy, Tom Crizer, Charles La Due, Jack Roberts, Jack Wood, Frank Pementel, Stanley Sargent, Bill Cato. Row three: Fritz Wintermeier, True Boardman, Lee Willard, Victor Potel, G. M. Anderson, Harry Todd, Jerome Anderson, Carl Stockdale. Row two: Ira Morgan, Evelyn Selbie, Mararet Joslin. Front: Shorty Martin, Marguerite Clayton.

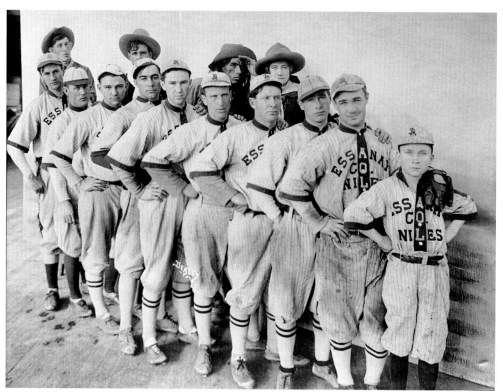

Another line-up: Kite Robinson, Martin Killilay, Eddie Fries, Duke Deiterle, Robert Burroughs, Mervyn Breslauer, Frank Dolan, Rollie Totheroh, Earl Esola and bat boy Dewey McCarthy. The western bunch are: Joe Cassidy, Bill Cato, Tom Crizer and Florence Cato.

Francisco's Mission District, formed the Progressive Film Producing Company. Jack L. Warner, manager of the All Star Theater on Sutter and Fillmore, produced his first film, a one-reel baseball comedy called *The Bleacher Hero. Moving Picture News* announced in May, 1914: "San Francisco Looms as Producing Center."[40] It appeared to be true.

That year the Niles baseball team played right up to the end of November. They had refused to participate in a new league that had been formed out of the ruins of the previous year's under-financed association. Instead, they toured all over the Bay Area: south to San Jose, north to Richmond and Martinez, east to Livermore, and west to San Francisco. Out of 28 games, they won 22. The team was following Anderson's independent nature, and this was not lost on the *Washington Press*; in June it posted a notice on the sports page:

> "This is logic:
> 1913—Niles
> 1914—Niles-Essanay
> 1914—Essanay-Niles
> 1915—Essanay."[41]

The paper was right.

Chapter Nine
Chaplin

After two feature film tie-ins between the Essanay Chicago studio and *Ladies'
World* magazine, Broncho Billy finally got the chance to star in his own three-reel
film; *The Tell-Tale Hand* was released on November 19, 1914. It was produced in
a very short time, but, nevertheless, the production was handled skillfully; all of
the movie trade magazine reviews were favorable. The event was long-awaited by
western movie fans, a view reflected by James McQuade's comments in *Moving
Picture World*: "It is quite a time since I have reviewed a 'Broncho Billy' film, and
for that reason, perhaps, I was an eager spectator of the wild scenes as they were
unfolded. The break-neck speeding of horses along winding roads, the harsh
atmosphere in which the men and women of the west moved some forty years
and more ago, the triumph of the hero, the rescue of the innocent, fair maiden
and the punishment of the low-down critter who tried to send her to the gallows,
had each a special appeal."[1] Before *The Tell-Tale Hand* was released, Anderson was
already making a follow-up feature, *When Love and Honor Called*, once again
filming at a quick pace.

The story for both films was written by Frank Blighton, who had done the
same thing for the Edison Company with the serial *What Happened to Mary?* in
1912. *Ladies' World* readers were invited to submit their interpretation of a missing
paragraph in the story after reading the rest of the tale in the magazine and seeing
the movie; the best dramatic representation would win $100. This "mystery play"
angle was a clever way to stimulate interest, but it was a strange way to present a
western movie. *When Love and Honor Called* didn't generate nearly as much interest
from the critics as *The Tell-Tale Hand* received, and that lack of enthusiasm probably
carried over to the public. The Chicago studio produced more tie-ins with *Ladies'
World* but the Niles studio didn't.

Bill Cato, Lee Willard, Leo West, G. M. Anderson, Darrell Wittenmyer, Tom Crizer, Warren Sawyer.

Marguerite Clayton.

G. M. Anderson. William Coleman Elam, Tom Crizer, Bill Cato, Jack Roberts, Leo West, Fritz Wintermeier, Gertrude Cassidy, Frank Dolan, Joe Cassidy, Darrell Wittenmyer, Harry Todd, Lee Willard, Martin Killilay, ?, Robert Burroughs, Ernest Van Pelt, Mervyn Breslauer, Warren Sawyer.

Harry Todd, Lee Scott, Warren Sawyer, G. M. Anderson, William Coleman Elam, Mervyn Breslauer.

Victor Potel, Mildred Pam Potel, Fritz Wintermeier and canine friend on an Essanay set.

A few days later, on November 23, 1914, Snakeville veteran Victor Potel and Mildred Pam were married in San Francisco. It was a whirlwind courtship that began when Mildred visited the Essanay studio in Niles with her father, Leopold Pam, a movie theater manager. Victor was at the studio that day, acting in another Snakeville comedy. As soon as he saw this dark-haired beauty, only twenty years old and nearly two feet shy of his six-foot two-inch frame, the action on-camera ceased. Potel, who had just turned twenty-five, approached her.

She hoped to win a scholarship to a music institution by selling magazine subscriptions, with each sale counting toward a vote in a contest, and her first words to him were a question: "Won't you buy a vote?"

"A vote — one vote — why, say little girl, I'll elect you!" said Slippery Slim, and he proceeded to sign up every person in sight. But the scholarship was forgotten eleven days later as they stood before Justice of the Peace Charles Creighton, who solemnly pronounced them man and wife.

Other Essanay men had married: the first was Kite and Malvina; Malvina's sister Ida married Rollie Totheroh; Louis Morisette eloped with a Berkeley girl, but it was annulled by her parents; two other Niles sisters tied the knot with Darrell Wittenmyer and Fodder Dolan, and Audrey Orpin, daughter of Niles merchant Frank Orpin, became the wife of Tom Crizer. But Victor's status as a movie comedian made it news, and his fun-loving humor made it newsworthy.

This reception awaited Victor Potel and his bride when they returned to Niles.

During the ceremony he took note of the judge's serious mood and tried to lighten it: "Excuse me, Judge," he said, "this is no tragedy. It may not exactly be a comedy, this little girl and me are going to get a lot of fun out of this." The Judge laughed, and Mildred approved, saying, "That's better. It's not going to be sad. Cheer up, there's nothing to worry about."[2]

This spirit of fun continued with the couple's arrival in Niles, where an immense crowd at the train depot escorted them to a donkey cart with a sign on the back: "To Victor Belong the Spoils." From the depot they were led to their home on the reservation, and Victor was heard to say: "I have figured in a great many marriages for the Essanay people, but none of them proved so satisfactory to me as this."[3] Only five days later they were in the public eye again when they attended the first Motion Picture Industry Ball in San Francisco at the Coliseum on Baker Street.

Sponsored by the Screen Club of San Francisco, the event attracted more than 8,000 people hoping to see their favorite movie stars in person. Among those invited by Sid Grauman, president of the Screen Club, were Lillian Gish, Roscoe "Fatty" Arbuckle, Minta Durfee, Mabel Normand, Bobby Harron, Dustin Farnum, Max Asher, Beatriz Michelena and most of the people from the Niles Essanay studio, including G. M. Anderson. Roy Clements demonstrated the making of a Snakeville Comedy with Slippery Slim, Mustang Pete and Sophie Clutts, and a new dance step, "The Movie Tango," was introduced for the first time by Dorothy Gish and a rising new comedian, Charlie Chaplin.

Moviegoers recognized his talent near the very start of his film career. *Motion Picture News* reported on March 21, 1914: "One pantomimist who is making his mark on the screen is Charles Chaplin, the hero of four Keystone comedies, and on his way to be a comedian of the films of country-wide popularity."[4]

Charles Chaplin.

Chaplin's contract with Keystone was only days short of its conclusion at the time of the San Francisco event, and the sums bandied about for his re-signing with Keystone or moving to another company were reaching unusual proportions. Chaplin had just finished his last Keystone film, *Getting Acquainted*, on November 22nd (although the film he made before it, *His Prehistoric Past*, would be released last), and now he was just waiting for the right proposal.

It's possible he came to town with Arbuckle earlier in the week to relax after his last film. Did he meet with Anderson to talk business? Probably not. Essanay wasn't in the habit of bidding large amounts of money for actors. This was the company Mary Pickford approached in 1909, offering her acting talent for ten dollars more than her $35 Biograph salary, and George Spoor was almost proud to admit he'd turned her down.[5]

Anderson was capable of making a bold move in the other direction, given the right circumstances, and that's what happened when Chaplin returned to Los Angeles. Chaplin was determined to get at least $1000 a week if he renewed his contract with Keystone, and, according to a letter he wrote to his brother Sydney, there were other offers of salary plus percentage coming in at around this same figure. Then Jess Robbins got involved. His offer was unique — it included a $10,000 signing bonus. Chaplin wrote in his autobiography: "I had never thought of a ten-thousand-dollar bonus until he mentioned it, but from that happy moment it became a fixation in my mind."[6] That's what pushed Chaplin in Essanay's direction.

Robbins called Anderson and convinced him this was the chance of a lifetime. Anderson figured he should inform the Chicago studio of his intentions: "So I telegraphed Spoor. 'I'm going down to Los Angeles and I'm going to sign a comedian. I may have to pay him $1000 a week.' And then I got a wire back; he says, 'What, are you crazy? Paying anybody $1000 a week! Don't do it.' But anyway, I went down there."[7]

Anderson and Robbins met with Charlie and Syd Chaplin the second week of December, 1914, and negotiated a final figure of $1250 a week plus the $10,000 bonus. Anderson recalled: "Yeah, well, when I offered him $1250 I didn't know where the $1250 was coming from..."[8] He waited until he was back in Niles to telegraph Spoor.

Spoor, in New York on other business, read the news and was not happy; he was furious. The Chaplin salary was astronomical; even Francis X. Bushman, the Chicago studio's most popular star, received only a fraction of that amount.

Spoor wasn't the only person to question Anderson's decision; Herbert Choynski, Anderson's San Francisco lawyer, refused to draw up the contract, calling the salary too generous, but Anderson stood firmly by his agreement with Chaplin, the contract was written, and Chaplin signed.[9]

Bound by Anderson's commitment, Spoor announced from New York on Monday evening, December 14th, that Chaplin was now with Essanay. The news came to Niles the same day. The *Press* wrote: "Members of the Essanay Film Company at Niles are jubilant over the addition to their staff of Charles Chaplin, comedian. Chaplin was with the Keystone company for some time, and is by far one of the most popular comedy artists in the motion picture industry."[10]

Adding to the pressure now on Anderson, he discovered that his leading lady, Marguerite Clayton, was leaving, hired away by the Liberty Film Company in San Mateo to star in feature films. Marguerite wasn't the only one to seize this opportunity; actors True Boardman and his family, Emory Johnson, Carl Stockdale, Vera Hewitt, and crew members Ira Morgan, Earl Sudderth and Perc Pembroke went with her.[11]

On a positive note, the chance to work with a comedian of Chaplin's ability was irresistible to Jess Robbins, so Robbins dissolved his struggling Robbins Photo Plays Company and joined Essanay once again to produce the Chaplin films. It was just the kind of support Anderson needed to fight Spoor's opposition to this new venture.

Chaplin recalled in his autobiography that he left for Niles immediately after finishing his last Keystone film. This was plainly not true since he didn't sign the contract until two weeks later. More likely, he left immediately after signing, which means he and Anderson arrived in the bustling city of San Francisco on December 14th, ate lunch at the St. Francis Hotel and were driven by Anderson's chauffeur, Joe Flynn, to the Ferry Building as he described. Crossing the bay to Oakland, they drove south through the countryside for an hour. They passed Hayward, curved to the left around the hills north of Niles, and headed directly toward their destination — the Essanay studio. Chaplin remembered: "When I saw it my heart sank, for nothing could have been less inspiring. It had a glassed-in roof, which made it extremely hot when working in the summer."[12] Chaplin didn't like the studio (never mentioning the other stage within the building, completely dependent upon artificial light), he didn't like Niles (it was out in the middle of nowhere), and Anderson's bungalow (which Anderson offered to share) was a mess. Chaplin described it: "The place was empty and drab. In his room was an old iron bed with a light bulb hanging over the head of it. A rickety old table and one chair were the other furnishings. Near the bed was a wooden box upon which was a brass ashtray filled with cigarette butts. The room allotted to me was almost the same, only it was minus the grocery box. Nothing worked. The bathroom was unspeakable. One had to take a jug and fill it from the bath tap and empty it down the flush to make the toilet work."[13] By the end of the week Chaplin was thoroughly depressed.

Anderson suggested the Chicago studio might be more to Chaplin's liking and Chaplin agreed to try it. They took an eastbound train on Sunday, December 20th, and arrived in Chicago on December 23rd.[14] They were met by Anderson's wife, Mollie.

It must have been a surprise to most people that Anderson had time for a wife, or the inclination to marry. A photo donated by Anderson to the Hollywood Museum suggests Mollie was working as a newsstand cashier in Chicago at the Sherman House (hotel) when they met. Two years younger than Anderson, she was born in Russia, but raised in St. Cloud, Minnesota. They probably married

Francis X. Bushman, Charles Chaplin and G. M. Anderson in Chicago, December, 1914.

during the summer of 1910. Their only child, Maxine, was born in Chicago on January 29, 1912, and Mollie brought her up in a comfortable apartment at 1027 Lawrence Avenue near the Essanay studio. Anderson saw them only on his infrequent trips east.[15]

Mollie recalled this particular arrival: "It was... bitterly cold out. I met G. M. and there was the little fellow with him. He had no luggage, no handbag at all, just a small roll of clothes. He had no overcoat, and there was a severe wind. You know how vicious Chicago weather can be. Well, we all rode back to my Chicago apartment. When I could get G. M. alone, I asked him, 'Who is this little chap?' He answered, 'I find him clever and amusing. I think he could be a great comedian. He's being wasted in Los Angeles.'"[16]

Chaplin entered a world unknown to him when he stepped inside that apartment. There before him was the Anderson's baby daughter, tended by a maid, and beside her was a Christmas tree. Mollie remembered: "He walked around the tree with a radiant expression on his face. And he kept exclaiming: 'A Christmas tree, a baby, a Christmas tree! It's wonderful!'"[17]

Chaplin stayed with the Andersons for the next two weeks, and they entertained him around town. On at least one night the public was also amused; dressed as moviegoers knew them, Anderson as Broncho Billy, Chaplin as The Tramp, the two men danced "The Broncho Billy Waltz" at a charity event. People talked about this weird and comical stunt for weeks.

As for work, Chaplin kept busy until the new year with studio publicity staff and a mass of reporters eager for information. Everyone wanted an interview. Clarence Caine, writing for *Motography* magazine, described the scene: "He seldom moved as fast while on the screen as he did during his first few days of his stay in the Windy City. 'Charlie' was wanted here and 'Charlie' was wanted there, from the time he arrived in the studio in the morning until he left at night. Therefore it was a rather difficult task to catch him, but I managed to corner him in the advertising department of the big studio on Argyle street for an interview."[18]

Just what it took to corner Charlie was told in more detail by Mae Tinee of the *Chicago Tribune*: "The man who was to introduce us looked at me rather blankly as we shook hands. 'Yes, he's here somewhere,' he said, 'but where he is I haven't an idea. You may not believe him, but he is scared to death of publicity, and I had my hands full, I can tell you, to pry permission out of him for this interview. Come on, we'll see if we can find him for you.'

"We started out. All over the place we went — through the big studio where pictures were being taken, through the business offices, out in the yard — everywhere. No Mr. Chaplin. I sighed. Had I made the trip for nothing? Oh dear! My guide looked at me dubiously.

"'There's one place we haven't been—that's the projecting room,' he said. 'There's a chance that he might be there. Anyhow, Mr. Bushman, G. M. Anderson, and a lot of others are, so come on down,' (Francis Bushman and G. M. Anderson, girls! Did I go!)

"In the projection room of the Essanay there are two rows of seats facing the screen. The seats are schoolroom seats with desks attached — you know the kind? Well, seated at one little desk was Mr. Bushman; seated at another little desk — fairly scrooged in, the seat was so little and he was so big — was Mr. Anderson. A lot of other people of more or less importance were at the other desks.

"My guide looked around.

"'Is he here?' I asked anxiously. Still eagle eye peered. Suddenly he touched me. 'Yes,' he said. 'Over there!'

"Over in the corner was a little man. And the little man in the corner was Charles Chaplin!

"Just then the lights went on and Mr. Anderson's latest picture, *When Love and Honor Called*, was started. My guide pushed me into one of the little seats.

"'Sit there till the picture's over,' he said, 'and I will stand at the door and see that Mr. Chaplin doesn't get out.'"[19]

While Mae Tinee sat during the movie she had a chance to observe Anderson. Her comments give an indication of how Anderson could sympathize with Chaplin, a younger man faced with the extreme admiration of complete strangers, something only another celebrity would know: "Believe me, girls, Mr. Anderson in the flesh is some winner! He has the nicest eyes and the whitest teeth in the world, and the kind of manner that makes you wish he was a friend of the family. You know what

I mean? All through the picture he just sat and looked at himself in a shy sort of way. Everybody else in the room kept exclaiming 'Great!' 'Wonderful!' and so on. But Mr. Anderson never said 'Boo!' Just sat and acted sort of as if he wished he were anyplace but there."[20]

When the film was over Tinee moved swiftly: "I made a dive and got in front of Mr. Chaplin just as he was about to run away under the barring arm of my guide.

"'Mr. Chaplin?' I said. And he answered: 'I guess there's no denying it. Glad to meet you. Now where shall we go for our talk?"[21]

They went to the guide's office and Tinee pressed Chaplin for the details of his life, but he avoided that.

Everyone who interviewed him wanted to know his life story, and the repetition must have taken on the aura of a police grilling. Chaplin became adept at shortening that story to a minimum, or avoiding it all together, but gave each reporter a slant on his life that made up for it.

In Tinee's case it was that, in his case, being interviewed was not a good idea: "You see, people aren't strong for celebrities that are already made. When a man's been boosted to the skies, they're apt to sit back in their seats and say: 'I don't see anything so wonderful about that chap. Nothing to make a fuss about. He's overrated.' But, if the man is not made, they take joy and pride in discovering him. They say: 'Now there's a man that can act. He's a comer.' Later, when the man's made good they have all the joy of saying: 'I told you so.' Get me?"[22]

With Clarence Caine, Chaplin revealed that it wasn't until he was working in films that he reconciled himself to being a comedian; before that he desired to become a dramatic leading man. Then he turned to a theory about comic source material that neatly wrapped up these two opposing forces in acting: "I believe that a plot which could easily become a dramatic subject, but which is treated in an amusing manner and which burlesques events of daily life, with which the average person is familiar, depending principally upon its humorous action for laughs, is the one to make a successful farce comedy."[23]

After the endless conversations at the studio about his life and work, Chaplin left it behind, and was doted on and entertained by the Andersons. Mollie said: "He slept late. Very late. And when he appeared, it was without a shirt collar. He had curly hair and never ran a comb through it. The maids kept his food waiting. We heard no apology from him. So I simply did what I could. I was a young person too, and I told him, 'Charlie, run a comb through your hair, and make yourself a little more presentable, and we'll have breakfast."[24]

It wasn't as if Chaplin was unaware of his appearance to other people; he himself commented about it in one his many interviews at the time: "I don't care anything about dress. As I got off the train a newsie spotted me. 'What do you think of that hamfat?' he yelled to his companion. 'One hundred thousand bucks a year, and he looks like a tramp.'"[25]

On January 2, 1915, Anderson left Chicago to meet Sam Rork, his theatrical manager, in New York. Anderson wanted to put together a musical comedy, send it west on a tour, and finish up at his Gaiety Theatre in February. While in New

York Anderson was recognized, as usual, and asked about his new comedian, Charles Chaplin. Anderson would only say that Chaplin was working in Chicago under the guidance of Jess Robbins.[26]

Robbins was indeed in Chicago, smoothing the way for Chaplin. It wasn't easy. The Chicago studio was much different than Niles, or Keystone for that matter. Scripts were usually assigned to directors; there were forms to fill out during production; budgets were very tight. The regimented atmosphere troubled Chaplin: "In the upstairs office the different departments were partitioned like tellers' cages. It was anything but conducive to creative work. At six o'clock, no matter whether a director was in the middle of a scene or not, the lights were turned off and everybody went home."[27]

No mention was made of Robbins, who must have found himself in a difficult position trying to bridge the gap between Essanay and its new star. Spoor's absence didn't help any either. It's not clear when Spoor finally arrived to face Chaplin for the first time, but when he did, it was too late to sooth the comedian's frustrations, as Chaplin's bitter comments reveal. It was too bad mostly for Spoor, who never did learn how valuable Chaplin could be to him, even as the demand for these new comedies kept escalating and the money rolled in. But it wasn't just the money; Chaplin's presence put Essanay in a higher class, the top echelon of the industry, and Spoor didn't even know it.

The personnel at the Chicago studio knew better. A crowd of veteran Essanay performers spent their off-time watching Chaplin from the sidelines while he worked. Charles J. McGuirk, writing for *Motion Picture* magazine, described the scene as Chaplin hopped around doing vigorous dance steps in the morning: "He did it so seriously that everybody wondered if he was out of his mind, because it seemed entirely uncalled for. Francis X. Bushman was among the interested bystanders — just a wee bit peeved, perhaps, to see this great bidder for world-popularity stepping into the Essanay studio, where he had been monarch o'er all he surveyed — and he inquired the cause of Chaplin's peculiar antics.

"'Ah!' he said, sotto voce. 'Got to limber up. A little pep, everybody; a little pep. Come on, boys. Shoot your set. I'm ready.' The last sentence was shouted. Charlie went thru a few other steps, and then sized up the situation. He examined his set and then his actors. He gave them their instructions as to just what they should do and just when they should do it. He looked down on those $50,000 feet of his, picked up one of them and stood like a stork as he examined a shoe, put it down again, straightened up and started to shoot a rapid-fire of directions, musings and comments on the world of today. When any actor went thru a piece of 'business' that appealed to Charlie, he was quick to step out, pat him on the back and tell him: 'You're a bear. Good stuff. You're goin' along right, old top. Keep it up — keep it up.'"[28]

It's plain to see that Chaplin was on exhibition this day, and making the most of it. He was also directing attention to Leo White, Charlotte Mineau and Ben Turpin, people who would work with him in more films. They were all featured prominently in this first Essanay film, *His New Job*. Even Chaplin's producer, Jess

Robbins, got into the act; he's the cameraman on-screen during the shooting of the movie within the movie.

One cast member who didn't seem to fit in was Gloria Swanson, seen briefly in the background as a very serious office secretary. She was a newcomer to Essanay who wanted to be a dramatic actress and Chaplin's slapstick antics didn't appeal to her. Ironically, she'd move to Los Angeles later that year and find work at Mack Sennett's Keystone studio doing exactly what she refused to do in *His New Job*.

Chaplin's film, set in a movie studio, was shot entirely on Essanay's newest stage (completed in 1914).[29] His cameraman was Jackson Rose, one of the best men on the lot.[30] Clearly, the Chicago studio was trying to get past the initial confusion, but Chaplin's way of working was simply foreign to them.

In describing Chaplin's methods, McGuirk continued: "It took a little while, but Chaplin finally injected enough enthusiasm into his people to make them work hours without thought of time. The proof of it came at the noon hour. Nobody knew it was twelve o'clock. The first inkling Chaplin had of it was when he noticed the augmented crowd that eyed his efforts with all sorts of expressions on their faces. 'What's the idea? Why the party?' Charlie exclaimed, during a lull in the work. 'By George! I'll bet it's twelve o'clock, aint it, boys? Twelve o'clock, sure as you live. That's all for a while. Get out and get your lunches.' The actors filed out, tired but very happy."[31]

That didn't mean everything was perfect; far from it. A hint of the continuing conflict was voiced by Edward Arnold, relaying the observations of Essanay writer H. Tipton Steck: "Chaplin's acting, even in those days, fascinated everyone. He was so dynamic, yet subtle. Whenever he was doing a scene, the other members of the cast would behave as though they were hypnotized. Everybody stood still, and watched him. Even the stage hands would leave their work and gather around. It became a standard joke in the company that 'this fellow Chaplin had better be dropped. He disrupts the whole organization with his antics.'"[32]

Anderson returned to Chicago from New York on Tuesday, January 12th, just as Chaplin was finishing *His New Job*. The movie appeared to be in fine shape, but not Chaplin. Anderson could see the Englishman was unhappy: "He didn't like the cameraman and he didn't like the fellow who painted the scenery and he didn't like this and he didn't like that."[33] The situation was driving Chaplin crazy. The only other option was a return to Niles. Two days later, Anderson and Chaplin left Chicago by train, heading west.[34]

Chapter Ten
The Tramp Out West

Although Chaplin berated the Chicago Essanay studio, two of its comedians, Ben Turpin and Leo White, met with his approval, and he brought them along to Niles.

Like Chaplin at Keystone, Ben Turpin didn't really fit in at the Chicago studio; no one seemed to know what to do with Ben's unique attribute, his crazy eyes When the studio took a series of group photographs in 1914 he stood in the back row with his eyes shut. Worst still, his employment with the company during its early years worked to his detriment; on his return to the studio in 1913 after four difficult years in vaudeville, he was very reluctantly hired back by George Spoor at his old salary of twenty dollars per week. For nearly two years thereafter, Turpin's supporting work in countless farce-comedies, the George Ade Fables and Wallace Beery's Sweedie Comedies went largely unnoticed despite the oddball look about him that begged to be exploited. *His New Job* changed Ben's life; he was suddenly recognized as an out-of-kilter twin to Chaplin, funny in his own unique way. Things were finally looking up for him.

Leo White claimed to be a Manchester, England, native, but there's evidence he was born in Graudenz, Germany.[1] His acting career began in 1902, the year of his twentieth birthday, and ten years later he made his movie debut with Essanay in Chicago. White was a go-getter, and was able to stand out at times from the crowd of comics at the studio. In *One Wonderful Night*, for instance, his portrayal of a fussy French count brought him favorable notice; however, like Turpin, it took Chaplin's intervention for White to significantly advance from there.

Ben Turpin.

Leo White.

Margie Rieger.   *Edna Purviance.*

Hazel Applegate was another member of the group heading west. She came from the Chicago studio to replace Marguerite Clayton when Anderson failed to find a suitable co-star in New York. But her presence in Niles was short-lived; three months later she returned to Chicago.

Chaplin's new leading lady was still to be decided when he came to Niles on January 18th. No one at the studio fit the bill, and the chorus line at Anderson's Gaiety Theatre was also rejected.[2] The next day there was an ad in the *San Francisco Chronicle*: "WANTED — THE PRETTIEST GIRL IN CALIFORNIA to take part in a moving picture."[3] George V. White (a freelance promoter) was the contact person. It seems likely this was an attempt to find Chaplin's co-star; after all, Anderson discovered Marguerite Clayton through a similar ad. The advertisement's link is further supported by its timing to the arrival of the leading contenders for the position in Niles; just two days later, on January 21st, Sade (pronounced Saydee) Carr, Margie Rieger (pronounced Reeger) and Edna Purviance (rhymes with reliance) signed in together at the Belvoir Hotel.[4]

Which woman Chaplin would choose was by no means a foregone conclusion; at various times each of them was publicly announced to fill the bill.[5] Sade Carr was a vivacious twenty-five-year-old singer (born in London) who'd worked in Al Jolson's *Honeymoon Express* and at Anderson's Gaiety Theatre in the Rock and Fulton musical revue *The Candy Shop*. By contrast, Margie Rieger and Edna Purviance were both younger and neither had film or stage experience.

Chaplin said that he decided to hire Edna before his first Niles movie, *A Night Out*, began production, that he was anxious to get busy, but hadn't thought of a story yet, so he ordered a cafe set built for inspiration. The set may have still been under construction, but on the day Edna came to Niles, production was already under way. Chaplin was in Oakland with Ben Turpin to film street scenes at the entrance to a real cafe, and in the process they were nearly arrested.

The action took place at the doorway to the Hotel Oakland's cafe on Harrison Street. The rehearsal gathered a large crowd and this caught the attention of officer Robert Lyons. He forced his way through the onlookers to see two men, apparently drunk, rolling around on the sidewalk. He grabbed both men by their collars, pulled them upright, then heard the whir of the camera and the cameraman shouting, "Good stuff, good stuff. A real arrest. Keep it up." Lyons studied the situation and realized to his embarrassment that he was participating in a movie. Letting go of his would-be prisoners, he backed away, apologizing and blushing. This scene never reached the screen, but did become the genesis for a running gag between Chaplin and a policeman (played by Fritz Wintermeier) stationed outside a saloon in the finished film.[6]

Chaplin probably met his three choices for leading lady that evening or the next day, but it appears he didn't make a decision immediately; the *Chronicle* ad was repeated on the 21st, 23rd and 24th. Chaplin never mentioned any rivals to Edna in his autobiography, but he did express a hesitation to hire her: "She was quiet and reserved, with beautiful large eyes, beautiful teeth and a sensitive mouth. I doubted whether she could act or had any humor, she looked so serious. Nevertheless, with these reservations, we engaged her. She would at least be decorative in my comedies."[7]

Olga Edna Purviance was born in Lovelock, Nevada, on October 21, 1895. She grew up in nearby Paradise Valley, and was a recent business school graduate living in San Francisco with older sister Bessie Hill when the movies beckoned. Later sources claim she was working as a secretary at the time, but it appears just as probable, even likely, that she was working at the Tait-Zinkand Cafe (a popular hangout in the heart of the theater district) on O'Farrell Street right next to Anderson's Gaiety Theatre. According to Anderson's sister Leona, who was living only a block away at the St. Francis Hotel: "Miss Purviance was a waitress in San Francisco at the time. My brother phoned me in San Francisco from his Niles studio and told me to go get her and bring her down for a film test."[8]

As it turned out, Sade Carr returned to San Francisco, Margie Rieger stayed in Niles to work at Essanay, and Edna Purviance became Chaplin's leading lady. After Edna was hired, she went to Oakland with Turpin and Chaplin to film on location in front of the Peralta Apartments building at 184 13th Street, standing in for the first hotel in *A Night Out*. The Sierra Apartments at 1502 Alice Street represented the second hotel. Along with them was William "Bud" Jaimison, another newcomer to the movies, playing Edna's husband.

Bud Jamison (as his last name was spelled for the movies) was born in Vallejo, California, in 1894.[9] After high school he worked at the local telephone company, then moved to San Francisco and performed in cafes. From there he went on the road touring with stock companies and appearing in vaudeville. He was living

Edna Purviance, Charlie Chaplin and Lincoln Beachey on the sidewalk in front of the Essanay studio in Niles, January 29, 1915.

again in San Francisco when word came that performers were needed for Chaplin's Essanay company. Jamison's imposing six-foot, two-hundred-seventy-pound frame no doubt helped him get the job.

News that Chaplin was working in the area intrigued the organizers of the Celebrities Ball, who were looking for movie stars to bring crowds into San Francisco's new Civic Auditorium. Lincoln Beachey, a world-famous aviator and chairman for the event, was scheduled to lead the grand march, but he surrendered the honor to Charles Chaplin, personally going to Niles and presenting the comedian with an invitation to the event. Edna, swept up in Chaplin's whirlwind rise to fame, was invited to be his partner at the ball, and she accepted.[10]

Two days after the ball, Chaplin's Chicago Essanay film, *His New Job*, was released. It received good reviews, but more important for Essanay, the public was clamoring to see it. The company suddenly became swamped with requests for two, then three times the number of prints usually made for distribution. Theaters that normally didn't book with the General Film Company service were trying to outbid the regular subscribers.[11]

In the cafe from A Night Out, *Bud Jamison tries to get a grip on Ben Turpin's neck while Charlie Chaplin and Leo White look on. In the background are Eddie Fries, Hazel Applegate, Charles Allen Dealey and behind Leo's shoulder is William Coleman Elam.*

With this surprising success, Spoor saw his investment in Chaplin paying off quickly — if the comedian would hurry up and make more films. Pressure was put on the Niles studio to ship the next Chaplin film immediately, and its release was announced for February 11th. But the film wasn't ready.

Rollie Totheroh remembered: "After Charlie finished his first picture, he wanted to rest and go to San Francisco for a couple of days over the weekend … Anderson decided he was going to cut it so he got ahold of me and we went in and we started to cut on the first reel of Charlie's picture. Lo and behold! Chaplin didn't go to San Francisco. He decided not to at the last minute and came walking in on us. We were cutting the first reel, and Charlie said, 'Take your hands off that.' At that time we never had a print made; we used to do the cutting on negative. If we scratched it, it was just too bad. So Charlie said, 'And furthermore, I want a print.' At that time we had our own little laboratory, but we never had a printing machine because we never used it. Our laboratory man didn't know anything about a printing machine. So they had to send all the way back to Chicago to get one.

"By the time we sent out for it with express, it was two weeks before we got it. Then they went to make a print and they had forgotten to send the blower for the

Ben Turpin marries Margie Rieger and Tom Crizer in A Bunch of Matches. *Behind them: Harry Pollard, Florence Cato, Pat Rooney, an unknown woman and Bill Cato.*

Harry Pollard, Robert McKenzie and Ed Armstrong in A Countless Count.

machine. The blower would contact each frame on the aperture when it went through the printing machine; it held the film firm. So this laboratory man made the print with everything going in and out of focus. So Charlie said, 'How am I going to cut with that thing?'"[12] Jess Robbins had to make a quick trip back to Chicago to get the pieces that should have been sent in the first place.

When *A Night Out* was finally released on February 15th, Chaplin's latest triumph brought further recognition to Ben Turpin. Here was someone who, if he didn't actually steal a scene from Chaplin, could collaborate with the Englishman in a way that no one else had done before, except perhaps Roscoe Arbuckle. It put Ben in a new comic class. Briefly. Ben recalled: "You heard that gossip about Charlie having killed a man in a picture, didn't you? Huh? Well, that was me. I was the guy he killed. Some bump, believe me."[13]

Ben may have referred to a physical bump that put him out of commission temporarily, but in a greater sense the blow was more deadly. Chaplin decided, and rightly so for his own future, that he didn't need a partner. Turpin had to go.

The logical new home for Turpin was in the Snakeville comedy unit, but this series had suffered a setback in January when Roy Clements was hurt in an Oakland car accident. Production of the films continued, fitfully, with Fritz Wintermeier directing, then stopped when Anderson decided it was better to wait for Clements' recovery. Finally, the comedies resumed with *The Undertaker's Uncle* starring Ben Turpin in the title role. The *Dramatic Mirror* stated: "At last the efforts of Victor Potel and Harry Todd have been rewarded with a third partner equally successful in making the orchestra ring. No less than Ben Turpin is the undoubtedly ludicrous gentleman who adds new life to Snakeville doings. All this is no disrespect to the powers of Margaret Joslin, bless us."[14] Ben was bouncing back.

G. M. Anderson, however, wasn't doing too well; his new musical revue, *The Arcadian's*, was losing money in its Los Angeles run and had to be shut down.[15] This left Anderson in a difficult position with several performers who were guaranteed a longer run by contract. Anderson tried to make do by bringing them to San Francisco for his show at the Gaiety Theatre. That show, *Tillie's Nightmare* (starring May Boley), closed in less than a month, and the first to sue Anderson for breach of contract was Percival Knight, one of the performers. In the financial squeeze Anderson was forced to turn over the Gaiety to a management firm, Ackerman & Harris, and they reopened it as a vaudeville theater, the Hippodrome.[16]

In Niles, Chaplin's presence seemed to attract other skilled comedians. Robert McKenzie and his wife Eva Heazlett (her stage name) arrived just in time to join in the revived Snakeville Comedies. Soon, musical comedy stars Ed and Billy Armstrong were in Niles, too, as was Harry "Snub" Pollard, previously associated with the Pollard Juvenile Opera Company. The question was what to do with all of these talented newcomers; the answer was to make more comedies. *A Bunch of Matches*, *A Hot Finish* and *A Countless Count* were the first of these.

While the Snakeville series was temporarily sidelined, Ernest Van Pelt became one of the few regulars to join the Chaplin unit. He played the first boxer in *The Champion*, Chaplin's second film in Niles.

Ernest Van Pelt and Charlie Chaplin face off (Bill Cato between them in the background) in
The Champion. *Note the large pile of film cans on the far left by the darkroom door.*

The Champion included no trips to Oakland this time. Nearly everything was shot at the studio or within a block of it. The fence surrounding the studio yard was used frequently in the film. When Van Pelt runs past a gate escaping from Chaplin, the two-story *Township Register* building can be seen in the distance, identifying that location as the G Street entrance. The front of the studio is seen when Chaplin encounters the first cop, played once again by Fritz Wintermeier, and Van Pelt's getaway down the dirt road was shot just to the right of the studio sidewalk in that same direction. The closeup of Edna Purviance was taken two blocks to the east near Front Street; the building in the background is the Southern Pacific freight shed (still there today).

When *The Champion* came out, reviewers delightedly pointed out another face on the screen — a bulldog. The dog figures in the story right from the beginning; Chaplin, out of work and hungry, shares a meal with the animal. At the end of the film the dog helps the tramp win a big boxing match against Chaplin's opponent, Bud Jamison, by chomping into the seat of Jamison's pants and hanging on to the finish.

Turpin and Anderson had already perfected this trick with a dog years before at the Chicago Essanay studio. With both men on the scene it would have been easy

The Champion: *Warren Sawyer stands on the left, Chaplin is the blur in the center. Edna sits in costume at the right with the bulldog beside her.*

to work out the routine and minimize the danger to Jamison's rear end. Anderson even claimed, years later, to have directed *The Champion*, while Chaplin, in turn, directed a Broncho Billy western. There's no proof to that story, but either man could have provided the idea for *The Champion*. Anderson and Chaplin were both boxing fans, and had previously worked the sport into films, Chaplin with *The Rounders*, Anderson with *"Spike" Shannon's Last Fight*. However, the only firm evidence connecting Anderson to the film is within the film itself; he appears as a spectator in the fight scene.

As with *"Spike" Shannon's Last Fight*, the boxing ring spectators were all men. Although the crowd wasn't enormous, it was still unusually large for films made in Niles, and it's certain this was another occasion when Niles residents were rounded up to fill the seats. Some Essanay people even doubled up their roles; Jess Robbins is a spectator in the second row of the bleachers, just behind Anderson, and he also loosens up Chaplin between rounds in the ring, while other people in the bleachers stand by at ringside, too. One newcomer, Lloyd Bacon, played two significant roles in the film: Van Pelt's first sparring partner, and the referee.

Bacon came to Niles from the Liberty Film Company in San Mateo. While business was booming with Essanay, Liberty couldn't pay their bills and production

Lloyd Bacon in His Regeneration.

The Champion.

Edna Purviance and Charlie Chaplin In the Park.

had stopped. True Boardman went from Liberty to the Kalem Company in Los Angeles, but Marguerite Clayton returned to Niles. Some of her old colleagues from Niles followed her lead, including cameraman Ira Morgan, scenic painter Earl Sudderth and actor Perc Pembroke, but for Bacon it was a new experience.

Lloyd Francis Bacon, born on December 4, 1889 in San Jose, California, was the son of the popular and respected stage actor, Frank Bacon, who had a farm called "Baconia" in Mountain View. This is where Lloyd grew up. Lloyd took to the stage himself, but his greatest success came in the movies. Working in Essanay westerns at first, he soon discovered comedy with Chaplin.[17]

It took nearly all of February to complete *The Champion*, and it's likely that *In the Park*, a one-reel film, was rushed through production to amend for it. The movie is notable for two reasons: Edna is relaxed and natural for the first time on screen, and Chaplin can't take his eyes off her. Something was going on here. That something was love, and it changed the way Chaplin treated her character. She came through unscathed while everyone else was knocked about and manhandled. Filmed, as implied by its title, in San Francisco's Golden Gate Park, it led naturally to another movie in the same setting — *A Jitney Elopement*.

Just at that time, San Francisco was experiencing jitney fever. Owners of touring cars, to make extra money, picked up strangers and delivered them to their destination. It was, in effect, a taxi service run by private individuals with time on their hands, and the newspapers were running daily accounts of what the public thought of this business, and what the city government was going to do about it. As the developing "jitney" story was endlessly played out in the local newspapers, Chaplin made the most of it by using the name for his film even though the movie had nothing to do with the subject.

Ernest Van Pelt played a sausage vender *In the Park*, but for *A Jitney Elopement* he reverted to type; instead of being the father of Sophie Clutts, he was Edna's father. Lloyd Bacon was the butler and Leo White became Charlie's rival. Interiors were filmed in Niles, exteriors in Golden Gate Park. The company stayed in San Francisco while filming the park scenes (they attended the newly-opened Panama Pacific International Exposition for fun), then returned to Niles on March 15th.[18] *Jitney* was released barely two weeks later, on April 1, 1915.

This short turnaround time became standard procedure with the Chaplin Essanay films for the rest of the year. The publicity department was fortunate in one respect: the films didn't need boosting to the skies; they were already in the stratosphere.

For his next film, *The Tramp*, Chaplin finally yielded to the rural atmosphere of Niles. Begun in Niles Canyon and ending there, production remained in the vicinity throughout its three-week shooting schedule. Here, Chaplin crafted a story with a range of emotions that was unusual for a comedy.

Harris Ensign was the cameraman on Chaplin's previous Niles films, but may have been temporarily absent for at least part of *The Tramp*; otherwise Chaplin's core production team continued to work with him — Mervyn Breslauer as assistant cameraman, Danny Kelleher handling props and W. P. Gordon assisting, Fritz Wintermeier as assistant director and Alfred Griffin as set carpenter. Ernest Van

Pelt once again played Edna's father, Leo White, Bud Jamison and Lloyd Bacon were the thieves, Paddy McGuire the farm hand, Billy Armstrong a minister, and Lloyd Bacon cleaned himself up for another role as Edna's boyfriend.

Kitty Kelly, columnist for the *Chicago Tribune*, stopped in Niles in time to see him figuring out a scene for *The Tramp*: "If I were a motion picture company I would shadow Mr. Chaplin with a moving picture camera, for he is positively just as funny directing as he is acting — which most people must admit is about the topnotch of funniness." The scene was shot behind the studio in an open field of grass surrounded by a fence. With him was Billy Armstrong (in his first film), dressed as a minister holding a book. Chaplin studied the scene: "'Now let me see what action I have got,' he said after rehearsing the minister, whose business was to look soulfully at the sky while Chaplin approached.

"'Get me a bad egg — no, a good one,' ordered Chaplin, and a blue overalled person arose from the grass and trotted toward the studio, returning soon with the required prop. Through the motions they went several times, Chaplin laughing and grimacing and holding the egg carefully down to the minister's book, where ultimately it was to be dropped.

"'I think it ought to run a little bit,' he decided, so somebody picked a hole in one end and arranged an animated extraction of the yolk.

"'Now, let's see,' Chaplin mused, not exactly tearing his hair, but certainly racking his brains. 'Smell, smell, we must have something about smell.' Striking an oratorical attitude, he declaimed, 'The divine fragrance, the glorious perfume of the — here, get me a flower, not red, something white,' and the prop boy scattered to a neighboring garden, returning with an apple blossom.

"Then the directing and acting went on with the minister smelling the flower and looking to heaven, while Chaplin slipped humorously up, dropped the egg, which fell with a satisfyingly pictorial smashup on the book, and waltzed off, the egg emphasizing things by running — without any direction — in driblets down the front of the ministerial coat."[19]

Kitty Kelly could see that behind the fun of creating was also the work and stress of it. She decided that, despite Chaplin's youth, just days short of his twenty-sixth birthday, tension and anxiety were bringing on gray hairs at his temples.

The Tramp was in its last few days of production, and everyone knew this would be Chaplin's last film in Niles. He'd made up his mind to return to Los Angeles, and Anderson went along with it for practical reasons; space at the small Niles studio was limited, and Chaplin's extensive use of interior and exterior sets tied up much of the crew. To maintain a measure of control, Jess Robbins and a core group of the Niles studio staff would go with Chaplin to Los Angeles and from there, at moment's notice, competent people could be hired as needed for the short term from a vast pool of technicians and actors. Studio space in Los Angeles could easily be rented, too, along with all the necessary equipment. Dozens of production companies dotted the Los Angeles landscape; by 1915 it was clearly the center of film production in the United States, and this was the environment Chaplin preferred.

Chaplin, born and raised in London, was a city person, and although Los Angeles wasn't like London, it was more so than Niles. One difference between these environments was of particular importance: in a big city there could be anonymity; in a small town everyone was on display.

But just how often was Chaplin in Niles? He worked there, of course, but where did he stay? Not with Anderson, according to Rollie Totheroh: "...Charlie wasn't real satisfied with the bungalow. Later on, he didn't stay there. They got him a room in a little hotel that was across the tracks, so he didn't stay at Anderson's."[20] The only hotel across the tracks was the Belvoir. In a conversation with Marie Sharpe Bishop, Hal Angus said: "I don't think Charlie Chaplin lived in Niles at all. I think he went back and forth from San Francisco."

"Not all the time," said Marie.

"Well, most of the time."

"They loaned him a cottage or something," she said. "He never stayed at the Belvoir."[21]

Local legend mentions him living downtown at the Wesley Hotel, but there's no concrete evidence of that either. He did, however, like many of the other Essanay people, eat lunch there.[22]

Wherever he stayed, Chaplin, by his very nature, was someone who stuck out in Niles. Innately shy, he tried to overcompensate for this by constantly performing in public. This exhibitionism was another trait he had in common with Ben Turpin.

Ben Turpin would do backflips in front of saloons or fall into a horse trough just for the fun of it. Niles resident Lillian Scott said: "He always wore baggy pants. One day he was walking down the street, and his pants fell down and he just kept right on walking. It was a trick he could do, you know. He was never dirty — just funny."[23] Alameda County motorcycle cop Leon Solon said: "Ben was a favorite of everybody in town. I can still see him climbing out of a trough, looking like a drowned rabbit with those crazy eyes of his going in two directions at once."[24] Hal Angus remembered: "He was really cockeyed, a real funny duck. You give him a couple of shots of booze and you'd have the time of your life."[25] Bert Silveria, bartender at Silva's Corner, recalled how Ben's evenings in the bar would end with the entrance of his wife Carrie: "Ben would see her coming through the swinging doors. Right away he'd call out: 'Gee, I'm glad to see you, dear. You must know how I hate to walk home alone.' He would lock arms with her and they'd peacefully go home together.[26]

Ben's extroverted ways made it seem like he and the people witnessing his antics were sharing in the fun, but Chaplin's methods somehow antagonized. The ill feelings felt by the people of Niles still erupt on occasion, handed down by the generations, passions so strong it can be quite a shock to the uninitiated. Sam Marshall, who acted in two Chaplin films, expressed himself with surprising anger: "On or off the set he had to keep doing his tricks, flipping his hat, hopping about grotesquely in the big shoes, bouncing the cane and grimacing, though not more than two or three persons were gathered to see him."[27] Chaplin's constant effort to perfect his signature skills could understandably get on some people's nerves after

Ben Turpin, on the running board of Ed Rose's car, leads a procession to the Rose garage. Ed's brother George is in front of the car beside their father, constable Frank Rose. Lloyd Easterday, in overalls, stands at the Rose garage entrance. The building with the awning, just down the street, is Silva's Corner.

awhile, but one could imagine Chaplin doing these same things alone in his room at night. The trouble came when he actively stepped forward, as Marshall related: "He would come in his silly tramp suit to the ball park when we were having a practice game, walk to third or first base, grab the player's mitt, put it on his left hand and pantomime playing the position, thereby stopping all of us. He thought it was enormously funny when he got in everyone's hair, and none of us would do anything about it because he was too much the PPP (precious piece of property) for any of us to manhandle."[28] Marshall called Chaplin "endlessly meddling," but what perhaps bothered him the most was Chaplin's treatment of Ben Turpin when Turpin starred in two Essanay comedies after *A Night Out*: "Chaplin held up their release; he wanted no rival. And Ben didn't even know who and what were working against him."[29]

Another aspect of the general dislike toward Chaplin stemmed from his enormous salary. The people of Niles didn't begrudge him his wealth so much as how he handled it: never tipping waitresses, letting Anderson pay for his pool games at Billy Moore's, mooching walnuts at the Murphy and Briscoe general store. One time he and Sam Marshall walked together to the Niles movie theater and Chaplin took so long in front of the ticket booth searching through his pockets for the price of admission that the fourteen-year-old boy, in disgust, paid for both of them. Marshall graphically exclaimed: "His pockets were fish-hook lined; nothing came therefrom."[30] Mollie Anderson laughed about it, but said: "Charlie has the first nickel he ever earned. I'm certain of that."[31] Later in life Chaplin could be generous to people he cared for; it's been said that Edna Purviance received money from Chaplin until the day she died, many years after she stopped acting with him. But at this early stage in Chaplin's film career he was rightfully worried about the longevity of his fame (Augustus Carney was one of the many who demonstrated this downside), and the fear of returning to the extreme poverty he'd experienced as a child must have strongly influenced his actions. Unfortunately, it also contributed to the general dislike of him in Niles.

It was inevitable that Chaplin would leave Niles, and he soon had the clout to do so. Reports in the movie trade magazines tracked a Chaplin fever that swiftly spread across the United States. In Portland, Oregon, his films were held over for a week while other films on the program changed every other day.[32] In Detroit a sign in front of theaters announcing "Charlie Chaplin today" resulted in packed houses.[33] Even with 250 prints in circulation, an astounding six times what Essanay usually required for a typical release, there were still not enough copies to go around.[34] Chaplin, it seemed, could do no wrong with the movie-going public, whatever else might be happening in Niles. So Chaplin chose to leave. The *Register* spoke vaguely and coldly about the reason for the move: "Mr. Chaplin finds that conditions in the south are more to his liking for the class of pictures he presents than they are in Niles."[35]

It's important to note that his cast and crew remained loyal. Danny Kelleher was proud to be working with Chaplin: "If you did, you were in."[36] Kelleher remembered when Chaplin asked him if he would like to go down to Los Angeles and continue with the Chaplin unit there. Overwhelmed, all that Kelleher could manage to say was, "Wonderful." The conversation happened on April 6th, and they were to leave the next day: "I didn't have anything to pack, and he didn't either. We put it all in Chaplin's trunk, and the next morning we caught the 9 o'clock train to San Francisco and boarded the 'Harvard.'"[37] On that passenger ship were Harris Ensign, M. A. Breslauer, Lloyd Easterday (a local boy graduating from chauffeur to business manager), Lloyd Bacon, Jess Robbins, Edna Purviance, Bud Jamison, Harry and Jack Pollard, Margie Rieger, Tom Crizer, Fritz Wintermeier, Mr. & Mrs. Ernest Van Pelt, William P. Gordon, Paddy McGuire, Tom Wilson, Alfred Griffin, William Gorham, Mr. & Mrs. Leo White, and the Armstrongs, Billy and Ed.[38]

Chaplin did not leave right away; he stayed overnight, frolicking in San Francisco with Anderson and Roscoe "Fatty" Arbuckle. During the day Roscoe was working on three movies back-to-back with Mabel Normand, one each featuring the Panama Pacific Exposition, Golden Gate Park and Idora Park in Oakland, but at night he was free to have fun. The three men went to Sid Grauman's Empress Theater to catch the vaudeville show and were spotted in their box seats by the audience. Enthusiastic applause brought them to the stage and they entertained the crowd for forty minutes. They also attended the first meeting of the San Francisco Screen Club at the Tivoli Theater building on Eddy Street. That night Sid Grauman was elected president. Chaplin left for Los Angeles the next day.[39]

Chaplin didn't completely turn his back on the San Francisco Bay Area. He was back at the end of the month to appear at the opening of the new Oakland Municipal Auditorium. He and seven Charlie Chaplin imitators led the grand march, and he was also a judge in deciding which of them impersonated him best. But he wasn't alone in deciding; his co-judge was G. M. Anderson.

Anderson and Chaplin were friends, and that friendship grew in the coming months. He frequently visited Chaplin in Los Angeles, and Chaplin traveled north a few times. There was a mutual admiration. Chaplin said: "I liked Anderson; he had a special kind of charm."[40] Anderson spoke of Chaplin simply: "I knew him, and knew him well."[41] It marked a turning point in both their lives, Chaplin's rise to international fame, and Anderson's slide to obscurity.

Chapter Eleven
The Final Year

Zelbert Goza aimed his .38-caliber Smith & Wesson at Charles Evans, the Niles State Bank cashier, and commanded: "Throw up your hands." Instead, Evans ran to the front door. Goza fired his gun, and the bullet hit Evans in the back of his shoulder. He collapsed on the floor. Goza, in a panic, ran toward the door, jumped over Evans and dashed outside. For fifteen minutes confusion reigned in Niles while Goza was chased through the town by Niles residents and Essanay cowboys. Then, in an alley, a car drove up beside Goza, and Charles Sillers, a Southern Pacific night operator, disarmed Goza and forced the fugitive into the vehicle also occupied by Ernest Salter, A. V. Butler and Al Roderick. Goza was delivered to constable Frank Rose, who locked the would-be bank robber in the Niles jail. This happened on March 9, 1915, and two months later Goza was serving a six year sentence in San Quentin penitentiary. The four men who participated in his capture received reward money in July.[1]

Niles had never experienced anything like this before, nothing this bold. Goza had come all the way to Niles from San Francisco. Why Niles? Was the town's prosperity now attractive to this kind of criminal?

The population had grown from 1,400 to 1,900 in three years, a far cry from a local prophet's prediction in 1910, inscribed on Oscar Walpert's barn: "Watch Niles Grow – Population 1915, 10,000." (Some critic added an "L" to make it Watch Niles Growl" before the old barn was dismantled in 1914.)[2] Nevertheless, this rapid increase in size was unprecedented for Niles.

The movie business, however, was in a slump due to the war in Europe. American films had been growing in popularity on the continent, especially western films, but now that foreign trade was curtailed, no one knew when the economy would rebound. Essanay had even stopped listing its European offices in advertisements.

G. M. Anderson was going through some difficult times himself; he set his Broncho Billy character aside to search for a new identity, one that wasn't a cowboy. Throughout the year he experimented, playing a modern-day husband caught in a love triangle, a top-hatted man about town, a Raffles-like gentleman burglar, and an out-and-out crook. He was credible in these parts, but people continued to see him as Broncho Billy, not these strangers. It didn't help that these films were one-reelers.

Lloyd Bacon and G. M. Anderson head for trouble over Belle Mitchell (at the table) in His Regeneration. *In the background from Anderson's left shoulder are Ben Turpin, Victor Potel, Carrie Turpin, Robert McKenzie and Bud Jamison wearing the cap and dark coat.*

G. M. Anderson lives it up before the tragic end of Wine, Women and Song.

Despite appearances, gentleman burglar G. M. Anderson solves the marriage problems of Marguerite Clayton and Lee Willard in The Face at the Curtain.

Ruth Saville and husband G. M. Anderson have their own difficulties in Too Much Turkey.

One-reel dramas were becoming a thing of the past; no one was interested. Even comedies were threatened. *Variety* spelled it out — "ONE-REELERS GOING" — reporting that Keystone was discontinuing one-reel comedies, Vitagraph had already stopped. Feature films were what everyone wanted, and some companies were concentrating exclusively on those.[3]

Struggling to meet the demand for features, the Chicago Essanay studio was caught short by the General Film feature release arrangement; it was still a mess. Spoor went to New York and met with his old competitor William Selig of Selig Polyscope, Albert Smith of Vitagraph and Ira Lowry of Lubin, and together they formed the VLSE film distribution system, releasing directly to theaters.[4] The *Chicago Tribune's* Kitty Kelly asked Selig about the new agreement; he replied: "We had to have some way to get our big pictures adequately before the public, so we created this organization especially for features. It doesn't indicate anything inimical to the General at all. The General tried to handle features and found it couldn't, because it hadn't been organized for that purpose, so we have just relieved it of the strain, and think it will be better all around."

She queried: "You don't think, then, the day of the little picture is done?"

"Oh, no, we'll always have little pictures, just as we'll always have vaudeville."[5]

With the additional features added to the schedule, Essanay was now releasing about thirty films each month. Unfortunately it created havoc in the studio's publicity department. *Essanay News,* the company's bi-weekly newspaper, reflected the turmoil that was going on. One issue would show a photograph to illustrate each film release, another issue would drop the photos completely. Images would be attached to the wrong release, or repeated in later issues with other films. Publicity photos from *Broncho Billy and the Lumber King,* for instance, became attached to three different films.

The Chaplin unit in Los Angeles complicated matters. Whenever they finished a film it was shipped with little warning to Chicago, and the staff had to scramble to get it out for distribution as quickly as possible. This meant setting aside other work to do so.

By the Sea, Chaplin's last one-reeler, was made at the beach in Santa Monica, and on a stage at the former Bradbury mansion. The house faced 147 North Hill Street, a side entrance at 406 Court Street led to offices, and an open-air stage occupied the backyard. The stage was recently used to make a series of films on a shoestring budget by a young producer/director — Hal Roach.

Harold Lloyd, one of the actors working for Roach just weeks before Essanay arrived, described the studio a few years later: "The big Bradbury house stands atop the abrupt Court Street Hill, looking down on downtown Los Angeles, and is just about the best surviving example in the city of pre-stucco California architecture. It is a place of many turrets, bay windows, wood carvings and curlicues, a grand staircase, sixteen-foot ceilings, brocaded wall papers, stained glass, parqueted floors, hardwood finish, sliding doors and all the other elegancies of the '80s. In the yard a giant palm soars 110 feet and a rubber tree has grown so huge now that its roots

Tom Crizer and Hal Roach on a set for Mustaches and Bombs.

Ed Armstrong, Jean Jarvis and Tom Crizer in The Drug Clerk.

Charlie Chaplin and Charles Inslee at Work.

are pushing up the cement walks. We called it Pneumonia Hall, from its wide and windy spaces... There was not another building in Los Angeles so combining location and magnificence."[6]

Not everyone in Chaplin's unit was actively involved with *By the Sea*, but they had to be kept busy or they'd go elsewhere, which is where Roach came in. He was completely broke after producing and directing an unsold string of one- and two-reelers, and was hired by Robbins to direct one-reel comedies with the otherwise-idle actors. The first of these films was *Street Fakers* with Bud Jamison, James T. Kelly and Margie Rieger. Each week Roach finished another film.[7]

Meanwhile, with his casual, inspiration-based approach, Chaplin struggled for week after week on *Work*, his second project at the Bradbury studio. It began with Danny Kelleher and his assistant collecting all sorts of tools for props. What Chaplin would do with them was anybody's guess. *Work* evolved endlessly.

Back in Niles, Anderson suddenly received a telegram from Chaplin requesting a two-week vacation. This was a curious time to ask for such a thing; the demand for Chaplin films was so great that the old Keystone films were being released indiscriminately through fly-by-night operations, sometimes with new titles to imply they were the latest releases. There was talk of Chaplin producing a feature film for release through the new VLSE outlet to combat these deceitful competitors. A vacation was not advisable.

Finally the reason came out: Madison Square Garden in New York had installed a projection system and wanted Chaplin to fill its 13,000 seats by appearing on stage, fifteen minutes in the afternoon and fifteen minutes at night. For this they would pay him $12,500 a week for two weeks. Chaplin wanted to go, and it looked like a loophole in his Essanay contract allowed it.

Spoor and Anderson panicked.

Spoor took a train to Niles, met Anderson and both men went to Los Angeles. Chaplin received his $25,000, but it was drawn from Essanay's bank account. Chaplin also got a new contract calling for him to receive a $10,000 bonus (over and above his $1,250 weekly salary) for each film he completed. Trying to speed up the output, this new contract specified there would be ten films made by Chaplin between June 1, 1915, and January 1, 1916, including the film he was still working on, *Work*. Chaplin signed the contract, Spoor took a train back to Chicago and Anderson returned to Niles.[8] Peace reigned once again, briefly.

The Court Street studio was proving to be too small for the Chaplin unit now that Hal Roach was back in business with his own company. A new location was found, the old Majestic studio at 651 Fairview Avenue in Boyle Heights, and the company moved in during the first week of June. By the end of the month Chaplin was completing *A Woman*. Chaplin also began work on a six-reel comedy feature, part of the reason for the move to larger quarters, but little information was given to the press. A reporter for *Moving Picture World* complained: "We had to use a pass key, a 'shelaleh,' and a stick of dynamite to get into the sanctum sactorum of the great pooh bah this week."[9]

Security at the studio was absolutely necessary, for without it Chaplin would be mobbed. Chaplin fever was rising, and nowhere was it more evident than in Los Angeles. One exhibitor stationed a Chaplin imitator outside his thater to attract crowds, and it was so effective that it was copied vigorously. *Motion Picture News* noted: "Not only theaters, but automobile tire concerns and other agents have adopted the idea. It is not an uncommon sight to see as many as three or four Charlie Chaplins on one single block in the busy parts of the city."[10] The Chaplin unit might have done well to hire one, too, as a decoy.

Essanay, overwhelmed by their self-distribution of the Chaplin films, turned over the task to the General Film Company, which promptly boosted the price to nearly double its rate for first-run films, and tied their release to the less desirable General Film product line. There was an immediate outcry from exhibitors, but no one dared to start a boycott and risk being left behind. Even if they put the other General Film releases aside and refused to show them they could still profit from the Chaplin films.

Jess Robbins, Sydney Chaplin and Charles Chaplin take a break at the Fairview studio in July, 1915, as Charles receives his first $10,000 bonus on the revised contract.

Since the camera is set up…Edna steps in.

At the Fairview studio during The Bank: *Jess Robbins, Charlie Chaplin, Edna Purviance, Charles Inslee, Leo White, Billy Armstrong, Carl Stockdale, Fred Goodwins, Lawrence A. Bowes, ?, Paddy McGuire…*

…Danny Kelleher, William Gordon?, ?, ?, Alfred Griffin, George Green, ?, ?, William Gorham, Lee Hill…

…Tom Crizer, Lloyd Easterday, Jack Roach, Frank Stockdale, ?, George Cleethorpe, Harris Ensign, ?, ?, Shortie Wilson…

… and Jess Robbins again, next to their Pathe camera.

But for Anderson, his venture into three-reelers was over; *When Love and Honor Called* marked his last. The standard feature was now five reels (although the Chicago studio continued their three-reel productions into the next year), and yet, against the trend, Anderson went back to his one-reel Broncho Billy films: "There was no outstanding picture. The only thing that gave me the thrill was making these pictures and making them fast.... Maybe that was my downfall, that I didn't take it seriously..."[11]

Anderson did decide to inject some comic relief into his Broncho Billy one-reelers, bringing in Victor Potel, Harry Todd and Ben Turpin to help out. It harkened back to his days in San Rafael when his early Broncho Billy releases were played more for comedy than drama, but this time he depended upon others more heavily than taking it on himself. In fact, he almost retreated from acting. The *Dramatic Mirror* recognized this in *Broncho Billy Steps In*: "Plenty of comedy, plenty of heart interest, and a touch of the usual 'Western' fills this one-reel offering with merit far beyond that usually possessed by the one-reel Broncho Billy offerings. It is, essentially, the 'Girl of the Golden West' situation again, for the ranch foreman posts a sign advising that a school teacher will preside and essay to eradicate some of the ignorance which sets thick on the members of the ranch. The efforts of the jovial drunkards to do spelling, recitation, and other branches of erudition is interrupted by the bad man who is curbed in turn by Broncho Billy as sheriff. The excellent comedy of Ben Turpin and Victor Potel were the most successful in the comedy line, although even Mr. Anderson unbent enough to give, in the few feet that he worked, an excellent rendering of grim humor. Patrons will enjoy this."[12]

More often the reviews were less favorable, although few were negative. *Motion Picture News* pinpointed the problem with Anderson's career in comments for *Broncho Billy Evens Matters*: "Nothing revolutionary is ever expected of a Broncho Billy film, and if anything, this release is more conventional than usual.... G. M. Anderson and Marguerite Clayton will not disappoint their admirers, however."[13]

Anderson's flagging interest in his films hurt him badly, and he compounded it with repetition: *Broncho Billy's Mexican Wife*, released November 5th, 1915, was a remake of his 1912 production of the same name, and, in December, the title for *Broncho Billy's Marriage* was repeated only four months after it had been used for another film. This confusion was perhaps evidence of deeper problems. Marguerite Clayton left in October for Chicago to act in a feature, *A Daughter of the City*, and she remained there with the Essanay company through 1917.

Despite the problems within studio walls, the town of Niles remained spirited. A Fourth of July celebration lasted three days, with the traditional reading of the Declaration of Independence, school children singing the "Star Spangled Banner," fireworks, a masquerade ball, three baseball games, two broncho-busting exhibitions, a scramble for a greased pig, a "jitney dance," speeches and two parades. On the final day, Monday, July 5th, a crowd numbering 10,000 saw the "Parade of the Horribles" with Ben Turpin in a bathing suit riding a horse, leading a grotesque assortment of characters. It was a contest to see who could look the ugliest. Ben only won second place, beaten by Tony Silva as "the monkey boy."[14]

The comic tone is played up in Broncho Billy Steps In. *In the foreground: Lloyd Bacon, Marguerite Clayton, Eva Heazlett and G. M. Anderson. Charles Allen Dealey is the priest, witnesses are Bill Cato (with beard), Harry Todd, Victor Potel, Leo West, Darrell Wittenmyer, Warren Sawyer hidden by Robert McKenzie; Belle Mitchell and Ben Turpin are on the right.*

On the dramatic side: Broncho Billy's Marriage *(the December 17th version) with Marguerite Clayton protected by G. M. Anderson from Lee Willard.*

Humanity, *with Darrell Wittenmyer, Fritz Wintermeier, ?, Ruth Saville, Harry Todd holding Rodney Hildebrand, Robert McKenzie with beard, Henry Youngman, Bill Cato, G. M. Anderson.*

Rollie Totheroh shoots a scene for Humanity *with a barely-visible Bell & Howell 2709 camera.*

Anderson supported that event with equipment and personnel. He also sponsored a pageant at Mission San Jose to raise funds for restoring part of an old mission building. He also revived *The Man From Mexico* on stage as a benefit for the Niles Catholic church.

The play was his final appearance at a community event in Niles. He played the leading role again, just as he had in Petaluma, but only three other people repeated their roles from past performances: Harry Todd, Margaret Joslin, M. A. Breslauer. The other spots were filled by Robert McKenzie, Eva Heazlett, Rodney Hildebrand, Ben Turpin, Eddie Fries, Darrell Wittenmyer, Leo West, Fritz Wintermeier, Earl Esola, Lloyd Bacon, Ruth Saville, Belle Mitchell, Joe Cassidy, Lawrence Ganshirt, Allen Dealey, Henry Lilienthal, Arthur Jasmin, Robert Burroughs, Frank Harveson and Frank Dolan. The Western Essanay Film Company had changed considerably over the years, but these would be its last members.[15]

It was around then that Anderson tried one more time to break out of the rut Spoor had fashioned for him. Although Spoor refused to authorize any further feature films from Niles, Anderson secretly went ahead and made a six-reeler anyway.

The film was called *Humanity*. It was a Broncho Billy film photographed by Rollie Totheroh. Ruth Saville starred as Billy's wife; Rodney Hildebrand played his rival; Lee Willard, Bill Cato, Tom Crizer and Ella McKenzie played supporting roles, and probably everyone else at the studio had some connection to it. In part, the story was based upon Anderson's old solo effort, *What a Woman Can Do*. *Humanity* follows the earlier story of hardship and betrayal, but instead of Billy dying in his vault of gold, he fights the man who took his wife away then abandoned her for someone else. All the rage pent up in Billy over the years is unleashed and he's at the brink of strangling the man in a blind fury when the man's young daughter breaks the spell. It ends with Billy, in tuxedo and top hat, composing himself and calmly walking away.[16]

The Snakeville Comedies suffered a blow when director Roy Clements left Niles to work at Universal in Los Angeles. Even worse, Victor Potel went with him, and they promptly created a series starring Victor as "Slim" living in the town of Centerville. To replace Clements, thirty-year-old Wallace Beery came from the Chicago studio.

Beery had been at Essanay for two years, acting in a roughhouse series about a Swedish maid named "Sweedie"(he played the maid). He'd also starred in some of the George Ade fables, notably its first release, *The Fable of the Brash Drummer and the Nectarine*. He played a traveling salesman (the "brash drummer") and was singled out in reviews for his naturalism and restraint, a quality the Sweedie films lacked. Personally, Beery's relaxed and extroverted joviality put people at ease. He appeared to be nothing more than a friendly, straightforward kind of guy, but underneath he calculated with a single-minded determination to get exactly what he wanted. This could get him into trouble according Gloria Swanson, who was a teenaged newcomer at the Chicago studio just learning the ropes when Beery was there. Swanson believed that Beery got involved with a young, under-aged girl, and her parents complained to Spoor about him. The situation neared the

Wallace Beery in Niles.

Ben Turpin and Harry Todd appear slightly out of place in Taking the Count. *In the foreground beside them are Robert McKenzie, Eva Heazlett, Belle Mitchell, Leo White, Lloyd Bacon and Margaret Joslin.*

scandalous stage until Beery quietly put it to rest by skipping to Niles.[17]

Beery gained from the move by abandoning his Sweedie character to concentrate on directing the Snakeville Comedies. Swanson thought the Sweedie pictures "silly" and suspected Beery hated them as much as she did, but, from all indications, Beery pushed the Snakeville series toward the same, broad, slapstick humor as his Sweedie films, and even embraced its surreal quality. The main problem in evaluating Beery's directing style is that nothing remains of his work; all that one can go by are the plot lines printed at the time of release and the few photographs that exist. Nevertheless, these few clues speak loudly. In *The Merry Models*, for instance, Bloggie (Ben Turpin's character) and Mustang Pete pose as statues in an upscale cafe, but when their wives see them a riot ensues and the place is completely wrecked. In *Taking the Count*, two cabin stewards in somewhat-modified formal attire are mistaken for society people, but the bizarre slant presented puts it in the same catagory as the Three Stooges.

Ben Turpin took the lead in all six films that can be attributed to Beery, and Lloyd Bacon, who had mostly been working with Anderson, played a prominent role in the comedies. Bacon was given the name Hotch for yet another boxing film, *Snakeville's Champion*, and became Turpin's rival. They were both waiters in *A Waiting Game*. They were adversaries in *Taking the Count*. It could have led to an even closer association if time hadn't run out in Niles.

Ben Turpin has the advantage over Lloyd Bacon in Snakeville's Champion. *Awaiting the outcome: Darrell Wittenmyer, Rodney Hildebrand and Harry Todd.*

Ben Turpin and Lloyd Bacon demonstrate waiting technique in A Waiting Game. *The bellboy is Arthur Jasmin, Charles Allen Dealey hides under a beard, Eva Sawyer and Eva Heazlett wait for Lloyd. In the background on the left photo is Helen Dolan; on the right photo: the man wearing glasses is L. Allen Dealey, Robert Burroughs is near Bacon.*

Bloggie and Hotch.

Whatever Beery was thinking at the time, it could be argued that his mind wasn't completely on his work; when Gloria Swanson came west to join the Keystone Film Company, Beery went to Los Angeles to meet her. Swanson never came up north; Beery preferred to visit her, saying, "I use any excuse to get away from Niles.

Wallace Beery steps behind the wheel of his Mercer Runabout in Illinois. His passenger is Marvin Spoor (brother of George), a cameraman at the Chicago studio and Beery's friend.

That's like the Klondike up there."[18] Swanson wrote: "He couldn't wait to come down and get started in Hollywood once his contract with Essanay ran out."[19]

About once a month Beery made the eight-hour drive from Niles in his beloved Mercer Runabout, a car he had brought from Chicago. The highway in those days went from Niles to Mission San Jose, Warm Springs and on south. Between Warm Springs and the city of San Jose was a fast stretch of road. Policeman Leo Solon recalled: "Beery used to get on that road and open it up — he'd get up to 80 or 85 miles an hour. One day he was on his way back to Niles from San Jose and a traffic officer spotted him speeding and gave chase. He couldn't catch him, but he got his license number — I guess he knew who it was anyway — and the next day the Alameda County district attorney, Ezra Decoto, got the warrant for Beery's arrest."[20] According to the *Register*, Beery was law-abiding, and "when an officer says to halt he does so, however that San Jose deputy has a way of ordering a halt with a six-gun that will addle the nerves of anybody.... Beery didn't know whether it was a hold-up or an arrest. He decided to play safe and accordingly stepped on the throttle of his car and arrived in Niles several hours ahead of the deputy."[21]

The next day Solon was ordered to arrest Beery. Solon drove to the studio and presented Beery with the warrant. Beery asked how much the bail was. Solon told him $200. "Let's go to the bank," said Beery.

Anderson, a little worse for wear, in The Man in Him

Solon remembered: "You know, he got the money in gold — which wasn't too unusual in those days — and paid the bail. Of course, he never showed up in court."[22]

As the Niles studio entered its final months, the only thing holding it together was Anderson's will, such as it was. An indicator of his declining interest was revealed in *Moving Picture World*, a short paragraph on his arrival in Los Angeles: "G. M. Anderson, known on the curtain as Broncho Billy, was in town this week. He dropped down from San Francisco Tuesday and returned the following day. He said he came just to see what was going on. Charlie Chaplin and Jesse J. Robbins met him at the depot and escorted him to the Essanay studio on the mountain top."[23]

In January, 1916, Anderson struggled with his last picture, *The Man in Him*. He'd started it in October as a one-reeler, then picked it up again to add another reel. On January 16th, a Sunday, he worked on the last scene, a courtroom sequence. It was a final nod to the town he'd grown to know over the course of nearly four years. Members of the jury were played by prominent Niles townspeople, among them: Justice of the Peace Ralph Richmond. Then it was over. Anderson recalled: "I loved to make these pictures. I thought that was my life, as long as they were good. Finally, I got kind of tired of it, you know." [24] That week he left for Los Angeles.

Anderson at left, Charles Allen Dealey (index finger at his temple), Leo West behind the desk,

Ralph Richmond (below witness) and the Niles-businessmen jury in The Man in Him.

The *Register* got wind of what was about to happen next, and printed a notice in the paper that Friday, January 21st: "Big Shake-up in Local Essanay Co."[25] It wasn't known yet just what would happen, but a rumor claimed every performer in the company would be fired and replaced by new people. The rumor came to pass on Saturday and the *Oakland Tribune* picked up the story on Sunday: "News of the closing of the plant came as a complete surprise to the citizens of Niles. A notice had been planted before the door of the place announcing a temporary closing and reorganization of the business. Only eight people are on premises at present, watching the property and awaiting the arrival of the new director.

"Anderson opened the Essanay plant at Niles, presenting his famous Wild West pictures there. Lately the studio has been used instead for society plays, and this, according to the motion picture people, is the cause of Anderson's being recalled to the head office."[26]

Jess Robbins was to be the new director, supposedly on his way from Los Angeles with the remaining staff of the Chaplin unit to take over the Niles studio, but Chaplin was still working on his last film. Understandably, there was enormous interest and speculation about Chaplin's next step. Kitty Kelly managed to get a telling scoop for the *Tribune* that no one else followed up with: "His contract with Essanay expired Jan. 5, and high priced comedians usually do not linger long around without a contract.

"'But,' says Homer A. Boushey, general manager for Essanay, 'we are just waiting on Chaplin's pleasure — very patiently waiting. He is still out there working for us. We haven't received the *Carmen* negative yet, and he is finishing another picture, *Nine Lives*. If some other company doesn't come along and offer him a whole lot more money, I suppose he'll stay with us. If it does, probably he'll go.'"[27]

Elsewhere, rumors were flying. A *Variety* headline on page one announced: "CHAPLIN'S ENORMOUS OFFERS; TURNS DOWN $500,000 YEARLY." It claimed that his annual salary with Essanay was now $125,000 plus $10,000 for each release. However, Essanay had netted $1,380,000 from his films so far. Not surprisingly, Chaplin was getting offers from other companies, Keystone and Paramount among them, but there was no telling how high the figures would go.[28]

In Los Angeles, Chaplin and Anderson were leaving the Alexandria Hotel for the train depot when they were cornered by Mabel Condon, reporting for the *Dramatic Mirror.* Condon asked Chaplin to explain his situation: "As far as I know I'm still with the Essanay Company, and my understanding at present is that I shall be for the next year."[29] So he was still leaving his options open, but it was clear his demands would be heavy: "I think I've worked Los Angeles through and through, so would like to make pictures elsewhere for a while for a change of location, ideas and — temperment." Anderson agreed it was time for a change, and they would explore that territory together. Chaplin elaborated: "We are thinking of traveling around making pictures. If one wants to make pictures in the south of France, to locate there for three months or more and make them, then to move on to whatever other location one happened to feel like. That's the thing I want to do, and…"

Anderson finished the sentence: "…that's the thing to do."[30]

Chaplin and Anderson arrived in Chicago on January 28th. Anderson recalled that it was he who made the first move: "I said, 'Now Spoor I'm going to knock you off your seat. Charlie wants $10,000 a week.' He says, 'WHAT?' I said, 'Well, that's what he wants.'"[31]

Spoor didn't want to hear this; he had just invested heavily in the Chicago studio, building a whole new wing that doubled its production capacity, and its completion was scheduled for March. Whatever profit the Chaplin films might be expected to generate, Spoor simply had a hard time coming to terms with the figures involved in the negotiation.

Anderson's bitterness toward Spoor, and what happened in those final days, still burned brightly decades later. First off, he considered the Chicago studio's manager Homer Boushey "a smart aleck... who ruined it." As for the society pictures rumored to be causing the trouble between Anderson and Spoor, Anderson insisted the problem was with Chicago's five-reel society pictures, and Spoor's wife was getting "society-minded." Anderson claimed: "She had a fella name of Patterson. He was writing stories and this Patterson was the brother of Gil Patterson, see, that owns the *Tribune* in Chicago." Anderson reflected: "Well, anyway, I screwed up with Spoor."[32]

Anderson sold his share of Essanay to George Spoor — the numbers vary, anywhere from $500,000 to a million. All the negotiating was over in less than a week. Then Anderson left with Chaplin: "I went back to New York with Charlie, and we were going to form our own company, which didn't come off.... Charlie and I were going to make pictures. I was going to do Broncho Billy, and he was going to do the Chaplins. He had a brother named Sydney Chaplin. Pretty hard to take, Sydney is, but a nice fellow. Sydney advised Charlie to go on his own."[33]

Charlie sided with his brother, a wise choice; every studio wanted to talk business, including Essanay. Spoor followed Chaplin to New York, but didn't get any special treatment; if anything he had a tougher time, and returned to Chicago on February 17th, tired after the ordeal, Spoor confided to Kitty Kelly: "Unless Chaplin comes down on his demands he is out of the running for Essanay. He is asking altogether too much for any company. Why, now he wants $626,000 a year, which is $12,050 a week. If I could get together $12,000 for him I couldn't raise the $50. He is very friendly toward Essanay, but he'll have to ask for less money if he wants to come back, and there isn't much chance of that."[34]

Two days later, according to an inside report given to Kitty Kelly, Chaplin signed with Mutual for $10,000 a week and a $100,000 signing bonus, the bonus to be handed over on Wednesday, February 23th. But Kelly reported prematurely; the bonus escalated to $150,000, papers were signed on February 26th, and Chaplin was on his way.

In Niles, the future was not so rosy. Lawrence Abrott, head carpenter was there: "It was February 16, 1916 — I remember it well. We started a picture in the morning. That afternoon we got a wire from Chicago to stop work. That was the end. We never made another one in Niles."[35]

Just as suddenly as it had begun, the movies were over in Niles. The population of the town visibly shrank as actors and technicians scrambled to find other work. Most of them went to Los Angeles. Niles barber Bert Silveria recalled: "When they left, everything was dead."[36]

Epilogue
The Aftermath

The Niles studio building slowly crumbled in the years following its heyday, becoming a mute symbol of the town's once-active role in film history. For the rest of 1916 the building was unoccupied. In 1917 Essanay nearly revived it when a young director, just starting out, was hired to write and direct a series of western feature films. The young man, W. S. Van Dyke (later to gain fame at MGM with *The Thin Man* and many other films), was instead able to use Essanay's studio in Los Angeles, at Culver City, after it suddenly became available.[1]

The next year Essanay general manager Vernon Day arrived in Niles to settle a $740.65 debt owed to J. R. Kelly so the property could be released from an attachment. It was Day who arranged the sale of the property to Catherine Boysen, who planned, with San Jose promoter Fred S. Reed, to lease the studio to the Haworth Picture Corporation. When the deal with Haworth fell through she couldn't meet the payments on a $9,000 mortgage or settle a $1000 promissory note to Niles realtors F. V. Jones and Edward Ellsworth as they had arranged on the $12,000 sale.[2] Additional claims filed against her for unpaid bills put the studio in limbo for years.

In 1921 the Sympho Cinema Syndicate tried to reopen the studio, but nothing came of it.

In 1925, Niles car-dealer Ed Rose bought the property at auction for $1,500 in back taxes, but could do nothing with it because of disputes over ownership. He tried to arrange a lease for a hardwood floor company to set up a factory in the building (the rent being paid into a bank account held for whomever could clear the property title), but a compromise couldn't be reached.

Finally, in 1931, Rose settled all claims and held the deed. Hoping to bring the movies back to Niles, he traveled to Hollywood looking for someone to revive the old studio. The first person he met was Ben Turpin, who introduced Rose to "several prominent producers." Jess Robbins also helped Rose, guiding him around

The Essanay studio in 1928.

Ed Rose and Ben Turpin in front of Turpin's home in Beverly Hills, 1931.

Hollywood for four days of meetings at practically every studio.[3] In the end it all failed. Rose said: "I tried to breathe life back into the old dream, but it was too late. Producers are not interested in a studio that faces the state highway and only a few yards away from the puffing switch engines of a freight yard. The talkies have said the last word about the possiblities of making movies in Niles."[4]

Two years later, with the building still idle as the Great Depression worsened, Rose decided to tear the studio down to salvage its lumber and steel for resale.

Everything inside the building that could be sold was first auctioned off: from the prop department came wagons, furniture, Broncho Billy's saddle, and bamboo canes; from the set-building department came paint, brushes and nails; from wardrobe came suits, dresses, cloth and cowboy clothes. What couldn't be sold was given away or thrown out; rumor has it that much of what remained, including the old stagecoach, was buried in a pit on Rose's ranch.

It took the month of July, 1933, for the building to be dismantled. The *Register* reported: "At first, when the beams were exposed, the casual wayfarer might have remarked on the new building being erected in Niles, but a more careful scrutiny would have shown that this was death, not birth. At one time during its destruction, when the outer sheeting had been torn away, the historical place took on an unearthly essence at night; standing silently upright, like some obscure prehistoric skeleton."[5] One man who watched from the sidelines was Essanay cowboy Frank Pementel, who could only say: "I hate to see the old place go."[6]

An estimated 70,000 board feet of lumber were removed from the building, and all that remained for years was a concrete ramp that originally went up to the sliding front door of the studio stage. Imprinted in it were the outlines of horseshoes, decoratively arranged, made for a practical purpose, so people walking up the ramp wouldn't slip on its slick surface. By the 1970s that, too, was gone.

The Essanay studio, July, 1933. Ed Rose stands at the far right.

Behind Rose is the Niles Grammar School. Compare it with the view on page 126.

The old Essanay barn in the 1970s.

The old barn, Essanay's first studio in Niles, lasted longer. In 1914 it was moved to the back of the property to make way for a house that still stands today. Over time the barn began to show its age; shingles blew from the roof, boards fell off, the building sagged. Fearing its loss, the Mission Peak Heritage Foundation tried to register it for landmark status, but failed; in 1980 the barn was torn down. The owner claimed he'd tried to get money to restore it; failing that, he was afraid it would fall and hurt someone. All that remains is a door to the barn, on permanent display at Fremont's Museum of Local History.[7]

The Essanay bungalows have fared better; all ten houses still exist, although most of them have taken on a different look over the years, and three sit at other locations. Many houses in Niles have been moved to save them; in the case of the bungalows it was because Anderson ignored the lot lines and squeezed them together on his property. When they were sold, first to the California Nursery Company, then to the Jones and Ellsworth real estate company, the houses had to fit onto standard-sized lots, so two were removed from Second Street and relocated to School Street. The third house, on G Street, was moved to a lot near F Street on

Second, and a doctors's office was built adjoining the corner house on G. That office is now a residence too, as is Anderson's first home in Niles, the Silva cottage.[8]

Niles, now part of the city of Fremont, continues to have a character all its own, one that harkens back to those days. The hills around Niles are unblemished, imposing as ever. The business district retains much of the atmosphere from Anderson's era — four blocks long, with open space on the old railroad property now owned by the city.

Little is left of the wide-open spaces once marked by farm houses, dirt roads and orchards, but Niles Canyon has escaped major development due to its limited access. The one lane road is now two lanes, and Alameda Creek takes up most of the remaining area. Railroad tracks line both sides of the hills: the south track is the Union Pacific line for freight and Amtrak; the northern track was torn out and abandoned by Southern Pacific, and has since been relaid by the Niles Canyon Railroad, whose steam locomotives once again ply the route made famous by the Transcontinental Railroad. One almost expects Broncho Billy and a posse to emerge out of the woods and come riding by at full gallop.

As for other Essanay haunts, much has been lost. Aside from the Belvoir and Wesley in Niles, hotels seem to have fared badly: the Niles Hotel is gone, so is the Morrison Hotel in Morrison, Colorado, the Mascarel Hotel in Santa Barbara, the Lakeside Inn in Lakeside and the Hotel Lyndon in Los Gatos. Baseball fields have also disappeared: Mayhew's Field is a nursery; a parking lot, F Street and houses occupy Sullivan's Park; the Eastside Ballpark in San Rafael is a business block. In Los Angeles, the site of Arthur Mackley's Fleming Street studio is television station station KCET, but to even establish the location of Chaplin's Court Street and Fairview Avenue sites is difficult, the landscape has changed so dramatically.

The Chicago Essanay studio building still stands as a city landmark, owned for a time by the Bell & Howell Company and now home to St. Augustine College, but the company Spoor and Anderson formed in 1907 is long gone. George K. Spoor continued to run the studio until March, 1918. By then he'd had enough: "At that time we had fourteen operating units in Chicago. We were releasing a picture every day except Sunday, and six special five-reel pictures each month. The place was a madhouse and too difficult to stand up under. I tried a number of general managers with no success. I found I was running a high class school for directors and actors. I'd make stars out of them and other producers would offer them more money. I had to meet those offers or lose the stars. Had I met all the offers I would have gone broke myself, constantly doubling salaries. So I locked up the place and took a good, long rest."[9]

After a rest of about one month Spoor produced two feature films and began rereleasing the best films in his inventory: the George Ade Fables, the Snakeville Comedies, Broncho Billy westerns and Chaplin's comedies. Two Chaplin compilations were also produced, *Chase Me, Charlie* and *Triple Trouble*, the last of which produced a protest from Chaplin claiming it was made up of discarded portions of *Police*. Spoor said it was nothing of the kind: "The facts are that at the time of making the picture it went under the working title of *Life*."[10] Spoor may have been technically correct, *Life* was the original title, revived by Chaplin in January, 1916, as *Nine Lives*, but it was still as Chaplin described it, a rehash of *Police*.

Spoor kept busy otherwise by financing inventions. The first one was designed and built by Fredrick B. Thompson to develop, fix, wash and dry movie film in one continuous operation, and was a forerunner of today's film processing machines. In 1926, after ten years of work, Thompson received several patents on it, and Universal Pictures began using these machines in 1927.

But the invention that obsessed Spoor was his Natural Vision process, a design for three-dimensional films ("3-D") that also incorporated a wide-screen format. Johan Berggren began engineering the equipment in 1916, and Spoor plowed the rest of his fortune into it — four million dollars. By 1930 it was finally ready, but the timing was wrong; the talkie revolution had already stretched the movie industry to the limit, and, with the Great Depression picking up momentum, the Motion Picture Producers and Distributors Association agreed to a moritorium on wide-screen projection so exhibitors could catch up to the expense of wiring theaters for sound. Spoor couldn't wait, he was overextended financially, and it forced him into bankruptcy. Twenty years later Spoor might have been welcomed with open arms, but by that time he was embittered: "Laboratory equipment and projection machines for twelve theaters went into storage where it is now and where it will remain. If there ever was a commercial murder, this was it. And I was the victim at the hands of men, most of whom, I put into the picture business."[11]

In 1948, an honorary Academy Award recognizing him as a movie pioneer didn't soften him; he stayed in Chicago during the Los Angeles ceremony and the award was sent to him. In the end he was still tinkering away in his home basement at 908 Argyle Street when he died in 1953, just before his 82nd birthday.

Gilbert M. Anderson, it is said, never returned to Niles, but he might have passed through it. He spent years shuffling between the east and west coasts, spending his money. He co-financed a comedy play called *Nothing But the Truth* on Broadway, bought into the Longacre Theater in New York, bought land to build a second theater in San Francisco (the Casino), started the Andermat Aeroplane Company with Robert Matches in Sunnyvale, California, bought into the World Series-winning Boston Red Sox team when Babe Ruth was there, started a taxi company in San Francisco, made a movie (*Vera, the Medium*) in New Jersey for Lewis Selznick starring Kitty Gordon, and tried to release his Broncho Billy film, *Humanity*. All of these endeavors occurred in 1916.[12]

That year was a mix of good and bad news. *Nothing But the Truth* was a hit. The Casino opened to great acclaim, but within four years was turned over to a management company. Andermat produced one, gigantic two-engine airplane, almost got a government contract, then folded. The Boston Red Sox never won another World Series, and Babe Ruth was sold to the New York Yankees to raise capital, but even that influx of cash couldn't help Anderson or his partners; they had to sell the team. The man who ran his taxi company sold their only taxi and skipped town. *Vera, the Medium*, the first of what was supposed to be a series of

Kitty Gordon, Lowell Sherman and G. M. Anderson on the set of Vera, the Medium, *Fort Lee, New Jersey.*

movies, failed, and Kitty Gordon sued Anderson for breach of contract. George Spoor stopped the release of *Humanity* because Anderson no longer had the rights to his Broncho Billy character and allegedly had agreed to stay off the screen for two years. Anderson cut a reel from the film and tried to release it again in 1918 as *Naked Hands*, but the film failed. Anderson produced several plays on Broadway and toured them around the country, but they lost money. He and some wealthy San Franciscans formed Golden West Productions to produce a series of westerns starring him, but released them on a States Rights basis at absolutely the worst time for movies, during the big flu pandemic, when theaters and all public places were closed for fear of spreading this deadly disease. When theaters reopened his films were ignored, even though, judging by the two that still exist, they were well-made.

Anderson organized a new company, Amalgamated Producing Corp., with his old Essanay co-star Fred Church as president of the company, and stayed in the background because he was getting sued so often. Four more feature films failed, but a two-reel comedy series with Stan Laurel showed promise (and the initial film, *The Lucky Dog*, also marked Stan's first work with future co-star Oliver Hardy). The films were a breakthrough for Stan, but Anderson miscalculated: "I...made them in Louis B. Mayer's studio, and he liked them...wanted to become interested in them because Louis B. Mayer always wanted the big piece of pie in anything he went into, and I thought I could do it alone and I wasn't businessman enough. He was a great businessman."[13] The contract with Mayer made it impossible for Anderson to profit by it, and that stopped the series.

From 1920 until 1942 Anderson lived in San Francisco. He managed an apartment house on O'Farrell Street, just two blocks from his old Gaiety Theatre, and could have stepped onto the sidewalk and looked east to watch as the theater was torn down in 1936. The Casino, also close by, was sold in 1939. It's gone, too.

Anderson lived a solitary life, one he preferred, but he wasn't destitute. His daughter Maxine, a Stanford University graduate, helped him out in his later years when he needed it. She moved to Los Angeles, eventually becoming a successful casting agent. He moved south, too, but the public didn't know whether he was dead or alive until he sued Paramount Pictures for releasing *Star Spangled Rhythm*, claiming it portrayed him as "a washed up and broken down actor."[14] Three years later he was in court again to swear he didn't have the money to settle a debt he'd refused to pay for 27 years. After that Anderson kept such a low profile that he missed receiving an Academy Award in 1948 as "one of the small group of pioneers whose belief in a new medium, and whose contributions to its development, blazed the trail along which the motion picture has progressed, in their lifetime, from obscurity to world-wide acclaim."[15] Of the four who did receive it — William Selig, Albert E. Smith, George Spoor and Thomas Armat — Armat was the only one who hadn't materially benefited from an association with Anderson.

Ten years later, when Associated Press correspondent Bob Thomas discovered Anderson was still alive, the reporter attempted to interview him, but Anderson wanted nothing to do with it. "I wouldn't be interested," he said.[16] Thomas persisted, and a newspaper article he wrote paved the way for Anderson's recognition in March 1958 by the Academy of Motion Picture Arts and Sciences "for his contributions to the development of motion pictures as entertainment."[17]

Suddenly Anderson was a celebrity again, appearing on television, frequently interviewed and invited by the Niles Chamber of Commerce to be the center of attention at an Essanay celebration that June. Anderson couldn't be at the event because he went to New York, but his time in the spotlight was brief and he soon faded into obscurity again.

In 1964, Anderson entered the Motion Picture Country House in Woodland Hills, frail, wheelchair-bound and nearly deaf. It was another comeback of sorts, but this time he was greeted more personally by those within the film industry.

Director Robert Florey said: "Whenever I went to the Motion Picture Country House to see some old friends I always paid a visit to Broncho Billy, and often brought along some French movie writers such as Charles Ford or Fronval — they were always more anxious to meet Anderson than the great stars of the day. We found him one day terribly excited as he was going to be picked up and transported to the Paramount Studio for a cameo in a western quickie."[18] That film, *The Bounty Killer* (1965), was notable for its group of western stars (Dan Duryea, Richard

Rollie Totheroh and G. M. Anderson at the Country House.

Arlen, Rod Cameron, Bob Steele, Johnny Mack Brown, Buster Crabbe) gathered by the producer, Alex Gordon. Gordon thought it would be fitting to include Anderson, and, for the first time, his voice was heard on-screen (he spoke two sentences in a barroom scene). Thus ended a movie career that technically spanned 62 years.

One more person visited Anderson in his last years, and it brought back memories of Niles. Rollie Totheroh hurt himself in a fall at his home, came to the Motion Picture Country Home to mend and heard Anderson was there, too. Totheroh paid Anderson a visit: "I came in the room and introduced myself, not knowing if he'd remember me. And he stared at me, smiled, and said, 'Rollie... yes, Rollie. My old third-base man.'"[19]

Anderson's health worsened as the 1960s ended. He moved to the Academy's Brierwood Convalescent Hospital in 1970, and died there the next year. He was 90 years old.

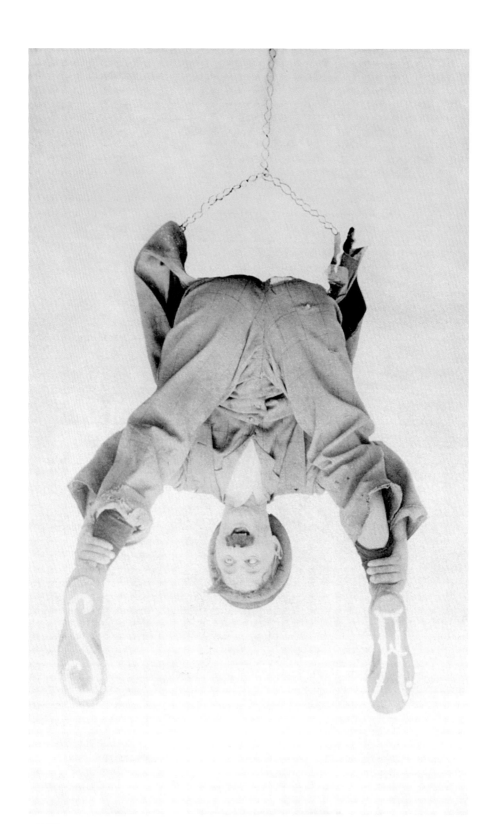

246

Essanay Personnel

This listing of Western Essanay staff includes people who worked with Anderson's division from Colorado to California. It's based on information in newspapers, trade magazines, films, photographs and from the families of Essanay personnel. Real names, if different than commonly reported, are in parentheses. This list is by no means complete; any additional information is welcome.

Lawrence A. Abrott 22 July 1888 Sunol, California - 9 August 1961 Oakland, California. He joined the company in Niles as a set carpenter in July 1912. By 1914 he was also appearing as an extra in films. His wife Alice appeared in at least one Essanay film, *A Waiting Game*. He remained with the company until the studio closed in 1916, then formed the Western Scenic Studio in Oakland, producing scenic backdrops, flats and theater curtains. It remained in operation into the 1990s.

Gilbert M. Anderson, George Maxwell Anderson, Broncho Billy (Max H. Aronson) 21 March 1880 Little Rock, Arkansas - 20 January 1971 Pasadena, California. His family moved to St. Louis in 1884. In 1902 he was listed as an actor in the St. Louis city directory. He acted in New York City in *Life* (seven performances beginning 31 March 1902). He joined the Edison Film Company in October 1903, and left in March 1904. He was back in St. Louis by 1905 as an actor. He joined Vitagraph as a director in July 1905, and left in May 1906. He produced films for the Harry Davis Company from May 1906 to July 1906. He worked as a director for Selig Polyscope from July 1906 to March 1907. At Essanay he was a minority stockholder, secretary of the company, producer, director, writer and editor. He began to star in westerns in October 1909. He sold his share of Essanay to George Spoor at the end of January 1916. Anderson entered into a theatrical partnership with H. H. Frazee (forming the Frand Theatre Company) in April 1916, buying the Longacre Theatre in New York City. In August he signed with Lewis Selznick to produce and direct a film, *Vera, the Medium*, starring Kitty Gordon. That same year he and Lawrence Webber begin producing a series of plays. He built two theaters in San Francisco: the Gaiety and the Casino. In 1918 he formed the Golden West Producing Company with several San Francisco businessmen. It failed. In late 1921 he formed the Amalgamated Producing Company to make feature films and Stan Laurel comedies. He quit the film business in 1923. Later films: *Red Blood and Yellow* (1918), *The Son of a Gun* (1918), *The Greater Duty* (1921), *The Bounty Killer* (1965).

Leona Anderson (Leona Aronson) 3 April 1885 St. Louis, Missouri - 25 December 1973 Fremont, California. G. M. Anderson's sister, she had modest success on Broadway in musicals from 1905 to 1908. She was an Essanay actress in Niles from January to August 1915. She married San Francisco real estate magnate Alfred Rosenstirn in 1916, but performed occasionally in plays and films produced by her brother. She revived her singing career in 1954 with Columbia Records, and in connection with it appeared on the Jack Parr, Ernie Kovacs and Steve Allen shows. Later films: *Ashes* (1918), *Mud and Sand* (1922), *The House on Haunted Hill* (1958).

Nathan Anderson (Nathaniel A. Aronson) 1878 Texas - ? G. M. Anderson's brother, he joined Essanay in Niles as an actor in 1913, then wrote scenarios there in 1915, heading that department. He was a theater actor in San Francisco in the early 1920s, and worked in various San Francisco bookstores from 1926 to 1928.

Hal P. Angus 23 August 1890 Oakland, California - 20 April 1977 Castro Valley, California. He acted at Ye Liberty Theatre in Oakland from 1909 to 1910, acted in Niles with Essanay in 1912-13 and married Essanay scenario writer Josephine Rector in 1914. He was elected the first secretary-treasurer of the California State Council of Cannery Unions in 1939.

Hazel Applegate 1886 - 30 October 1959 Chicago, Illinois. An actress at the Chicago Essanay studio from 1913, she came to Niles with Anderson and Chaplin in January 1915, and returned to Chicago in April.

Billy Armstrong (William Armstrong) 14 January 1891 Bristol, England - 1 March 1924 Sunland, California. His performing career began in music halls and burlesque with his father (Will H. Armstrong?). From 1910 to 1914 he was with Fred Karno's company in England. His first film was *The Tramp*. He left Niles with Chaplin for Los Angeles in April 1915 and stayed until the unit disbanded. In 1916 he starred in Horsley's Cub Comedies, worked at Keystone, then Rolin. His life was cut short by tuberculosis. Later films include: *The Defective Detective* (1916), *A Royal Rogue* (1917), *Beach Nuts* (1918), *Do Husbands Deceive?* (1918), *Call the Cops* (1919), *Chicken a la Cabaret* (1920).

Ed Armstrong England - ? A music hall and burlesque comedian, he was touring in 1908 throughout the United States and Canada with his brother Will H. Armstrong in their act "A Busy Night." They settled at the Unique Theater in Los Angeles later that year with their Armstrong Musical Comedy Company. In April 1915, he joined Chaplin's unit for the Essanay film *By the Sea*.

Lloyd Bacon 4 December 1889 San Jose, California - 15 November 1955 Burbank, California. A vaudeville and stock company actor, he began film work with the Liberty Film Company in San Mateo. He joined Essanay as an actor in February

Warren Sawyer and Lawrence Abrott pose with their handiwork, a finished set on the stage.

Hal Angus surrounded in an unidentified Essanay film. The other cowboys are True Boardman, Jack Wood, Slim Padgett, Charles La Due, Freddie Bridges and ?.

Leona Anderson and Ella McKenzie in Suppressed Evidence.

G. M. Anderson and Vedah Bertram in Broncho Billy and the Indian Maid. *Fred Church is the sheriff beside the body (Brinsley Shaw); the cowboys are Louis Morisette and Al Parks.*

1915, left Niles with Chaplin in April, returned to Niles in July, and stayed until January 1916. He acted with Chaplin at Mutual, then began directing. He made Lloyd Hamilton comedies for Mack Sennett, westerns at Fox and Universal, and a string of musicals at Warners. As an actor: *The Vagabond* (1916), *Easy Street* (1917), *Blue Blazes Rawden* (1918), *Wagon Tracks* (1919); as a director: *The Singing Fool* (1928), *42nd Street* (1933), *Marked Woman* (1937), *Boy Meets Girl* (1938), *It Happens Every Spring* (1949).

Charles Barton 25 May 1902 Sacramento, California - 5 December 1981 Burbank, California. Although he acted in one 1915 Broncho Billy film, it was his stage career that boosted him into film work in Los Angeles. Following a period of disenchantment, he became an office boy at the Lasky studio, and slowly moved up the ladder to become a director. In 1951 he began directing in television with the "Amos and Andy Show," and later, "McHale's Navy," "Petticoat Junction" and "The Smothers Brothers Show." As an actor: *County Fair* (1920), *Beau Geste* (1939); assistant director: *Duck Soup* (1933), *Union Pacific* (1939); as director: *Wagon Wheels* (1934), *Abbott and Costello Meet Frankenstein* (1948), *The Shaggy Dog* (1959).

Wallace Beery 1 April 1885 Kansas City, Missouri - 15 April 1949 Beverly Hills, California. He ran away to the circus as a kid, performing with elephants for the Ringling Brothers. From there he went into acting, working on Broadway, then touring with The Yankee Tourist in 1907. He was in Redlands with The Red Rose company only a few months after Essanay left there in 1911. His older brother William, an office worker at the Chicago Essanay, got him a job at the studio in August 1913. He starred in the Sweedie Comedies playing a Swedish maid, and in the George Ade Fables. He came to Niles in October 1915 to direct the Snakeville Comedies. When the studio closed he went to Keystone in Los Angeles. His fame as an actor grew in the 1920s and blossomed in the 30s. His films include: *The Last of the Mohicans* (1921), *Robin Hood* (1922), *The Sea Hawk* (1924), *The Lost World* (1925), *Chinatown Nights* (1929), *Min and Bill* (1930), *The Champ* (1931), *Grand Hotel* (1932), *Dinner at Eight* (1933), *Treasure Island* (1934), *China Seas* (1935), *The Man from Dakota* (1940), *Big Jack* (1949).

Vedah Bertram (Adele Buck) 1 December 1891 Brooklyn, New York - 26 August 1912 Oakland, California. She was discovered by G. M. Anderson in December 1911. Beginning with *The Ranch Girl's Mistake* (2 March 1912) and ending with *Broncho Billy Outwitted* (14 September 1912) she made twenty-two films before her entry into Oakland's Merritt Hospital in July 1912.

Peggy Blevins (Eleanor Blevins) Lincoln, Nebraska - ?   A young stage actress working in Northern California, she intermittently worked in Niles for Essanay in 1913 and 1914, and in Los Angeles with the Chaplin unit in 1915. Other films: *Yankee Doodle Dixie* (1913), *The Dead Soul* (1915), *The Beggar King* (1916).

True Boardman (William True Boardman) 21 April 1882 Oakland, California - 28 September 1918 Norwalk, California. A stock company actor since 1903, his first film work was with Selig in Chicago. He came to Niles with his wife (actress Virginia Eames) and their son True Eames Boardman in August 1912. He distinguished himself in leading and supporting roles. He left in December 1914 for the Liberty Film Company in San Mateo, and when that under-financed company failed he went to Kalem in Glendale to star in the Stingaree film series and other films. Some of his films: *When Thieves Fall Out* (1915), *On the Brink of War* (1916), *The False Prophet* (1917), *The Doctor and the Woman* (1919).

True Boardman (True Eames Boardman) October 1909 Seattle, Washington. Like his father, True acted first at Selig, then Essanay from 1912 to 1914, went on to the Liberty Film Company and Kalem. But he didn't stop there. Films include: *A Boy at the Throttle* (1915), *Shoulder Arms* (1918), *Daddy Long Legs* (1919). He's written for movies (*The Arabian Nights*, 1942), radio ("The Lux Radio Theater") and television ("Perry Mason," "Bonanza").

Fred W. Bogan ? - ? He was "Soldier" Elder's boxing trainer, and that association brought him to Essanay in Niles as an actor in 1912.

Lois Boulton ? - ? In 1910 she worked during the day as an actress with Essanay in Santa Barbara while performing at night with the Elleford Stock Company.

Lawrence A. Bowes 1 January 1885 Newark, California - 5 June 1955 Glendale, California. He was an actor on stage with the Ferris Hartman Company before joining Chaplin's Essanay unit in Los Angeles in May 1915. He remained there until November 1915. Other films: *Picture Pirates* (1916), *A Warm Reception* (1917).

M. A. Breslauer, Harris Breslauer, B. Harris (Mervyn A. Breslauer) April 1886 California - ? He was a stringer for the San Francisco Call newspaper and a catcher on the San Rafael baseball team in 1911. He was hired in July 1912 as a press agent for Essanay, and played on the Niles baseball team until he left in November 1912. He returned to Niles in September 1913, worked in the prop department and acted. He switched to camera assisting in 1914 and worked with Harris Ensign on the Chaplin films in Niles. He left Niles with Chaplin's Essanay unit in April 1915 and wrote press releases.

Texas George Briggs ? - ? A cowboy and rifle marksman for the Kalem Company in 1911, he came to Essanay when they were at Lakeside in January 1912. He remained with Essanay in Niles until the summer of 1913. In 1914 he was with the California Motion Picture Company in San Rafael and their Boulder Creek location in the Santa Cruz Mountains.

Peggy Blevins and some Niles children in The New Schoolmarm of Green River.

True Boardman, True Boardman and Evelyn Selbie in The Reward for Broncho Billy.

Vincent Bryan 22 June 1878 St. Johns, Newfoundland - 27 April 1937 Hollywood, California. A vaudeville sketch writer (for Lew Dockstader, Eddie Foy, Bert Williams) and songwriter ("Budweiser's a Friend of Mine," "Merry Oldsmobile"), he joined Chaplin's Essanay unit in Los Angeles to work on scenarios. He continued with Chaplin at Mutual. He also worked at Mack Sennett's Keystone Film Company. His writing work includes: *The Fireman* (1916), *The Scrub Lady* (1917), *Ambrose's Day Off* (1919).

Al Bundrick ? - ? An electrician with Essanay in San Rafael from 1911, he left Niles with Arthur Mackley's unit for Los Angeles in November 1912, staying until the company disbanded in March 1913.

Robert Burroughs ? - ? He was a catcher on the Essanay baseball team, a propman at the studio and an actor from July 1914 to January 1916.

George Cantwell ? - ? He was assistant scenario writer from late 1913 to 1914. Other writing work: *The Golden Heart* (1913).

Neva Don Carlos 1888 Kansas - ? She joined Essanay as an actress in November 1909 and left after they returned to Chicago in June 1910. She worked with the Star and Garter company on tour in the fall of 1910, was in San Francisco for six months in 1911 and entertained at a Los Angeles cafe later that year.

Augustus F. Carney 1870s? Ireland - ? Carney said he came to America when he was sixteen to live on an uncle's California ranch. When he was twenty-one he went to New York and got a comedy role on stage. He was in a stage production of *The Goddess of Liberty* in Chicago (10 August 1909 to 15 January 1910) when he got an offer from Essanay. Anderson latched onto him for the Hank and Lank series, then took him west. He became a star as Alkali Ike, and was lured away by Universal in October 1913. As Universal Ike he lasted until May 1914. He appeared in *The Absentee, The Failure, The Straw Man, The Martyrs of the Alamo* (all 1915), *Blue Blood and Red* (1916). After that he disappeared.

Sade Carr 13 April 1889 London - 17 November 1940 Carmel, California. In the Ziegfeld *Follies of 1911*, Al Jolson's *Honeymoon Express* in 1913 and *The Candy Shop* at Anderson's Gaiety Theatre later that year, she came to Niles in January 1915 as a possible choice for Chaplin's new leading lady. Her stay was brief. She married an architect and moved to Carmel in 1929, opening a little restaurant, "Sade's," a popular gathering spot for artists and writers.

Helen Carruthers 1892 - ? She acted at Selig and Keystone before joining Essanay in Niles in February 1915, and supposedly appeared in *The Champion* and other films before leaving in April.

Joe Cassidy (Thomas Joseph Cassidy) ? - ? He joined the company as a stagecoach driver and cowboy in March 1911, trained horses to do tricks after the Niles studio opened, and stayed until the studio closed in 1916. His wife Gertrude also appeared in films occasionally.

Bill Cato (William S. Cato) 16 April 1887 Wyoming - 9 January 1965 Los Banos, California. He was Broncho Billy's stunt double in Niles beginning in June 1912. He became the boss cowboy of the company and stayed until the studio closed in 1916. He may have worked in Los Angeles briefly, but by 1920 he was on a ranch in Los Banos.

Florence Cato (Donna Florence Perkes) 2 June 1892 South Bend, Oregon - 12 May 1969 Carmel, California. As Florence Perkes she was hired for her horse riding skills in August 1912. She married Bill Cato (in 1913?) and stayed with the company until the studio closed in 1916.

Charles Chaplin 16 April 1889 London - 25 December 1977 Switzerland. The actor/director/writer came to Essanay in December 1914 after a year with the Keystone Film Company. *His New Job* was made in Chicago, followed by five films (including *The Tramp*) in Niles, and eight in Los Angeles. He signed with Mutual on 26 February 1916. Later films include: *The Kid* (1921), *The Gold Rush* (1925), *Modern Times* (1936), *Limelight* (1952).

Lillian Christie ? - ? An actress with Vitagraph, Kalem and Bison, she came from the American Film Company to work in Niles around November 1913. She married Fred Church in December and they left the company together just before Christmas. Other films: *The Half-Breed's Daughter* (1911), *Custer's Last Raid* (1912), *A Rose of Old Mexico* (1913).

Fred Church 17 October 1889 Ontario, Iowa - 7 January 1983 Blythe, Califonia. He was living with his family in Denver when he first worked in the movies with Selig in the summer of 1908. He worked with Essanay on Anderson's first western series in January 1909. He joined Essanay full-time in October 1909 and, except for two months at Pioneer Park in Wyoming during the summer of 1910, he remained with the company until December 1913. Besides working in Anderson's westerns he was Rawhide Bill and Coyote Simpson in the Snakeville Comedies. In 1914 he worked for the Frontier company in Santa Paula, Universal in 1915-16, Fox in 1917, and Anderson's Golden West company in 1918. His theatrical stage experience dated from 1906, and he took it up again in 1919, managing several touring companies for Anderson's Frand Theatre Company. In October 1921 he became president of the Amalgamated Producing Company, overseeing the Stan Laurel comedies Metro releases and a few features directed by and/or starring G. M. Anderson. Amalgamated ended with *The Woman in Chains* (1923).

Bill Cato at work.

Lillian Christie, Fred Church, an unknown friend and the Niles movie theater in the background.

Marguerite Clayton, Gertrude Cassidy and Evelyn Selbie in Niles Canyon.

Church acted with the Casino Players at San Francisco's Casino Theatre in 1924. In the 1920s and early 1930s he acted and directed for many short-lived film companies: Major Film Productions, Great Northern Pictures, Golden Eagle Pictures, Bell Film Production and others. He also starred in the Montana Bill series. He retired to a ranch in Victorville after a car accident in 1935. For the last 35 years of his life he was the caretaker for the Williams Mill lead mine in Quartzite, Arizona. His later films include: *The Long Chance* (1915), *A Knight of the Range* (1916), *Du Barry* (1918), *Red Blood and Yellow* (1918), *The Son of a Gun* (1918), *Stacked Cards* (1926), *Secrets of the Range* (1928), *Western Methods* (1929), *Wild West Whoopee* (1930), *Riders of the Cactus* (1931), *Border Guns* (1935).

Marguerite Clayton (Margaret Fitzgerald) 12 April 1892 Salt Lake City, Utah - 20 December 1968 Los Angeles, California. Aspiring to be an actress, she answered an ad placed by Essanay in a San Francisco newspaper, was hired in May 1913 and became Anderson's leading lady in September. In December 1914 she went to the Liberty Film Company, but returned in March 1915. She left Niles for good to work in features at the Chicago Essanay studio in October 1915 and stayed there until December 1917. After that she worked at Fox, Universal, FBO, Pathe and Paramount. She retired in 1928. In 1930 she married Victor Bertrandias, an aviator who served with Eddie Rickenbacker in World War I. Her films include: *Hit-the-Trail Holliday* (1918), *The Pleasure Seekers* (1920), *Forbidden Love* (1921), *What Love Will Do* (1923), *Flashing Spurs*(1924), *Straight Through* (1925), *Wolf Blood* (1925), *The Palm Beach Girl* (1926), *Inspiration* (1928).

Scotty Cleethorpe (George Cleethorpe) 1893 Ireland - ? He was an actor and propman for Chaplin's Essanay unit in Los Angeles in 1915 and went with Chaplin to Mutual. He worked for G. M. Anderson's Golden West company in 1918 and was an assistant director at Jess Robbins Productions in 1921.

Roy Clements 12 January 1877 Sterling, Illinois - 15 July 1948 Hollywood, California. A long-time stock company actor hired by Essanay to direct the Snakeville comedy series in December 1913, he produced around seventy films by the time he left for Universal in September 1915. In 1917 he directed the Lyons and Moran Nestor Comedies. He worked at the Hal Roach Company in the 1920s. Films include: *When Slim Picked a Peach* (1916), *A Proxy Elopement* (1917), *The Light of the Western Stars* (1918), *The Tiger's Coat* (1920), *Nobody's Fool* (1921), *Uncensored Movies* (1923), *The Devil Horse* (1926).

Eugenia Clinchard 5 July 1904 California - 15 May 1989 Panorama City, California. A well-known child actress in the San Francisco Bay Area from 1910 to 1917, she acted with Essanay in San Rafael in October and November 1911, and again off-and-on in Niles from August 1912 to December 1914. One of her granddaughters is actress Rebecca De Mornay.

Lee Willard and Marguerite Clayton in a tense moment from The Face at the Curtain.

Roy Clements, Margaret Joslin and Victor Potel get front row seats in How Slippery Slim Saw the Show. *In the next row: Robert McKenzie, Carrie Turpin, Elizabeth Scott, Belle Mitchell, Pat Rooney, Leo West, Madrona Hicks, Gertrude Cassidy. Behind them: Tom Crizer, ?, ?, Joe Cassidy, Ida Totheroh, Eddie Fries, Florence Cato, Perc Pembroke, Bill Cato, Ralph Richmond, Harry Pollard.*

Frank J. Coleman ? - ? He was an actor at Chaplin's Essanay unit in Los Angeles, and continued with Chaplin at Mutual. His later films include: *The Fireman* (1916), *The Tenderfoot* (1917), *A High Diver's Last Kiss* (1918), *A Fresh Start* (1920).

George Creel 1 December 1876 Lafayette County, Missouri - 2 October 1953 San Francisco, California. At eighteen he was a newspaper reporter in Kansas City, then editor of the Kansas City Independent from 1899 to 1909. He was editor at the Denver Post later in 1909 when he met G. M. Anderson and discovered the movies, but his one-film career remained a footnote in an active life, as a Denver police commissioner, chairman of the Committee on Public Information for President Woodrow Wilson during World War I, an appointee by Franklin Roosevelt to the Works Progress Administration national advisory board, and chairman of the San Francisco Regional Labor Board. A bid to become governor of California in 1934 was short-lived, but his marriage to famed actress Blanche Bates lasted nearly thirty years, until her death in 1941.

Thomas J. Crizer 28 October 1889 Virginia - 13 November 1963 Los Angeles, California. He started in Niles as a cowboy with Essanay in 1912, then learned to edit, probably on the Snakeville comedies. He edited Chaplin's Niles films, and went with him to Los Angeles. In July 1915 he married Audrey Orpin, a Niles girl, and took her to Los Angeles. After the Chaplin unit disbanded he became the film editor for Hal Roach, working on, among others, Harold Lloyd's Lonesome Luke Comedies. He stayed with Lloyd through the transition to feature films, editing *Grandma's Boy* (1922), *Safety Last* (1923), and also working on Stan Laurel's two-reelers for Roach. He co-wrote the story for Lloyd's *The Kid Brother* (1927). His last writing effort was for the Tom Mix feature *My Pal, The King* (1932).

Shorty Cunningham (Samuel Cunningham) 1858 Iowa - ? Cunningham operated a candy and cigar store in the 1890s at Golden, Colorado. By 1902 he was in partnership with Joe Dennis at Dennis's livery stable. Cunningham also became the mayor of Golden for awhile. He and Dennis were all for the movies, working with G. M. Anderson on his first trip to Golden in 1907 and participating during his return in 1909.

Charles Allen Dealey 21 July 1867 Nevada - 9 August 1930 Oakland, California. A San Francisco photographer since the 1890s, he gradually took over all photographic operations at the Niles studio beginning in 1913. In 1915 he played small parts in several Essanay films and acted in Anderson's last Niles film, *The Man in Him* (1916). In 1925 he helped set up the short-lived Hayward Film Company in Hayward, California.

L. Allen Dealey 6 August 1898 San Francisco, California - 26 May 1978 Oakland, California. One of Charles Allen Dealey's sons, he acted at Essanay from January 1914, and possibly took still photos when his father was otherwise occupied.

Leo White in the drink; Tom Crizer, Frank Dolan, Ben Turpin and Charles Allen Dealey nearby, in A Night Out.

L. Allen Dealey amid the merchandise.

Joe Dennis (Joseph Dennis Jr.) 1862 England - ? He came to the United States when he was five, settled in Golden, Colorado at sixteen. For ten years he worked in the grocery business, then opened a livery stable. By 1902 he and Shorty Cunningham were partners. Their stable supplied the horses for G. M. Anderson's Selig Polyscope westerns in Colorado, and they also worked with Francis Boggs at Selig after Anderson left that organization. Anderson used them again in 1909 with his first Essanay westerns. Dennis was good to have around, a deputy sheriff for nine years who knew just about every person and road in the county.

Orrin Denny 14 March 1882 Lewisville, Indiana - 6 August 1969 Alameda, California. He was the still photographer for Anderson's unit beginning in October 1910, also responsible for the Negative Car, a railroad baggage car converted into a rolling laboratory. In April 1912 he joined the Nestor Film Company in Hollywood, then started his own lab in 1914. In 1916 he outfitted a railroad car as a lab for the Signal Film Corporation. By the 1920s he was a wildlife cameraman.

Joe Derlin ? - ? He was an Essanay cowboy in San Rafael (1911).

Fodder Dolan (Frank Dolan) 1892 California - ? Recruited as a pitcher for the Niles baseball team in April 1913, he also found work in the Essanay prop department. Despite offers to play elsewhere, he remained with Essanay until the studio closed in 1916, then immediately signed with the Pacific Gas and Electric baseball team. That year his team won the Tribune League pennant. He married local Niles girl Helen Enos in 1915, and she appeared in some of the last films made in Niles.

Virginia Eames (Virginia Eames Boardman) 23 May 1889 Fort Davis, Texas - 10 June 1971 Los Angeles, California. An actress since 1906, she married actor True Boardman in 1909. She worked in Essanay films from 1912 to 1914, then went to the Liberty Film Company, Kalem and others. Her son is actor/writer True Eames Boardman, her great-granddaughter is television actress Lisa Gerritsen. Her films include: *A Blind Bargain* (1922), *Penrod* (1922), *The Village Blacksmith* (1922), *The Third Alarm* (1922), *The Mailman* (1923), *The Tomboy* (1924), *The Road to Ruin* (1934), *The Fugitive Sheriff* (1936).

Lloyd Easterday 21 May 1891 California - 15 November 1962 San Francisco, California. He started with Essanay as Chaplin's chauffeur and graduated to business manager with the unit in Los Angeles in 1915.

William Coleman Elam 7 May 1888 Orosi, California - 4 July 1945 Los Angeles, California. He joined Essanay as an actor in April 1912, and worked there until the studio closed in 1916. Later on he was a machinist and carpenter.

True Boardman, Virginia Eames and Fred Church help Arthur Mackley in The Miner's Request.

William Coleman Elam.

Soldier Elder (Willis Elder) 1889 Evansville, Indiana? - ? A heavyweight boxer, he acted with Essanay beginning in June 1911, and also handled props. He stayed until mid-1913.

Thomas Elliott 24 July 1882 Canada - 2 January 1980 Fremont, California. Hired as a set carpenter and blacksmith in November 1912, he stayed until the studio closed in 1916. He was the master mechanic for the Kraftile Company in Niles for over thirty years.

Harry Ensign (Harris Newton Ensign) 5 October 1883 Waterbury, Connecticut - 11 October 1943 Hollywood, California. Hired as a cameraman for the Snakeville Comedies in September 1913, he left with Jess Robbins in April 1914 to work at Robbins Photo Plays. He returned to Niles in late 1914, was assigned to Chaplin's unit in January 1915 and shot Chaplin's first four Niles films. He left with Chaplin in April 1915 for Los Angeles, staying until that company disbanded in 1916. He eventually became the head of Paramount's film lab.

Earl Esola (Joseph Earl Esola) 13 May 1892 California - 15 November 1968 Eugene, Oregon. A shortstop with the Essanay baseball team, he acted in films from August 1914 to January 1916.

William A. Evans ? - ? He was at Niles as a cameraman in September 1912, back from a trip to the Far East filming documentaries for Essanay. He went with the Mackley unit to Hollywood in November and stayed there when the company disbanded in March 1913.

Gladys J. Field 1889 San Francisco, California - August 1920 Mount Vernon, New York. She was an actress at Ye Liberty Theatre in 1909, living in Alameda. In September 1909 she began acting with the Elleford Stock Company. She joined Essanay in Santa Barbara in January 1910. She left Essanay in late August 1911 when they were in San Rafael, but worked with the Mackley Essanay unit in Hollywood in 1913. By 1915 she was married to director John B. O'Brien. She died during childbirth. Her other films include: *Dr. Jekyll and Mr. Hyde* (Sheldon Lewis, 1920).

Edna Fisher (Edna Levi) 14 August 1891 Omaha, Nebraska - 23 April 1978 Los Angeles, California. She was with the company in San Rafael as an actress from August to December 1911. She went to Vitagraph in Santa Monica, married director Rollin Sturgeon and retired from films in October 1912. In the 1940s she played small parts in films. A few of her films: *At the End of the Trail, The Greater Love, The Prayers of Manuelo* (all 1912).

Joe Flynn (John J. Flynn) ? - ? Anderson's chauffeur from 1912 to 1916, he also acted in Essanay films, and did so again at Golden West.

William A. Evans helps his assistant in the Orient.

Gladys Field.

Edna Fisher.

Eddie Fries (Edward W. Fries) ? - ? He played center field with the Niles baseball team, acted in films from August 1914 to December 1915 and wrote a sports column for the Township Register.

Lawrence T. Ganshirt 9 January 1892 San Jose, California - 19 June 1966 Yosemite, California. He acted with the company during the last few months of 1915.

Denver Jack Geyer ? - ? A heavyweight boxer who worked briefly with Essanay in 1912, he blamed Soldier Elder for getting him fired and beat Elder soundly in a match at the West Oakland Club in August 1912.

Marta Golden ? - ? A Ye Liberty Theatre actress from June 1913, she had substituted briefly for Marie Dressler during the Gaiety Theatre flap in 1914. She wrote a script that was bought by Essanay in March 1915 (possibly *A Bunch of Matches*) and came to Niles to assist on it. She acted in the Chaplin Essanay films *A Woman* and *Work* in Los Angeles, then moved to the Keystone studio. By 1917 she was back on stage in San Francisco.

Fred S. Goodwins 1891 London ? - 1923 London ? A stage actor, he was in New York when Chaplin signed with Essanay. He started with the Chaplin Essanay unit in Los Angeles beginning with *The Bank* and continued with Chaplin at Mutual as a press agent. After a renewed period of acting, he returned to England and began directing. Films as an actor: *Amarily of Clothes-Line Alley* (1918), *For Husbands Only* (1918), *Common Clay* (1919), *The Scarlett Kiss* (1920), *Her Winning Ways* (1921).

William P. Gordon ? - ? He had been working at the Idora Park Theater in Oakland when he was hired as an assistant propman in February 1915. He joined the Chaplin unit and went with them to Los Angeles.

William M. Gorham February 1874 California - ? Anderson's long-time accountant, he worked in that capacity with the Chaplin unit in Los Angeles. He later handled Anderson's books in New York, and was secretary/treasurer of the Amalgamated Producing Company.

Robert Henry Gray, Bob Gray 1882 Houlton, Maine - ? He joined Essanay as an actor while they were in Colorado in April 1910, traveled with them to Chicago and left in February 1911 to work for Lubin in Los Angeles. He was with Lasky in 1916-17. Films include: *Fate and Fugitive* (1914), *Jealousy* (1915), *Unprotected* (1916), *The Chorus Lady* (1917), *The Ranger* (1918), *The White Rider* (1920).

Robert Henry Gray (Henry Virtue Goerner) 17 July 1891 Oakland, California - 26 April 1934 Los Angeles, California. An actor with Ye Liberty in 1910, he came to Essanay in San Rafael in June 1911. He left for the American Film Company in

March 1912, but returned to Essanay in September 1913. In early 1914 he left again, for Los Angeles, and subsequently worked for Balboa, Kalem and Pathe. Later films include: *The Disappearance of Harry Warrington* (1915), *Twin Souls* (1916), *Feet of Clay* (1917), *Petticoats and Politics* (1918).

George Green ? - ? He worked as a set carpenter(?) with the Chaplin unit in Los Angeles.

Alfred T. Griffin 25 July 1888 California - 10 September 1920 Los Angeles, California. An architect, he supervised the construction of the Niles Essanay studio and may have been involved with building Anderson's bungalows in Niles. He also worked as a set carpenter at Essanay. In April 1914 he left with Jess Robbins to work at Robbins Photo Plays in Los Angeles. He returned to Niles in December 1914, then left with the Chaplin unit in April 1915 and worked there until Chaplin left in 1916. He went to Fort Lee, New Jersey, to work on Anderson's Selznick picture *Vera, The Medium* in May 1916 and stayed on in anticipation of more work until February 1917. Returning to Los Angeles, he joined the Rolin Company in September as a set designer and probably was still working there when he died of acute appendicitus.

Frank Hall (Franklyn A. Hall) 1880 Oakland, California - ? He started acting at sixteen at the Grand Opera House in San Francisco. He married actress Clara Williams in 1909, probably when they were working together at the Charles King Stock Company. In August 1909 they were touring with "The Turning Point," a playlet Hall wrote with Carl Birch. They joined Essanay in December. Hall and his wife left in October 1910 for an engagement on stage in Chicago, then went to Lubin in Philadelphia. He worked at Selig beginning in 1912 and was there at least until 1914. In 1919 he was in charge of the scenario department at the National Film Company. His later films include: *Tess of the D'Urbervilles* (1913), *Life's Crucible* (1914), *A Boy at the Throttle* (1915), *A Branded Soul* (1917), *The Confession* (1920).

Audrey Hanna 1906? - ? She was a child actress with the company from April 1912. She left Niles with her father Jay Hanna in November as part of the Mackley unit, then went elsewhere at the end of March.

Jay Hanna ? - ? He joined Essanay as an actor in April 1912, went to Hollywood with the Mackley unit in November and stayed through March 1913. In April 1914 he joined the Dick Wilbur stock company in Stockton for a tour through the San Joaquin Valley.

Eldon Hatch 3 November 1886 Sandy, Oregon - 26 September 1947 Los Gatos, California. He was a Los Gatos resident who acted with Essanay while they were in town from October 1910 to February 1911.

Jack Hawks (John G. Hawks) 13 October 1874 San Francisco, California - 10 April 1940 Hollywood, California. He worked as a scenario writer in 1911 and 1915 with Essanay. In 1914 he wrote for the Vim Film Company in Alameda, California. Later he directed, wrote or edited films for Ince, Universal, Goldwyn, FBO and Metro. Some of the films he worked on: *Mr. Silent Haskins* (1915), *The Cold Deck* (1917), *Blue Blazes Rawden* (1918), *Shadows* (1919), *The Penalty* (1920), *A Blind Bargain* (1922), *The Sea Hawk* (1924), *The Last Warning* (1929), *Aloha* (1931).

Eva Heazlett (Eva B. McKenzie) 5 November 1889 Cecil, Ohio - 15 September 1967 Hollywood, California. A stock company actress since 1899, she joined Essanay in March 1915 with her husband Robert McKenzie and worked there until January 1916. Her later films include: *Knight of the West* (1921), *Virtuous Husbands* (1931), *The Wrong Miss Wright* (1937), *You Can't Take It With You* (1938), *Heavenly Days* (1944).

E. Hellwig ? - ? She was a scenerio department assistant in September 1913.

Jack Henderson 1878 Syracuse, New York - 1 January 1957 New York City. He acted with the Chaplin unit in October 1915. His other films include: *A Royal Rogue* (1917), *Scars and Bars* (1918), *Jiggs in Society* (1920).

Al Herman (Adam Herman Foelker) 22 February 1894 Brooklyn, New York - 28 September 1958 Los Angeles, California. A boxer who began with Essanay as a propman and actor in late 1913, he left for Liberty Films in August 1914. He returned in February 1915 and went with the Chaplin unit to Los Angeles. He became a director in the 1920s and continued doing so for television. His films include: *Beyond the Trail* (1926), *Sporting Chance* (1931), *Gun Play* (1935), *The Clutching Hand* (1936), *The Utah Trail* (1938), *Arizona Frontier* (1940).

Madrona Hicks 1 January 1879 California - 4 July 1954 Oakland, California. The wife of Orlando Hicks, in May 1914 she began acting at Essanay, and worked until the studio closed in 1916.

Orlando Lee Hicks 19 January 1870 Kentucky - 10 February 1947 Oakland, California. He joined the company as a set carpenter in October 1914, sometimes filling in as an extra in crowd scenes, and remained at Essanay until the studio closed in 1916.

Rodney Hildebrand 22 March 1892 Illinois - 22 February 1962 Los Angeles, California. A long-time stage actor, he joined Essanay in October 1915 and stayed until the studio closed in 1916. His later film work includes: *Early to Wed* (1926),

Snakeville's Weak Women: *Eva Sawyer, Madrona Hicks, Margaret Joslin, Elizabeth Scott, Carrie Turpin and Eva Heazlett.*

Ella McKenzie fingers Rodney Hildebrand in The Escape of Broncho Billy. *The witnesses are Lloyd Bacon, Darrell Wittenmyer, Warren Sawyer, Joe Cassidy and Bill Cato.*

Mother Macgree (1928), *Bright Eyes* (1934), *Life Begins at Forty* (1935), *The Whole Town's Talking* (1935), *It Could Happen to You* (1937).

Lee Hill Minneapolis, Minnesota - ? He acted with the Chaplin unit from June 1915, and also worked at Majestic, Vogue, Ince, Selig and Universal. His films include: *The Witness* (1915), *To Him That Hath* (1918), *Girls* (1919), *The Deceiver* (1920), *Guilty* (1922).

Earl H. Howell 1883 Missoula, Montana - 18 July 1918 Boston, Massachusetts. He worked for years in vaudeville with his wife/partner May McCaskey. From November 1909 to March 1910 they acted with Essanay. His last two years were with the Temple Players in Maiden, Massachusetts.

Orral Humphrey 3 April 1878 Louisville, Kentucky - 12 August 1929 Hollywood, California. A stage actor since 1890, he worked for ten years with Ye Liberty in Oakland and with Essanay from June 1913 to February 1914. He later acted at Universal, Keystone and Paul Gerson Pictures. His films include: *Beauty and the Rogue* (1918), *Huckleberry Finn* (1920).

Fred Ilenstine 13 November 1889 Santa Maria, California - 16 February 1968 Santa Barbara, California. He was an actor/cowboy with Essanay beginning in January 1910, traveling with them to Chicago. He probably left the company when they were in Santa Monica in 1911, returning to Santa Barbara. He worked with the American Film Company when they came to Santa Barbara in 1912.

Lloyd Ingraham 30 November 1874 Rochelle, Illinois - 4 April 1956 Woodland Hills, California. A stock company actor since he was fifteen, his first film work was with Universal in mid-1912. He joined Essanay in April 1913 as an actor and director, then returned to Universal in March 1914. He directed for Majestic-Reliance, Fine Arts and American with stars Mae Marsh, Douglas Fairbanks, Lillian Gish and Mary Miles Minter. Among his many films as director: *Hoodoo Ann* (1916), *American Aristocracy* (1916), *Mary's Ankle* (1920), *Hearts and Fists* (1926), *Arizona Nights* (1927), *Kit Carson* (1928) As an actor: *Intolerance* (1916), *A Front Page Story* (1922), *Scaramouche* (1923), *The Spoilers* (1930), *Modern Times* (1936), *Never Give a Sucker an Even Break* (1941), *The Savage Horde* (1950).

Lois Ingraham 24 June 1908 Nebraska - 3 June 1955 Los Angeles, California. She and her sister Zella (three years older) were Lloyd Ingraham's daughters. While Zella is credited with only one Essanay film, Lois was on the screen frequently in 1913. Lois later married writer Ken Gamet. Her other films: *Hearts and Fists* (1926), *Heroes of the Night* (1927).

Charles E. Inslee ? - ? He was in films from 1908 with Edison, Biograph, Bison and Kalem. He acted with the Chaplin Essanay unit in *Work* and stayed until

October 1915. A few films: *The True Heart of an Indian* (1909), *Little Dove's Romance* (1911), *The Little Fat Rascal* (1917), *Cold Steel* (1921), *The Man Who Woke Up* (1921).

Ann Ivers ? - ? She acted with the Chaplin unit in July 1915. Her films include: *Martin Eden* (1914).

Bud Jamison (William Edward Jaimison) 15 February 1894 Vallejo, California - 30 September 1944 Hollywood, California. He began performing in cafes, found work in stock companies, went into vaudeville and joined Essanay in January 1915. *A Night Out* was his first film. He went to Los Angeles with the Chaplin unit and that's when he met Hal Roach. After the Essanay Chaplin unit folded Jamison joined Roach's Rolin Film Company for Harold Lloyd's Lonesome Luke Comedies, and from there seemed to specialize in short comedy films, working in an incredible number of them. His films include: *Luke's Movie Muddle* (1916), *Lonesome Luke, Messenger* (1917), *Beach Nuts* (1918), *A One Night Stand* (1918), *Just Rambling Along* (1918), *Do Husbands Deceive?* (1918), *Hoot Mon* (1919), *Dante's Inferno* (1924), *Buck Privates* (1928), *The Dentist* (1932), *Wonder Bar* (1934), *Men in Black* (1934), *It Always Happens* (1935), *The Wrong Miss Wright* (1937), *Pest from the West* (1939), *Li'l Abner* (1940), *Phony Express* (1943).

Arthur Jasmin 9 June 1896? - August 1971 Springfield, Massachusetts? He acted in Niles from August 1915 to January 1916. His films include: *A Tokio Siren* (1919), *Salome* (1923).

Bud Jerome, Jerome Anderson (Jerome W. Aronson) September 1872 New York City - ? Another of G. M. Anderson's brothers to work in Niles, he acted with the company from early 1913 to January 1916. He was a shoe salesman in New York in the 1920s.

Emory Johnson (Albert Emory Johnson) 16 March 1894 San Francisco, California – 18 April 1960 San Mateo, California. An architecture student from the University of California at Berkeley, he came to Niles out of curiosity and asked for a job. He was hired as a camera assistant in September 1913, but got interested in acting and stepped in front of the camera. He went with Jess Robbins to Los Angeles as a camera assistant for the Robbins Photo Plays Company in April 1914. In September 1914 he went to the Liberty Film Company to star, and when that company failed he returned to Los Angeles. After acting at Pathe, Universal and Paramount he started directing and became highly successful in the 1920s, but his career declined in the 1930s. In 1945 he moved to San Mateo to operate a portrait studio. He died from severe burns after falling asleep while smoking in bed. His films include: *The Way of the World* (1916), *Prisoners of Love* (1921), *The Third Alarm* (1922), *The Mailman* (1923), *The Last Edition* (1925), *The Lone Eagle* (1927), *Phantom Express* (1932).

Margaret Joslin (Margaret Lucy Gosling Todd) 6 August 1883 Cleveland, Ohio - 14 October 1956 Glendale, California. Married to Essanay actor Harry Todd, she began appearing in films when the company was in Colorado in September 1910. She made a hit a few months later in *Alkali Ike's Auto* and from then on became a regular in the Snakeville Comedies. She stayed with Essanay until the Niles studio closed in 1916, then moved with her husband to Universal briefly before settling in at Rolin to work in the Toto, Lonesome Luke and Stan Laurel comedies. She retired to raise her daughter. Films include: *Lonesome Luke, Messenger* (1917), *Just Rambling Along* (1918, *Beach Nuts* (1918), *Do Husbands Deceive?* (1918), *Hoot Mon* (1919).

Harry G. Keenan 15 June 1867 Indiana - 18 April 1944 Santa Ana, California. An actor since the 1890s, he joined Essanay sometime in 1911, but was gone by the end of the year. He returned in April 1913 and left again in January 1914 for American. He resumed stage acting in November 1916. His films include: *The Cup of Life* (1915), *Soul Mates* (1916).

Danny Kelleher (Daniel P. Kelleher) 13 May 1896 Califonia - 26 April 1958 Los Angeles, California. A Niles boy, he gradually worked his way in with Essanay as an assistant propman in 1913. He was in charge of props with the Chaplin unit and went with them to Los Angeles. He worked as a lighting technician in the 1920s, switched to sound with RKO and continued at that job for 27 years.

James T. Kelly 10 July 1854 Castlebar, Co. Mayo, Ireland - 12 November 1933 Los Angeles, California. His stage-acting experience dated from 1876. He joined the Chaplin Essanay unit in Los Angeles in September 1915, and continued with Chaplin at Mutual. He later worked for Universal and Hal Roach. Films include: *Easy Street* (1917), *The Immigrant* (1917).

Thomas Kelly ? - ? He joined the company as an actor in October 1911, and left some time in 1912 after he came to Niles with his daughter Violet.

Violet Kelly ? - ? A child actress and daughter of Thomas Kelly, she occasionally worked as Baby Kelly from 1911 to 1912.

Martin A. Killilay 17 June 1883 Kansas - 28 March 1964 Sacramento, California. A centerfielder on the Niles baseball team, he also acted for Essanay on occasion from October to December 1914 and was an assistant cameraman that year.

David S. Kirkland (David Swim) 26 November 1878 San Francisco, California - 27 October 1964 Vista, California. He'd acted for years on the stage before joining Essanay in June 1911. He left in December but was back in November 1912 and was directing by September 1913. He also acted in a few Snakeville Comedies, as Dr. Hippy, Dr. Dopeum or Dr. Killem. In December he left for the Burr McIntosh

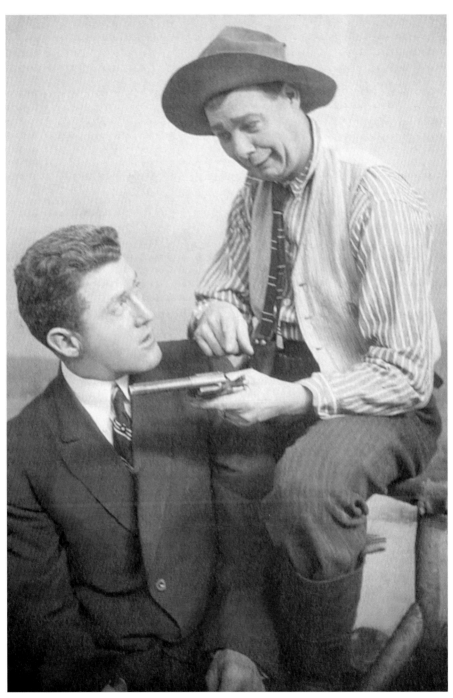

Martin Killilay and Harry Todd.

Film Company in Pleasanton. In March 1914 he was directing Universal Nestor dramas, then Sterling Comedies, Keystone Comedies in 1915 and Fox Sunshine Comedies in 1917. After World War I he directed features with Constance Talmadge, Fred Thompson and others. Films include: *The Crippled Hand* (1915), *A Virtuous Vamp* (1919), *The Perfect Woman* (1920), *Nothing But the Truth* (1920), *The Ladder Jinx* (1922), *The Tomboy* (1924), *The Tough Guy* (1926), *The Gingham Girl* (1927), *Riders of the Cactus* (1931), *El Impostor* (1937).

Charles La Due ? - ? He worked at Essanay as a cowboy from September 1913 to the spring of 1914.

Dee Lampton 6 October 1890 Ft. Worth, Texas - 2 September 1919 New York City. He was working as an actor for Keystone before he joined the Chaplin unit in September 1915. He later worked at Rolin in his own series. Films include: *Luke's Movie Muddle* (1916), *Skinny Gets a Goat* (1917), *Kicking the Germ Out of Germany* (1918), *Do Husbands Deceive?* (1918), *Hoot Mon* (1919).

Robert S. Lawler 14 September 1884 California - 20 July 1967 San Francisco, California. At the age of twenty he was on stage as an actor at Ye Liberty with Lloyd Ingraham, D. W. Griffith and Landers Stevens (father of film director George Stevens). He tried the movies in May 1912 with Essanay in Niles. Other films include: *Hoodoo Ann* (1916), *Casey at the Bat* (1916), *The Babes in the Woods* (1917), *Common Property* (1919).

Benjamin P. Lee 20 August 1858 Peoria, Illinois - 16 April 1937 Los Angeles, California. Stage manager at the Columbia Theater in Chicago, he was hired as a set carpenter by Anderson in September 1910. He went with Mackley's unit to Los Angeles in November 1912 and stayed there when the company disbanded in March 1913. Later he was the stage carpenter at the El Capitan Theater in Los Angeles.

Bonnie Leonard ? - ? She was an actress with the Chaplin unit in September 1915.

Henry Lilienthal (Carl Henry Lilienthal) ? - ? He was an occasional stagecoach driver and full-time night watchman at the Niles studio from 1914 to 1916.

Anna Little 7 February 1891 Siskiyou Co., California - 20 June 1984 Los Angeles, California. An actress with Ferris Hartman in 1908, her first movie work was with Essanay from April to August 1911. She was at Bison the next month, then went to Universal. She later worked at Triangle, American, Fox and Paramount. Her films include: *Custer's Last Raid* (1912), *Damon and Pythias* (1915), *Man Afraid of His Wardrobe* (1915), *Rimrock Jones* (1918), *Blue Blazes Rawden* (1918), *The Roaring Road* (1919), *The Love Expert* (1920), *Chain Lightning* (1922).

Elsa Lorimer ? - ? She acted with Essanay from January to March 1914.

Arthur Mackley (Arthur James Mackley) 3 July 1865 Scotland - 21 December 1926 Hollywood, California. An actor since the 1880s, he was working in Chicago when Anderson asked him to join his company. Mackley and his wife Elhilda went west in September 1910 and his first role was as a sheriff. He started directing in 1911, but it was a series of films in 1912-13 beginning with *The Sheriff's Luck* (him in the lead) that made his reputation. After running a unit in Hollywood from November 1912 to March 1913, he left Essanay in May for a European vacation. In August he returned to direct for Reliance-Majestic, but towards the end of his life only acted. Films include: *Loot* (1919), *The Sheriff's Oath* (1920), *Shootin' for Love* (1923), *The Hurricane Kid* (1925).

Julia Mackley (Elhilda Loretta Mackley) 30 October 1878 Virginia - 2 July 1964 Los Angeles, California. In 1910 she began playing small roles at Essanay. In 1912 she was even singled out, notably in *The Loafer's Mother*. When her husband Arthur began his sheriff series she played opposite him. Other films include: *Intolerance* (1916), *The Mother and the Law* (1919).

Marguerite Marsh, Margaret Loveridge 1892 Lawrence, Kansas - 8 December 1925 New York City. A Biograph actress and sister of May Marsh, she worked at Essanay when Vedah Bertram was incapacitated in March 1912. Her films include: *Blue Blood and Red* (1914), *Intolerance* (1916), *The Americano* (1916), *Casey at the Bat* (1916), *Fields of Honor* (1918), *The Mother and the Law* (1919), *Women Men Love* (1921).

Sam Marshall (Samuel Lyman Atwood Marshall) 18 July 1900 Catskill, New York - 17 December 1977 El Paso, Texas. He and his family settled in Niles by 1913. When he was in the eighth grade he was screen-tested and got a job with Essanay. In 1914 and 1915 he acted in the Snakeville Comedies and two Chaplin films. His career was cut short when he moved with his family to El Paso. He was a reporter for the El Paso Herald and Detroit News, served as a military historian in the U. S. Army and retired as a brigadier general.

Shorty Martin ? - ? He was a Niles resident recruited as an actor in May 1914.

Adolph H. Mayer 12 January 1872 San Francisco, California - 19 January 1944 San Francisco, California. A film projectionist since 1898, he was the operator in the Niles studio screening room. He was still a projectionist in 1941 at the Embassy Theater in San Francisco.

Emil T. Mazy 27 December 1865 Belgium - 6 June 1943 Los Angeles, California. He joined the Chaplin unit in Los Angeles in April 1915 as a scenic painter and followed Chaplin to Mutual.

May A. McCaskey ? - ? She and her partner/husband Earl Howell came to Essanay in November 1909 from the Curtis Stock Company, and acted in films until Essanay left Santa Barbara in March 1910. She was with her husband as a member of the Temple Players in Maiden, Massachusetts, when he died in 1918.

Lila McClemmon ? - ? She came from Oakland to act on occasion from 1913 to 1915. She was seriously hurt in a stagecoach accident in Niles Canyon in November 1914.

Vera McCord 1872 Iowa - 3 March 1949 New York City. Her parents were living in Oakland, California, when she joined Essanay as an actress in June 1913 after several years in New York working on Broadway. In July she was on stage at Ye Liberty in Oakland, in October at the Oriental Theater in San Francisco.

Paddy McGuire 1884 Ireland - 16 November 1923 Norwalk, California. He reportedly worked on stage with the Kolb and Dill company for five years before joining the Chaplin unit in February 1915 as an actor. He went with Chaplin to Los Angeles, and joined Vogue Films in November. By 1917 he was with Fox. His films include: *Bungling Bill, Detective* (1916), *The Iron Mitt* (1916), *Bing! Bang!* (1917), *Ladies First* (1918).

Ella McKenzie 9 April 1911 Oregon - 25 April 1987 Hollywood, California. A niece raised by Robert and Eva McKenzie, she became an actress at Essanay in May 1915. Her cousin Ida got in the act too and they became known as the McKenzie Twins. She continued film acting into the 1930s, and married film comedian Billy Gilbert. Her films include: *Jane Goes A'Wooing* (1919), *The Last Warning* (1929), *Alice Adams* (1935), *Riders of the Dawn* (1937), *The Wrong Miss Wright* (1937).

Ida Mae McKenzie 15 January 1911 Oregon - 29 June 1986 Los Angeles, California. She came to Niles with her parents Robert and Eva McKenzie in March 1915 and worked in her first film in May 1915. She acted at Essanay until January 1916, was in the Educational Film Company Chester Comedies in 1920, was a regular on "The Red Skelton Show" TV show and a contestant coordinator for "Hollywood Squares." Films include: *Jane Goes A'Wooing* (1919), *The Village Blacksmith* (1922), *Abraham Lincoln* (1924), *The Godless Girl* (1929), *International Squadron* (1941).

Robert McKenzie 22 September 1883 Ballymena, Ireland - 8 July 1949 Matunuck, Rhode Island. An actor on stage for years, he was at Ye Liberty in Oakland in June 1913, played leads with the Dick Ferns-Florence Stone Company in Long Beach in May 1914 and joined Essanay in Niles for his first film roles in March 1915. He stayed in Niles until January 1916, then moved his family to Los Angeles. His wife Eva Heazlett and daughters Ella, Ida and Fay also acted in films, and worked

Eva Heazlett, Ida Mae, Robert, and Ella McKenzie.

in his McKenzie Players stage productions. He died while in rehearsals for a play in Matunuck. A few of his many films include: *Oliver Twist* (1916), *A Western Demon* (1922), *Single-Handed* (1923), *Bad Man's Bluff* (1926), *Cimarron* (1931), *Tillie and Gus* (1933), *Six of a Kind* (1934), *It Always Happens* (1935), *Life Begins at Forty* (1935), *The Wrong Miss Wright* (1937), *Buried Alive* (1939), *Saps at Sea* (1940), *The Spoilers* (1942), *Duel in the Sun* (1946).

Larry Medeiros 8 July 1889 Honolulu, Hawaii - 22 July 1963 Fremont, California. He joined Essanay as a set carpenter in 1913, went to Los Angeles on 13 April 1914 with Jess Robbins to work at Robbins Photo Plays, returned to Niles, then went to Liberty Films in September 1914. Back in Niles by February 1915, he probably worked at the Essanay studio until it closed in 1916. He became a carpenter at Pacific States Steel in Niles.

Paul Miller ? - ? He was an actor with Essanay in November-December 1909.

Charlotte Mineau 24 March 1891 Bordeaux, France (or 24 March 1887 Michigan) - ? She came to the Chicago Essanay from Selig to act in the summer of 1914. She appeared in Chaplin's one film there, then joined his Essanay unit in Los Angeles. She acted in his Mutual comedies and later worked with Mary Pickford. Films include: *Easy Street* (1917), *Carolyn of the Corners* (1919), *You Wouldn't Believe It* (1920), *The Extra Girl* (1923), *Sparrows* (1926).

Belle Mitchell 24 September 1889 Michigan - 12 February 1979 Woodland Hills, California. She acted on stage extensively before and after her work with Essanay, which began in September 1915 and continued until the Niles studio closed in 1916. In the 1930s she worked at Paramount, Republic, MGM and Universal. Some of her films: *Just Rambling Along* (1918), *Hoot Mon* (1919), *The Leavenworth Case* (1936), *The Firefly* (1937), *The Mark of Zorro* (1940), *One Night in the Tropics* (1940).

Ira H. Morgan, Joe Morgan 2 April 1889 Fort Ross, California - 10 April 1959 San Rafael, California. His first work in the movie business was with Gaumont as a projectionist in Portland, Oregon, where he also shot newsreels. In April 1913 he opened a nickelodeon theater in Sunnyvale, California, with his father-in-law. He joined Essanay that year as a cameraman, left Niles for San Mateo and the Liberty Film Company in August 1914, met and married actress Rena Carlton after the death of his first wife, then returned to Niles after the Liberty Company failed. In 1916 he joined the American Film Company in Santa Barbara and was there until entering the U. S. Signal Corps in 1918. On his return from World War I he worked with King Vidor, Marion Davies and many other famous names at MGM. He shot dozens of films in the 1930s, 40s and 50s before his retirement in 1957. He was a longtime member of the American Society of Cinematographers. Films include: *Dust* (1916), *The Jack Knife Man* (1920), *When Knighthood Was in*

Flower (1922), *Janice Meredith* (1923), *Tell It to the Marines* (1926), *The Taxi Dancer* (1927), *Sinner's Holiday* (1930), *The Vampire Bat* (1933), *Modern Times* (1936), *Fighting Valley* (1943), *Leave It to the Irish* (1944), *The Lost Tribe* (1949), *Devil Goddess* (1955).

Louis J. Morisette ? - ? With Kalem in early 1911 as a cowboy, he joined Essanay in San Rafael that June. He left Niles with the Mackley unit in 1912 and stayed in Los Angeles when it disbanded in March 1913. He worked at the American Film Company in 1916 on the Art Acord "Buck Parvin" series and other films at least to 1920.

Corbett Morris (Louis Thompson) ? - ? In May 1909 he acted with the Charles King Stock Company in Long Beach. He worked as an actor with Essanay in February 1910 while acting at night as a member of the Girton Stock Company.

Chick Morrison (Charles P. Morrison) 3 April 1878 Morrison, Colorado - 20 June 1924 Hollywood, California. He worked in Colorado as a cowboy with Selig director Francis Boggs in the summer of 1908, and with Essanay in Anderson's first western series in January 1909. In September he joined Essanay full-time and traveled with them until April 1911, switching to the American Film Company. He later worked in *The Squaw Man* (1914), in *The Half-Breed* (1916) with Douglas Fairbanks and many others until an accident at the Hal Roach Studio ranch; a horse he was riding stumbled, fell on him and crushed him to death.

Pete Morrison (George D. Morrison) 8 August 1890 Westminster, Colorado - 5 February 1973 Los Angeles, California. Like his brother Chick, Pete also worked with Selig and Essanay in Colorado as a cowboy in 1908, 1909 and 1910, but stayed home until summoned by his brother to the American Film Company at La Mesa in late 1911. He went with the company when it settled in Santa Barbara and remained with them until 1916. He worked in westerns at Triangle in 1917, just as it was floundering, but he kept busy all through the 1920s. In 1935 he retired and moved back to Colorado to live on his ranch. A few films: *Man Afraid of His Wardrobe* (1915), *Fighting Back* (1917), *The Law's Outlaw* (1918), *The Fighting Brothers* (1919), *The Better Man Wins* (1922), *Mystery of Lost Ranch* (1925), *Chinatown Nights* (1929), *Five Bad Men* (1935).

Frank Murphy 1882 NY - ? He was a set carpenter and actor with Essanay from December 1909 to April 1910.

Anita Murray ? - ? She acted in a stock company with Essanay actor Lee Willard in 1909. In April 1913 she acted at Essanay.

Jack O'Brien (John B. O'Brien) 13 December 1884 Roanoke, Virginia - 15 August 1936 Los Angeles, California. Before joining Essanay in Chicago in June 1909 he was with the Augustus Thomas Stock Company. He went to Colorado in September 1909 with Anderson as actor and business manager, left to make *The Life of Buffalo Bill* in July 1911. He later directed with the Circle Ranch Film Company, Universal, Mutual, Powers, Famous Players, Metro, Thanhouser, De Luxe and his own company, O'Brien Productions. Films include: *Captain Macklin* (1915), *Hulda from Holland* (1916), *The Foundling* (1916), *Lonely Heart* (1921), *The Outlaw's Daughter* (1925).

Sophie Osborn (Sophia Osborn) 1900 California - ? A child actress, she and her brother Gordon were acting with the Elleford Stock Company in Santa Barbara when Essanay arrived and she worked with them in February and March 1910.

Hazel Padgett (Hazel Mitchell Padget) 1895 Kentucky - ? With Pathe in 1911 as Hazel Mitchell, she married Slim Padgett in January 1912 and worked with him and other cowboys (including Hoot Gibson, Dick Parker, Wallie Padgett, Wolf Verdugo, Jim Cathcart, Inez Clampitt and Hart Hoxie) in the traveling Frontier Days wild west show. She and Slim acted with Arthur Mackley's unit in Los Angeles starting in November 1912 and came to Niles when Mackley returned in April 1913. They stayed until September 1913, went back to Los Angeles and worked in films there. She was at Fox in *Bing! Bang!* (1917).

Slim Padgett (Harrington W. Padgett) 3 August 1887 Spearville, Kansas - 11 July 1964 Los Angeles, California. He and his brother Wallie were working as cowboys with Kalem in 1911. They quit along with Dell Eagles, Jessie Snow, George Souards, Hoot Gibson and Dick Parker in April to work elsewhere and some of them joined the Frontier Days wild west show that toured in 1912. After Slim and his wife Hazel worked with Essanay from November 1912 September 1913, Slim had a long career in westerns with William S. Hart, Buck Jones, Hoot Gibson, Pete Morrison, Jacques Jaccard, Fred Thompson and Tom Mix. He retired in 1945 after breaking his hip in a fall. Some of his films include: *Wild and Woolly* (1916), *Sunset Sprague* (1920), *Just Pals* (1920), *West of Arizona* (1925), *Shootin' Irons* (1927), *My Pal, the King* (1932).

Al Parks ? - ? He joined Essanay as a cowboy in the summer of 1911, played on the Niles baseball team in 1913 and left Essanay that year. He was working at Universal in 1916.

Earl B. Pearson ? - ? He joined Essanay as a scenic painter in 1912. In November he went to Los Angeles with the Mackley unit and stayed in that city when Mackley closed the unit in March 1913.

Perc Pembroke, Stanley Pembroke, Scott Pembroke (Percy Stanley Pembroke) 13 September 1889 San Francisco, California - 21 February 1951 Alhambra, California. He acted on stage at the Alcazar Theatre in San Francisco in 1913 and came to Essanay in Niles in October 1913 for his first film work. He acted at the Liberty Film Company in San Mateo in February and March, 1915, and returned to Niles after that, working behind the scenes more frequently (possibly as an assistant director), staying until the studio closed. At Golden West he was an assistant director to Jess Robbins from May to September 1918. He was also an assistant for the Amalgamated Producing Company shorts with Stan Laurel in 1922, and directed Laurel in 1923 for Hal Roach, then for Joe Rock in 1924, and directed at Century in 1925. In July 1927 he was signed by Columbia to direct comedies as Scott Pembroke, a name given to him by his wife, actress Gertrude Short. (Scott was a family name on his mother's side.) In the 1930s and 40s he was a writer, often working with William Anthony McGuire. Some of his films include: *The Son of a Gun* (1918), *Shootin' Mad* (1918), *Mud and Sand* (1922), *Uncensored Movies* (1923), *Rupert of Hee Haw* (1924), *Dr. Pyckle and Mr. Pride* (1925), *Polly of the Movies* (1927), *The Black Pearl* (1928), *Shanghai Rose* (1929), *The Medicine Man* (1930), *The Oregon Trail* (1936).

Frank Pementel 28 March 1889 Decoto, California - 1 February 1934 Niles, California. He was recruited as a cowboy in April 1912 and remained with the company until it closed in 1916. He was a horse dealer with his brother Manuel for the rest of his life.

Arthur A. Penn 1876 London - 6 February 1941 New London, Connecticut. He was a Niles Essanay publicity writer in September 1913, wrote the lyrics to Marie Dressler's *Merry Gambol* stage production, the music for the Essanay song "Broncho Billy" in 1914, composed more than thirty operettas, and a popular song, "Smilin' Through," which served as the basis for the 1932 movie *Smilin' Through*.

Harry Pollard, Snub Pollard (Harold Fraser) 9 November 1893 Melbourne, Australia - 19 January 1962 Burbank, California. An actor with stage experience from 1910, he joined Essanay in Niles in March 1915. He went with the Chaplin unit to Los Angeles and moved to Rolin for the Lonesome Luke Comedies. He starred in his own films for Hal Roach and acted in many, many films until his death. A few of his films: *Lonesome Luke, Social Gangster* (1915), *Luke's Movie Muddle* (1916), *Lonesome Luke, Messenger* (1917), *Bees in His Bonnet* (1918), *His Royal Slyness* (1920), *The Dumb Bell* (1923), *Do Your Duty* (1927), *Midnight Patrol* (1934), *The White Legion* (1937), *Arizona Days* (1938), *Phony Express* (1943), *Limelight* (1952), *Pete Kelly's Blues* (1957), *Pocketful of Miracles* (1963).

Jack Pollard ? - ? An actor at the Gaiety Theater in December 1914, he worked in Niles in 1915 and went with Chaplin's unit to Los Angeles, but mostly worked in Hal Roach's Essanay films.

Victor Potel 12 October 1889 Lafayette, Indiana - 8 March 1947 Hollywood, California. Anderson hired him in Chicago on 20 July 1910 to play Lank in his

Hank and Lank Comedies. He went west with Anderson's division in September, played supporting roles in westerns, then became Slippery Slim in the Snakeville comedy series created by Anderson. He left Essanay on 1 September 1915 to work in a comedy series directed by Roy Clements at Universal, similar to Potel's character roles at Essanay. He subsequently worked for many companies, among them Triangle-Keystone, Sunshine Comedies, the Victor Potel Homespun Comedy Company, MGM, Goldwyn and Paramount. Films include: *When Slim Picked a Peach* (1916), *Mary's Ankle* (1920), *Quincy Adams Sawyer* (1922), *The Law Forbids* (1924), *The Virginian* (1929), *Doughboys* (1930), *Ruggles of Red Gap* (1935), *Three Godfathers* (1936), *Christmas in July* (1940), *Sullivan's Travels* (1941), *Hail the Conquering Hero* (1944), *The Egg and I* (1947).

Dean Preston 1890 California - ? He was a Niles studio clerk in August 1913.

Eva Prince ? - ? She worked as an actress in Niles in August 1915.

Edna Purviance (Olga Edna Purviance) 21 October 1895 Paradise Valley, Nevada - 13 January 1958 Woodland Hills, California. She was hired as an actress in January 1915 and came to Niles to play opposite Chaplin in *A Night Out*. She remained for all of his Essanay films and went with him to Mutual, then First National. Her last film opposite him was *The Pilgrim*, then he directed a starring film for her, *A Woman of Paris*, both released in 1923. She married aviator John P. Squire.

John F. Rand 19 November 1871 New Haven, Connecticut - 25 January 1940 Hollywood, California. An acrobat and vaudeville performer, he joined Chaplin's unit in Los Angeles as an actor in July 1915, and worked with Chaplin several times over the years. Films include: *Easy Street* (1917), *Bow Wow* (1922), *The Circus* (1928), *City Lights* (1931), *Modern Times* (1936)

Josephine Rector 25 September 1885 Indiana - 1 October 1958 Castro Valley, California. She sold her first scripts to Essanay when the company was in Los Gatos in 1910-11, worked again with them in San Rafael and took over the scenario department in Niles when they arrived in April 1912. She also acted in small parts in San Rafael, then took on leads in Niles. She quit Essanay in April 1914 and married Hal Angus later that year. She was with the Pacific Motion Picture Company in May 1914 and the Yolo Film Company in March 1915.

Margie Rieger ? - ? She joined Essanay in January 1915 as an actress, went with the Chaplin unit to Los Angeles in April and ended her film career in July.

Hal Roach 14 January 1892 Elmira, New York - 2 November 1992 Los Angeles, California. He got his start in films by answering a want ad in a Los Angeles paper for extras in Universal westerns. In 1914 he inherited $3,000 and decided to produce films with a partner, Dan Linthicum. Their company, Rolin, was broke by early 1915 so Roach found a job for a month at Charlie Chaplin's Los Angeles-based Essanay studio at the Bradbury mansion, directing a series of one-reel films with the cast members Chaplin didn't need each week. When Rolin got a distribution contract with Pathe, Roach was back in business producing Lonesome Luke Comedies with Harold Lloyd. After a slow buildup to success, Linthicum was bought out and the company became Hal Roach Studios, a formidable rival to Mack Sennett and one that would outlast the Keystone Company.

Spider Roach (James F. Roach) 22 September 1893 San Francisco, California - 10 December 1956 Agnew, California. A lightweight boxer, he was with Essanay in February 1912 at Lakeside, played right field on the Niles baseball team, and acted with the company until November 1914. He continued to fight professionally in the 1920s, then became a trainer and worked with the United States Olympic boxing team in 1932. He was a coach for the Olympic Club in San Francisco for 28 years.

Jess Robbins (Jesse Jerome Robbins) 30 April 1888 Galion, Ohio - 11 March 1973 Los Angeles, California. He managed a nickelodeon theater in Middletown, Ohio, as a teenager in 1907. In 1908 he became a cameraman with Essanay, at the end of that year going west with Anderson to shoot the company's first films in California. His first wife Nancy came along, playing small parts during his second trip with Anderson in 1909. Anderson's division settled in Niles in 1912 and Robbins became the general manager of that studio in 1913. He left a year later to start the Robbins Photo Plays Company in Los Angeles, but returned to supervise the Charles Chaplin films for Essanay in December 1914. When Anderson sold out to Spoor, Jess was supposed to take over the Niles studio, but it closed in February 1916, and Robbins went to New Jersey to set up Anderson's studio space in Fort Lee for the feature film *Vera, The Medium*. Robbins worked again with Anderson in 1918, directing Golden West films. Jess also directed Anderson's first Amalgamated film, *The Lucky Dog*, with Stan Laurel and Oliver Hardy. Jess spent the rest of the 1920s directing Lupino Lane, Jimmy Aubrey, Syd Chaplin, Baby Peggy, Ben Turpin and others. He quit the movie business in 1929, but kept busy running a taxi service, a machine screw factory and, in his eighties, he was a machinist at a water purifying equipment company. Some of his films: *When a Woman Loves* (1914), *The Son of a Gun* (1918), *The Backyard* (1920), *Too Much Business* (1922), *The Ladder Jinx* (1922), *A Front Page Story* (1922), *The Law Forbids* (1924), *Skirts* (1928).

Jack Roberts (John A. Roberts) 5 September 1890 San Francisco, California - 17 September 1960 Ben Lomond, California. In his youth he worked on several cattle ranches including the Hayes Ranch and the Miller and Lux Ranch. He participated in the last cattle drive at the Chowchilla Ranch in 1912. He was a cowboy with Essanay from the spring of 1913 to 1915.

Edna Robinson ? - ? An actress at Ye Liberty in Oakland from 1908, she worked at Essanay in November 1915.

Edward R. Robinson ? - ? He was a set carpenter for Essanay in 1914.

Ethel G. Robinson 16 March 1886 Oakland, California – 16 March 1971 Forestville, California. She acted with Essanay in San Rafael in 1911. Her father, Merritt Robinson, owned a livery stable in town.

Kite Robinson (Raymond Robinson) 1889 South Dakota - ? He was a propman, an actor and a first baseman on the Niles baseball team. He got his start at the Chicago studio in 1909 and traveled west with Anderson in September 1910. He married Niles girl Malvina Chaix in October 1912. When the Niles studio closed he got a job with the Orpheum Theatre in Oakland as an electrician, but by 1920 he was in Los Angeles as a propman in the movie business.

Patrick T. Rooney (Frederick E. Ratsch) 28 April 1889 Chicago, Illinois - 15 January 1933 Hollywood, California. He joined Essanay as an actor in June 1911. He replaced Anderson's chauffeur, Richard Young, in November 1911 after Young had an accident, then had an accident of his own in February 1912. He left Niles for Lubin in May 1915, later working with Douglas Fairbanks. He was briefly married to actress Grace Darling. His films include: *The Actors' Boarding House* (1915), *Some Medicine Man* (1916), *A Pirate Bold* (1917).

Wesley Ruggles 11 June 1889 Los Angeles, California - 8 January 1972 Santa Monica, California. After touring the Pacific Coast in stock companies he began his film work as an actor at Keystone in 1914. He joined the Essanay Chaplin unit in July 1915, stayed until it disbanded, worked as an actor at Vitagraph, and a director at FBO, Paramount, Universal, RKO, Columbia and MGM. His films include: *The Plastic Age* (1926), *Silk Stockings* (1927), *Cimmarron* (1931), *I'm No Angel* (1933), *Arizona* (1940).

William A. Russell 1878 Illinois - 11 January 1914 Hollywood, California. He began as a propman with Essanay in Chicago in 1909, left with Anderson for Colorado in September, and also filled in as an actor. He left Niles with the Mackley unit for Los Angeles in November 1912. Tuberculosis prevented him from returning in 1913, and he never recovered.

Bessie Sankey 1891 Oakland, California - ? She began acting with Ye Liberty in Oakland in April 1907, toured with the Marjorie Rambeau Company in 1912, and joined Essanay in Niles in November 1912. She left in May 1913, toured with Oliver Morosco's stage production of *The Traffic* and continued in the theater until at least 1917. Her films include: *Blue Grass* (1915), *The Heart of New York* (1916).

Bessie Sankey and G. M. Anderson in Broncho Billy and the Western Girls.

Jack Wood, Frank Pementel, Charles La Due, Perc Pembroke, ?, ?, Harry Todd, and Lee Willard in A Borrowed Identity.

Pat Rooney towers over the Essanay boxing contingent: Al Herman, Spider Roach, Red Watson and two unknowns in front of Victor Potel on the right.

Stanley Sargent 31 March 1895 California - 28 September 1949 Los Angeles, California. The son of a Monterey superior court judge, he joined Essanay as a cowboy in October 1912 and stayed until October 1914.

Ruth Saville 7 June 1892 Allessandro, California - 31 March 1985 Los Angeles, California. She began acting on the stage in 1905 and was with the Belasco Stock Company by 1909. She came to Essanay in September 1915 and stayed until January 1916. Her long career included many appearances on stage, radio and television. Films include: *None So Blind* (1916), *Never Too Late* (1965).

Bernice Sawyer (Nellie Bogdon) 25 May 1911 San Francisco, California - 17 March 1978 Brooklyn, New York. She was a child actress in *Broncho Billy and the Baby,* the first of her three 1915 Anderson westerns when she was staying with friends of her family, the Sawyers. As Sally Phipps she began a second movie career (named as a Wampas Baby Star in 1927) working in several Fox films until 1930, when she took a part in the Kaufman and Hart play *Once in a Lifetime.* Her films include: *Bertha the Sewing Machine Girl* (1926), *The Cradle Snatchers* (1927), *None But the Brave* (1928).

Eva Sawyer ? - 27 May 1955 Oakland, California. Wife of Essanay set designer Warren Sawyer, she acted in Niles from the fall of 1914 to the closing of the studio in 1916, except for two months recovering from a stagecoach accident in Niles Canyon in November 1914.

Warren Sawyer 4 August 1877 Ohio - 11 April 1952 San Leandro, California. On the stage crew at the Orpheum and Ye Liberty theaters in Oakland, he joined Essanay in June 1913, took charge of the prop department, and occasionally acted in small parts until the studio closed in 1916. Thereafter, he once again worked in Oakland theaters.

Ruth Schrock ? - ? She acted for Essanay in Morrison, Colorado, in September and October 1909.

Dick Scott (Richard Scott) ? - ? He was an actor at Essanay in Santa Barbara in February 1910 while performing at night with the Girton Stock Company.

Lee Scott (Edmund Lee Scott) 16 August 1863 Milpitas, California - 27 March 1940 Redwood City, California. The owner of the Live Oak saloon in Niles Canyon, he became the janitor at the Essanay studio in July 1913, when his business failed. He also acted in films until the studio closed in 1916. His wife Elizabeth was an extra with the company in late 1915.

Evelyn Selbie, Jet Selbie (Evelyn Selby) 6 July 1880 Louisville, Kentucky - 7 December 1950 Los Angeles, California. An actress on stage since the 1890s, she

Bernice Sawyer in Broncho Billy and the Baby.

Warren Sawyer, Tom Crizer, True Boardman, Fritz Wintermeier, Jack Roberts and Bill Cato in Broncho Billy and the Escaped Bandits.

came to Essanay from the Melies Film Company in October 1912. She stayed until March 1915, then went to Universal. She later played small roles in a variety of films: *The Devil to Pay* (1920), *Cafe in Cairo* (1924), *Camille* (1927), *King of Kings* (1927), *Wings* (1929), *The Return of Fu Manchu* (1930), *The Merry Widow* (1934), *Two in a Crowd* (1936), *Tower of London* (1939).

Edna Sharpe 23 July 1890 Oakland, California – 27 January 1967 San Francisco, California. An actress at Ye Liberty in 1910, she joined Essanay in September 1912 and worked off and on until July 1913. Her grandmother owned the Belvoir Hotel in Niles.

Brinsley Shaw (Sheldon Brinsley Shaw Jr.) 1876 New York City - ? An actor on stage since the 1890s, his first film work was with New York Cameraphone. He joined Essanay in Chicago in May 1910 and left in October 1913 for Vitagraph, later acting at Lubin, Universal and Metro. He returned to the Broadway stage in the late 1920s. His films include: *The Man of Mystery* (1917), *The Hornet's Nest* (1919), *Hearts Are Trumps* (1920), *The Four Horsemen of the Apocalypse* (1921), *Three Wise Fools* (1923), *Bucking the Truth* (1926).

Arthur Smith ? - ? He was an actor with Essanay from September 1909 to June 1910.

Joseph G. Smith ? - ? In January 1909 he was a car mechanic in Denver; in October he was an Essanay actor, and remained so until March 1911.

Carl Stockdale (William Carlton Stockdale) 19 February 1874 Worthington, Minnesota – 15 March 1953 Woodland Hills, California. He acted in many Essanay western dramas with Anderson and played Dr. Bealy Byers (his real-life wife was Clara Byers) in the Snakeville Comedies. He went to the Liberty Film Company in February 1915, returned to Niles in March, acted in Chaplin's *The Bank* in Los Angeles, and appeared in Essanay features directed in 1917 by W. S. Van Dyke. Like his stage career, his movie career was long and active. A few films include: *Intolerance* (1916), *Open Places* (1917), *Molly O* (1921), *The Extra Girl* (1923), *The Love Parade* (1929), *The Vampire Bat* (1933), *Lost Horizon* (1937), *The Devil and Daniel Webster* (1941).

Frank Stockdale (Franklin E. Stockdale) 30 November 1870 Fairfield Co., Ohio - 31 December 1950 Los Angeles, California. The brother of Carl Stockdale, he was an actor with Essanay from March to October 1914. He had very small parts in many films, among them: *The Gold Rush* (1925).

William T. Stockdale 16 July 1845 Pennsylvania - 24 June 1923 Los Angeles, California. The father of Carl and Frank, he was an actor in Niles during the summer of 1914.

Brinsley Shaw and Evelyn Selbie in The Last Shot.

Earl Sudderth (Robert Earl Sudderth) 14 September 1891 Lenoir, North Carolina - 10 June 1957 Oakland, California. A student of the artist A. D. M. Cooper, he was a scenic painter with Essanay beginning in November 1913. He went to the Liberty Film Company in September 1914, but returned to Niles by March 1915. He later worked at Lawrence Abrott's Western Scenic Studios in Oakland.

Frank Sund 1893? Dundee, Illinois - 4 April 1933 Long Beach, California. He was a scenic painter, a catcher on the Essanay baseball team and an actor from October 1913 to June 1914.

Beth Taylor 28 June 1888 New York City - 1 March 1951 Hollywood, California. She acted with the Belasco Stock Company in Los Angeles in 1909, Ye Liberty in Oakland in 1911, played opposite Charles Ruggles at the Alcazar Theatre in San Francisco later that year. She joined Essanay in August 1912 and left in December for the Redmond Stock Company in Sacramento. She went to Hollywood in 1921.

May Thorn ? - ? She acted in *Broncho Billy and the Sisters* as one of the sisters in 1914.

Elmer C. Thompson 1884 Nebraska - ? He joined the Essanay company in Santa Barbara as an actor in January 1910, traveled to Chicago with them and returned west with the company, leaving them by May 1911.

Harry Todd, William Todd (John Nelson Todd) 13 December 1863 Allegheny Co., Pennsylvania - 15 February 1935 Glendale, California. His stage career began in 1877 in a production of *Uncle Tom's Cabin*. He acted with Essanay in its early days, went to Selig in 1909, then returned to Essanay by February 1910. Anderson took him west in September 1910. He acted in many Essanay western dramas and also appeared as Mustang Pete in the Snakeville Comedies, as did his wife Margaret Joslin. Their daughter Marguerite was sometimes an extra in films. Harry stayed with Essanay until the Niles studio closed in 1916, then worked at Universal, Rolin, Golden West, Metro, Columbia and many others. Among his many films: *Luke's Movie Muddle* (1916), *Lonesome Luke, Messenger* (1917), *Skinny Gets a Goat* (1917), *Red Blood and Yellow* (1918), *The Son of a Gun* (1918), *Hoot Mon* (1919), *Fickle Women* (1920), *The Jack Knife Man* (1920), *Penrod* (1922), *The Hurricane Kid* (1925), *King of the Congo* (1929), *The Fighting Legion* (1930), *The Texas Ranger* (1931), *It Happened One Night* (1934).

Rollie Totheroh (Roland H. Totheroh) 29 November 1890 San Francisco, California - 17 June 1967 Hollywood, California. He came to Niles to play on the baseball team in August 1912, and became an actor with Essanay. He learned to operate a movie camera and took up that profession with Essanay in June 1913, working on Broncho Billy westerns and Snakeville Comedies. His wife Ida (a sister of Kite Robinson's wife Malvina) appeared in some of the last Essanay films in 1915, and Rollie's son Jack was the baby in *The Bachelor's Baby*. When the studio closed in 1916 he went to Los Angeles, was hired by Chaplin for his Mutual films and continued to work with him until retirement in 1954. He was a member of the American Society of Cinematographers. Some of the films he photographed: *Easy Street* (1917), *A Dog's Life* (1918), *The Kid* (1921), *A Woman of Paris* (1923), *The Gold Rush* (1925), *City Lights* (1931), *Modern Times* (1936).

J. Travers ? - ? He was an actor with Essanay from January to August 1910.

Ben Turpin (Bernard Turpin) 19 September 1869 New Orleans, Louisiana - 1 July 1940 Santa Monica, California. A vaudeville veteran, he was discovered by Anderson and became Essanay's first actor (1907). He went with Anderson on his first trip to California in 1908 and acted in Essanay's Colorado westerns in January 1909, but quit the company that spring and returned to vaudeville in his "Happy Hooligan" act. He came back to Essanay in 1913, worked in the Sweedie Comedies and the George Ade Fables, and acted in Chaplin's first Essanay film, *His New Job*. He came to Niles with Chaplin, appearing in Chaplin's first two Niles films. His wife Carrie often acted with him at Essanay in Niles. After the Niles studio closed in January 1916, he worked in the expanded version of *Burlesque on Carmen*, then went to Vogue Films for a year. At Mack Sennett's Keystone studio he reached his greatest success. Some of his films: *A Clever Dummy* (1917), *East Lynne with Variations* (1919), *A Small Town Idol* (1921), *Three Foolish Weeks* (1924), *Million Dollar Legs* 1932), *Keystone Hotel* (1935), *Saps at Sea* (1940).

Carrie Turpin 1878 Quebec, Canada - 1 October 1925 Beverly Hills, California. The wife of Ben Turpin, she acted at Essanay in Niles from March 1915 until the studio's closing in 1916.

Reina Valdez 1890? Springfield, Massachusetts - ? A dancer, she went into movies with Lubin, joined Essanay as an actress in September 1913 and left in March 1914. She also worked at Kalem, Lasky, Eclair and directed at Ideal. Her films include: *The Weaker Mind* (1913), *The Woman He Married* (1915), *Mismated* (1916).

Ernest Van Pelt 31 March 1883 Kansas - 1 July 1961 Los Angeles, California. He began his theatrical career at the Burbank Theater in Los Angeles, working there three and a half years. He was with the Keating and Flood Musical Comedy Company in Portland, Oregon, in 1911. He and his wife Ella partnered in a vaudeville routine, "The Chattering Chums." For two years he was an actor with Dillon and King in the San Francisco Bay Area, then he came to Essanay as an actor in July 1914. He played Hiram Clutts in the Snakeville Comedies, and acted in several of the Chaplin Niles films. He left Essanay in April 1915. For twenty years he worked in the public relations department at Loew's, Incorporated, a theater management company. His films include: *Bring Him In* (1921), *Avenging Fangs* (1927), *I Live for Love* (1935).

Carrie Clark Ward 9 January 1862 Virginia City, Nevada - 6 February 1926 Hollywood, California. A veteran stage performer, she joined the Chaplin Essanay unit in Los Angeles as an actress in July 1915 and stayed until October. Later films include: *The Honor System* (1917), *Penrod* (1922), *Scaramouche* (1923), *The Eagle* (1925).

Red Watson ? - ? He was a boxer who joined Essanay in San Diego in January 1912. He acted, and played on the Niles baseball team before leaving in late 1913.

Charley West ? - ? He was an electrician with Essanay in December 1913.

Hazel West 1896 Louisiana - ? She was an actress with Essanay in August 1915. Her husband was Essanay scenic painter Leo West.

Howard Dunbar West 21 September 1880 San Francisco, California – 5 November 1965 Yountville, California. He was an Essanay assistant cameraman from 1913 to 1916.

Leo Goden West 1 June 1891 Sacramento, California – 23 September 1966 Santa Cruz, California. A student of artist A. D. M. Cooper, he was an Essanay scenic painter and actor from January 1914 to January 1916. He worked at the Strand Theater in San Diego from 1919 to 1924, in Hollywood after that, and then at CBS television until his retirement in 1959. He moved to Santa Cruz and taught classes in art to senior citizens during his last years. His son Davis West was a scenic painter for the San Francisco Opera.

Neva West (Neva West Clements) 10 September 1883 California - 5 October 1965 Glendale, California. The wife of Essanay director Roy Clements, she'd been a stage actress before their marriage, and signed with Francis Boggs in May 1909 when he was visiting San Francisco with Selig Polyscope, but in June 1910 she was back on stage with the Girton Stock Company at the Grand Theater. She played small roles at Essanay in 1914 and 1915.

Arthur S. White 11 September 1881 England - 27 September 1924 Los Angeles, California. He was a scenic painter and actor with Essanay from September 1909 to March 1912. In May he was with Bison, then worked for the American Film Company and, lastly, the Fox Film Company.

Leo White 10 November 1882 Manchester, England (or Graudenz, Germany) - 20 September 1948 Hollywood, California. He made his debut as an actor on stage in 1902, and came to Essanay in Chicago in July 1912. His first film was

Three to One. He appeared in some of Essanay's George Ade Fables and many other comedies for the company. He was in Chaplin's Essanay film *His New Job*, came to Niles with Chaplin and went with Chaplin to Los Angeles. After Chaplin left Essanay Leo reportedly directed additional scenes for *Burlesque on Carman* to expand it from two reels to four reels. He originated his character of the French count in the Chaplin Essanay films and kept playing the role in the King Bee films of Chaplin imitator Billy West. He also acted with Chaplin in some of Chaplin's Mutual films, worked at the Hal Roach Studios and was a contract player with Warner Brothers for fourteen years. A few of his many films: *Dough-Nuts* (1917), *The Handy Man* (1918), *The Chauffeur* (1919), *The Devil's Passkey* (1920), *Blood and Sand* (1922), *Why Worry* (1923), *Ben-Hur* (1925), *Roarin' Ranch* (1930), *Rasputin and the Empress* (1932), *The Kennel Murder Case* (1933), *The Thin Man* (1934), *A Night at the Opera* (1935), *The Great Dictator* (1940), *Meet John Doe* (1941), *Arsenic and Old Lace* (1944), *In Old New Mexico* (1945), *My Wild Irish Rose* (1947).

May White ? - ? She acted with Essanay in Niles briefly before leaving with the Chaplin unit for Los Angeles. She continued with Chaplin at Mutual. Films include: *The Beauty Hunters* (1916), *The Adventurer* (1917).

Lee Willard (Asa Lee Willard) June 1873 Illinois - 9 December 1940 San Francisco, California. A stage actor beginning in 1903, he joined Essanay in April 1913 and remained with the company until the studio closed in 1916. He continued acting both in Los Angeles and in the San Francisco Bay Area for the rest of his life. Films include: *The Mediator* (1916), *The Last Edition* (1925), *The Fourth Commandment* (1927), *The Man with Nine Lives* (1940).

Clara Williams, Clara Hall (Clara Williams Hall) 3 May 1888 Seattle, Washington - 8 May 1928 Los Angeles, California. An actress on stage since 1908, she came to Essanay in December 1909 with her husband Franklyn Hall. Her first film was *The Cowboy and the Squaw*. She and Hall left Essanay in October 1910, went back to Chicago for an engagement on stage and returned to films with Lubin in Philadelphia. After a year she came to California and joined the New York Motion Picture Corporation studio in Santa Monica, known as Inceville. She worked there until signing with Paralta in 1917. She retired after marrying director Reginald Barker in 1920. Some of her films: *The Bargain* (1914), *The Italian* (1915), *Hell's Hinges* (1916), *The One Woman* (1918).

Shortie Wilson (Tom Wilson?) ? - ? He was an actor with Essanay from December 1914, and went to Los Angeles with the Chaplin unit in April 1915.

Fritz Wintermeier (Fred C. Wintermeyer) 15 April 1892 Muscatine, Iowa - 18 March 1970 Newport Beach, California. He came to Niles as an actor in the

Clara Williams tends Jack O'Brien under the watchful eyes of bandits Fred Church, G. M. Anderson, Frank Hall and Arthur Smith in The Pony Express Rider.

Things look bad for Harry Todd when Margaret Joslin and Victor Potel want to get married in Sophie and the Man of Her Choice.

summer of 1912, left for Los Angeles in 1913, returned in March 1914. He stayed with Essanay until February 1916, when he brought the rough-cut of G. M. Anderson's feature, *Humanity*, to New Orleans and then assisted him in New York and Fort Lee during the making of *Vera, the Medium*. As Fred Windermere he directed films in the 1920s, and married actress Belle Bennett in 1924. His films include: *The Prince Chap* (1916), *Won By a Nose* (1920), *The Verdict* (1925), *Broadway After Midnight* (1927), *Devil Dogs* (1928).

Darr Wittenmyer (Darrell Wittenmyer) 10 October 1888 California - 6 Dec 1940 Yountville, California. Raised in Oakland, California, he joined Essanay in February 1914 as a bookkeeper, actor and baseball player (second base) and stayed until the studio closed in 1916. He married Niles girl Mae Enos.

Jack Wood (John A. Wood) ? - ? He was a cowboy for the Mackley unit in Los Angeles in 1912, came to Niles when the unit disbanded and stayed until May 1914. He worked at Universal in 1916.

Marie Woods ? - ? She was an Essanay actress in 1914.

Martin Woods ? - ? He was an Essanay actor in 1914.

Richard Young ? - ? He was an Essanay cowboy and Anderson's chauffeur from June to November 1911 until a car accident nearly killed him. He was alone, driving at night when the car went off the road and rolled over into water. He would have drowned if a passerby hadn't pulled him free, but he was in a hospital for a month and never rejoined the company.

Henry Youngman 7 November 1846 Shelbyville, Indiana - 24 December 1940 San Francisco, California. He was a Civil War veteran and Niles resident, hired when the Essanay studio opened in June 1913 to take care of the horse stable. He also acted in many Essanay films until the studio closed in 1916.

Filmography

The following list represents both the output of Gilbert M. Anderson and the members of his Western Essanay company. Film titles are listed in chronological order by release date, when known. Where the release date is uncertain a "?" follows the date. Copyright dates are listed beginning in December, 1914. Any two consecutive films with the same date were released together (known as a split reel). All films are one reel (35mm, 1000 ft.) unless otherwise noted. Unknown film length is indicated by "? ft." Filming locations follow if known. Anderson is assumed to be the producer, director, editor and writer of his films until late 1909, when he added acting to his duties, and began to use, on occasion, scenarios written by other people. His directing credit followed by a "?" indicates uncertainty as to his involvement with a film. Anderson's cameraman from 1907 to mid-1908 was Gilbert P. Hamilton, then Jesse J. Robbins took over until he became manager of the Niles studio in 1913. Rollie Totheroh and Ira Morgan worked on later films. Other crew people (never credited on screen at Essanay) can roughly be determined by their dates of employment; for that information, when not listed, see the personnel section. Ben Turpin was the only regularly employed actor at first, but his credit in each film is only listed when comfirmed. Cast credits have been compiled from trade magazine listings, and through visual sightings in still photographs and movies that have survived. Character names or descriptions follow in parentheses. A synopsis of the film is given when known. Remake information follows the synopsis in parentheses. When the film is known to exist in some form the film title is preceeded by an "*" and the viewing source is contained in brackets at the end of the listing. Sources include: George Eastman House [GEH], The Museum of Modern Art, New York [MOMA], Library of Congress [LOC], University of California at Los Angeles [UCLA], National Film and Television Archive, London [NFTA], Nederlands Filmmuseum, Amsterdam [NFMA], Pacific Film Archive, Berkeley [PFA], video dealers [video]. Abbreviations: D: director, P: photographer, ST: story, SC: scenario, C: cast, S: synopsis.

1907

An Awful Skate; or, the Hobo on Rollers 27 July 1907 683 ft. Chicago D: G. M. Anderson C: Ben Turpin (hobo) S: A hobo runs into people on the street while rollerskating. [GEH]

Slow But Sure 10 August 1907 647 ft. Chicago D: G. M. Anderson S: A messenger, distracted by life in the city, delivers a boy's theater invitation to a girl too late and is beaten up by the boy.

Mr. Inquisitive 24 August 1907 647 ft. Chicago D: G. M. Anderson C: Ben Turpin S: A man's curiosity creates havoc until he releases a prisoner from a patrol wagon and is arrested.

Life of a Bootblack; or, The Street Urchin 7 September 1907 926 ft. Chicago D: G. M. Anderson S: A boy lives on the street after running away from an abusive stepfather.

The Dancing Nig 21 September 1907 390 ft. Chicago D: G. M. Anderson S: A black man can't help dancing when he hears music, even though he's fired from his job each time because of it.

99 in the Shade 28 September 1907 300 ft. Chicago D: G. M. Anderson S: A plumber puts his soldering furnace under a chair, making it uncomfortably hot for the unsuspecting people who sit on the chair.

Hey There! Look Out! 19 October 1907 400 ft. Chicago D: G. M. Anderson S: Two youngsters drive recklessly.

The Vagabond 26 October 1907 770 ft. Chicago D: G. M. Anderson S: A wealthy man ruins the life of a family man, turning the man into a thief.

A Free Lunch 2 November 1907 ? ft. Chicago D: G. M. Anderson C: Ben Turpin

The Street Fakir 2 November 1907 ? ft. Chicago D: G. M. Anderson

Where Is My Hair? 14 December 1907 400 ft. Chicago D: G. M. Anderson S: A bald-headed man pulls the hair of many people while looking for his stolen toupee.

The Bell Boy's Revenge 28 December 1907 385 ft. Chicago D: G. M. Anderson S: A bell boy escorts a cheapskate man to the wrong room and mayhem follows.

1908

The Football Craze 4 January 1908 650 ft. Chicago D: G. M. Anderson S: Football players chase a bouncing ball through the streets.

Jack of All Trades 11 January 1908 650 ft. Chicago D: G. M. Anderson S: Jack fails as a coachman, expressman, painter, paperhanger, baker and plumber.

Novice on Stilts 18 January 1908 400 ft. Chicago D: G. M. Anderson S: A young man on stilts disrupts everyone's life until a bulldog latches onto his pants.

A Home at Last 18 January 1908 250 ft. Chicago D: G. M. Anderson S: A stray dog suffers on the streets until taken home by a lady after recovering her purse. (remake of Anderson's Selig

Polyscope film *The Tramp Dog*, released 12 January 1907)

The Hoosier Fighter 1 February 1908 800 ft. Chicago D: G. M. Anderson S: A young man saves the family farm by winning a prize fight.

Babies Will Play 8 February 1908 750 ft. Chicago D: G. M. Anderson S: A child creates mischief in the house until put to bed.

Louder Please 15 February 1908 350 ft. Chicago D: G. M. Anderson S: A deaf old man is repeatedly informed, to no avail, by pedestrians that his frightened horse has run away, until it is learned, by written note, that the horse isn't his.

The Dog Cop 22 February 1908? 585 ft. Chicago D: G. M. Anderson

All is Fair in Love and War 4 March 1908 823 ft. Chicago D: G. M. Anderson S: Three young men woo a lady, each sabotaged by the other two, until they are chased off by a policeman, who escorts the lady away.

Well-Thy Water 11 March 1908? 310 ft. Chicago D: G. M. Anderson

Juggler Juggles 11 March 1908? 418 ft. Chicago D: G. M. Anderson

Hypnotizing Mother-in-Law 18 March 1908? 552 ft. Chicago D: G. M. Anderson S: A newly married man tries to get his live-in mother-in-law out of the house by using a mail order course in hypnotism.

A Lord for a Day 25 March 1908? 889 ft. Chicago D: G. M. Anderson

James Boys in Missouri 8 April 1908? Riverview Park in Chicago and Scotdale, Michigan D: G. M. Anderson C:Harry McCabe S: The major events in the lives of Frank and Jesse James are presented.

Don't Pull My Leg 6 May 1908 425 ft. Chicago D: G. M. Anderson S: A dealer in cork legs searches for the person who stole one from his inventory.

Ker-Choo 6 May 1908 400 ft. Chicago D: G. M. Anderson S: A boy gives people sneezing fits with snuff.

Just Like a Woman 20 May 1908? 500 ft. Chicago D: G. M. Anderson S: A woman pokes people with a parasol, runs a car backwards, spends a dollar at a sale to save one cent and steals money from her sleeping husband.

I Can't Read English 20 May 1908? 400 ft. Chicago D: G. M. Anderson

The Gentle Sex 10 June 1908 750 ft. Chicago D: G. M. Anderson

Little Mad-Cap; or, Oh, Splash! 17 June 1908 600 ft. Chicago D: G. M. Anderson S: A child runs wild, notably putting a baby in a can of milk.

The Tragedian 17 June 1908 400 ft. Chicago D: G. M. Anderson S: A woman overhears an actor rehearsing, thinks its a robbery and calls the police.

Oh, What Lungs! 1 July 1908 ? ft. Chicago D: G. M. Anderson C: Ben Turpin

S: A doctor pumps an emaciated man's lungs with compressed air to beef him up, and he uses his lung power for good and evil around town.

Wouldn't it Tire You? 1 July 1908 ? ft. Chicago D: G. M. Anderson S: A messenger boy rolls a car tire to a distant location so carelessly that it's useless by the time he gets there.

An Enterprising Florist 8 July 1908 504 ft. Chicago D: G. M. Anderson

Checker Fiends 8 July 1908 322 ft. Chicago D: G. M. Anderson S: Two checker players play the game on everything resembling a checker board.

The Directoire Gown 15 July 1908 455 ft. Chicago D: G. M. Anderson S: A mob of men trail a woman wearing a scandalous gown until she hoses them down.

Stung; or, What Can It Bee? 15 July 1908 428 ft. Chicago D: G. M. Anderson S: A boy bottles some bees and unleashes them at intervals.

Mama's Birthday 22 July 1908? 450 ft. Chicago D: G. M. Anderson

A Distastrous Flirtation 22 July 1908? 274 ft. Chicago D: G. M. Anderson S: A young man winks at every woman he sees and gets punished by them for it.

The Escape of the Ape 5 August 1908 578 ft. Chicago D: G. M. Anderson S: An ape escapes from a circus and rambles around town.

The Baseball Fan 19 August 1908 989 ft. Chicago D: G. M. Anderson S: A fan tries to sneak into a baseball park to see a sold-out game.

Lost and Found 26 August 1908 634 ft. Chicago D: G. M. Anderson?

Oh, What an Appetite 2 September 1908 600 ft. Chicago D: G. M. Anderson? S: An actor suffers from indigestion.

Breaking into Society 9 September 1908 ? ft. Chicago D: G. M. Anderson C: Ben Turpin S: A poor man and wife inherit a fortune and go on a spending spree, but a mistake was made and the money has to be returned.

The Bully 16 September 1908 ? ft. Chicago D: G. M. Anderson?

Hired - Tired - Fired 23 September 1908 500 ft. Chicago D: G. M. Anderson S: A man fails as a laborer, porter, bartender and shoe clerk. (remake of Jack of All Trades, released 11 January 1908)

Never Again 23 September 1908 325 ft. Chicago D: G. M. Anderson? S: A man takes a disastrous trip to Coney Island.

Soul Kiss 30 September 1908 450 ft. Chicago D: G. M. Anderson? S: A young man, inspired by a long, drawn-out kiss in a play, attempts it with every woman he sees, then an old woman meets him more than half way.

Beg Pardon 30 September 1908 450 ft. Chicago D: G. M. Anderson? S: An individual bumps into people and begs their pardon.

The Impersonator's Jokes 21 October 1908 550 ft. Chicago D: G. M. Anderson? S: A destitute man impersonates a celebrity at a banquet. (repeated or remade for release on 25 November 1908)

The Effect of a Shave 21 October 1908 400 ft. Chicago D: G. M. Anderson? S: A man is shaved hairless after losing a bet, and is unrecognizable by his wife and chased by his dog. A reverse camera trick restores his hair and all is well.

He Who Laughs Last, Laughs Best 11 November 1908 500 ft. Chicago D: G. M. Anderson? S: A girl's aunt intercepts a note from a boy proposing elopement, disguises as the girl to foil it and marries a tramp sent in the boy's place. The young couple then wed.

If It Doesn't Concern You, Let It Alone 11 November 1908 550 ft. Chicago D: G. M. Anderson? S: A young man tries to help people, but gets in trouble.

The Tale of a Thanksgiving Turkey 18 November 1908 615 ft. Chicago D: G. M. Anderson S: A man pawns his clothes, except his overcoat, to buy a turkey while his wife pawns his other suit to buy one. (remade as *Too Much Turkey*, released 19 November 1915)

The Hoodoo Lounge 18 November 1908 315 ft. Chicago D: G. M. Anderson? S: A tramp, chased by a policeman, hides in a folding sofa at a second-hand shop. A series of owners believe it's haunted when the tramp moves around inside. The policeman eventually buys it, finds the tramp inside and arrests him. (reworked or modified as *The Haunted Lounge,* released 6 January 1909)

An All Wool Garment 25 November 1908 400 ft. Chicago D: G. M. Anderson? S: A man's itchy wool underwear drives him and everyone around him crazy.

The Impersonator's Jokes 25 November 1908 550 ft. Chicago D: G. M. Anderson? A repeat or remake of the 21 October 1908 film.

An Obstinate Tooth 2 December 1908 165 ft. Chicago D: G. M. Anderson? S: A man removes a bad tooth by tying it to a car.

The Installment Collector 16 December 1908 550 ft. Chicago D: G. M. Anderson? S: A man purchases a book on the installment plan and is hounded by the collector wherever he goes.

A Battle Royal 16 December 1908 396 ft. Chicago D: G. M. Anderson?

Bill Jones' New Year Resolutions 23 December 1908 600 ft. Chicago D: G. M. Anderson? S: A wife flounts Bill's list of resolutions at him every time he's about to stray.

Who Is Smoking That Rope 23 December 1908 400 ft. Chicago D: G. M. Anderson? S: A man is given a box of cheap cigars by his wife.

1909
* *The Neighbors' Kids* 6 January 1909 550 ft. Chicago D: G. M. Anderson C: Ben Turpin (servant) S: Two little girls

create mischief in a household. (remake of Anderson's Selig Polyscope film *The Tomboys*, released 11 August 1906) [LOC]

* The Haunted Lounge 6 January 1909 370 ft. Chicago D: G. M. Anderson? C: Ben Turpin (tramp) S: A tramp being chased by a policeman hides in a folding lounge on the street. The cop takes the sofa home and is confounded by it. (reworking of *The Hoodoo Lounge*, released 18 November 1908) [LOC]

Professor's Love Tonic 13 January 1909 490 ft. Chicago D: G. M. Anderson? S: A man discovers a liquid which provokes uncontrolled hugging and kissing when sprinkled on a victim.

The Actor's Baby Carriage 13 January 1909 467 ft. Chicago D: G. M. Anderson? S: An actor dons a convict's uniform in place of overalls to paint a baby carriage. The carriage is swiped by two boys. A real convict escapes from prison. Complications ensue.

A Cure for Gout 27 January 1909 540 ft. Chicago D: G. M. Anderson? S: An old man offers a $500 reward to anyone who can cure his gout.

Too Much Dog Biscuit 27 January 1909 400 ft. Chicago D: G. M. Anderson? S: A man eats dog biscuits thinking it's his breakfast and he begins acting like a dog.

Educated Abroad 10 February 1909 970 ft. Chicago D: G. M. Anderson? S: A young American man returns home with an English lord.

In December, 1908, G. M. Anderson, Jess Robbins and Ben Turpin left Chicago for California. Their one-month trip eventually brought them to Santa Monica, where they produced the following films.

Tag Day 17 February 1909 560 ft. Santa Monica D: G. M. Anderson C: Ben Turpin (tramp?) S: A tramp sees some young ladies tagging men's coats when receiving money for charity, so he steals some tags, dresses like a woman and collects money for himself.

Bring Me Some Ice 17 February 1909 350 ft. Santa Monica D: G. M. Anderson S: A housewife making ice cream sends her son to get more ice, but he takes so long in bringing a block of it back that it shrinks to the size of an ice cube.

Shanghaied 3 March 1909 Santa Monica D: G. M. Anderson S: A young man is kidnapped so a rival can marry his girlfriend, but the young man foils the plot and marries the girl himself.

An Expensive Sky Piece 10 March 1909 500 ft. Santa Monica D: G. M. Anderson S: A man puts money in his hat for safekeeping, the hat is stolen by a tramp and the man goes on a wild search for it.

The Crazy Barber 10 March 1909 500 ft. Santa Monica D: G. M. Anderson S: A prize of $100 for working fast prompts a barber to shave everything in sight including a dog, a girl and a tree.

After returning to Chicago, Anderson traveled west again, to Colorado, and filmed four westerns. They were released over the next two months while Anderson resumed his comedies in Chicago at Essanay's new studio on Argyle Street.

The Road Agents 17 March 1909 Morrison and/or Golden, Colorado D: G. M. Anderson S: Two outlaws rob a stagecoach, but an argument over dividing the spoils leads to their downfall.

A Midnight Disturbance 24 March 1909 525 ft. Chicago D: G. M. Anderson? C: Ben Turpin (burglar) S: A woman with a revolver chases a burglar all through her house, but it's a bulldog that catches him, on his rear end.

The Energetic Street Cleaner 24 March 1909 450 ft. Chicago D: G. M. Anderson? C: Ben Turpin S: A street cleaner sweeps up everything in his path, including people.

* **A Tale of the West** 7 April 1909 Morrison, Colorado D: G. M. Anderson S: A young cowboy steals a horse to pay the mortgage on his mother's home, but is chased and caught. (remade as *Broncho Billy's Reason*, released 12 April 1913) [LOC]

The Rubes and the Bunco Men 14 April 1909 430 ft. Chicago D: G. M. Anderson? S: Two bunco men sell a carriage and horses to two naive country boys.

A Pair of Garters 21 April 1909 250 ft. Chicago D: G. M. Anderson? S: A pair of garters travels from one owner to another.

A Mexican's Gratitude 5 May 1909 Morrison and/or Golden, Colorado D: G. M. Anderson C: Ben Turpin S: A sheriff is saved by a Mexican he'd helped years earlier. (remade as *The Lucky Card*, released 27 May 1911)

The Bachelor's Wife 12 May 1909 550 ft. Chicago D: G. M. Anderson? S: A young man borrows money from a relative with the excuse he has a wife and child to support, but when the relative arrives for a visit the young man must find a wife and baby to play those parts.

* **Mr. Flip** 12 May 1909 450 ft. Chicago D: G. M. Anderson? C: Ben Turpin (Mr. Flip) S: Pain and rejection doesn't stop Mr. Flip from flirting. [video]

The Indian Trailer 19 May 1909 Morrison and/or Golden, Colorado D: G. M. Anderson S: An Indian tracks down a ranchman's kidnapped daughter.

Scenes from the World's Largest Pigeon Farm 26 May 1909 150 ft. Pasadena, California P: Jess Robbins S: This documentary on the pigeon farm was filmed during Anderson's 1908 trip.

The Sleeping Tonic 2 June 1909 625 ft. Chicago D: G. M. Anderson? C: Ben Turpin S: A doctor's tonic makes an insomniac sleep anywhere.

The Dog and the Sausage 2 June 1909 350 ft. Chicago D: G. M. Anderson? S: Two messengers play marbles and accidently switch delivery baskets. A customer expecting a dog gets the sausages and the sausage customer gets a dog.

A Hustling Advertiser 16 June 1909 550 ft. Chicago D: G. M. Anderson C: Ben Turpin (young man) S: A soap manufacturer hires a young man to paint advertising signs and he paints on everything he sees.

The Policeman's Romance 30 June 1909 ? ft. Chicago D: G. M. Anderson? S: A policeman's sweetheart constantly distracts him from his duty.

The Slavey 30 June 1909 ? ft. Chicago D: G. M. Anderson? S: The slavey and an iceman go to a ball, do a comedy dance and get thrown out.

The Black Sheep 7 July 1909 Chicago D: G. M. Anderson? S: The "bad" brother is banished from home for his wild ways. The "good" brother becomes a successful grain broker. The parents go broke in old age and the good brother refuses to help. The bad brother strikes it rich in a gold mine, bankrupts the good brother and saves his parents from the poor house. (remade as *The Good-for-Nothing*, released 8 June 1914)

The New Cop 14 July 1909 550 ft. Chicago D: G. M. Anderson? C: Ben Turpin? S: A new cop enforces the law too literally, but it's ok; he ends up with a bulldog on the seat of his pants.

* *A Case of Seltzer* 28 Jul 1909 210 ft. Chicago D: G. M. Anderson? C: Ben Turpin S: A masher follows a lady home and her brothers seltzer him. [GEH]

The Mustard Plaster 4 August 1909 445 ft. Chicago D: G. M. Anderson? S: A man with a mustard plaster tries to cool off.

On Another Man's Pass 25 August 1909 950 ft. Chicago D: G. M. Anderson? S: A tramp steals a railroad president's pass and lives it up, but is reformed by a Salvation Army girl.

Sleepy Jim 8 September 1909 ? ft. Chicago D: G. M. Anderson? S: A tramp dreams he and a policeman have traded places.

A Case of Tomatoes 15 September 1909 495 ft. Chicago D: G. M. Anderson? S: Boys find a box of tomatoes and throw them at people.

Three Reasons for Haste 15 September 1909 485 ft. Chicago D: G. M. Anderson? S: A traveling salesman hurries to get home. A telegram in his hand speeds him past people who initially try to stop him. It announces the birth of triplets.

A Birthday Affair 6 October 1909 550 ft. Chicago D: G. M. Anderson? S: A man forgets to mail invitations to his wife's birthday.

The Widow 20 October 1909 520 ft. Chicago D: G. M. Anderson? S: A friend in the country invites a man over to meet "the widow" which disturbs the man's wife, but it turns out the widow is a horse.

Anderson and Jess Robbins returned to Colorado in September and began making westerns, some dramatic, others with comedy, all filmed entirely outdoors. Throughout this and subsequent travels they managed to keep, more or less, two months ahead of the release schedule.

The Best Man Wins 20 November 1909 875 ft. Morrison, Colorado D: G. M. Anderson C: John B. O'Brien, Fred Church, William A. Russell, Chick Morrison, Pete Morrison, Shorty Cunningham S: A young woman, tired of waiting for her cowboy lover to return from the east, announces she'll marry the first cowboy to bring her a marriage license from town.

Judgement 27 November 1909 988 ft. Morrison D: G. M. Anderson C: Pete Morrison (Tom Ripley) S: Ripley, in love with a ranchman's daughter, is framed by Robert Gray for a murder and lynched, but his ghost returns to avenge the injustice.

His Reformation 4 December 1909 Morrison D: G. M. Anderson C: G. M. Anderson (Tom Carlton), Fred Church, Pete Morrison, John B. O'Brien, William A. Russell S: Tom Carlton, an outlaw, is unable to reform until his mother sees him holding up a stagecoach. Note: Filmed a week after *The Ranchman's Rival.*

* *The Ranchman's Rival* 11 December 1909 Golden and Morrison working title: *Won Back* D: G. M. Anderson C: G. M. Anderson (Jim Watson), John B. O'Brien (Walter Milton), Fred Church (Mexican), Joseph Smith (girl's father), William A. Russell (cowboy whittling wood) S: Ranchman Jim Watson decides to leave town when easterner Walter Milton wins the love of Watson's girl, then Watson discovers Milton's wife at the train depot. (remade as *The Ranch Girl's Mistake*, released 12 March 1912) [LOC] Note: This was Anderson's first leading role in an Essanay western.

The Spanish Girl 18 December 1909 975 ft. Denver and Boulder? D; G. M. Anderson C: G. M. Anderson (Tom Wilson), Pansy Perry (Lola), Fred Church (Pedro) S: Tom and Martha love each other, but Lola, jealous, arranges with Pedro for Tom to see Martha in Pedro's arms. When Tom saves Pedro from being hung unjustly, Pedro confesses the deception and the lovers are reunited.

The Heart of a Cowboy 25 December 1909 959 ft. Morrison D: G. M. Anderson C: G. M. Anderson (Honest Steve), George Creel (Bad Steve), Loma Besserer (Kitty Blair), Fred Church, Arthur Smith, William A. Russell, John B. O'Brien S: Bad Steve frames Honest Steve for cattle rustling. A posse is about to hang Honest Steve when Kitty rides to his rescue.

1910

A Western Maid 1 January 1910 875 ft. Golden D: G. M. Anderson C: G. M. Anderson, Pete Morrison S: A man's daughter witnesses three bandits robbing him of the mine payroll. She takes a bandit's horse, gets the sheriff and the money is recovered.

Electric Insoles 12 January 1910 502 ft. Denver? D: G. M. Anderson C: John B. O'Brien, Joseph Smith, William A. Russell S: A man with tired feet buys a pair of electric insoles and moves along at high speed.

Won by a Hold Up 19 January 1910 629 ft. Golden D: G. M. Anderson C: G. M. Anderson (old rancher), Fred Church (Bill), John B. O'Brien (Bill's friend), Arthur Smith (Bill's friend),

William A. Russell S: Bill arranges with two friends to rob an old rancher so Bill can step in to save the day. This is done to impress the old man, who objects to the marriage of Bill and his daughter.

Essanay left Colorado for El Paso, Texas, on 15 November 1909, but they only stayed there briefly. By 1 January 1910 they were in Santa Barbara, California.

Flower Parade at Pasadena, Cal. 19 January 1910 292 ft. P: Jess Robbins This is a documentary on Pasadena's famous parade, probably a combination of the 1909 and 1910 events.

An Outlaw's Sacrifice 29 January 1910 996 ft. El Paso D: G. M. Anderson C: Fred Church (Walt Malone), William A. Russell (girl's father), John B. O'Brien (rival) S: The outlaw Walt Malone forces his girlfriend to turn him in to the sheriff so she can collect the reward money and pay off the mortgage on her father's property.

* **Western Chivalry** 12 February 1910 568 ft. Golden D: G. M. Anderson C: G. M. Anderson, Shorty Cunningham, Joe Dennis, William A. Russell, Clara Williams S: The ranch boss's niece from the city is rescued by a cowboy when her horse is spooked, then she shows off her horseriding skills to prove she can ride as well as the cowboys. [NFTA]

Aviation at Los Angeles, California 16 February 1910 600 ft. Dominguez Field P: Jess Robbins S: Louis Paulhan, Glenn Curtis, Lincoln Beachey, G. M. Anderson and others are seen in this documentary of the first aviation meet in the United States. [GEH]

The Cowboy and the Squaw 19 February 1910 935 ft. El Paso and Santa Barbara D: G. M. Anderson C: G. M. Anderson (Tom Ripley), Clara Williams (Lightfeather), Fred Church (bartender), Chick Morrison, John B. O'Brien, Fred Ilenstine, William A. Russell S: Tom Ripley, a cowboy, defends Lightfeather, an Indian girl, from the insults of Jim Simpson, another cowboy. She returns the favor by saving Ripley when Simpson tries to kill him.

* **The Mexican's Faith** 26 February 1910 925 ft. Santa Barbara D: G. M. Anderson C: G. M. Anderson (Mexican), Joseph Smith (rancher), Clara Williams (rancher's daughter), John B. O'Brien (scoundrel), Charles Morrison, Fred Church (scoundrel's accomplice), Frank Hall (daughter's boyfriend), William A. Russell S: A Mexican who loves a rancher's daughter saves her from a city-bred scoundrel. [NFTA]

The Ranch Girl's Legacy 5 March 1910 825 ft. El Paso and Santa Barbara working title: A Refusal D: G. M. Anderson C: G. M. Anderson (Jack Tyler), Clara Williams (Carrie Perkins), Joseph Smith, Frank Hall, Fred Ilenstine S: Jack Tyler stands to lose a fortune under the terms of his uncle's will if he refuses to marry his distant cousin, so he schemes to make her refuse him instead. [LOC]

* **The Ostrich and the Lady** 5 March 1910 175 ft. P: Jess Robbins This is a documentary of a Santa Barbara ostrich farm. [LOC]

* **The Fence on "Bar Z" Ranch** 12 March 1910 950 ft. Santa Barbara D: G. M. Anderson C: G. M. Anderson

(Robert Graham) S: A property line dispute between Graham and a widow ends in compromise after she accidentally shoots her little girl while aiming for him, and he saves the girl's life by rushing her to a doctor. (remade as *A Romance of the West,* released 9 March 1912) [LOC]

Method in His Madness 16 March 1910 302 ft. filmed 24-25 January 1910 on State Street, Santa Barbara D: G. M. Anderson C: Joseph Smith (first man having fit), Earl Howell (first tramp), William A. Russell (second tramp), Frank Hall (first pedestrian, second bartender) Fred Church (pedestrian at second bar, third bartender), Neva Don Carlos (first stout woman), John B. O'Brien (man outside third bar), Clara Williams (woman outside third bar), Fred Ilenstine (pedestrian in last scene), G. M. Anderson (pedestrian with seltzer bottle) S: Tramps fake epileptic fits in front of several barrooms to get free drinks after they see an old man revived by this method. [LOC, UCLA, PFA]

The Girl and the Fugitive 19 March 1910 950 ft. Mission Canyon, Santa Barbara D: G. M. Anderson C: G. M. Anderson (Ross White), Clara Williams (Minnie Harding), Fred Church (cowboy), John B. O'Brien, William A. Russell, Frank Hall, Joseph Smith, J. Travers, Fred Ilenstine, Dick Scott, Corbett Morris, Frank Murphy S: Ross saves Minnie from the clutches of a cowboy, and later Minnie saves Ross from a mob.

A Ranchman's Wooing 26 March 1910 651 ft. Santa Barbara D: G. M. Anderson C: G. M. Anderson, Clara Williams,

Gladys Field, William A. Russell, Elmer Thompson, Joseph Smith, Arthur Smith, John B. O'Brien, Fred Church, Nancy Robbins, Neva Don Carlos, Fred Ilenstine, Lois Boulton S: An old ranchman wants to marry a widow but she won't as long as his four daughters are single, so he chases off their boyfriends to encourage them to elope. (remade in part as *The Ranch Widower's Daughters,* released 12 March 1912)

The Flower of the Ranch 2 April 1910 Santa Barbara D: G. M. Anderson C: G. M. Anderson (Frank Wendell), Neva Don Carlos, Fred Church S: Cowboys save a girl from a rich man who had once run off with her mother.

The Ranger's Bride 9 April 1910 750 ft. Santa Barbara D: G. M. Anderson C: G. M. Anderson, Fred Church, Earl Howell S: A Texas Ranger sends for a mail order bride, but is tricked by his cowboy friends when one of them disguises himself as a woman. [GEH]

The Bad Man and the Preacher 16 April 1910 422 ft. Goleta, California D: G. M. Anderson C: G. M. Anderson (James Smyth), John B. O'Brien (Snake Williams), Frank Hall, Fred Church, Arthur Smith, Joseph Smith, Earl Howell, Lois Boulton, Mae McCaskey, J. Travers, Frank Murphy, Fred Ilenstine S: Williams and his cowboy pals try to get Smyth, a preacher, to drink whiskey. When he refuses they disrupt his church service until he fights and wins.

The Mistaken Bandit 16 April 1910 578 ft. Hoff Heights, Santa Barbara D: G. M. Anderson C: G. M. Anderson (innocent cowboy), Fred Church, John

B. O'Brien, Clara Williams, Frank Hall, Joseph Smith, Fred Ilenstine S: A young woman guarding a strong box at an isolated express company way station disarms and locks up an innocent cowboy thinking he's a bandit, then she's held up by outlaws. She arms the cowboy and he holds them off until the express agent arrives. (remade as *Broncho Billy and the Bandits*, released 4 May 1912)

The Cowboy's Sweetheart 23 April 1910 Santa Barbara D: G. M. Anderson C: G. M. Anderson (Jesse Farson), Clara Williams (Jennie), John B. O'Brien, Neva Don Carlos S: Jesse asks Jennie for his engagement ring back after he falls for a city girl, but Jennie finds out the girl is happily married and contrives a way to win Jesse back.

A Vein of Gold 30 April 1910 Santa Barbara D: G. M. Anderson C: G. M. Anderson, Fred Church, Clara Williams S: A convict is allowed to visit his sick mother, but steals money from a storekeeper to pay her doctor bills. After he serves his prison term he finds a vein of gold and repays the storekeeper. (remade as *Broncho Billy Evens Matters*, released 22 October 1915)

The Sheriff's Sacrifice 7 May 1910 950 ft. Santa Barbara D: G. M. Anderson C: G. M. Anderson, Earl Howell, Clara Williams, William A. Russell S: A sheriff who loves a ranchman's daughter gives her thieving ranch-foreman husband another chance to make good.

The Cowpuncher's Ward 14 May 1910 965 ft. Santa Barbara D: G. M. Anderson C: G. M. Anderson, Sophie Osborn (ward), Gladys Field (grown up ward),

Fred Church, John B. O'Brien, Clara Williams, Frank Hall, Neva Don Carlos, Joseph Smith, Fred Ilenstine, Earl Howell, Lois Boulton, Nancy Robbins, Mae McCaskey S: The ward of some cowboys is implicated in a murder and one of the cowboys assumes the guilt to protect her.

The Little Doctor of the Foothills 21 May 1910 935 ft. Santa Barbara D: G. M. Anderson C: G. M. Anderson, Clara Williams (Miss Burton), John B. O'Brien, Frank Hall, Fred Church, Joseph Smith (Alkali Ike) S: A woman doctor arrives in town and the cowboys suddenly have all kinds of ailments. (remade as *Snakeville's New Doctor*, released 10 January 1914)

The Essanay company returned to Morrison, Colorado in late March, 1910.

The Brother, Sister and the Cowpuncher 28 May 1910 ? ft. Morrison D: G. M. Anderson C: G. M. Anderson, Fred Church, Clara Williams S: A cowboy tries to recover his girlfield's money, stolen by her brother and given to his Mexican girlfriend, but when the cowboy's girl sees him flirting with the Mexican girl to get the money back, she rejects him.

Away Out West 4 June 1910 Morrison D: G. M. Anderson C: G. M. Anderson, Frank Hall (prospector), John B. O'Brien (prospector) S: A dying miner gives a map showing the location of his valuable mine to two prospectors, setting one man against the other.

The Ranchman's Feud 11 June 1910 989 ft. Morrison D: G. M. Anderson

C: G. M. Anderson (doctor), Clara Williams (ranchman's daughter), John B. O'Brien (other ranchman's son), Neva Don Carlos (son's mother), Fred Church (sheriff), Elmer Thompson, Robert Gray, Fred Ilenstine, Pete Morrison, Chick Morrison S: The son and daughter of two feuding ranchmen fall in love, prompting the girl's father to shoot and wound the young man, but the boy refuses to press charges and the feud ends.

The Bandit's Wife 18 June 1910 956 ft. Morrison D: G. M. Anderson C: G. M. Anderson S: A bandit's wife falls for another gang member and turns her husband over to the sheriff to get him out of the way.

The Forest Ranger 25 June 1910 969 ft. Morrison D: G. M. Anderson C: G. M. Anderson (Charles Wentworth), Fred Church, John B. O'Brien S: Deputy marshall Charles Wentworth goes undercover to track down lumber thieves.

The Bad Man's Last Deed 2 July 1910 Morrison D: G. M. Anderson C: G. M. Anderson (bad man), John B. O'Brien, Fred Church (sheriff), Pete Morrison, Frank Hall, William A. Russell, Chick Morrison, Joseph Smith S: A drunk bad man is escorted to the county line by the sheriff and warned never to return. The man helps recover money a boy gambled away, takes the boy home and is shot by the sheriff. (remade at Anderson's Golden West Producing Company as *The Son of a Gun*, released 20 October 1918)

The Unknown Claim 9 July 1910 997 ft. Morrison D: G. M. Anderson C: G. M. Anderson (Bartwell), Fred Church (ranch hand), Frank Hall (Walker), Gladys Field S: Bartwell and Belle Ellis, a rancher's daughter, pay the loan on her father's land before Walker, a moneylender, can foreclose and profit by an unmined gold vein on the property.

Trailed to the Hills 16 July 1910 983 ft. Morrison D: G. M. Anderson C: G. M. Anderson (Harry Forsyth), Frank Hall S: Forsyth goes after the man who stole his wife away then abandoned her, kills him and is helped in eluding the law by a miner who went through the same experience.

The Desperado 23 July 1910 Morrison D: G. M. Anderson C: G. M. Anderson (new sheriff), Fred Church (Black Bart), Clara Williams, Frank Hall S: The new sheriff goes out alone to capture the notorious Black Bart after a posse fails miserably.

Anderson and company returned to Chicago on 30 June 1910, finished interiors on several westerns, including the first Broncho Billy film (started in December, 1909, in El Paso) and began producing a series of comedies.

Broncho Billy's Redemption 30 July 1910 950 ft. El Paso and Chicago D: G. M. Anderson C: G. M. Anderson (Broncho Billy), Clara Williams (Millie Merrill), Frank Hall, Chick Morrison S: The outlaw Broncho Billy risks his freedom to save the lives of Millie Merrill and her father, both of whom are unconscious and dying on the prairie.

* *Under Western Skies* 6 August 1910 Morrison C: G. M. Anderson (cowboy), Fred Church (cowboy), Joseph Smith (cowboy & minister), Clara Williams, Frank Hall (old sweetheart), Chick Morrison, John B. O'Brien (bartender), Fred Ilenstine (marriage witness), William A. Russell (second witness) S: A woman promises to marry one of three drunks who are about to molest her if he will protect her from the other two. [LOC, NFTA, NFMA]

The Girl on Triple X 13 August 1910 Morrison D: G. M. Anderson C: Clara Williams (Nellie Monroe), G. M. Anderson S: Nellie and an Indian cowboy save Jack Hartley, framed by Red Williams, from hanging as a horse thief.

The Dumb Half-Breed's Defense 20 August 1910 Colorado D: G. M. Anderson C: G. M. Anderson (half-breed), Frank Hall, John B. O'Brien S: A half-breed, on trial for killing his brother-in-law, argues his own case in court.

The Count That Counted 17 August 1910 Chicago D: G. M. Anderson C: Augustus Carney (reporter), Martha Spier (his sweetheart), G. M. Anderson, J. Warren Kerrigan, John B. O'Brien S: A lowly reporter pretends to be a count so his sweetheart's father will consent to their marriage.

Take Me Out to the Ball Game 24 August 1910 990 ft. Chicago D: G. M. Anderson C: Augustus Carney (the fan), Neva Don Carlos (his wife), J. Warren Kerrigan, John B. O'Brien, Arthur White, Chick Morrison, Elmer Thompson, Fred Ilenstine S: A fan takes his wife and dog to the game.

* *The Deputy's Love* 27 August 1910 Morrison and Chicago alternate title: The Deputy's Duty D: G. M. Anderson C: G. M. Anderson (Bob Dean), Clara Williams (Nance O'Brien), Frank Hall (Walt), Chick Morrison (stagedriver), Elmer Thompson (guard), Fred Church (passenger), John B. O'Brien, Joseph Smith, Robert Gray S: Deputy Bob Dean finds a pair of gloves he'd given to Nance at the scene of a stagecoach robbery and knows he's obliged to arrest her. (remade as *Broncho Billy's Capture*, released 7 June 1913) [NFTA]

The Millionaire and the Ranch Girl 3 September 1910 987 ft. Colorado D: G. M. Anderson C: G. M. Anderson (Milton Rodd), Clara Williams (Nellie Blair), Frank Hall S: An agent for millionaire Milton Rodd forecloses on a ranch mortgage when the rancher's daughter refuses to marry the agent, but Rodd finds out and sets things right. (remade as *An Unexpected Romance,* released 24 September 1915)

A Dog on Business 7 September 1910 940 ft. Chicago D: G. M. Anderson C: Augustus Carney, Victor Potel S: A hobo rounds up stray dogs and sells them to suckers in a dog-reward scam. (remake of Anderson's Selig film *The Grafter,* released 26 January 1907)

An Indian Girl's Awakening 10 September 1910 Morrison D: G. M. Anderson C: G. M. Anderson, Clara Williams S: An Indian girl, saved by a white man from an Indian man she detests, tries to stay with the white man until she finds out he's married.

While in Chicago, Anderson produced a series of comedies based upon the Mutt and Jeff comic strip characters, but uncredited as such. In this short flurry of films, Augustus Carney (Hank) was paired with newcomer to films Victor Potel (Lank).

Hank and Lank — Joy Riding 17 September 1910 233 ft. Chicago D: G. M. Anderson C: Augustus Carney (Hank), Victor Potel (Lank) S: Hank gets a free ride in a limo by faking an epileptic fit, but when Lank tries the trick he gets caught.

The Pony Express Rider 17 September 1910 750 ft. Colorado and Chicago D: G. M. Anderson C: G. M. Anderson (Jim Allison), John B. O'Brien ("Pony" O'Brien), Clara Williams (Mary Holmes), Fred Church, Frank Hall, Joseph Smith, Elmer Thompson S: Jim Allison must prove his allegance to a gang by robbing a pony express rider.

A Close Shave 21 September 1910 553 ft. Chicago D: G. M. Anderson C: Augustus Carney, J. Warren Kerrigan, John B. O'Brien S: Mr. Marc is sold some phony stocks by Mr. Bunco, but Marc's check is delayed in being cashed and Bunco is caught.

A Flirty Affliction 21 September 1910 416 ft. Chicago D: G. M. Anderson C: John B. O'Brien, Gladys Field S: A girl's nervous tick is mistaken by a succession of men as a come-on.

The Tout's Remembrance 24 September 1910 Chicago, Juarez and Santa Barbara D: G. M. Anderson C: G. M. Anderson ("Bullets" Brown), Ethel Clayton, J. Warren Kerrigan, Victor Potel,

Augustus Carney, Frank Hall, Fred Church, Arthur Mackley, Gladys Field, Jimmie McIntyre (jockey) S: Brown, a racetrack tipster, tries to reform, gets a job at a grocery store, is fired, and returns to the track to score in a long shot.

* Hank and Lank Dude Up Some 28 September 1910 307 ft. Chicago D: G. M. Anderson C: Augustus Carney (Hank), Victor Potel (Lank) S: Hank accidently falls down a coal-chute and is paid to avoid a lawsuit, but Lank fails at the scam and is kicked out. [LOC]

* Curing a Masher 28 September 1910 660 ft. Chicago D: G. M. Anderson C: Augustus Carney (masher), Clara Williams, J. Warren Kerrigan, Frank Hall S: A woman allows a masher to carry her many shopping purchases home, then he gets kicked down four flights of stairs by her husband. [LOC]

Early in September the Western Essanay returned to Colorado with a larger troupe that included Arthur Mackley, Brinsley Shaw, Harry Todd, Margaret Joslin, Augustus Carney and Victor Potel.

Patricia of the Plains 1 October 1910 Morrison D: G. M. Anderson C: G. M. Anderson (Dick Martin), Arthur Mackley (Sheriff Dixon), Clara Williams (Patricia Watkins), Augustus Carney (Mr. Watkins), Fred Church, Victor Potel S: Patricia Watkins runs her drunken father's saloon, a place that outlaw Dick Martin intends to rob until he meets her. She saves him from being arrested.

The Bearded Bandit 8 October 1910 950 ft. Colorado D: G. M. Anderson

C: G. M. Anderson (Curt), Gladys Field (Nan Conners), Harry Todd (Mr. Conners), Victor Potel, Fred Church S: Curt, the sheriff, wants the $5000 reward for capturing the Bearded Bandit so he can marry Nan Conners, not knowing the bandit is Nan's father.

Hank and Lank — They Get Wise to a New Scheme 12 October 1910 302 ft. Chicago D: G. M. Anderson C: Augustus Carney (Hank), Victor Potel (Lank) S: Hank babysits while a woman shops, but when Lank babysits for a husband who enters a saloon, he's beaten by the mother.

A Cowboy's Mother-in-Law 15 October 1910 Colorado D: G. M. Anderson C: G. M. Anderson, Gladys Field, Victor Potel, Augustus Carney, Harry Todd S: Pete, a cowboy on Nellie's uncle's ranch, dresses up as Nellie's mother to tame her abusing husband.

Hank and Lank: (Uninvited Guests) 19 October 1910 539 ft. Chicago D: G. M. Anderson C: Augustus Carney (Hank), Victor Potel (Lank) S: Hank and Lank winter in a summer house, but smoke from their campfire sends out the fire department and they're hosed down.

* *Pals of the Range* 22 October 1910 Morrison and Golden D: G. M. Anderson C: G. M. Anderson (Jack Smythe), John B. O'Brien (Jack Hartley), Clara Williams (Clara), Fred Church (Indian), Augustus Carney, Robert Gray, Chick Morrison S: Hartley switches a letter from Clara accepting Smythe's marriage proposal for a letter rejecting him and Smythe goes prospecting in the desert.

When Clara finds out about Hartley's scheme she sends Hartley after Smythe. [NFTA]

Hank and Lank: They Take a Rest 26 October 1910 298 ft. Chicago D: G. M. Anderson C: Augustus Carney (Hank), Victor Potel (Lank) S: A boy ties Lank's ankles to a policeman's.

A Silent Message 29 October 1910 960 ft. Colorado D: G. M. Anderson C: G. M. Anderson, Clara Williams, Arthur Mackley (fugitive), John B. O'Brien, Harry Todd, Elmer Thompson, Frank Hall, Victor Potel S: A woman being molested by a fugitive signals to her deaf and dumb Indian servant to get the sheriff. (remade as *The Man in the Cabin*, released 16 August 1913)

A Westerner's Way 5 November 1910 Morrison D: G. M. Anderson C: G. M. Anderson (Big Bill Hastings), Arthur Mackley (sheriff), Harry Todd, Frank Hall, Chick Morrison, Victor Potel, Augustus Carney, William A. Russell, Arthur White S: A sheriff arrests Hastings for robbery, but loses the robbery money in a poker game. Hastings robs the gambler, returns the money to the sheriff and is set free. (remade in 1914 by William S. Hart as *The Bargain* and by Anderson as *Broncho Billy's Double Escape*, released 28 November 1914)

Hank and Lank: Life Savers 8 November 1910 560 ft. Chicago D: G. M. Anderson C: Augustus Carney (Hank), Victor Potel (Lank), Harry Todd, Gladys Field S: Lank saves Hank from drowning and is rewarded, but when Hank falls asleep instead of saving Lank the reward money goes to real lifeguards.

The Masquerade Cop 8 November 1910 428 ft. Chicago D: G. M. Anderson C: Arthur Mackley, John B. O'Brien, Fred Church, Brinsley Shaw S: A man on his way to a masquerade ball is arrested for impersonating an officer. Stripped, he goes home in a barrel.

The Marked Trail 12 November 1910 Colorado D: G. M. Anderson C: G. M. Anderson (doctor), Clara Williams (Marie Canby), Fred Church, Brinsley Shaw S: A blindfolded doctor taken by bandits to tend a kidnapped woman, scatters pills along the trail as a guide to their escape. (remade as *Broncho Billy's Scheme,* released 21 November 1914)

The Little Prospector 19 November 1910 960 ft. Colorado D: G. M. Anderson C: G. M. Anderson (Hal Martin), Clara Williams (Nell Kendall), Brinsley Shaw, Harry Todd, Fred Church S: Old, halfwit miner Silas Kendall shows off some ore from his gold strike to everyone in the town store, but his daughter Nell and Hal Martin manage to stake Kendall's claim on the land before anyone else can. (remade as *The Crazy Prospector,* released 3 May 1913)

* Hank and Lank: Sandwich Men 22 November 1910 389 ft. Colorado D: G. M. Anderson C: Augustus Carney (Hank), Victor Potel (Lank), Arthur Mackley (restaurant manager), John B. O'Brien (cook) Fred Ilenstine, Harry Todd, Margaret Joslin, Gladys Field, Frank Hall, Julia Mackley S: Hank and Lank spy a sandwich-board man getting a free meal for his efforts, and Hank works the same deal at another restau-

rant, but Lank gets beaten up on his detail. [LOC]

A Western Woman's Way 26 November 1910 Colorado D: G. M. Anderson C: Harry Todd, Clara Williams, Fred Church, Frank Hall S: A woman made crazy by the murder of her husband goes after the killer.

Circle C Ranch's Wedding Present 3 December 1910 Colorado D: G. M. Anderson C: G. M. Anderson, Clara Williams, John B. O'Brien, Victor Potel, Harry Todd, Augustus Carney, Fred Church, Robert Gray, Joseph Smith S: A ranchman decides his cowboys should go to school and hires a woman to teach them. (remade as *Broncho Billy Steps In,* released 13 August 1915)

A Cowboy's Vindication 10 December 1910 960 ft. Colorado D: G. M. Anderson C: G. M. Anderson (Frank Morrison), Clara Williams (Faro Nan), Brinsley Shaw (Jesse Gibbs), Frank Hall (Will Morrison), Harry Todd, William A. Russell, John B. O'Brien, Fred Church, Victor Potel, Chick Morrison S: When Will Morrison is murdered by Jesse Gibbs, Will's brother Frank goes after Jesse.

The Western Essanay left Colorado for Los Gatos, California, in mid-October.

The Tenderfoot Messenger 17 December 1910 997 ft. Los Gatos D: G. M. Anderson C: Augustus Carney (Shorty Blair), Arthur Mackley, Fred Church, Victor Potel, Harry Todd S: Bandits underestimate the cleverness of a messenger transporting a gold shipment.

Hank and Lank - Blind Men 20 December 1910 275 ft. Los Gatos? D: G. M. Anderson C: Augustus Carney (Hank), Victor Potel (Lank) S: Hank and Lank imitate a phony blind man's scheme to get money, but Lank gets caught.

The Bad Man's Christmas Gift 24 December 1910 975 ft. Los Gatos? D: G. M. Anderson ST: based on O. Henry's "A Chaparrel Christmas Gift" C: G. M. Anderson (Andy Carson), Gladys Field (Gladys Pierce), Brinsley Shaw (Jack Brinsley), Arthur Mackley, Fred Church, Victor Potel, Margaret Joslin, Augustus Carney, Harry Todd S: Andy Carson, jealous when Jack Brinsley marries Gladys Pierce, resolves to kill Brinsley on Christmas eve. (remade as *A Christmas Revenge,* released 18 December 1915)

A Gambler of the West 31 December 1910 Colorado D: G. M. Anderson C: G. M. Anderson (Halsted), Gladys Field (Alice Thomas), Frank Hall, Arthur Mackley, Brinsley Shaw S: Alice Thomas asks gambling house owner Halsted for help to stop her father from gambling all of their cattle ranch money away. Halsted robs Thomas and gives the money to his daughter.

1911
The Count and the Cowboys 7 January 1911 Los Gatos D: G. M. Anderson C: Victor Potel (the count), Augustus Carney ("Stump" Carney), Arthur Mackley, Fred Church, John B. O'Brien, Harry Todd, Joseph Smith S: A French count arrives in Rawhide and irritates the local cowboys when he shows them the French way to duel.

Carney shows him the American way.

The Girl of the West 14 January 1911 990 ft. Los Gatos and Alma D: G. M. Anderson C: G. M. Anderson, Arthur Mackley, Gladys Field S: Deputy Morris has the difficult task of arresting the brother of the girl he wants to marry.

The Border Ranger 21 January 1911 985 ft. Los Gatos D: G. M. Anderson C: G. M. Anderson (ranger), Gladys Field (ranger's girl), Arthur Mackley, Victor Potel S: A band of smugglers kidnap a ranger's girlfriend to exchange for one of their number who is in jail.

The Two Reformations 28 January 1911 996 ft. Los Gatos and Alma D: G. M. Anderson C: G. M. Anderson, Gladys Field, Fred Church, Arthur Mackley, Augustus Carney, Chick Morrison, Robert Gray, Margaret Joslin, Brinsley Shaw, Harry Todd, Victor Potel, Eldon Hatch S: Frank McLain loses his job and decides to prospect for gold out west, but falls on hard times and into bad company.

Hank and Lank — They Make a Mash 31 January 1911 360 ft. Los Gatos D: G. M. Anderson C: Augustus Carney (Hank), Victor Potel (Lank) S: Hank flirts with a man dressed as a woman who is on his way to a masquerade ball.

Carmenita the Faithful 4 February 1911 995 ft. Los Gatos D: G. M. Anderson C: G. M. Anderson S: After Frank Dougherty is crippled in an accident, a rich Mexican threatens to kill Frank unless Frank's wife will go away with him, so she goes. A doctor tending the husband finds out about the situation, gets the sheriff, and a posse saves her.

The Bad Man's Downfall 11 February 1911 Los Gatos D: G. M. Anderson C: G. M. Anderson (Harry Perkins), Brinsley Shaw ("Bad" McGrew), Harry Todd, Gladys Field, Victor Potel S: "Bad" McGrew, an outlaw, tangles with Harry Perkins, a deputy marshall, over a woman. Perkins arrests McGrew.

The Cattleman's Daughter 18 February 1911 Los Gatos D: G. M. Anderson C: G. M. Anderson (Frank Carpenter), Gladys Field (Gladys Brown), Arthur Mackley (Jim Brown), Brinsley Shaw S: Jim Brown objects to the marriage of his daughter Gladys to Frank Carpenter. Following hard times, Gladys gets sick and Frank steals money from Brown to pay a doctor. Brown has Frank arrested for the theft, but dismisses the sheriff when he learns of Gladys's illness.

The Western Essanay left Los Gatos on 4 February 1911 for Redlands.

* **The Outlaw and the Child** 25 February 1911 Los Gatos and Redlands? D: G. M. Anderson C: G. M. Anderson (Dan Warrington), Arthur Mackley (sheriff), Harry Todd (deputy), William A. Russell (prisoner), Joseph Smith (prisoner), Fred Church, Chick Morrison S: Dan Warrington, an escaped outlaw, sacrifices his life to save the sheriff's little daughter in the desert. [NFTA]

On the Desert's Edge 4 March 1911 990 ft. Mohave desert and Los Gatos D: G. M. Anderson C: G. M. Anderson (Hal Morley), Harry Todd (Ed Sawyer), Fred Church, Augustus Carney, Victor Potel,

David Kirkland S: Ed Sawyer, a gambler in trouble, is pursued into the desert by Hal Morley, a deputy sheriff.

The Romance on "Bar O" 11 March 1911 Redlands D: G. M. Anderson C: G. M. Anderson (Wells), Arthur Mackley (rancher) S: Wells saves a rancher's daughter from a dangerous horse and she persuades her father to hire him, but the foreman sees him as a rival and frames him for horse theft. (remade as *Broncho Billy's Narrow Escape*, released 6 July 1912)

The Faithful Indian 18 March 1911 Redlands D: G. M. Anderson C: G. M. Anderson (Will Talbot), Brinsley Shaw (Indian), Arthur Mackley, Fred Church, Harry Todd, John B. O'Brien, Joseph Smith S: A doctor treats miner Will Talbot, hurt in an mine explosion, finds flecks of gold on the miner and tries to bully Talbot's Indian friend into telling him where the mine is located. (remade as *Broncho Billy and the Red Man*, released 7 February 1914)

A Thwarted Vengence 25 March 1911 Redlands D: G. M. Anderson C: G. M. Anderson (Bob Griswald), Brinsley Shaw (Mexican), Gladys Field (Nell Ollcott) S: Griswald, a miner, saves Nell, a saloon owner, from an annoying Mexican. The Mexican kidnaps Nell, ties her to a post outside Griswald's shack and tries to stab Griswald. When he is stopped, he tries to stab Nell and Griswald shoots him.

* **Across the Plains** 1 April 1911 990 ft. Redlands D: G. M. Anderson SC: Josephine Rector C: G. M. Anderson (cowboy), Gladys Field (Jennie Lee),

Arthur Mackley (drunken father), Fred Church (Indian and cowboy), John B. O'Brien (cowboy's friend), Harry Todd, Brinsley Shaw, Victor Potel S: A cowboy aids a woman in a covered wagon pursued by Indians, while his friend rides for help. [NFTA]

The Sheriff's Chum 8 April 1911 Redlands D: G. M. Anderson C: G. M. Anderson (sheriff Will Phelps), Gladys Field (Jessie Phelps), Brinsley Shaw (George Arden), Fred Church (prisoner), Harry Todd, Victor Potel, Chick Morrison, John B. O'Brien S: George, once Will's rival for Jessie, is invited to dinner, and when Will is called away on business George makes advances on her. [LOC]

The Bad Man's First Prayer 15 April 1911 Redlands D: G. M. Anderson C: G. M. Anderson (Dan Quigley), Gladys Field (Alice Selling), Harry Todd (sheriff), Arthur Mackley, Julia Mackley S: Bad man Dan Quigley takes the blame for a stagecoach holdup done by Alice's father Joe. Alice gives Dan a bible to read in jail.

* *The Indian Maiden's Lesson* 22 April 1911 Redlands D: G. M. Anderson C: G. M. Anderson (Rev. Warren Addington), Anna Little (Red Feather), Arthur Mackley (Jack Beardsley), Harry Todd, Victor Potel, John B. O'Brien, Fred Church S: When gold is discovered by Beardsley, he pistol-whips his partner Rev. Addington and leaves him in the desert to die. Red Feather finds Addington, nurses him back to health and, when a confrontation with Beardsley arises, she stops Addington from killing Beardsley with the com-

mandment he wrote on a slate: "Thou Shalt Not Kill." (remade as *Broncho Billy's Teachings*, released 13 March 1915) [NFTA]

What a Woman Can Do 29 April 1911 950 ft. Redlands D: G. M. Anderson C: G. M. Anderson (Frank Mills) S: Frank Mills has one ambition, to marry Helen Wilson. They marry and go west. After the hardships of prospecting he strikes gold and goes to their cabin to announce the news, but finds a note saying she has grown tired of their miserable life and has left with another man. Ten years later, Mills is a wealthy businessman, and gets a telephone call that Helen is dying in a hospital, but he refuses to go to her. Twenty years more and he visits his money in a vault, accidently gets locked in and dies. (the basis for *Humanity*, released in May, 1917, also known as *Naked Hands*, released in January, 1918)

The Bunco Game at Lizardhead 6 May 1911 Redlands D: G. M. Anderson C: Augustus Carney, Victor Potel, Gladys Field, Arthur Mackley, Fred Church, Harry Todd S: Jake and Millie Walters run a scam that enables them to sell dozens of "How to Make Love" books to every cowboy in Lizardhead, Arizona, before catching a train out of town.

* *The Puncher's New Love* 13 May 1911 Redlands D: G. M. Anderson C: G. M. Anderson (Harvey Barton), Gladys Field (city girl), Anna Little (Kate Bowers), John B. O'Brien, Augustus Carney, Harry Todd, Robert Gray, Margaret Joslin, Victor Potel, Brinsley Shaw S: Barton drops his girlfriend Kate for a city girl who rejects him. When he re-

turns to Kate asking forgiveness, she won't take him back. (remade as *Broncho Billy Well Repaid*, released 9 July 1915) [NFTA]

"Alkali" Ike's Auto 20 May 1911 Redlands D: G. M. Anderson C: Augustus Carney (Alkali Ike), Harry Todd (Mustang Pete), Margaret Joslin (Betty Brown), William A. Russell (auto owner), Arthur Mackley (man in apron), Victor Potel, John B. O'Brien, Fred Church S: Pete takes Betty on a buggy ride and Ike, Pete's rival, tries to one-up him by enticing Betty away with an old automobile of questionable merit. (reissued 15 November 1913) [UCLA, LOC, video]

The Lucky Card 27 May 1911 Redlands D: G. M. Anderson C: G. M. Anderson (George Maxwell), Gladys Field (the woman), Fred Church (Mexican), Harry Todd (Mexican), John B. O'Brien, Chick Morrison, Anna Little, Augustus Carney, Arthur Mackley S: Maxwell is kidnapped by three Mexicans after he beats one in a barroom brawl. The Mexicans plan to kill Maxwell, but he recognizes one of them as a prospector he saved some months earlier, and the man prevents the murder. (remake of *The Mexican's Gratitude*, released 5 May 1909)

The Western Essanay arrived in Santa Monica on 9 April 1911.

The Infant at Snakeville 3 June 1911 Santa Monica D: G. M. Anderson C: G. M. Anderson (Broncho Bill), Augustus Carney, Harry Todd, Victor Potel, John B. O'Brien, Arthur Mackley S: After a baby is accidently separated

from his mother during a stagecoach journey, some cowboys in Snakeville are recruited to care for the child.

Forgiven in Death 10 June 1911 Santa Monica D: G. M. Anderson C: G. M. Anderson (Jack), Brinsley Shaw (Ned), Arthur Mackley (Katy's father), Gladys Field (Katy), Harry Todd (minister), Julia Mackley (minister's wife), Fred Church (Indian) S: Jack and Katy are secretly married. On a prospecting trip, Ned hides the letters Katy sends to Jack because Ned is jealous, but when Indians attack their cabin and the miners are near death Ned confesses to Jack. [NFTA, LOC]

The Tribe's Penalty 17 June 1911 Santa Monica D: G. M. Anderson C: G. M. Anderson (Gray Wolf), Gladys Field (Dorothy Sloane), John B. O'Brien S: Gray Wolf helps a white woman to escape from an Indian camp and is killed by the tribe.

The Hidden Mine 24 June 1911 Santa Monica D: G. M. Anderson C: Arthur Mackley (William Hart), Brinsley Shaw (Indian), Harry Todd (Indian) S: Two Indians steal supplies from a miner's family and set fire to their house. When the miner sifts through the ashes he finds a streak of paydirt.

The Sheriff's Brother 1 July 1911 Santa Monica D: G. M. Anderson C: G. M. Anderson S: A sheriff tracks down a stagecoach robber and discovers it's his brother. The sheriff urges him to escape, but the bandit commits suicide rather than compromise the sheriff's honor. (remade as *The Calling of Jim Barton*, released 14 February 1914)

A Hungry Pair 5 July 1911 528 ft. Santa Monica D: G. M. Anderson C: Augustus Carney (Shorty), Victor Potel (Skinny) S: Two hobos steal a police uniform so they can get a free meal at a restaurant and safely escape by being "arrested." Skinny saves Shorty, but Shorty falls asleep when Skinny tries the trick and Skinny is arrested for real.

At the Break of Dawn 7 July 1911 Santa Monica D: G. M. Anderson C: G. M. Anderson (Gilbert Randal) S: On a surveying expedition, Gilbert Randal meets and marries Pepita, but he abandons her to return to New York. She waits five years for his return, and when Pedro, who has always loved her and spoken against the American, tells her he's seen Randal in town with a woman, Pepita runs toward the village, but is killed in an earthquake.

* The Corporation and the Ranch Girl 8 July 1911 Santa Monica D: G. M. Anderson C: G. M. Anderson (Gerald Todds), Gladys Field (Ann Newton), Arthur Mackley (H. Todds and H. M. Blake), Brinsley Shaw, Fred Church, John B. O'Brien, Victor Potel, Augustus Carney, Harry Todd, Margaret Joslin S: Railroad president H. Todds sends his son Gerald to trick Ann into selling her land to the railroad, but Gerald falls for her and writes to his father that "they" won't sell. [NFTA]

Mustang Pete's Love Affair 11 July 1911 Santa Monica C: Harry Todd (Mustang Pete), Augustus Carney (Alkali Ike), Margaret Joslin, Victor Potel, Fred Church, Gladys Field S: One of the two boarding houses in Snakeville gets an edge on the competition by hiring a young lady to attract the cowboys.

The Backwoodsman's Suspicions 15 July 1911 Santa Monica D: G. M. Anderson C: G. M. Anderson S: An author out west for his health teaches a backwoodsman's illiterate wife to read, making her husband jealous.

Essanay left Santa Monica 27 May 1911 for San Rafael, arriving on the 31st.

The Outlaw Samaritan 22 July 1911 San Rafael and Fairfax D: G. M. Anderson C: G. M. Anderson (Jack Mason), Arthur Mackley (Detective Clarington) S: Detective Clarington breaks an ankle in the hilly countryside while tracking express train robber Jack Mason, and Mason, although knowing Clarington's identity, nurses the detective back to health. (remade as *Broncho Billy's Cunning,* released 30 May 1914)

The Two Fugitives 29 July 1911 San Rafael D; G. M. Anderson C: G. M. Anderson (Jack Harvey), Arthur Mackley, Victor Potel S: Harvey is hired by a cattle company president to pick a fight with a squatter and kill him, but when Myrtle Dunn, the ranch superintendent's daughter, shows Harvey the squatter's cabin, child and sick wife, Harvey backs off.

The Ranchman's Son 12 August 1911 Santa Monica working title: *A Race With Death* D: Arthur Mackley S: A ranchman's son is wrongly accused of murder. The man who did it struggles with his conscience to confess.

* A Pal's Oath 19 August 1911 San Rafael D: G. M. Anderson C: G. M.

Anderson (Jack Manley), Brinsley Shaw (John French), Harry Todd (U. S. Marshall and a minister), Arthur Mackley (doctor), Gladys Field (Marie Wentworth) S: Manley robs a pony expressman to pay a doctor to save his sick friend John French, but French later betrays their secret when they become rivals over a woman. (remade as *Broncho Billy's Oath*, released 11 October 1913) [LOC]

"Spike" Shannon's Last Fight 26 August 1911 980 ft. San Rafael D: G. M. Anderson C: G. M. Anderson (Spike Shannon), Gladys Field (Nora Flannigan), Arthur Mackley (fight promoter), Lew Rushing (fighter), Glenn Shaver (referee), Margaret Joslin S: Before she agrees to marry Spike, Nora makes him promise to quit boxing, but when she needs an expensive, life-saving operation he tries to win the money with one last fight.

A Western Girl's Sacrifice 2 September 1911 San Rafael and Santa Monica D: G. M. Anderson SC: Arthur Mackley C: G. M. Anderson (Harry Farman), Gladys Field, Arthur Mackley, Fred Church, Harry Todd, Augustus Carney, William A. Russell S: When the western wife of a city-raised man realizes he still loves the woman he traveled from the east to forget, she begs the woman to marry her husband, then commits suicide. (remade as *The Other Girl*, released 14 May 1915)

Broncho Bill's Last Spree 9 September 1911 980 ft. San Rafael D: G. M. Anderson ST: based on "The Reformation of Calliope" by O. Henry C: G. M. Anderson (Broncho Bill), Victor

Potel, Augustus Carney (Alkali Ike) S: Bill gets drunk and shoots up the town for the last time after his mom unexpectedly arrives for a visit and the sheriff shoulders him with the responsibility of keeping the peace. (remade as *Broncho Billy's Mother*, released 31 October 1914

The Puncher's Law 14 September 1911 980 ft. San Rafael D: G. M. Anderson C: G. M. Anderson S: When the woman Tom Patterson loves marries a no-good gambler and dies from his abuse, Patterson goes after the gambler to avenge her death.

The Millionaire and the Squatter 16 September 1911 980 ft. San Rafael D: G. M. Anderson C: G. M. Anderson S: Silas Strong, a miner evicted from Gordon Olcott's property, goes after Olcott to shoot him, but when Olcott accidently falls off a cliff and pleads for help, it is Strong who aids him.

An Indian's Sacrifice 23 September 1911 980 ft. San Rafael D: G. M. Anderson C: G. M. Anderson (Grey Deer) S: On his deathbed, Sam Madden makes his daughter Emily promise to marry his friend Grey Deer, an educated Indian, and she does, even though she loves a cousin. A year later Grey Deer discovers them together and consents to a separation, but vows the cousin will be punished if his love is false.

The Power of Good 28 September 1911 San Rafael D: G. M. Anderson C: G. M. Anderson S: A wounded outlaw is taken in and cared for by a backwoodsman and his daughter. Their kindness brings from him a pledge to reform, and he gives himself up to the sheriff.

The Strike at the "Little Jonny" Mine 30 September 1911 San Rafael D: G. M. Anderson C: G. M. Anderson (Jim Logan), Arthur Mackley (J. C. Phillips), Gladys Field (Mrs. Logan), Victor Potel, Augustus Carney, Fred Church S: Logan, a mine worker, helps mine-owner Phillips fend off a mob of violent strikers until the sheriff arrives, and later negotiates an acceptable agreement between the two parties.

The Sheriff's Decision 6 October 1911 San Rafael D: G. M. Anderson C: G. M. Anderson (Steve Jameson), Robert H. Gray (Manuel Garcia) S: Jameson, a sheriff in love with Nita Sanchez, gives her up when she wants to elope with Manuel Garcia. Then Jameson receives a telegram ordering him to arrest Garcia for murder, and he does so.

Town Hall, Tonight 7 October 1911 San Rafael D: G. M. Anderson C: Victor Potel (tall Schultz brother), Augustus Carney (short Schultz brother), G. M. Anderson (Broncho Bill), Harry Todd (Mustang Pete), Arthur Mackley, Margaret Joslin, Fred Church S: The Schultz brothers, stranded vaudeville artists, perform in Snakeville hoping to earn enough to get to New York.

The Stage Driver's Daughter 14 October 1911 San Rafael D: G. M. Anderson C: G. M. Anderson (Tom Percival), Arthur Mackley (William or Pete or Jim Lacey), Gladys Field (Nell or Rose or Alice Lacey), Augustus Carney, Fred Church, Louis Morisette S: Stagecoach driver William Lacey is drugged by the Riley boys to prevent him from taking Tom Percival to the assay office to file a mining claim, so Lacey's daughter takes the reins while Tom holds off the scoundrels from the back of the coach. (remade as *Broncho Billy and the Claim Jumpers*, released 9 January 1915)

A Western Redemption 21 October 1911 San Rafael D: G. M. Anderson C: G. M. Anderson S: A father loses his job because his son is jailed for theft. The father and his wife go west to start over and the son follows after his release. The son unknowingly robs the store which his father manages, but when he finds this out he gives himself up to the sheriff. (remade as *Broncho Billy's Parents*, released 15 October 1915)

The Forester's Plea 28 October 1911 San Rafael D: G. M. Anderson C: G. M. Anderson (Rev. Small), Arthur Mackley (Henry Carter), Fred Church (sheriff), Gladys Field (Agnes), Victor Potel, Louis Morisette S: Carter, an alcoholic who has given up drinking with the help of Rev. Small, is forced to drink by saloonman Jake Easton and three cronies. When Easton is accidently killed in a fight with Carter, Small helps Carter again by making it look like self-defense.

Outwitting Papa 31 October 1911 San Rafael D: G. M. Anderson C: G. M. Anderson (Tom Phelps), Arthur Mackley (Col. Walker), Edna Fisher (Ethel Walker), Harry Todd (Rev. Jones or Rev. Arnold Smith) S: Walker is against the marriage of his daughter Ethel to Phelps. He bars the windows and locks the doors to make it difficult for her to escape, but a toothache sets the stage for the youngsters to outwit him and marry.

The Outlaw Deputy 4 November 1911 San Rafael D: G. M. Anderson C: G. M. Anderson (Buck Stevens) S: A young outlaw who's shown kindness by the sheriff serves his time in jail, then volunteers to go after a dangerous criminal who wounded the sheriff.

The Girl Back East 11 November 1911 San Rafael D: G. M. Anderson C: G. M. Anderson (Jack King) S: Jack and Tom, two prospecting buddies, get a letter asking for help from the girl back east that they both love. They flip a coin to decide who should go, but Tom, the loser, can't contain his jealousy and shoots Jack. The wound isn't serious, and Tom, feeling bad about what he did, urges Jack to go. They exchange guns as tokens of remembrance and Jack realizes who shot him, but surpresses his desire for revenge and goes east.

Hubby's Scheme 14 November 1911 San Rafael D: G. M. Anderson C: Augustus Carney (Hubby), Margaret Joslin (his wife), Harry Todd, G. M. Anderson S: Some male friends coax Hubby into a resort hotel vacation, but first he must get permission from his wife.

President Taft in San Francisco 16 November 1911 P: Jess Robbins S: This newsreel, taken on 13-14 October 1911, shows William Howard Taft, Lillian Nordica and Charles de Young breaking ground for the Panama Pacific International Exposition in San Francisco.

The following films were most likely directed by Arthur Mackley. He continued to direct, usually starring himself, when *Anderson was not the star. Anderson directed his own starring productions and the Alkali Ike films.*

A Cattle Rustler's Father 18 November 1911 San Rafael and Lake Tahoe D: Arthur Mackley? C: Arthur Mackley, Fred Church? S: The worthless son of a rancher is tracked by a sheriff's posse. He tries to hide at his father's ranch, but the old man turns him in. Realizing what a dope he's been, the son asks his father's forgiveness.

The Desert Claim 25 November 1911 San Rafael and Lake Tahoe D: Arthur Mackley? C: Arthur Mackley, Fred Church, Kite Robinson, Victor Potel, Augustus Carney S: An old prospector makes the mistake of showing ore samples of his gold strike around town, and two men attempt to ambush him, but Lee tricks them with a bedroll wadded up in his tent and overpowers them.

Papa's Letter 5 December 1911 San Rafael D: Arthur Mackley? C: Fred Church (Papa), Edna Fisher (his wife), Eugenia Clinchard (Johnny) S: Unable to comprehend the death of his papa in a train accident, little Johnny asks his mother if he can write a letter to his father. Without thinking, his mother puts a stamp on his forehead and says he is a letter to papa. He goes outside to wait for the mailman and is hit by a car. "Papa's letter went to heaven."

The Frontier Doctor 9 December 1911 San Rafael D: Arthur Mackley? C: Arthur Mackley, Eugenia Clinchard (daughter) S: Jameson, a widower with a five year old daughter, proposes to Nan Warren, but she marries another man.

When her husband is hurt and needs an operation she sends for the doctor. The doctor realizes a chance for revenge, but resists the temptation.

* *The Cowboy Coward* 16 December 1911 San Rafael D: G. M. Anderson C: G. M. Anderson (Steve), Gladys Field (Katie), Brinsley Shaw (Cash Wilkins) S: Wilkins, a bully, insults Katie, a rancher's daughter, then takes her revolver and says if she wants it back her boyfriend Henry will have to get it. Henry, a coward, asks his fellow cowboy Steve to go. Steve thrashes Wilkins, gets the gun and gives it to Henry. Henry pretends to Katie that he did it, and Steve, disgusted, silently packs up and leaves the ranch. (remade as *Broncho Billy - Favorite*, released 24 October 1914) [NFMA, LOC]

* *Broncho Billy's Christmas Dinner* 23 December 1911 San Rafael D: G. M. Anderson C: G. M. Anderson (Broncho Billy), Arthur Mackley (sheriff), Edna Fisher (sheriff's daughter), Julia Mackley (sheriff's wife), Willis Elder (deputy), Brinsley Shaw (guard), Victor Potel, Kite Robinson, Harry Todd, Augustus Carney, Pat Rooney, Louis Morisette, Al Parks, Fred Church, Josephine Rector, Margaret Joslin, Robert H. Gray S: The stagecoach Billy intends to rob rushes by him out of control with a young woman alone in the driver's seat. Billy saves her by chasing down the coach. In gratitude she invites him to her home for Christmas dinner. When her father, a sheriff, thanks Billy, Billy is secretly shamed, and after a cheerful, law-abiding crowd gathers at the table he gives himself up, pledging to reform. [NFTA, NFMA]

A Story of the West 26 December 1911 San Rafael D: G. M. Anderson C: G. M. Anderson S: A paralysed prospector overcomes his disability and helps his wife as she struggles with an desperate outlaw. (remade as *Broncho Billy and the Escaped Bandit*, released 2 January 1915)

Broncho Billy's Adventure 30 December 1911 San Rafael D: G. M. Anderson C: G. M. Anderson (Broncho Billy), Arthur Mackley, Edna Fisher, Fred Church, Victor Potel, Kite Robinson, Pat Rooney S: Billy holds off a mob that wants to hang a tavern-owner who shot and wounded the sweetheart of the owner's daughter. (remade as *Broncho Billy Butts In*, released 19 September 1914)

1912

* *A Child of the West* 6 January 1912 San Rafael D: G. M. Anderson? C: Harry Todd (Jim Riley), Eugenia Clinchard (Riley's child), Arthur Mackley (sheriff), Augustus Carney (rancher), G. M. Anderson, Willis Elder, Pat Rooney, Victor Potel, Kite Robinson, Fred Church, Louis Morisette S: Riley, arrested for horse-stealing, is taken by an unruly mob to be hanged, but the sheriff gets Riley's little daughter to plead for her father's life. The mob weakens and returns Riley to the sheriff. (remade as *Broncho Billy and the Posse,* released 23 July 1915) [NFTA]

The Tenderfoot Foreman 11 January 1912 San Rafael D: G. M. Anderson C: G. M. Anderson (Jack Reed), Edna Fisher (Jane), Brinsley Shaw (Buck Brady), Harry Todd, Victor Potel, William A. Russell S: Jane hires an inexperienced foreman to run her ranch, and has to get a sheriff to save him from a cowboy mob.

The Sheepman's Escape 13 January 1912 San Rafael D: G. M. Anderson C: G. M. Anderson (Tom Harper), Brinsley Shaw (Buck Brady), Julia Mackley (Mrs. Harper), Edna Fisher S: Tom Harper and his widowed mother try to start a sheep ranch in cattle country.

* *The Loafer* 20 January 1912 San Rafael D: Arthur Mackley C: Arthur Mackley (Joe Simmons), Julia Mackley (Simmons' wife), Marguerite Todd (Simmons' daughter), Harry Todd (Jim Wrayburn), Margaret Joslin (Wrayburn's wife), Brinsley Shaw, Kite Robinson, Augustus Carney, Victor Potel S: Wrayburn leads a group of masked men that horse-whips lazy Joe Simmons, advising him to work and support his family. Simmons vows to get even when he finds out who they are. [NFTA]

Widow Jenkins' Admirers 23 January 1912 San Rafael D: G. M. Anderson C: Augustus Carney (Alkali Ike), Harry Todd (Mustang Pete), Edna Fisher (Widow Jenkins), Arthur Mackley, Victor Potel, Harry Keenan S: The menfolk of Snakeville swarm over the rich widow Jenkins, all of them aiming to marry her.

The Oath of His Office 27 January 1912 San Rafael D: G. M. Anderson C: G. M. Anderson (Bob Graham), Fred Church, Harry Todd, Arthur Mackley, Willis Elder, Brinsley Shaw, Victor Potel S: Bob Graham upholds the oath of his office as sheriff and stops a lynch mob from hanging a man who deceptively married the woman Graham was once engaged to wed.

Broncho Billy and the Schoolmistress 3 February 1912 San Rafael D: G. M. Anderson C: G. M. Anderson (Broncho Billy), Fred Church, Augustus Carney S: A rival of Billy for the schoolmistress contrives what appears to be a practical joke but in reality is set up for Billy to be shot and killed by the schoolmistress.

"Alkali" Ike's Love Affair 6 February 1912 San Rafael D: G. M. Anderson C: Augustus Carney (Alkali Ike), Harry Todd (Mustang Pete), Margaret Joslin (Betty Brown) S: Ike tries to show his bravery in front of Betty's father by staging the capture of two hold-up men (actually Ike's buddies), but it turns out the men he encounters are for real.

The Deputy and the Girl 10 February 1912 San Rafael D: G. M. Anderson C: G. M. Anderson (deputy), Edna Fisher (Edna Black), Brinsley Shaw (Frank Shaw), Arthur Mackley (sheriff), Fred Church S: Edna shields Shaw (her fiance) after a stagecoach robbery, but when he seriously wounds a deputy she becomes enraged at him and he leaves, only to be caught by a posse.

The Prospector's Legacy 17 February 1912 San Rafael D: G. M. Anderson? C: Harry Todd, Fred Church, Julia Mackley, Victor Potel, Kite Robinson, Harry Keenan (sheriff), Louis Morisette S: A horse trader kills a prospector for his gold, but is thwarted by a young couple who happen upon the scene.

Curiosity 20 February 1912 ? ft. San Rafael D: Arthur Mackley S: A man with a suspicious bag is chased through the streets, but it turns out he's just trying to catch a train.

The Biter Bitten 20 February 1912 ? ft. D: G. M. Anderson C: Augustus Carney, Victor Potel S: A nasty landlord takes a motorcycle in payment for back rent and tries to sell it.

A Western Kimono 24 February 1912 San Rafael at 4th and B St., Union Depot, and the tunnel D: G. M. Anderson C: Augustus Carney (Alkali Ike), Harry Todd (Mustang Pete), Edna Fisher (Ike's wife) S: Ike mistakenly believes his wife has caught the dreaded Kimonitis disease.

The Essanay Company arrived in Lakeside, California, 12 January 1912. Vedah Bertram's first film was made here.

* *The Ranch Girl's Mistake* 2 March 1912 Lakeside D: G. M. Anderson C: G. M. Anderson (Broncho Billy), Vedah Bertram (Nan Morgan), Brinsley Shaw, Victor Potel, Fred Church S: Billy and Nan are expected to marry, but a flashy Easterner shows up and turns Nan's head. Billy packs to leave town and meets the Easterner's wife at the train depot. She's looking for her husband, and Billy brings him to her. (remake of *The Ranchman's Rival,* released 11 December 1909) [GEH]

A Romance of the West 9 March 1912 Lakeside D: Arthur Mackley? C: Arthur Mackley, Julia Mackley S: A widowed woman fends off a landowner intent on removing her and her daughter from his land, but when she accidently shoots her child during a scuffle, and the land-

owner rushes the girl to a doctor, the adversaries have a change of heart. (remake of *The Fence on Bar Z Ranch,* released 12 March 1910)

The Ranch Widower's Daughters 12 March 1912 Lakeside D: G. M. Anderson C: Augustus Carney (Alkali Ike), Arthur Mackley (widower), Margaret Joslin, Vedah Bertram S: A widower with nine daughters seems determined to keep them all at home and unmarried, but the daughters have other ideas. (remake of *A Ranchman's Wooing,* released 26 March 1910)

The Bandit's Child 16 March 1912 Lakeside D: G. M. Anderson C: G. M. Anderson (Tom Fleming), Vedah Bertram (Mrs. Fleming), Arthur Mackley (a blacksmith), Augustus Carney, Harry Todd, Pat Rooney S: A reformed bandit, refused honest work because of his past, vows to take up armed robbery again, but the stagecoach he selects includes among its passengers his wife and child, who are on their way from the east to join him. (remade as *The Redemption of Broncho Billy,* released 3 June 1914, and *The Outlaw's Awakening,* released 27 March 1915)

The Deputy's Love Affair 23 March 1912 Lakeside D: G. M. Anderson C: G. M. Anderson (Bill Simpson) S: Dolores, jealous of Bill's love for Olive, schemes with Pedro to break the couple's engagement by having Bill discover Olive in an embrace with Pedro.

* *"Alkali" Bests Broncho Billy* 26 March 1912 Lakeside D: G. M. Anderson C: Augustus Carney (Alkali Ike), G. M. Anderson (Broncho Billy) S: Billy wins

a riding contest to take his boss's niece to the dance, but Ike tops him because he's in charge of the music and if he doesn't get the girl there won't be a dance. [GEH]

An Arizona Escapade 30 March 1912 Lakeside D: G. M. Anderson C: G. M. Anderson S: Brig Harris and a pal attempt to steal an ore shipment from the express headquarters in town, which is the home of Dr. and Mrs. Barnes. The doctor is lured to a shack and tied up. The bandits go to the house to overpower Mrs. Barnes, but she barricades herself in and holds them off until a posse arrives.

A Road Agent's Love 6 April 1912 Lakeside D: G. M. Anderson C: G. M. Anderson (Bob Farco or Andy), Vedah Bertram (Lucy Mackley), Arthur Mackley (John Mackley), Julia Mackley, Brinsley Shaw S: A notorious bandit, Bob Farco, sacrifices his freedom so that Lucy, the daughter of a down-on-his-luck rancher, can get the reward for his capture and pay the mortgage on her father's ranch.

Broncho Billy and the Girl 9 April 1912 Lakeside D: G. M. Anderson C: G. M. Anderson (Broncho Billy), Vedah Bertram (Nan Fowler) S: Nan stops bad man Billy from disrupting a dance and a romance begins to develop, but when he robs a cattleman of his wallet and finds a photo of Nan inside it, he goes to the ranch to give back the money regardless of the consequences.

Under Mexican Skies 13 April 1912 Lakeside D: G. M. Anderson C: G. M. Anderson (Pasquale), Vedah Bertram (Vedah Fowler) S: Pasquale, in love with Vedah, is rejected by her, but when an Eastern suitor, also rejected, tries to force her into marriage Pasquale rescues her. (remake of *The Mexican's Gratitude*, released 26 February 1910)

The Cattle King's Daughter 20 April 1912 Lakeside D: G. M. Anderson C: G. M. Anderson (Buck Brady), Arthur Mackley (the cattle king), Brinsley Shaw S: Two members of Buck Brady's gang kidnap the cattle king's daughter for ransom and take her to a shack where Brady is deliriously sick. She nurses Brady back to health and, in gratitude, he escorts her home.

"Alkali" Ike's Boarding House 23 April 1912 Lakeside D: G. M. Anderson C: Augustus Carney (Alkali Ike), Margaret Joslin (Bridget or Maggie), Arthur Mackley, Fred Church, Harry Todd, Kite Robinson, Al Parks, Louis Morisette S: Ike is chosen by the ranch cowboys to tell the cook that her food is inedible. She leaves and Ike is faced with the task of cooking.

The Indian and the Child 27 April 1912 Lakeside D: G. M. Anderson C: G. M. Anderson (Indian), Arthur Mackley (Jake Willis) S: Jake Willis, a timber-cutter, unjustly fires an Indian from his crew, and later discovers the Indian carrying his unconcious little daughter in the woods. Willis thinks the Indian tried to kidnap her and plans to shoot him, but the little girl revives to tell of being saved by the Indian just in time to save the Indian's life.

* Broncho Billy and the Bandits 4 May 1912 Lakeside D: G. M. Anderson C:

G. M. Anderson (Broncho Billy), Arthur Mackley (storekeeper), Marguerite Loveridge (storekeeper's daughter), Julia Mackley (storekeeper's wife), Fred Church (Arizona Kid), Brinsley Shaw, Harry Todd, Al Parks, Louis Morisette S: Billy is mistaken as the notorious Arizona Kid and is held prisoner by the storekeeper's daughter. Then the real Arizona Kid and his gang show up to steal an express shipment, and Billy holds them off. (remade as *Broncho Billy - A Friend in Need*, released 12 September 1914) [LOC]

"Alkali" Ike's Bride 7 May 1912 Lakeside D: G. M. Anderson C: Augustus Carney (Alkali Ike) S: Ike sends for a wealthy widow to marry him, but the ranch boys try to scare him off by disguising one of their number as the new bride.

* *The Dead Man's Claim* 11 May 1912 Lakeside D: G. M. Anderson C: G. M. Anderson (Jim Durkin), Fred Church (his partner Black), Arthur Mackley (the prospector), Brinsley Shaw (Indian) S: A dying prospector tells Durkin about his rich claim, but Black double-crosses Durkin when they're on the way to locate the claim far out in the desert. [LOC]

The Sheriff and His Man 18 May 1912 Lakeside and San Rafael D: G. M. Anderson C: G. M. Anderson (Arizona Kid), Arthur Mackley (Sheriff Matthews), Harry Todd (Sheriff Todd and Mexican), Fred Church (Mexican) S: Sheriff Matthews is escorting the Arizona Kid across the desert to jail when two Mexicans attack, shoot the sheriff and take their horses. The Kid carries

Matthews to town then goes after the Mexicans.

* *A Western Legacy* 21 May 1912 Lakeside D: G. M. Anderson C: G. M. Anderson (Walter Johnson), Marguerite Loveridge (Alice), Margaret Joslin (Alice's Mother), Harry Todd (Alice's father) S: Walter Johnson is bound by an uncle's million-dollar will to marry a cousin he's never seen before, or forfeit the money to the woman. The woman is also notified: marry or forfeit. They both dress up as odd characters to repulse their cousin and get the money, but otherwise meet and fall in love. [LOC]

The Desert Sweetheart 25 May 1912 Lakeside D: G. M. Anderson C: G. M. Anderson (Jim Morris), Vedah Bertram (Mary), Fred Church (Wells) S: Wells takes a letter from Morris at a desert prospecting camp to Mary, who is engaged to Morris. Mary and Wells fall in love and go away to the desert, but run short of water and Wells dies. Mary is saved by Morris.

Broncho Billy's Bible 1 June 1912 Lakeside and Niles D: G. M. Anderson C: G. M. Anderson (Broncho Billy), Fred Church ("Quick-Draw" Kelly), Harry Todd, Josephine Rector S: Billy and a pal rob a stagecoach. Billy takes a Bible as part of his share of the loot. Later, Billy and Kelly get in a argument during a poker game, and the Bible, tucked in Billy's shirt, stops a bullet from Kelly's gun. Billy goes after Kelly and catches him on a mountain ledge, but as Billy is about to push Kelly over the edge the Bible falls open to "Thou shalt not kill." Billy lets Kelly go and ponders the worthless life he's led.

On El Monte Ranch 4 June 1912 Lakeside D: G. M. Anderson C: G. M. Anderson (foreman), Vedah Bertram (Mary Trent), Robert H. Gray (Dave Trent), Fred Church, Harry Todd, Pat Rooney, Kite Robinson, Al Parks, Louis Morisette S: When Dave Trent cheats at cards, his fellow cowboys on the Big O ranch insist the foreman fire him. Trent lies to his sister Mary about it and she breaks off her engagement to the foreman. But after the foreman saves Trent from hanging as a cattle rustler, Trent writes to Mary telling the truth, and the couple reunite. [NFTA]

The Western Essanay moved from Lakeside to Niles on 1 April 1912. A Child of the Purple Sage *was probably their first film made completely in Niles.*

A Child of the Purple Sage 8 June 1912 Niles D: G. M. Anderson C: G. M. Anderson (Bart Darrow), Violet Kelly (little girl) S: Darrow becomes an outlaw when a woman he loves leaves him for another man. Years later he saves a little girl alone in a covered wagon beside the dead body of that same woman.

Western Hearts 15 June 1912 Lakeside and the desert near Yuma, Arizona D: G. M. Anderson C: G. M. Anderson (Sam Hardy), Vedah Bertram (Vedah), Marguerite Loveridge (Mabel), Harry Todd, Fred Church S: Vedah, a poor cripple saving money for an operation, uses the money to pay for the release from jail of Hardy, whom she secretly loves. (remade as *Broncho Billy and the Sisters*, released 16 January 1915)

Broncho Billy's Gratitude 18 June 1912 Niles working title: Broncho Billy and the Schoolmarm's Kid D: G. M. Anderson C: G. M. Anderson (Broncho Billy), Vedah Bertram (Mrs. Hart), Brinsley Shaw (Dan Hart), Audrey Hanna (the Hart's child) S: Billy, a wounded outlaw, is tended by Mrs. Hart. While he heals he makes friends with the woman's child. Later, the woman's estranged husband, Dan Hart, kidnaps their child and escapes by stagecoach, one that is soon held up by Billy. Billy realizes something is wrong and takes the child back to her mother, but is arrested by a posse and taken to jail. (remade as *Broncho's Surrender*, released 29 July 1915)

The Foreman's Cousin 22 June 1912 Niles D: G. M. Anderson C: G. M. Anderson (Bob Knight), Robert Lawler (Bob Lawlor), Vedah Bertram (Sue Jordan) S: Bob Knight, the foreman of a ranch, welcomes his cousin Bob Lawlor, there for a vacation. Knight's girlfriend Sue Jordan falls for Lawlor. Lawlor gets in with the wrong crowd, rustles cattle and Sue protects Lawlor by directing a posse to arrest Knight. When Lawlor finds out he gives himself up.

Broncho Billy and the Indian Maid 29 June 1912 Niles D: G. M. Anderson C: G. M. Anderson (Broncho Billy), Vedah Bertram (Laughing Fawn), Arthur Mackley (her father), Brinsley Shaw (Bart McGrew), Fred Church (sheriff), Louis Morisette, Al Parks S: Billy stops McGrew from punishing Laughing Fawn for foiling a scheme to sign over her father's land. Vengeful, McGrew attempts to sneak up on Billy and shoot him, but Laughing Fawn shoots McGrew first. Billy makes it look like self-defense, and the sheriff buys it.

On the Cactus Trail 2 July 1912 Niles D: G. M. Anderson C: G. M. Anderson (Jim Andrews), Vedah Bertram (Vedah Powers), Fred Church (Dan Clayton), Brinsley Shaw, Victor Potel, Willis Elder, Pat Rooney S: Vedah comes west to marry her boyfriend Dan Clayton and discovers he's a murderer on the loose.

* *Broncho Billy's Narrow Escape* 6 July 1912 Niles D: G. M. Anderson C: G. M. Anderson (Broncho Billy), Vedah Bertram (Lois Martin), Arthur Mackley (Ben Martin), Brinsley Shaw (Baxter), Fred Church, Victor Potel, Harry Todd, Jack Roberts, Pat Rooney, Willis Elder S: Billy gets work at Ben Martin's mine claim and befriends his daughter Lois to the dismay of Baxter, who wants to marry her. Billy takes Ben's horse to file a claim and Baxter reports it stolen, expecting Billy to be lynched. Vedah finds out and saves Billy. (remake of *The Romance on "Bar O"*, released 11 March 1911) [NFTA, NFMA]

A Story of Montana 13 July 1912 Niles D: G. M. Anderson C: G. M. Anderson (Jim Burrows), Arthur Mackley (Clayton), Vedah Bertram (Clayton's daughter), Harry Todd (sheriff), Brinsley Shaw (Dan Morris), Victor Potel, Al Parks, Louis Morisette, Julia Mackley S: When Morris, jealous of the love between Burrows and Clayton's daughter, discovers Clayton dead of a heart attack, Morris shoots the body and plants Burrows' hand-made gauntlets nearby to get revenge. (remade as *The Escape of Broncho Billy*, released 10 December 1915)

* *The Smuggler's Daughter* 16 July 1912 Niles D: G. M. Anderson C: G. M. Anderson (Brant Graham), Vedah Bertram (Vedah Gregg), Arthur Mackley (Silas Gregg), Fred Church (sheriff), Brinsley Shaw, Harry Todd, Augustus Carney, Louis Morisette, Al Parks, Pat Rooney, Frank Pementel, Hal Angus? S: Deputy sheriff Brant Graham is engaged to Vedah Gregg, daughter of Silas, who Graham discovers is a smuggler. Vedah prevents Graham from arresting her father, then she finds out the gang plans to kill Graham. She gets the sheriff and a posse saves Brant at the last moment. [NFTA]

* *A Wife of the Hills* 20 July 1912 Niles D: G. M. Anderson C: G. M. Anderson (Bart McGrew), Arthur Mackley (sheriff), Brinsley Shaw, Vedah Bertram S: Bart McGrew's wife and Bart's fellow bandit, Dan Trent, turn McGrew over to the sheriff. McGrew escapes from jail, followed by the sheriff, and is about to shoot through the window of a shack at Trent, who is with McGrew's wife, when the sheriff fires at McGrew. The bullet misses McGrew but kills Trent. [NFMA]

A Moonshiner's Heart 27 July 1912 Niles D: G. M. Anderson C: G. M. Anderson, Vedah Bertram (Vedah Stevens), Arthur Mackley (Seth Stevens), Robert H. Gray (minister) S: Tom Jackson, a moonshiner working with Vedah's father, discovers Vedah in the arms of Ross Chalmers, a revenue agent posing as an artist. When Tom learns Chalmers' true identity he decides to kill him, but Vedah promises to marry Tom if he'll let Chalmers go. Instead, Tom takes them to a minister and orders them to be married. (remade as *The Revenue Agent*, released 21 May 1915)

Broncho Billy's Pal 30 July 1912 Niles D: G. M. Anderson C: G. M. Anderson (Broncho Billy), Vedah Bertram (Vedah Craig), Brinsley Shaw (Tom Shelby), Arthur Mackley (Sheriff Craig), Fred Church (Quick-Draw Kelly), Pat Rooney, Victor Potel S: Notorious outlaw Quick-Draw Kelly seriously wounds Sheriff Craig, but no one in town is brave enough to go after Kelly. Craig's daughter Vedah recruits Tom, her fiance, to do it, but Tom confesses to his pal Broncho Billy he's not up to it, so Billy captures Kelly and lets Tom take the credit.

* *The Loafer's Mother* 3 August 1912 Niles D: Arthur Mackley C: Fred Church (Gregg Wilson, the loafer), Julia Mackley (his mother), Harry Todd (thief), Arthur Mackley (Phillips), Victor Potel, Louis Morisette, Pat Rooney, Al Parks, Frank Pementel, Robert H. Gray S: Wilson and his thieving pal plan to rob old Phillips of his Civil War pension money, but Wilson's mother delays him and the pal goes on alone. Wilson arrives in time to see Phillips about to be murdered and shoots the thief. The thief escapes and Wilson is arrested, but Phillips later identifies the real culprit and Wilson's scare sets him on a straighter path. [NFTA]

The Little Sheriff 10 August 1912 Niles D: Arthur Mackley C: Arthur Mackley (sheriff Jim Watson), Audrey Hanna?, G. M. Anderson? S: The widow Felton is assulted by a cowboy on her ranch and her little son goes for help.

* *Broncho Billy's Last Hold-Up* 13 August 1912 Niles D: G. M. Anderson C: G. M. Anderson (Broncho Billy), Vedah Bertram (Vedah Barclay), Harry Todd (sheriff), Arthur Mackley (stage driver), Julia Mackley (Mrs. Barclay), Fred Church (doctor) S: The outlaw Broncho Billy holds up a stagecoach to get Mrs. Barclay and her daughter to a doctor, and is shot by the sheriff of the town just after doing his good deed. [MOMA]

On the Moonlight Trail 17 August 1912 Niles working title: The Express Package and the Child C: Arthur Mackley (Jim Murray), Julia Mackley (his sick wife), Audrey Hanna (their youngest daughter), Harry Todd (tramp), Fred Church (tramp) S: Two tramps knock out express agent Jim Murray, intent on stealing a package of money from his house, but Murray's youngest daughter delays them while her older sister races to get the sheriff.

Broncho Billy's Escapade 24 August 1912 Niles D: G. M. Anderson C: G. M. Anderson (Broncho Billy), Fred Church, Vedah Bertram S: Billy shoots a cheat in a saloon card game then escapes and is chased by a posse. Wounded in the arm, he finds refuge in a young woman's home, is nursed by her, then saves her from a lusting cowboy.

"Alkali" Ike Plays the Devil 27 August 1912 Niles D: G. M. Anderson C: Augustus Carney (Alkali Ike), Margaret Joslin, Harry Todd, Arthur Mackley S: When Ike dresses up as a devil one night to go to a masquerade ball, he's pursued by a posse.

Broncho Billy for Sheriff 31 August 1912 Niles D: G. M. Anderson C: G. M. Anderson (Broncho Billy), Arthur Mackley (Jim Dunn), Fred Church, Victor Potel, Pat Rooney, Louis Morisette, Al Parks S: County sheriff Jim Dunn vows to kill Broncho Billy if he runs against him during their election race for the office, and on election day Dunn shoots him. Then Dunn discovers Billy has just saved Dunn's little daughter from death, and Dunn pins his badge on Billy.

The Ranchman's Trust 7 September 1912 Niles D: G. M. Anderson C: G. M. Anderson S: The son of a ranchman's friend comes to the ranch for a visit and falls for the ranchman's daughter, a situation that makes the ranch foreman jealous. The foreman is fired for trying to get the young man drunk, then he shoots the boy in the shoulder and escapes. The rancher and a posse capture him, intent on a hanging, but the boy insists the foreman is too cowardly for that kind of punishment and should instead be exiled across the state line.

*** A Woman of Arizona*** 10 September 1912 Niles D: Arthur Mackley C: Arthur Mackley (Jim Hardy), Harry Todd (sheriff), Brinsley Shaw (Dixon), Pat Rooney, Frank Pementel, Fred Church, Al Parks, Augustus Carney, Victor Potel S: When Dixon, a homeless stranger, is fed and given money for a new start by Hardy, he repays Hardy by knocking him out and stealing his wallet. Mrs. Hardy goes gunning for Dixon. [LOC]

Broncho Billy Outwitted 14 September 1912 Niles D: G. M. Anderson C: G. M. Anderson (Broncho Billy), Vedah Bertram (Vedah Trent) S: Silas Trent wounds a man in an argument, and it's up to Broncho Billy, the sheriff, to bring him in, but Trent's daughter outwits Billy by locking him up when he searches the house, allowing Silas to escape. Billy doesn't get mad; instead he shakes her hand for being clever, and she admires him. (remade as *Broncho Billy Misled*, released 1 October 1915)

"Alkali" Ike's Pants 21 September 1912 Niles D: G. M. Anderson C: Augustus Carney (Alkali Ike), Margaret Joslin (Sophie), Fred Church (Coyote Simpson), Harry Todd (Mustang Pete), True Boardman, Kite Robinson, Pat Rooney, Willis Elder, Victor Potel S: Ike and Simpson fiercely compete for Sophie's attention, but when Ike gets the nod to escort her to the dance his pants are stolen.

Across the Broad Pacific 24 September 1912 P: William A. Evans This documentary shows life in the Philippines.

****An Indian Sunbeam*** 28 September 1912 Niles D: G. M. Anderson C: Edna Sharpe (Sunbeam), True Boardman (Bob Harris), Fred Church (Bob's pal), Brinsley Shaw (Big Wolf), G. M. Anderson (Indian), Victor Potel (Indian and cowboy), Spider Roach S: Sunbeam, a white girl raised by Indians after her parents die in a covered wagon accident, is tied to a wild stallion by Big Wolf, who is jealous of her love for Bob Harris. While she roams the hills, helpless on the horse's back, Big Wolf tries to kill Harris. [LOC]

Love on Tough Luck Ranch 5 October 1912 Niles D: Arthur Mackley? C: Augustus Carney (Carney), Arthur Mackley (Parsons), Margaret Joslin (Mrs. Parsons), Josephine Rector (Ethel Parsons), Fritz Wintermeier (Horace Winton) S: Ethel's father wants her to marry old man Carney, but she likes Horace. Ethel and Horace elope in a horsedrawn rig, chased by Parsons and Carney in an automobile, but the young couple win out because Carney doesn't know how to drive.

"Alkali" Ike Stung 8 October 1912 Niles D: G. M. Anderson C: Augustus Carney (Alkali Ike), Margaret Joslin (Sophie), Harry Todd, Victor Potel, Pat Rooney, Fred Church, Edna Sharpe, True Boardman S: All the cowboys rush to become boarders at Sophie's new establishment, but by the time Ike gets there, after leaving his old place, there are no rooms left and he ends up bedding down in a stable.

The Shotgun Ranchman 12 October 1912 Niles D: Arthur Mackley C: Arthur Mackley (Jake Nixon), True Boardman (doctor), Audrey Hanna (widow Morgan's child) S: The unconditional love of the widow Morgan's little girl for the bitter and gruff ranchman Jake Nixon transforms him into a human being.

The Outlaw's Sacrifice 19 October 1912 Niles D: Arthur Mackley C: Arthur Mackley (Jim Barton), True Boardman (Bud Layton), Harry Todd (Mexican), Julia Mackley (Barton's wife), Hal Angus S: The outlaw Bud Layton saves sheriff Barton's wife and daughter from a thief, but dies pulling Mrs. Barton

from her burning home to safety.

* *The Tomboy on Bar Z* 22 October 1912 Niles D: G. M. Anderson C: G. M. Anderson, Arthur Mackley, Rollie Totheroh? S: Arthur Springer, an easterner, convinces ranchgirl Letty King to elope with him. The sheriff is informed that Springer is wanted for wife abandonment, so the cowboys of the ranch race down the road to catch the stagecoach Letty and Springer are on. [NFMA]

The Ranch Girl's Trial 26 October 1912 Niles D: G. M. Anderson C: G. M. Anderson (Dave Price), Evelyn Selbie (Pepita), Fred Church (Big Moose), Brinsley Shaw (Jake Harding), Beth Taylor (Millie Farnum), Arthur Mackley, Harry Todd S: Big Moose shoots Harding dead with Millie's revolver when he catches Harding molesting Pepita. Millie is arrested, but at the trial Pepita reveals the truth.

The Mother of the Ranch 2 November 1912 Niles D: Arthur Mackley C: Julia Mackley (Mrs. Hart), Virginia Eames (the shorter daughter), Arthur Mackley (Dan Hart) S: Four rebels take over a farm house occupied by Mrs. Hart and her daughters, but Mrs. Hart manages to escape and bring back a posse. The rebels are shot as they flee to the woods.

The Ranchman's Anniversary 7 November 1912 Niles D: Arthur Mackley C: Arthur Mackley, Harry Todd, Augustus Carney, Julia Mackley, Rollie Totheroh? S: Jake Simpson is tricked by the cowboys on his ranch into thinking he's shot and killed a cowboy kissing his wife. When Simpson escapes by train the cowboys race to catch him at the next station and bring him back so he can see it was a joke.

An Indian's Friendship 9 November 1912 Niles D: G. M. Anderson C: G. M. Anderson (Broncho Billy), Brinsley Shaw (Dan Runnion), Fred Church (Yellow Wolf), Harry Todd, Victor Potel, Arthur Mackley S: Dan Runnion vengefully plants a note that incriminates Billy as a cattle rustler, but Billy's friend Yellow Wolf finds out and gets the sheriff in time to prevent Billy from being hanged by a rancher and his cowboys.

Cutting California Redwoods 14 November 1912 P: Jess Robbins S: This film documents the cutting and processing of redwood trees in Northern California.

"Alkali" Ike's Close Shave 16 November 1912 Niles D: G. M. Anderson C: Augustus Carney (Alkali Ike) S: After getting hit by a car, a doctor shaves Ike's long beard off to treat his face and nobody in town recognizes him.

The Dance at Silver Gulch 19 November 1912 Niles D: Arthur Mackley? SC: Josephine Rector C: Josephine Rector (Mildred), Harry Todd (Jim Silver), Arthur Mackley, Julia Mackley S: Joe Barton and Jim Silver get in an argument at a dance over Mildred, and later, when Silver accidently shoots himself, Barton is arrested and put on trial for attempted murder, but escapes. Meanwhile, Silver regains consciousness and admits Barton's innocence.

* *Broncho Billy's Heart* 23 November 1912 Niles D: G. M. Anderson C: G. M. Anderson (Broncho Billy), Fred Church (Jim Davis), Arthur Mackley (Silas Jordan), Julia Mackley (Mrs. Jordan), True Eames Boardman (Jordan's son), Audrey Hanna (Jordan's daughter), Victor Potel, Willis Elder, Pat Rooney S: Silas Jordan's poor horse can no longer pull his covered wagon so Jordan steals a horse owned by Jim Davis. Billy meets the family on the trail, plays with the kids and joins them for dinner, then later is confronted by Davis and a posse looking for the horse. Billy finds Jordan and trades Davis's horse for his own, then turns the stolen horse loose and Davis finds it. [NFTA]

The Boss of the Katy Mine 28 November 1912 Niles D: Arthur Mackley? C: True Boardman (Joe Benson), Virginia Eames (Mrs. Benson), Brinsley Shaw (Bushnell), Harry Todd S: Benson quits working at the mine after he hits Bushnell, the mine boss, for accosting Mrs. Benson. She pleads with Bushnell to hire Benson back, but he will only do so if she leaves Benson. Benson goes to Bushnell intent on killing him, but finds him dead of natural causes.

* *Broncho Billy's Mexican Wife* 30 November 1912 Niles D: G. M. Anderson C: G. M. Anderson (Broncho Billy), Bessie Sankey (Lolito), Arthur Mackley (Pietro), Harry Todd (sheriff), Fred Church (Manuel), Victor Potel, Willis Elder, Texas George Briggs S: Lolito's father Pietro, on his deathbed, makes Billy promise to marry his daughter, but after the marriage she falls for a Mexican singer and has Billy arrested on an assault charge to get him out of the way.

Billy escapes to kill them, but finds them dead, killed by the singer's girlfriend. (remade as *Broncho Billy's Mexican Wife*, released 5 November 1915) [GEH]

Western Girls 3 December 1912 Niles D: Arthur Mackley? C: Josephine Rector, Bessie Sankey?, True Boardman, Fred Church S: Two ranch girls dress up as cowboys with bandanas on their faces to hold up two bandits who have robbed a stagecoach. The girls recover the money and turn the men over to the sheriff.

Broncho Billy's Love Affair 7 December 1912 Niles D: G. M. Anderson C: G. M. Anderson (Broncho Billy), Evelyn Selbie (Winnie Allen), Brinsley Shaw (Dan Wild), David Kirkland (rancher), Jay Hanna, Texas George Briggs, Willis Elder, Pat Rooney, Victor Potel, Frank Pementel S: Dan Wild gets Billy fired as foreman of a ranch as part of a plan to marry Winnie, the rancher's daughter. Years later Billy is a sheriff and tracks down Wild for a murder. Wild, near death from the shootout, confesses his deception to Billy and before dying makes Billy promise to take care of Winnie. [NFTA]

The Prospector 12 December 1912 Niles D: Arthur Mackley? C: Fred Church (Jim Clayton), Arthur Mackley (Sam Dunn), Evelyn Selbie (Dunn's daughter), Audrey Hanna (Dunn's granddaughter) S: Clayton, on his way to file a mining claim, stops for the night at Dunn's house to rest. Dunn plots with his son to rob Clayton, but Dunn's widowed daughter and child overhear it and Clayton is warned. To save the woman and her daughter from abuse, Clayton escapes with them, then marries the woman.

"Alkali" Ike's Motorcycle 14 December 1912 Niles D: G. M.Anderson C: Augustus Carney (Alkali Ike), Margaret Joslin (Sophie), Fred Church, Harry Todd?, Danny Kelleher, Frank A. "Fat" Rose S: Ike buys a motorcycle to impress Sophie, a visitor from Lizardhead.

The Sheriff's Luck 19 December 1912 Niles D: Arthur Mackley C: Arthur Mackley (sheriff), Julia Mackley S: While pursuing a bandit headed for the Mexican boarder, the sheriff comes across the widow Barrett, unconscious beside her overturned carriage. Under doctor's orders she must remain in the sheriff's office until she recovers, and there a romance develops.

Broncho Billy's Promise 21 December 1912 Niles D: G. M. Anderson C: G. M. Anderson (Broncho Billy), Brinsley Shaw (Snake), Bessie Sankey, Harry Todd, Victor Potel, Willis Elder S: Billy's sweetheart makes him promise not to shoot Snake, a failed suitor, regardless of how much Snake taunts Billy into action, but Billy is sorely tempted.

The Sheriff's Inheritance 24 December 1912 Niles D: Arthur Mackley C: Arthur Mackley (sheriff), Julia Mackley (his wife), David Kirkland (rancher), Evelyn Selbie (rancher's wife), Jay Hanna, Fred Church, Pat Rooney, Louis Morisette, Audrey Hanna, Eugenia Clinchard, Jem Rector S: A deputy kills a rancher trying to escape from jail. The sheriff promises the rancher's dying wife that he will care for her three children.

The Reward for Broncho Billy 28 December 1912 Niles D: G. M. Anderson C: G. M. Anderson (Broncho Billy), Evelyn Selbie, True Boardman, True Eames Boardman S: Billy robs a stagecoach and kills a sheriff trying to arrest him. Years later, Billy is near death when a woman and her young son take him into their home, and he recognizes her husband's portrait as the sheriff he killed. He takes a wanted dead or alive poster of himself that he keeps in his pocket and writes a note on it to the current sheriff stating the widow deserves the $5000 reward for his capture, then he dies.

1913

The Miner's Request 2 January 1913 Niles D: Arthur Mackley C: Arthur Mackley (Davis), Virginia Eames (Leonie Davis), True Boardman (Tom), Fred Church (an easterner) S: Davis suffers a fatal accident mining for gold, but before dying makes his daughter Leonie promise to marry Tom. She does so even though she loves an easterner in town. She consents to go away with the easterner, but she discovers him robbing the mine claim. After she chases him off at gunpoint, she decides to remain with her husband.

* *Broncho Billy and the Maid* 4 January 1913 Niles D: G. M. Anderson C: G. M. Anderson (Broncho Billy), Bessie Sankey S: Billy gets into a gunfight with a rancher who cheats at cards. Both men are wounded and the rancher's daughter nurses them back to health. The rancher attempts to kill Billy, but the daughter defends him and that ends the feud. [once available through Breakspear Films]

Broncho Billy and the Outlaw's Mother 11 January 1913 Niles D: G. M. Anderson C: G. M. Anderson (Broncho Billy), Fred Church (Jim Dawson) S: After robbing a stagecoach, Dawson kills a sheriff, but Billy, his deputy, seriously wounds Dawson. Dawson managed to get home where his mother prepares to tend his wound. In her absence Billy enters and Dawson tells him his mother doesn't know he's a criminal and his dying wish is that it remain so. Dawson dies in her arms, and Billy quietly leaves.

China and the Chinese 14 January 1913 P: William A. Evans S: This documentary was filmed in Shanghai.

Broncho Billy's Brother 18 January 1913 Niles D: G. M. Anderson C: G. M. Anderson (Broncho Billy), Fred Church (Dick), Bessie Sankey (Nell Parsons), Brinsley Shaw S: Billy's brother Dick loses his girl to a mining engineer from back east, but Billy plays cards with the engineer and wins everything, including a note to the girl from the man bowing out of her life.

On 1 November 1912 Arthur Mackley took part of the western company to Hollywood as a buffer against bad weather in Niles. Mackley directed "sheriff" films, a series he started in Niles, and all of the other films starring him.

The Sheriff's Child 22 January 1913 Hollywood D: Arthur Mackley C: Arthur Mackley (Tom Mackley), Julia Mackley, True Boardman, Audrey Hanna S: Sheriff Mackley arrests Terrible Dan and jails him, then goes after another outlaw. In his absence Dan tries to escape, but the sheriff's six-year-old daughter holds him at gunpoint until her father's return.

Broncho Billy's Gun-Play 25 January 1913 Niles D: G. M. Anderson C: G. M. Anderson (Broncho Billy), True Boardman (Carl Waters), Fred Church (Hawk Eye), Brinsley Shaw, Evelyn Selbie, David Kirkland, Frank Pementel, Victor Potel S: Billy is called in by Sheriff Waters to round up and arrest a fierce camp of bandits led by Hawk Eye.

The Sheriff's Story 30 January 1913 Hollywood D: Arthur Mackley C: Arthur Mackley (Sheriff Coverdale), David Kirkland, Louis Morisette, Jay Hanna S: On a visit to New York City, Sheriff Coverdale tells the members of a club about a prisoner who escaped from jail.

* *The Making of Broncho Billy* 1 February 1913 Niles D: G. M. Anderson C: G. M. Anderson (Broncho Billy), Brinsley Shaw (Wilkes), Harry Todd (sheriff), Victor Potel, Pat Rooney, Fred Church, Willis Elder, Kite Robinson, Joe Cassidy, Rollie Totheroh, Frank Pementel, Texas George Briggs S: Billy, a dude from the east, orders a soda in a western barroom and is chased off by Wilkes with a six-shooter. Billy buys a gun, but can't hit a bottle at five paces. After some practice he becomes a marksman and goes looking for Wilkes. In a showdown he wounds Wilkes, then he rides to the sheriff's office to give himself up. Some cowboys friendly to Wilkes chase him and overpower the sheriff, but Wilkes arrives and calls them off. [LOC, video]

The Ranchman's Blunder 4 February 1913 Hollywood D:Arthur Mackley C: Arthur Mackley (Jed Mackeley), True Boardman (Sam Beasley), Bessie Sankey (Mabel Mackeley), Brinsley Shaw (Jack Harrington), David Kirkland, Jack Wood, Slim Padgett S: When rancher Jed Mackeley is informed by his foreman Jack Harrington that Mackeley's daughter Mabel is secretly seeing cowboy Sam Beasley, Mackeley goes after them with a shotgun, but as he climbs a fence the gun goes off, leaving him wounded and unconscious. Harrington, wanting Mabel for himself, tries to blame Beasley, but Mackeley, not so seriously hurt, revives, figures out the situation and fires Harrington.

* *Broncho Billy's Last Deed* 8 February 1913 Niles D: G. M. Anderson C: G. M. Anderson (Broncho Billy), Brinsley Shaw (Clarence Jenners), Carl Stockdale S: Billy, seriously wounded by a vengeful Indian, is nursed by Mr. and Mrs. Jenners, an old couple about to be evicted and sent to a poor home by their son Clarence. Billy, informed by a doctor he will die, kills Clarence and urges Mr. Jenners to turn him in for a big reward. [NFMA]

Across the Great Divide 13 February 1913 Hollywood D: Arthur Mackley C: Arthur Mackley, True Boardman (Walter Jordan), Bessie Sankey (Mrs. Jordan) S: Walter Jordan, his wife and two children are stranded in their wagon out in the desert. He goes to get help. Outlaws find one daughter, then the wagon with Mrs. Jordan dead and the youngest still alive in her arms. A posse arrests the outlaws and reunites Jordan and his children.

Broncho Billy's Ward 15 February 1913 Niles D: G. M. Anderson C: G. M. Anderson (Broncho Billy), Bessie Sankey (Bess Brady), Brinsley Shaw (Art Diamond) S: Billy's old friend dies and Billy becomes the guardian of the man's daughter Bess. When she grows up and asks his consent to marry Art Diamond, Billy nods yes even though he desires to marry her himself.

Where the Mountains Meet 19 February 1913 Hollywood D: Arthur Mackley C: Arthur Mackley S: When Ben Stapleton deserts the daughter of Dad Melton, Melton tracks him down and shoots him. At Melton's trial for attempted murder, Stapleton is remorseful and promises to right his wrong.

*** Broncho Billy and the Sheriff's Kid** 22 February 1913 Niles D: G. M. Anderson C: G. M. Anderson (Broncho Billy), Eugenia Clinchard (the kid), Evelyn Selbie (the sheriff's wife), Harry Todd (the sheriff), Victor Potel (jailer), Josephine Rector (teacher), Fred Church (Dr. Brush) S: Billy escapes from jail. While hiding in the back county he finds the sheriff's child unconscious from a fall over a cliff. He takes her to the sheriff's home and the little girl's mother thanks him. Later, the sheriff wounds Billy and he returns to the house for aid. When the sheriff comes home he discovers Billy, but the wife arms Billy, and he escapes to freedom. (remade as *Broncho Billy and the Baby*, released 23 January 1915) [NFTA]

The Western Law That Failed 25 February 1913 Hollywood D: Arthur Mackley C: Arthur Mackley (rancher), True Boardman (Dave Morgan),

Charles La Due, Slim Padgett, Jack Wood S: Morgan, intent on returning to his home back east, steals a horse, but is caught. About to be hanged, he tells a story of a wife and baby in the east that he was desperate to see, producing another man's letter that came into his possession accidentally. The cowboys give him money and let him go.

Beginning with the next film, all Niles releases were assigned a still code number during production, starting at 00100. These are listed when known. The Mackley films in Hollywood were unnumbered.

The Influence on Broncho Billy 1 March 1913 Niles 00100 D: G. M. Anderson C: G. M. Anderson (Broncho Billy), Bessie Sankey (Bessie Hendricks), Eugenia Clinchard (Bessie's daughter), Fred Church S: The outlaw Broncho Billy comes upon Bessie Hendricks and her young daughter stranded by the road. He takes them to her father's home. After staying the night, Billy is about to depart to rob a stagecoach, but following a long talk with Bessie he decides to quit his life of crime.

A Montana Mix-Up 6 March 1913 Hollywood D: Arthur Mackley C: Arthur Mackley (Mr. Mackley), Julia Mackley (Mrs. Mackley), Gladys Field (Maizie Mackley) S: Bud Stone, in love with Maizie, travels to her parents' house to ask her hand in marriage, but the cowboys who meet him at the station pick up a bundle with a baby in it instead of his suitcase, putting Bud in a difficult situation.

Broncho Billy and the Squatter's Daughter 8 March 1913 Niles 00101

D: G. M. Anderson C: G. M. Anderson (Broncho Billy), Bessie Sankey (Mabel Clark), Victor Potel, Willis Elder S: Billy, an alcoholic, is found by Mabel, a squatter's daughter, in the back country and nursed to health. Later, Billy saves her and her father from being evicted by a disappointed suitor.

*** Old Gorman's Gal** 13 March 1913 Hollywood D: Arthur Mackley C: Arthur Mackley (Gorman), Virginia Eames (Dorothy Gorman), True Boardman (Jim), Jay Hanna (the stranger) S: Dorothy Gorman, abused by her father, decides she will only marry a rich man, which leaves out her former sweetheart Jim. She goes off with a stranger, but he's killed and she's hurt when a train hits their buggy. Later, Jim gets a job as the foreman of a ranch and that brings Dorothy back to him. [LOC]

Broncho Billy and the Step-Sisters 15 March 1913 Niles 00102 D: G. M. Anderson C: G. M. Anderson (Broncho Billy), Bessie Sankey (Agnes Shepard), Evelyn Selbie (Evelyn), Harry Todd S: The step-sisters are both in love with Billy, but Agnes breaks her engagement to him when Evelyn schemes to be discovered in his arms. Billy is shot by an enemy and Evelyn confesses her deception to Agnes. Billy dies in Agnes's arms.

The Housekeeper of Circle C 18 March 1913 Hollywood D: Arthur Mackley C: Arthur Mackley S: A rancher is so desperate to retain a new housekeeper that he proposes marriage to "her," only to discover the housekeeper has a beard, and it belongs to one of his cowboys playing a trick on him.

Broncho Billy's Sister 22 March 1913 Niles 00109? D: G. M. Anderson C: G. M. Anderson (Broncho Billy), Fred Church (Fred Church), Bessie Sankey (Geraldine), Victor Potel S: Against Billy's better judgement, his sister goes away with Fred Church. A year later she returns with a baby son, having been deserted. Billy goes after Church and finds him in hiding, a fugitive from justice. Billy brings him back, forces him to marry his sister, then turns him over to the sheriff.

The Sheriff's Honeymoon 25 March 1913 Hollywood D: Arthur Mackley C: Arthur Mackley (Tom McCarthy), Julia Mackley (Soffie Clutts) S: Sheriff McCarthy, disgusted with bachelor life, finds a bride by mail order and leaves town to claim her, but must deal with some wild goings on when he gets back.

*** Broncho Billy's Gratefulness** 29 March 1913 Niles 00105 D: G. M. Anderson C: G. M. Anderson (Broncho Billy), Brinsley Shaw (John Harding), Evelyn Selbie (Mrs. Harding), Fred Church (Fred Church), Harry Todd (sheriff), Victor Potel (Dr. Huff) S: Church tries to blackmail Mrs. Harding with love letters he got from her before her marriage. Harding finds out, kills Church and is arrested. Mrs. Harding goes to Broncho Billy, whom the Hardings once nursed through a bad illness, and Billy holds up the sheriff so Harding and his wife can escape to Mexico. [NFTA]

The Sheriff's Son 1 April 1913 Hollywood D: Arthur Mackley C: Arthur Mackley S: The sheriff is injured investigating the explosion of a safe in a bank robbery and his daughter-in-law goes after the bandits. One of them is her husband, the sheriff's son. A few months later the son is released from prison and vows to mend his ways.

Broncho Billy's Way 5 April 1913 Niles 00106 D: G. M. Anderson C: G. M. Anderson (Broncho Billy), Evelyn Selbie (Billy's wife), Brinsley Shaw (Mexican) S: Billy, warned that his wife and a Mexican plan to run away together, finds them both at his home and orders them at gunpoint to go.

The Sheriff's Wife 9 April 1913 Hollywood D: Arthur Mackley C: Arthur Mackley (sheriff), Julia Mackley (his wife) S: Two thieves attempting to steal a bag of gold stored at the sheriff's home are kept at bay by the sheriff's wife until a posse arrives.

Broncho Billy's Reason 12 April 1913 Niles 00103 D: G. M. Anderson C: G. M. Anderson (Broncho Billy), Fred Church, Josephine Rector, Bessie Sankey S: Billy steals twelve horses and sells them to a stock dealer to pay the debts on his mother's home. The horses are found by a posse and returned to the owner. Later the dealer gets a check from Billy to square the account. (remake of *A Tale of the West*, released 7 April 1909)

The Accusation of Broncho Billy 15 April 1913 Niles 00107 D: G. M. Anderson ST: based on "Friends in San Rosario" by O. Henry C: G. M. Anderson (Broncho Billy), Harry Todd (sheriff), Victor Potel, Brinsley Shaw, Texas George Briggs, Kite Robinson S: Billy, a saloon-owner, is given a bag of gold by some miners for safekeeping, and

while sleepwalking he hides it. When the miners come back Billy can't find the gold and is nearly lynched, but while in jail he sleepwalks again and the door is opened by the sheriff so Billy can reclaim the gold.

Augustus Carney returned to Niles after five months in Chicago to resume his Alkali Ike Snakeville Comedies. "Alkali" Ike's Homecoming *also marked the first appearance of the "Slippery Slim" and "Sophie Clutts" characters.*

"Alkali" Ike's Homecoming 19 April 1913 Niles 00121 D: G. M. Anderson C: Augustus Carney (Alkali Ike), Victor Potel (Slippery Slim), Margaret Joslin (Sophie Clutts) S: During Ike's absence from town Slim courts Spohie, and to insure his continued success Slim claims Ike is dead. When Ike comes home he chases off Slim and reclaims Sophie.

The Unburied Past 22 April 1913 Niles 00112 D: ? C: Victor Potel, Fred Church S: Walter Morris loves Margaret Phillips but she marries the wealthy Jack Wright, who, unknown to her, is unfaithful. When Jack dies Margaret asks Walter to help settle his estate, and he discovers the truth about Jack's life, but keeps it hidden from Margaret.

City of Mexico 24 April 1913 P: Jess Robbins? Possibly a documentary shot when the company was in Mexico in December, 1909, but released later to capitalize on the bombardment of the National Palace and murder of President Madero in February, 1913.

Broncho Billy and the Rustler's Child 26 April 1913 Niles 00110 D: G. M. Anderson C: G. M. Anderson (Broncho Billy), Brinsley Shaw (David Morgan), Eugenia Clinchard (Morgan's child), Evelyn Selbie S: Morgan steals horses for money to move his sick wife to a better climate, but Broncho Billy (the sheriff) finds him at his cabin. Between Morgan's confession and his little daughter's pleas for mercy, Billy lets the family escape, and he pays for the stolen horses himself. [MOMA, NFMA]

The Story the Desert Told 1 May 1913 Hollywood D: Arthur Mackley C: Arthur Mackley, Slim Padgett S: The sheriff and his prisoner save a young girl from dying in the desert.

The Crazy Prospector 3 May 1913 Niles 00125 D: G. M. Anderson C: G. M. Anderson (Broncho Billy), David Kirkland (JohnHarlan), Evelyn Selbie, Brinsley Shaw, Eugenia Clinchard S: John Harlan discovers gold and tells everyone in a saloon. His daughter pleads with Billy to help her file the claim first and Billy drives her in his stagecoach to a mountain pass where he can guard the road while she rides to the claim agent. (remake of *The Little Prospector*, released 19 November 1910)

Two Western Paths 8 May 1913 Hollywood D: Arthur Mackley C: Arthur Mackley (John Lynch) S: Lynch marries a dancer, but she longs to return to the stage, so Lynch sacrifices his love for her by giving her money and bidding her a fond farewell.

"Alkali" Ike's Mother-in-Law 10 May 1913 Niles D: G. M. Anderson C: Augustus Carney (Alkali Ike), Margaret Joslin (the mother-in-law), Evelyn Selbie (Ike's wife) S: Ike's mother-in-law visits to whip him into shape and he retaliates by learning hypnotism.

Arthur Mackley returned to Niles in April, 1913, and continued to direct until May, then left for a vacation in Europe and work elsewhere.

The Ranch Girl's Partner 13 May 1913 Niles D: Arthur Mackley C: Arthur Mackley (sheriff), Fred Church (John Kelton), Brinsley Shaw, Mervyn Breslauer, Tom Crizer, Willis Elder S: Stevens tries to edge out Kelton for the hand of Marjorie Wayne by stealing a horse and blaming Kelton for it, but the sheriff arrests the right man.

Broncho Billy's Grit 17 May 1913 Niles D: G. M. Anderson C: G. M. Anderson (Broncho Billy) S: A woman helps Billy through a scrape. He repays her by retrieving her brother's money from a gambler, and escorting him home.

A Widow of Nevada 22 May 1913 Niles D: Arthur Mackley C: Arthur Mackley (Jim Ryder), Evelyn Selbie (Widow Gale), Fred Church (Foster) S: Ryder leases a played-out mine and discovers gold. Foster, the owner, steals the lease and declares Ryder's claim on it expired. The Widow Gale gets the lease from Foster and hands it over to Ryder, who marries her.

Broncho Billy and the Express Rider 24 May 1913 Niles 00123 D: G. M. Anderson C: G. M. Anderson (Broncho Billy), Fred Church (Ralph Spaulding), Bessie Sankey (Bessie Hendricks) S:

Billy refuses to help some men rob Spaulding, a Pony Express rider, of some gold, even though Spaulding has gotten the better of Billy in his bid for the love of Bessie, a ranchman's daughter. Billy even holds up the robbers and restores the money to Spaulding.

The New Sheriff 27 May 1913 Niles D: Arthur Mackley C: Arthur Mackley (Daffy Blinton) S: Blinton, a seemingly half-witted character, captures the notorious Sheppard gang when everyone else refuses to volunteer for the job.

"Alkali" Ike's Misfortunes 31 May 1913 Niles 00126 D: G. M. Anderson C: Augustus Carney (Alkali Ike), Margaret Joslin (Sophie Clutts), Harry Todd, Victor Potel S: With the aid of an electric belt, Ike battles three other suitors for Sophie's hand.

The Last Shot 5 June 1913 Niles 00118 D: ? SC: Josephine Rector C: Evelyn Selbie (Helen), Brinsley Shaw (Tom), Fred Church S: Helen tries to intervene in a feud between her brother, whose testimony sent her father-in-law to jail, and her husband Tom, who swears vengeance. She is killed.

Broncho Billy's Capture 7 June 1913 Niles 00130 D: G. M. Anderson C: G. M. Anderson (Broncho Billy), Evelyn Selbie (Evelyn), Fred Church (Juan Yukas), Bill Cato (deputy), Lloyd Ingraham (expressman), Frank Pementel (guard) S: Billy discovers Evelyn, the woman he loves, is in on a stagecoach robbery with Juan, and he must arrest them both. (remake of *The Deputy's Love*, released 27 August 1910) [video, LOC, MOMA]

Jess Robbins probably directed films before The Shadowgraph Message, *but existing information does not confirm any specific titles. When Lloyd Ingraham began directing dramas, Robbins probably made the first two-reel films in Niles, beginning with* "Alkali" Ike's Gal, *and the non-Broncho Billy two-reel dramas. Robbins also directed one-reel comedies.*

The Shadowgraph Message 10 June 1913 Niles D: Jess Robbins C: Harry Keenan (Texas), Brinsley Shaw (Dan Morgan), Harry Todd (Yuma), Evelyn Selbie S: Dan Morgan wins a bag of gold from Hugh Haines in a poker game and Haines decides to steal it from Morgan's house. Yuma, a deaf and dumb Indian friend of Morgan's, sees Haines, signals a sign language message on the curtain of Morgan's house that Morgan sees, and Morgan captures the thief.

The Ranch Feud 14 June 1913 Niles D: G. M. Anderson C: G. M. Anderson (Broncho Billy), Anita Murray (Billy's sweetheart), True Boardman (doctor) S: Billy and his sweetheart are caught in a feud between their fathers, and Billy is shot. The doctor says the only thing that will save him is a reconciliation enabling Billy's girl to help him fight for his life, and this prescription comes true.

The Rustler's Spur 19 June 1913 Niles 00117 D: Jess Robbins? C: Harry Todd (Harry), Bessie Sankey (Bessie Hargon), Brinsley Shaw, Fred Church, True Boardman S: Sheriff Bradley follows a clue leading to the whereabouts of a horse thief, and the trail leads to his girlfriend's house.

"Alkali" Ike and the Hypnotist 21 June 1913 Niles 00122 D: G. M. Anderson C: Augustus Carney (Alkali Ike), Margaret Joslin (Sophie Clutts), Harry Todd (Mustang Pete), Victor Potel (Slippery Slim), David Kirkland (Professor Hippy), Brinsley Shaw, Fred Church, Bessie Sankey, Josephine Rector, Kite Robinson, Evelyn Selbie, Tom Crizer, Spider Roach, Bill Cato, Lawrence Abrott, Texas George Briggs, Willis Elder, Marguerite Todd S: Ike is hypnotized by Professor Hippy on stage at the Snakeville Opera House.

Across the Rio Grande 24 June 1913 Niles D: Jess Robbins? C: Brinsley Shaw (Brinsley Shaw), Evelyn Selbie (Evelyn Selbie), Texas George Briggs, Bill Cato S: Shaw, who went west to make his fortune twenty years ago, recognizes his son by the engagement ring he gave the boy's mother back then, and protects the boy from a posse by giving himself up after the boy is safely across the Mexican boarder.

Broncho Billy's Strategy 28 June 1913 Niles 00135 D: G. M. Anderson C: G. M. Anderson (Broncho Billy), Lloyd Ingraham, Evelyn Selbie, Fred Church, Pat Rooney, Stanley Sargent, Slim Padgett S: Billy helps a woman get her wayward husband out of trouble when the man turns to gambling and robbery.

The Life We Live 3 July 1913 Niles 00129 D: Arthur Mackley C: Arthur Mackley (Joe Mackey), Fred Church, Evelyn Selbie, True Boardman, David Kirkland S: An old man out of work is about to hock his wife's wedding ring when he finds a package of money on the railroad tracks. His wife insists he turn it in to the authorities and this saves a railroad expressman accused of stealing the money from going to prison.

At the Lariat's End 5 July 1913 Niles 00128 working title: *A Victim of Gossip* D: Jess Robbins? C: Bessie Sankey (Bessie), Evelyn Selbie (Jet), Bill Cato (sheriff), Fred Church, Augustus Carney, Harry Todd S: A jealous rival for Bessie is shot and killed, and Bessie's beau is blamed, but the sheriff manages to set things right.

The Daughter of the Sheriff 8 July 1913 Niles D: Arthur Mackley C: Arthur Mackley (Sam Morley), Evelyn Selbie (his daughter) S: Sheriff Sam Morley's daughter captures an outlaw who comes to the house, the same man the sheriff is searching for.

* *Broncho Billy and the Western Girls* 12 July 1913 Niles 00127 D: G. M. Anderson C: G. M. Anderson (Broncho Billy), Bessie Sankey (Irene Courtney), Evelyn Selbie (Evelyn Courtney), Lloyd Ingreaham (Mr. Courtney), Victor Potel (outlaw), Harry Todd (outlaw), Fred Church (gang leader), Pat Rooney (stagecoach mail carrier) S: A sack of gold and letters are delivered to a general store post office and is seen by the leader of an outlaw gang. The gang breaks in to steal the gold, but one of ther storekeeper's daughters escapes with the sack. After a chase through the woods and underbrush, Billy saves her and holds the men at gunpoint until a posse arrives. [video, LOC]

The Heart of a Gambler 17 July 1913 Niles D: Jess Robbins? C: Harry Todd (John Gould), Harry Keenan (Dan Jordan) S: A gambler, Dan Jordan, stakes improverished gold miner John Gould to a claim for half the proceeds, but when the mine is profitable and the gambler needs money the miner refuses to honor the agreement. Nevertheless, the gambler helps out when an explosion injures the miner.

The Two Ranchmen 19 July 1913 Niles D: Arthur Mackley C: Arthur Mackley, Evelyn Selbie, Edna Sharpe S: Neighboring ranchmen quarrel over a hole in a fence that allows chickens on one side to dig up the seeds on the other side.

Rollie Totheroh claimed The Dance at Eagle Pass *was his first film as a cameraman, and Lloyd Ingraham's first as a director. It also marked the first use of the interior stage at the new Essanay studio in Niles.*

The Dance at Eagle Pass 23 July 1913 Niles 00133 D: Lloyd Ingraham P: Rollie Totheroh SC: Josephine Rector C: Josephine Rector (Florence Wessel), Brinsley Shaw (Joe Scott), Harry Todd (Sheriff Wessel), Fred Church (Jim Barton), Harry Keenan (doctor), True Boardman, Evelyn Selbie, Pat Rooney S: Joe Scott, a gambler, robs a post office, but is discovered by the sheriff, who previously favored him over cowboy Jim Barton to court his daughter Florence. Scott shoots the sheriff and fixes the blame on Barton, but the bullet that wounds the sheriff is found to fit Scott's gun.

Broncho Billy and the Schoolmam's Sweetheart 26 July 1913 Niles 00134 D: G. M. Anderson C: G. M. Anderson (Broncho Billy), Bessie Sankey

(Marjorie Wayne) S: Billy loses out when a man from the city marries Marjorie Wayne, but when the man is caught by a posse for horse stealing, Billy, for the sake of Marjorie, holds up the posse so the man can escape.

The Call of the Plains 29 July 1913 Niles 00136 D: Arthur Mackley C: Arthur Mackley (Bud Wheeler), Marguerite Clayton S: Bud Wheeler, rejected by Jane Barton because her father is very old, goes west. She writes a letter to Bud repenting her decision, but the letter is lost. Years later Bud finds the letter, sends for Jane and she comes to him.

The Tenderfoot Sheriff 2 August 1913 Niles D: G. M. Anderson C: G. M. Anderson (Broncho Billy), True Boardman (sheriff), Harry Todd (Snake) S: The notorious outlaw Snake causes two sheriffs to resign, but when a $1000 reward is offered Billy brings him in.

Their Promise 6 August 1913 Niles 00137 D: Jess Robbins? C: Fred Church, Evelyn Selbie S: Two pals go west to seek their fortune and they find it, but meet a young lady and quarrel over her.

Broncho Billy and the Navajo Maid 9 August 1913 Niles 00142 D: G. M. Anderson C: G. M. Anderson (Broncho Billy), Evelyn Selbie (Navajo maid), Bessie Sankey (Billy's sweetheart), Fred Church S: Billy saves an Indian woman from a prospector and gets shot. The woman tends his wound and falls in love with him, but gets jealous when Billy's sweetheart arrives in town.

The Edge of Things 12 August 1913 Niles 00143 D: Lloyd Ingraham? C: Harry Todd (Charles Rogers), Evelyn Selbie (Evelyn Rogers), Fred Church (George Clayton) S: Charles Rogers, a ranchman, receives a visit from his eastern partner, George Clayton. Rogers' wife Evelyn falls for Clayton. Jealous, the ranchman takes Clayton on a hunting trip up in the hills, planning to throw Clayton over a cliff.

"Alkali" Ike's Gal 15 August 1913 two reels Niles 00144 D: Jess Robbins? C: Augustus Carney (Alklai Ike), Victor Potel (Slippery Slim), Margaret Joslin (Sophie Clutts), Harry Todd (Mustang Pete), Fred Church (Rawhide Bill), David Kirkland (Dr. Dopeum) S: The Dotty Matrimonial Agency is offering reduced rates on June brides and Snakeville's four most eligible bachelors decide now is the time to act. Note: This was the first two-reeler produced by the Western Essanay.

The Man in the Cabin 16 August 1913 Niles D: G. M. Anderson C: G. M. Anderson (Broncho Billy), Evelyn Selbie S: Billy, a dangerous outlaw, escapes during his trial and goes to Evelyn's house in the woods, intent on forcing his affections on her. She tells her Indian servant in sign language to get help and a posse rescues her in the nick of time. (remake of The Silent Message, released 29 October 1910)

The Sheriff of Cochise 21 August 1913 Niles 00141? D: Lloyd Ingraham? C: Victor Potel (sheriff), Harry Todd, Harry Keenan, Kite Robinson S: A ranchman offers a huge reward for the capture of two horse thieves, and two sheriffs from neighboring towns become rivals to collect it.

Broncho Billy's Mistake 23 August 1913 D: G. M. Anderson C: G. M. Anderson (Broncho Billy), Vera McCord, Evelyn Selbie S: An artist from New York City arrives at Billy's house with a letter of introduction and stays to do some painting. He sees Billy's wife as an excellent subject and paints her portrait, in the process becoming her friend. A telegram calls him home and Billy's wife takes him to the station in a buggy, but Billy fears the worst. He overtakes them and fights the painter until his wife stops it and sets him straight.

* The Episode at Cloudy Canyon 28 August 1913 Niles D: Lloyd Ingraham? C: True Boardman (Charles Harris), Fred Church (Fred Harris), Evelyn Selbie (Mrs. Harris), Lee Willard (Mexican), Carl Stockdale (drunken cowboy), Kite Robinson (bartender), Stanley Sargent, Bill Cato, Tom Crizer, Willis Elder, Spider Roach S: A vengeful Mexican plants evidence that a drunken cowboy shot Fred Harris. The sheriff, Fred's brother Charles, arrests the cowboy and nearly kills him, but is saved by the arrival of a posse with the villain.

A Western Sister's Devotion 30 August 1913 Niles D: G. M. Anderson C: G. M. Anderson (Broncho Billy), Lloyd Ingraham (Sheriff Hardley), Harry Todd, Evelyn Selbie S: Billy is deputized to capture two horse thieves and finds one of them to be the brother of the girl Billy's engaged to. Billy goes after the brother, but captures the sister, who has dressed up to fool Billy and allow her brother to escape.

Hard Luck Bill 4 September 1913 Niles 00179 working title: Flustered and Frustrated (from a scenario bought by Anderson in a contest sponsored by the San Francisco Bulletin) D: ? ST: Harry A. Buerkle C: Victor Potel (Bill), Margaret Joslin (Mrs. Swatt), Carl Stockdale (judge), Pat Rooney (cop), Harry Todd (tramp), Marguerite Clayton (beautiful girl), Josephine Rector, Lee Willard, Emory Johnson, Tom Crizer, Harry Keenan S: Bill borrows ten dollars from his neighbor Tom to pay his rooming house rent. Seeing a beautiful new tenant, he decides to borrow Tom's new suit to take her to lunch. When it's time to pay the bill he realizes his money is in his old suit pocket, thrown out by the landlady and retrieved by a tramp.

Broncho Billy's Conscience 6 September 1913 Niles 00160 D: G. M. Anderson C: G. M. Anderson (Broncho Billy), Fred Church (Tom Warner), Carl Stockdale (rancher), Marguerite Clayton (rancher's daughter) S: Billy frames a rival for the death of a rancher so he can marry the rancher's daughter. The rival is hanged for the crime and the specter of the dead man haunts Billy until he dies from a fall.

Bonnie of the Hills 11 September 1913 Niles D: Lloyd Ingraham? C: Fred Church, Marguerite Clayton, Lee Willard S: When an easterner is hurt in a fall, a cowboy is enraged by the concern his fiancee shows the easterner. This leads to their breakup and the cowboy's desire for revenge.

Broncho Billy Reforms 13 September 1913 Niles 00170 D: G. M. Anderson C: G. M. Anderson (Broncho Billy), Marguerite Clayton (storekeeper's daughter), Lloyd Ingraham (storekeeper), Victor Potel (thief), Carl Stockdale (thief), Lee Willard (thief) Fred Church, Evelyn Selbie, True Boardman, Harry Todd, True Eames Boardman, Pat Rooney S: Billy and some pals plan to rob a general store, but when Billy sees a beautiful girl working there he changes his mind. He tells his pals he won't do it and they tie him up, planning to go ahead without him, but he foils their plan. (almost re-released as *His Regeneration*, 7 May 1915)

The Broken Parole 18 September 1913 Niles 00176? D: Lloyd Ingraham? C: Fred Church (Red Lewis), Harry Todd (detective), Eleanor Blevins (Lewis's wife), Lee Willard, Lloyd Ingraham, Stanley Sargent, Texas George Briggs, Bill Cato, Jack Roberts, Jack Woods S: Red Lewis, a thief, is released on parole and skips town to go west. After a five year search, a detective traces him to Lewis's ranch. Lewis bids farewell to his wife and small daughter, and it touches the detective so much that he gives up and goes back east alone.

The Redeemed Claim 20 September 1913 Niles 00172 D: G. M. Anderson C: G. M. Anderson (Mr. Orr), Marguerite Clayton, Harry Keenan, Harry Todd S: A rancher is refused a loan on his land until a lender discovers a gold vein on the property. The lender keeps it a secret and makes an agreement giving him the land after a certain date if the money isn't repaid. Mr. Orr, a government assayist fond of the rancher's daughter, stops the takeover at the last minute with his own money.

Days of the Pony Express 25 September 1913 Niles 00153 D: Arthur Mackley P: Arthur Mackley? C: Carl Stockdale (Farley), Harry Todd (postmaster), Evelyn Selbie (postmaster's daughter), Lee Willard (clerk), Bill Cato (sheriff), True Boardman, Jack Roberts S: The postmaster's daughter receives a telescope from her boyfriend Farley, a pony express rider. One day Farley is robbed by outlaws and arrested for the loss when he gets to town, but she saves him, thanks to the telescope, when she sees the outlaws on his route at a mountain pass as they divide up the loot.

* Why Broncho Billy Left Bear County 27 September 1913 Niles 00173 D: G. M. Anderson C: G. M. Anderson (Broncho Billy), Marguerite Clayton (Marion Rivers), Lloyd Ingraham (old man Rivers), Harry Todd (bartender), Victor Potel (druggest), Fred Church (sheriff), Slim Padgett (deputy), Frank Pementel, Stanley Sargent S: Billy helps Marion Rivers bring home her drunken father and later, Marion stops Billy from robbing a stagecoach. But her father robs the coach, and Billy saves the day by riding with the money to the county line, where he leaves it for a posse to recover, while he crosses the boarder to safety. [GEH]

The Belle of Siskiyou 2 October 1913 Niles D: Lloyd Ingraham? C; Marguerite Clayton (May Reidy), Harry Todd (her father), True Boardman (Black Moody), Evelyn Selbie (Moody's wife), Fred Church (sheriff) S: May leaves home to escape her father's cruelty and gets a job as a barmaid in a saloon, but the saloon-owner's wife is jealous of her and turns the saloon man over to the

sheriff for a stagecoach robbery he committed. The sheriff meets May and a romance develops.

The Struggle 4 October 1913 Niles 00164 D: G. M. Anderson C: G. M. Anderson (Dr. Sharp), Marguerite Clayton (Gretchen Sharp), True Boardman (Sharp's brother), Fred Church (sheriff), Carl Stockdale, Tom Crizer, Slim Padgett S: Dr. Sharp catches his wife and his brother together, which enrages him. The two men get into a gun battle and both are wounded, the brother more seriously, and Dr. Sharp operates to save his brother's life.

Love and the Law 9 October 1913 Niles D: Lloyd Ingraham? C: Marguerite Clayton (Ruth), Eleanor Blevins, Fred Church, Harry Todd, Carl Stockdale S: Several men, including the sheriff and deputy, are in love with Ruth, but Ted Magee wins out. When the other men hear the news there's an argument and a man is shot. Ted is blamed and he goes to Ruth's house to hide out. The sheriff and deputy show up, they argue over Ruth and she escapes with Ted.

Broncho Billy's Oath 11 October 1913 Niles 00178 D: G. M. Anderson C: G. M. Anderson (Broncho Billy), Marguerite Clayton, Tom Crizer, Bill Cato, Victor Potel S: Billy saves his friend Jim by stealing money in a stage holdup to pay for a doctor. Later, when Billy becomes engaged to Geraldine, Jim is jealous and turns Billy over to the sheriff for the crime. Billy escapes from jail to kill Jim, but a sheriff's bullet meant for Billy kills Jim. (remake of *A Pal's Oath*, released 19 August 1911)

A Borrowed Identity 16 October 1913 Niles 00171 D: Lloyd Ingraham? C: Marguerite Clayton, Evelyn Selbie, True Boardman, Harry Todd, Lee Willard, Frank Pementel, Joe Cassidy, Jack Wood S: A young man on a visit to a ranch changes clothes with a cowboy for a joke. The real cowboy is mistaken by the family for their guest and the young man is arrested for horse rustling.

Broncho Billy Gets Square 17 October 1913 two reels Niles 00155 D: G. M. Anderson C: G. M. Anderson (Broncho Billy), Evelyn Selbie (White Feather), Marguerite Clayton (Grace Todd), David Kirkland (Dave Kirkland), Harry Todd, Lee Willard, Fred Church, True Boardman, Harry Keenan, Carl Stockdale, Victor Potel, Frank Pementel, Spider Roach, Tom Crizer, Pat Rooney S: Dave turns his outlaw partner Billy over to a sheriff to get immunity from the law and to clear the way to marry White Feather, an Indian they both love. Fifteen years later Billy gets out of jail and comes across Dave as he's arranging a marriage between himself and Grace in exchange for paying off her father's debt. Billy stops the marriage by bringing White Feather and two of her male relatives to the scene.

"Alkali" Ike and the Wildman 18 October 1913 Niles 00161 D:? C: Augustus Carney (Alkali Ike), Fred Church (the wildman) S: Ike is hired as a sideshow wildman after the real one escapes.

The Kid Sheriff 23 October 1913 Niles 00166 D: Lloyd Ingraham? C: Fred Church (Fred Church), Danny Kelleher (the kid sheriff), Harry Todd (sheriff), Nathan Anderson, Frank Pementel, Tom Crizer, Carl Stockdale S: Fred Church and his kid assistant arrest Reno Bill when they find him annoying a young woman. Bill tells them of another sheriff and an express agent who robbed a stage. Fred arrests those two and stations the kid to guard all three in jail while he visits the young woman.

Broncho Billy's Elopement 25 October 1913 Niles D: G. M. Anderson C: G. M. Anderson (Broncho Billy), Marguerite Clayton (Mary Johnson), Lloyd Ingraham (minister), Lee Willard S: Robert Johnson tries to force his daughter Mary into a marriage with Dave Morgan, but she elopes with Billy instead. (remade or re-released as *Broncho Billy's Marriage*, 20 August 1915)

Greed for Gold 30 October 1913 Niles 00159 D: Lloyd Ingraham? C: True Boardman (Bill Riley), Harry Todd (miser), Lee Willard (Indian), Earl Esola, Tom Crizer, Slim Padgett, Lee Scott, William Elam S: An Indian witnesses a miser shooting a man for his gold and saves the man's partner from getting jailed for the deed.

The Doctor's Duty 1 November 1913 Niles 00180 D: G. M. Anderson C: G. M. Anderson (Dr. Roland White), Marguerite Clayton (Marguerite), Fred Church (Fred Church), Carl Stockdale (postmaster) S: Dr. White must operate on a man who is engaged to marry the woman White loves.

The Rustler's Step-Daughter 6 November 1913 Niles 00154 D: Lloyd Ingraham? C: Marguerite Clayton, True Boardman, Evelyn Selbie, Stanley Sargent, Bill Cato, Carl Stockdale, Jack

Wood S: The sheriff goes on a hunt for some cattle rustlers and falls into their hands, but the step-daughter of the leader saves the sheriff by delivering a note to his deputies.

Broncho Billy's Secret 8 November 1913 Niles D: G. M. Anderson C: G. M. Anderson (Broncho Billy), Marguerite Clayton (Marguerite Clayton) S: Billy, a sheriff, discovers that the father of his wife-to-be is a notorious outlaw.

The Last Laugh 12 November 1913 Niles 00174 D: Jess Robbins? C: Margaret Joslin (landlady), Marguerite Clayton (landlady's daughter), Augustus Carney (W. Jones), Harry Keenan (minister), Victor Potel, Harry Todd S: A landlady and her daughter believe their new boarder, Mr. Jones, may be the heir to a fortune, and the mother outmaneuvers the daughter to marry him, then finds out he's not the right guy.

* *The New Schoolmarm of Green River* 13 November 1913 Niles 00163 D: G. M. Anderson? C: Fred Church (mailman), Eleanor Blevins (teacher), Harry Keenan (gambler), G. M. Anderson S: A gambler shoots a mailman, jealous of the mailman's relationship with a teacher. The teacher finds the mailman seriously wounded and directs the gambler at gunpoint to carry her sweetheart to town, then she delivers the gambler to the sheriff. [LOC]

"Alkali" Ike's Auto 15 November 1913 This is a reissue of the 20 May 1911 film.

The Cowboy Samaritan 20 November 1913 Niles 00175 D: Lloyd Ingraham?

SC: Josephine Rector C: Marguerite Clayton, True Boardman, Evelyn Selbie S: A cowboy cashes a check at a saloon on his way to buy medicine for his sick wife, but drinking leads to gambling and the loss of all his money to a stranger. A fight starts just as his little daughter comes looking for him, and she's shot. The stranger follows the cowboy home, and, seeing the situation, leaves the gambling money on a table.

The End of the Circle 21 November 1913 two reels Niles 00177 D: Jess Robbins? C: Fred Church (Will Davis), Eleanor Blevins (Eileen Sheridan), True Boardman (Don Wilson), Evelyn Selbie (Juanita), Lois Ingraham (child), Victor Potel, Tom Crizer, David Kirkland, Carl Stockdale, Jack Roberts, Slim Padgett S: The impending marriage between Will and Eileen is broken off when Don and Juanita conspire to make it appear Will is unfaithful. Don marries Eileen and becomes a drunken gambler. A child is born to them, and when Don dies from a fall and Eileen dies from illness, Will takes their daughter to raise as his own.

Broncho Billy's First Arrest 22 November 1913 Niles 00182 D: G. M. Anderson C: G. M. Anderson (Broncho Billy), Marguerite Clayton, Victor Potel, Harry Todd S: Billy makes his first arrest as a sheriff by pursuing a train and stopping an outlaw from leaving with the girl Billy loves.

The Naming of the Rawhide Queen 27 November 1913 Niles 00189 D: Lloyd Ingraham? C: Harry Todd (Reuben Glen), Evelyn Selbie (Martha Glen), Lois Ingraham (Cynthia Glen), True

Boardman (Rufe Peters), Lee Willard, Pat Rooney, Bill Cato, Kite Robinson, Emory Johnson, Nathan Anderson, Harry Keenan, Jack Wood, Jack Roberts, Frank Stockdale, Charles La Due S: Prospectors are dead set against letting another miner into their community until the miner's daughter wins their hearts, and they name the new mine in the town of Rawhide after her.

Sophie's Hero 29 November 1913 Niles 00190 D: Jess Robbins C: Margaret Joslin (Sophie Clutts), Augustus Carney (Alkali Ike), Victor Potel (Slippery Slim), Harry Todd (Mustang Pete), Fred Church (Rawhide Bill) S: Ike wins Sophie by dressing up in a bearskin and chasing his rivals away. [UCLA]

A Romance of the Hills 4 December 1913 Niles 00181 D: Lloyd Ingraham? C: Josephine Rector, Fred Church, Lee Willard, Evelyn Selbie, Carl Stockdale, Victor Potel, Harry Keenan S: Lucy Oliver is set to marry Caleb Breen, but when Will Drummond, an easterner, arrives to visit rancher Henry McLean, Lucy abandons Caleb for Will. Will, however, marries Ruth McLean, Henry's daughter, and after this heartbreak Lucy gladly accepts Caleb's offer of marriage.

Broncho Billy's Squareness 6 December 1913 Niles 00203 D: G. M. Anderson C: G. M. Anderson (Broncho Billy), Marguerite Clayton (Grace Woodward), True Boardman (Carl Underwood), Fred Church (Earl Briggs), Evelyn Selbie (Carl's sister), Frank Pementel (deputy), Emory Johnson, Frank Dolan, Victor Potel, Bill Cato, Josephine Rector, Joe Cassidy, Stanley Sargent, Spider Roach, Jack Wood S: During a stagecoach hold-

up, outlaw Broncho Billy is wounded, but escapes. Earl Briggs innocently helps Billy regain his health and Billy gives Earl a gold locket in appreciation. The sheriff's sister recognizes the locket as her own, stolen in the robbery, and tells her brother Carl. He arrests Earl. Billy finds out and gives himself up to free Earl. [NFTA]

Children of the Forest 11 December 1913 Niles and Suisun 00192 D: David Kirkland C: David Kirkland (Wahahtomah), Evelyn Selbie (Mahtomee) S: Bradford, a prospector, carelessly starts a forest fire, and Wahahtomah saves his sweetheart Mahtomee from death as the fire sweeps away everything in its path.

The Three Gamblers 12 December 1913 two reels Niles 00169 D: G. M. Anderson C: G. M. Anderson (Broncho Billy), Marguerite Clayton (Marguerite Corrington), Robert H. Gray (Robert Corrington), Tom Crizer, Bill Cato, Harry Todd, Fred Church, Victor Potel, Lloyd Ingraham, Harry Keenan, True Boardman, Jack Roberts S: Billy, a professional gambler, promises to give up gambling to marry Marguerite, but when her brother Robert steals money from the family-run express office and gambles it away, Billy steps to the roulette table to win it back. Marguerite finds out and breaks their engagement, but her brother explains Billy's motive, and she forgives him.

Sophie's New Foreman 13 December 1913 Niles 00194 D: David Kirkland? C: Margaret Joslin (Sophie Clutts), Augustus Carney (Alkali Ike), Victor Potel (Slippery Slim), Harry Todd

(Mustang Pete), Joe Cassidy, Stanley Sargent, Jack Roberts S: Ike is hired to work on Sophie's ranch, and she keeps her six-shooter handy to make sure he doesn't relax for a minute.

The Trail of the Snake Band 18 December 1913 Niles 00195 D: Lloyd Ingraham? C: True Boardman (Bob Coleman), Reina Valdez (Nell Bradley), Lee Willard (Chuck Peters), Bill Cato (Tex Connors), Harry Keenan, Carl Stockdale S: A snakeskin hatband that cattleman Bob Coleman finds on the road ties him to an express messenger holdup, but Bob manages to find the real bandit and turn him in.

Broncho Billy's Christmas Deed 20 December 1913 Niles 00207 D: G. M. Anderson C: G. M. Anderson (Broncho Billy), Harry Todd (poor husband), Marguerite Clayton, True Boardman, Fred Church, Josephine Rector, Frank Pementel, Victor Potel, David Kirkland, Emory Johnson, Tom Crizer, Stanley Sargent, Jack Wood, Jack Roberts, Eugenia Clinchard S: Billy, the sheriff, must arrest a poor husband who burglarized a store to get Christmas presents for his wife and child. Billy pays the storekeeper for the loss so that the man can spend the rest of the holiday with his family.

That Pair from Thespia 25 December 1913 Niles 00196 D: David Kirkland C: Augustus Carney (actor), Victor Potel (actor), Margaret Joslin, Evelyn Selbie, Josephine Rector, Harry Todd, Harry Keenan, Jack Wood S: Two down-and-out actors are hissed off the stage in a small town. To get revenge they pretend to be lawyers and scam

money from the townspeople.

A Snakeville Courtship 27 December 1913 Niles 00201 D: David Kirkland? C: Margaret Joslin (Sophie Clutts), Victor Potel (Slippery Slim), Harry Todd (Mustang Pete), Augustus Carney (Alkali Ike), Fred Church (Rawhide Bill) S: Sophie tries to corral a husband, but the men of Snakeville elude her.

1914

Through Trackless Sands 1 January 1914 Niles 00191 D: Lloyd Ingraham? C: True Boardman (John Bailey), Evelyn Selbie (Mrs. Bailey), Carl Stockdale (Clem Dayton), Reina Valdez (Mrs. Dayton), Zella Ingraham (Zella Bailey), Frank Pementel S: Mr. Dayton rescues Mrs. Bailey's daughter at a cliffside, and later gets a job on the Bailey's ranch. Mr. Bailey tries to seduce Mrs. Dayton, but comes to his senses when he sees her wearing the locket his little girl gave the Daytons for saving her.

The Awakening at Snakeville 2 January 1914 two reels Niles 00183 D: Jess Robbins? C: Augustus Carney (Alkali Ike), Margaret Joslin (Sophie Clutts), Harry Todd (Mustang Pete), Victor Potel (Slippery Slim), Fred Church (Rawhide Bill), David Kirkland (Dr. Dopeum), Lee Willard S: Sophie keeps her husband Ike on a short leash and only a trip to the grocery store gives him the chance to enter into a card game with the gang, but he falls asleep, drugged by a sleeping potion meant for her.

The Redemption of Broncho Billy 3 January 1914 Niles 00197? D: G. M. Anderson C: G. M. Anderson (Broncho

Billy), Carl Stockdale S: Billy and a pal scheme to rob a stagecoach, but his pal finds out Billy's wife is onboard for a visit from back east and Billy is informed in the nick of time. After this close call he resolves to lead a better life. (remake of *The Bandit's Child*, released 16 March 1912, remade as *The Outlaw's Awakening*, released 27 March 1915)

The Hills of Peace 8 January 1914 Niles 00202 D: Lloyd Ingraham? C: Fred Church (Fred Church), Carl Stockdale (Carl Stockdale), Marguerite Clayton (Fred's sister), Evelyn Selbie (Fred's mother), David Kirkland (doctor), Lee Willard S: Fred goes west for his health and joins a prospecting venture with Carl. They strike it rich, but Fred dies of tuberculosis. Carl sends Fred's share of the money to Fred's mother and sister each week. Fred's sister arrives for a visit, and a romance develops with Carl.

Snakeville's New Doctor 10 January 1914 Niles D: G. M. Anderson C: Marguerite Clayton (J. Rawlins), G. M. Anderson (Broncho Billy), Harry Todd (Harry Todd), Lee Willard (Lee Willard), Lloyd Ingraham (express agent), Danny Kelleher (boy), Evelyn Selbie (Harry's wife) S: When the boys in Snakeville find out the new doctor is a woman they all pretend to be sick. Billy gets shot and she thinks he's also pretending. (remake of *The Little Doctor of the Foothills*, released 21 May 1910)

The Story of the Old Gun 15 January 1914 Niles 00200 D: Lloyd Ingraham? C:Harry Todd (sheriff, Yuba County), Danny Kelleher (his nephew), Fred Church (former sheriff) S: A young

chap from the city visits his uncle, a sheriff, and dresses up in western clothes, but when the boy reaches for a gun on the wall his uncle asks him not to take it and tells the story of it. The boy falls asleep after his uncle goes to round up some outlaws and dreams he's the hero of his uncle's story.

The Cast of the Die 16 January 1914 two reels Niles 00168 D: Jess Robbins? C: Fred Church (Fred Church), Harry Todd (grocer), Josephine Rector (grocer's daughter), Evelyn Selbie (Church's mother), Lois Ingraham (Church's daughter), Eleanor Blevins (Church's wife), David Kirkland (detective), True Boardman (outlaw) S: Fred is unjustly accused of theft at a grocery store job and escapes to the west. Years later, as a married prospector with a wife, he's tracked down. But a dying outlaw helped by Fred impersonates Fred, saving him from imprisonment.

Broncho Billy — Guardian 17 January 1914 Niles 00208 D: G. M. Anderson C: G. M. Anderson (Broncho Billy), Carl Stockdale (Jim Haley), Lois Ingraham (Josie Haley), Marguerite Clayton (Josie Haley, grown up), Lloyd Ingraham, Victor Potel, Fred Church, Lee Willard S: Billy stops Jim Haley from beating his little daughter Josie, but can't stop Haley from being hanged for cattle rustling. The cowboys send Josie to school back east. She returns grown up and falls for Jim Patton, a wild cowboy, who assures Billy he will mend his ways and be a good husband.

A Night on the Road 22 January 1914 Niles 00213 D: Lloyd Ingraham? C: Fred Church (John Duncan), Victor

Potel S: John Duncan is saved from robbery and death at a village inn by the innkeeper's daughter.

Broncho Billy and the Bad Man 24 January 1914 Niles 00212 D: G. M. Anderson C: G. M. Anderson (Broncho Billy), True Boardman (bad man), Harry Todd (sheriff), Carl Stockdale (deputy), Marguerite Clayton (girl), Lee Willard (doctor), Victor Potel (storekeeper), Bill Cato, Stanley Sargent, Jack Wood, Frank Pementel S: Billy, an outlaw in jail, is given a chance to reform by the sheriff, who allows him to track down a very bad man and bring him back to justice. As a reward for this deed, Billy becomes a deputy.

What Came to Bar Q 29 January 1914 Niles 00210 D: Lloyd Ingraham? C: Fred Church (Fred Church), Lillian Christie (Miss Clemens), Emory Johnson (Clarence Clemens), Victor Potel (bartender) S: Clarence Clemens, the son of a ranchman, is given a hard time by the cowboys when he arrives on vacation, but Clarence's sister proves tougher by wearing western garb and making the cowboys dance to her six-shooter.

Broncho Billy and the Settler's Daughter 31 January 1914 Niles 00198 C: G. M. Anderson (Broncho Billy), Marguerite Clayton (Marguerite), Harry Todd (Harry Todd), Emory Johnson (soldier), Frank Pementel (soldier) S: Billy attempts to save a prospector and his daughter from Indians, but it's the cavalry that comes to the rescue.

A Gambler's Way 5 February 1914 Niles 00209 D: Lloyd Ingraham? C: True

Boardman (Jim Kane), Evelyn Selbie (Louise Carew), Reina Valdez (Grace Carew), Victor Potel (bartender), Carl Stockdale, Harry Todd, Josephine Rector, Emory Johnson S: A gambler and a rancher play cards; at stake is the gambler's wife and the rancher's ranch. The gambler loses.

Broncho Billy and the Red Man 7 February 1914 Niles 00220 D: G. M. Anderson C: G. M. Anderson (Broncho Billy), Harry Todd, Lee Willard (the red man), Victor Potel S: After Billy is hurt in a mine explosion, his partner, an Indian, refuses to reveal the site of their gold mine to an evil doctor and his henchmen. (remake of *The Faithful Indian*, released 18 March 1911)

The Weaker's Strength 12 February 1914 Niles 00213 D: Lloyd Ingraham? C: Reina Valdez (Madeline March), Josephine Rector (landlady), Evelyn Selbie (Madeline's mother), True Boardman (Dan Downing), Victor Potel (deputy) S: A woman shoots her husband for abandoning her, but a stranger who hears her story brings the couple back together.

* **Sophie Picks a Dead One** 13 February 1914 two reels Niles 00214 D: Jess Robbins? C: Margaret Joslin (Sophie Clutts), Victor Potel (Slippery Slim), Harry Todd (Mustang Pete), Carl Stockdale (Dr. Bealy Byers), Harry Keenan, Pat Rooney, Emory Johnson S: Slim, depressed because the cowboys don't like his cooking, pretends to hang himself. [GEH]

The Calling of Jim Barton 14 February 1914 Niles D: G. M. Anderson C: G.

M. Anderson (Jim Barton), Danny Kelleher (Jim Barton as a boy) Carl Stockdale (his father), Evelyn Selbie (his mother), Emory Johnson (his brother as a boy), True Boardman (his brother, grown up), Marguerite Clayton (girl), Lee Willard (half breed) S: Jim Barton, an outlaw, is cornered by a posse led by his long-lost brother, now a sheriff. Rather than disgrace his law-abiding brother, Jim commits suicide. (remake of *The Sheriff's Brother*, released 1 July 1911)

Italian Love 19 February 1914 Niles 00211 D:? C: Emory Johnson (Sylvana), Reina Valdez (Arrita), Evelyn Selbie (her mother), David Kirkland (Gato), Carl Stockdale (Petro) S: Arrita and Sylvana marry, despite family disapproval.

David Kirkland left in December. Roy Clements was hired that same month to direct Snakeville Comedies. Snakeville's Fire Brigade *was probably his first film.*

Snakeville's Fire Brigade 21 February 1914 Niles 00216 D: Roy Clements? C: Margaret Joslin (Sophie Clutts), Victor Potel (Slippery Slim), Harry Todd (Mustang Pete), Emory Johnson, True Eames Boardman, Evelyn Selbie, Eva Sawyer, Lee Willard, Frank Pementel, Jack Wood S: Snakeville gets a new fire engine, but during the first call to a fire the volunteers blow up the engine.

The Arm of Vengeance 26 February 1914 Niles 00223 D: Lloyd Ingraham? C: Carl Stockdale (Craig Bowman), Reina Valdez (Mrs. Bowman), Lois Ingraham (Lois Bowman), Lee Willard (Indian), Stanley Sargent, Jack Roberts, Jack Wood S: Craig Bowman refuses to

let his wife feed a starving Indian, but when their young daughter Lois gets lost in the woods it's the Indian who finds her.

Broncho Billy's Bible 28 February 1914 This is a reissue of the 1 June 1912 release.

The Conquest of Man 5 March 1914 Niles D: Lloyd Ingraham? C: True Boardman (Tom Frazier), Reina Valdez (Nora Frazier), Lee Willard (Tex Eaton), True Eames Boardman (Frazier's son) S: Tom Frazier's problem with drinking gets him fired from a ranch, and his wife's bid to the foreman to get him rehired is misinterpreted by Frazier as infidelity. An argument that night leads to a fire in their home and the foreman saves their young son, sobering Frazier and making him promise to reform.

Sophie's Birthday Party 7 March 1914 Niles 00221 D: Roy Clements C: Margaret Joslin (Sophie), Victor Potel (Slippery Slim), Harry Todd (Mustang Pete), Carl Stockdale, Josephine Rector, Bill Cato, Emory Johnson, Tom Crizer, True Eames Boardman, Joe Cassidy, Stanley Sargent, Jack Wood, Jack Roberts S: Slim decides to surprise his wife Sophie with a piano on her birthday, but while moving the instrument it falls on him, and he's late.

The Warning 12 March 1914 Niles 00225 D: Lloyd Ingraham? C: Marguerite Clayton (Nellie), Emory Johnson (Larry Dale), Carl Stockdale (Scott Lawson), Harry Todd (Pop Haney), Evelyn Selbie (Pepita) S: Nellie rigs a signal system so Larry can visit when her father isn't around because he disapproves of Larry. Scott Lawson enters the Haney household to steal money and moves the signal not knowing what it is. Larry sees it, comes in and rescues Nellie and her father, which changes Haney's opinion of Larry for the better.

The Interference of Broncho Billy 14 March 1914 Niles 00238 D: G. M. Anderson C: G. M. Anderson (Broncho Billy), Carl Stockdale (Carl Stockdale), Marguerite Clayton (Marguerite Stockdale), Tom Crizer S: Billy protects Marguerite's father from cowboys scheming to get the old man drunk after he's vowed to lay off liquor.

Single Handed 19 March 1914 Niles 00222 D: Lloyd Ingraham? C: True Boardman (Jack Travors), Reina Valdez (Reina Valdez), Carl Stockdale (Dr. Karl), Emory Johnson, Jack Roberts, Joe Cassidy, Stanley Sargent S: Jack breaks an arm bringing in two bandits and is treated by Dr. Karl, who is jealous of his relationship with Reina. The doctor drugs Jack and sets the bandits free. When Jack awakens he goes after the bandits again, brings them back and locks the doctor up too.

Love's Lottery never released filmed about March 1914 Niles 00224 C: Victor Potel, Reina Valdez, Josephine Rector, Lee Willard, Bud Jerome Anderson, Pat Rooney, Eva Sawyer

A Hot Time in Snakeville 21 March 1914 Niles 00228 D: Roy Clements C: Margaret Joslin (Sophie Clutts), Victor Potel (Slippery Slim), Harry Todd (Mustang Pete), Danny Kelleher (Herman), Virginia Eames (Minnie), Martin Woods (Brutus), Marie Woods

Castoria), Joe Cassidy, Bill Cato, Jack Roberts, Emory Johnson, Stanley Sargent S: Slim writes to a widow proposing marriage, but Pete meets her first when she arrives by stagecoach. The only thing that troubles Pete is the four kids she has with her. Pete asks Slim for help and Slim marries her after discovering the kids are in her Sunday school class.

The Atonement 26 March 1914 Niles 00227 working title: The Heritage of Evil D: Lloyd Ingraham? SC: Josephine Rector C: Carl Stockdale (Jim Marvin), Reina Valdez (Maizie), Emory Johnson, Josephine Rector, Harry Todd, True Boardman, Victor Potel, Jack Wood, Tom Crizer, Bud Jerome Anderson, Pat Rooney, Mervyn Breslauer, Al Herman, Lee Scott, Ira Morgan, L. Allen Dealey, Frank Stockdale, Jack Roberts, Bill Cato, Frank Pementel, Orlando Hicks, Fritz Wintermeier, Leo West S: A reformed thief, now the sheriff of a small town, is accused of stealing, but he's saved from prison when his daughter confesses to the crime.

Broncho Billy's True Love 28 March 1914 Niles 00236 D: G. M. Anderson C: G. M. Anderson (Broncho Billy), Marguerite Clayton (Marguerite Clayton), Elsa Lorimer (Elsa Lorimer), Evelyn Selbie, Emory Johnson S: Elsa, on a visit from the east, turns Billy's head and he forgets he invited Marguerite to a dance. Elsa sees Marguerite crying after Billy goes back on his promise to her, and Elsa tells Billy she's engaged so that Billy will forget her and go back to Marguerite.

Canning Industry in California 31 March 1914 Sacramento and Milpitas P: Ira Morgan This documentary shows the growing, harvesting and packing of peas and asparagus.

Dan Cupid, Assayer 2 April 1914 Niles 00204 D: David Kirkland? C: David Kirkland (Billy Cousins), Carl Stockdale (Silas Barker), Reina Valdez (Bessie Barker), Harry Keenan (Percival Cholmondoly), Victor Potel S: Billy Cousins, an assayer, is in love with Bessie Barker and doesn't have the heart to break the bad news that her father bought a worthless mine. He assigns the ore a favorable rate and buys it himself, but is forced to straighten out the situation when Barker decides to sell the claim.

The Coming of Sophie's "Mama" 4 April 1914 Niles 00234 D: Roy Clements C: Margaret Joslin (Sophie), Victor Potel (Slippery Slim), Harry Todd (Mustang Pete), Pat Rooney (Sophie's mama) S: When Slim becomes too domineering over his wife Sophie, she and Pete decide to put him in his place by having Pete disguised as Sophie's mama, in town for a visit. Then Sophie's real mama arrives for a surprise visit.

Snakeville's New Sheriff 9 April 1914 Niles 00228 & 00229 D: Roy Clements C: Victor Potel (Slippery Slim), Harry Todd (Mustang Pete), True Boardman (Reno Bill), Bud Jerome Anderson, Lee Willard S: As acting sheriff, Slippery Slim captures the notorious Reno Bill using a jug of whiskey.

The Treachery of Broncho Billy's Pal 11 April 1914 Niles 00240 D: G. M. Anderson C: G. M. Anderson (Broncho Billy), Carl Stockdale (Carl Stockdale), Lee Willard (Mexican Pete), Marguerite Clayton (Peggy Adams) S: Billy and Carl cut cards to see which one will claim Peggy in marriage. Billy wins and begins the long trip to her home, but Carl hires a Mexican with a grudge against Billy to stop him, and Billy is shot, although not fatally.

High Life Hits Slippery Slim 16 April 1914 Niles 00218 D: Roy Clements C: Victor Potel (Slippery Slim), Margaret Joslin (Sophie), Harry Todd (Mustang Pete), Joe Cassidy, Stanley Sargent, Jack Wood, Charles La Due, Jack Roberts S: Sophie accuses Slim of laziness and he retaliates by leaving her a suicide note, but a doctor changes his attitude with a treatment of Carbon Disulphide Highlife and that gets him moving.

Broncho Billy and the Rattler 18 April 1914 Niles D: G. M. Anderson C: G. M. Anderson (Broncho Billy), Marguerite Clayton (Billy's wife), Carl Stockdale (Carl Stockdale), True Eames Boardman (boy) S: Carl Stockdale, the sheriff, decides to steal a jewelry shipment, and to keep his deputy, Billy, from interferring, he removes the lead from the bullets in Billy's gun. Billy comes across a rattlesnake and finds out his gun has been tampered with, so he's ready when he has to draw against the sheriff. Billy captures him and becomes the new sheriff.

Slippery Slim and the Stork 23 April 1914 Niles 00229? D: Roy Clements C: Victor Potel (Slippery Slim), Margaret Joslin (Sophie Clutts), Harry Todd (Mustang Pete), Evelyn Selbie (baby's mother) S: Pete tries to stop the marriage of Slim and Sophie by depositing a misplaced baby in Slim's home and slipping a note to Sophie indicating Slim is the father.

Broncho Billy — Gun-Man 25 April 1914 Niles D: G. M. Anderson C: G. M. Anderson (Broncho Billy), Harry Todd (Harry Rawlins), Carl Stockdale (Jack Holmes), Marguerite Clayton (Margaret Holmes), Emory Johnson (Emery Rawlins), Lee Willard (foreman), Jack Wood (half-breed), Pat Rooney, Bill Cato, Tom Crizer, Joe Cassidy, Jack Roberts S: Billy is hired by Harry Rawlins to eject squatter Jack Holmes and his daughter Margaret from Rawlins' land. Billy is wounded by a half-breed and Margaret nurses him back to health. Billy then refuses to carry out Rawlins' order.

Pie for Sophie 30 April 1914 Niles 00251 & 00252 D: Roy Clements C: Margaret Joslin (Sophie Clutts), Victor Potel (Snicklefritz), Harry Todd (Jabberwat), Pat Rooney (bad man), Fritz Wintermeier (sheriff) S: Sophie captures Jabberwat, one of two starving musicians, after they steal her pies. Snicklefritz, the other guy, steals Sophie's clothes and tries to get Jabberwat out by posing as his wife to get sympathy. A bad man takes up a collection, but the scheme is foiled when Sophie appears.

Broncho Billy's Close Call 2 May 1914 Niles 00248 D: G. M. Anderson C: G. M. Anderson (Broncho Billy), Marguerite Clayton, True Boardman, Fritz Wintermeier, Harry Todd, Jack Wood, Bud Jerome Anderson, Joe Cassidy, Tom Crizer, Frank Stockdale, Pat Rooney,

Lee Scott, Jack Roberts S: Billy sees his wife in a stranger's arms, but instead of attacking, goes to a gambling house and gets himself shot in a fight. He refuses to let a doctor save his life until he finds out the man with his wife was her brother.

A Snakeville Epidemic 7 May 1914 Niles 00255 D: Roy Clements C: Victor Potel (Slippery Slim), Margaret Joslin (Sophie Clutts), Harry Todd (Mustang Pete), Lee Willard (doctor), Fritz Wintermeier (horse doctor), Emory Johnson (Zeke), Evelyn Selbie S: Sophie and a mule both get sick, and Zeke gets confused about who gets what prescription.

Broncho Billy's Sermon 9 May 1914 Niles D: G. M. Anderson C: G. M. Anderson (Broncho Billy), Carl Stockdale (minister), True Boardman (bad man), Victor Potel (sheriff), Harry Todd (bartender), Margaret Joslin, Mervyn Breslauer, Tom Crizer, Pat Rooney, Frank Stockdale, Bud Jerome Anderson, Josephine Rector, Evelyn Selbie S: After some bad men turn a minister out of his church, Billy brings them in and forces them to sit for a service.

Slippery Slim's Stratagem 14 May 1914 Niles 00259 D: Roy Clements C: Victor Potel (Slippery Slim), Harry Todd (Mustang Pete), Margaret Joslin (Sophie Clutts), Bill Cato (Laramie Joe), Pat Rooney (Texas Simpson), Bud Jerome Anderson S: Sophie sends her mother a postcard stating she will wed the man who gives her a ring for her birthday, and Slim, the postmaster, tries to capitalize on this inside information.

Broncho Billy's Leap 16 May 1914 Niles 00251 & 00252 D: G. M. Anderson C: G. M. Anderson (Broncho Billy), Marguerite Clayton (Marguerite Wilson), Carl Stockdale (John Wilson), Victor Potel, Joe Cassidy S: Billy, about to rob a stagecoach, instead saves Marguerite, who is alone on the coach as it runs out of control. (remake of *Broncho Billy's Christmas Dinner*, released 23 December 1911)

A Snakeville Romance 21 May 1914 Niles 00250 D: Jess Robbins? C: Marguerite Clayton (Nell Canby), True Boardman (Dick), Fritz Wintermeier (Bud), Harry Todd (Mr. Canby) S: Dick and Bud are rivals for Nell. Dick, the honorable one, triumphs over Bud, a thief who robs a safe in the Canby home.

Red Riding Hood of the Hills 23 May 1914 Niles D: G. M. Anderson C: G. M. Anderson (Broncho Billy), Marguerite Clayton (Marguerite), Carl Stockdale, Harry Todd, Lee Willard S: Marguerite is left stranded in the woods during a train stop, wanders into Billy's cabin to rest, and is defended by Billy from abuse by his drunken partner.

Sophie Starts Something 28 May 1914 Niles D: Roy Clements C: Margaret Joslin (Sophie Clutts), Victor Potel (Slippery Slim), Harry Todd (Mustang Pete), Emory Johnson, Jack Roberts, Joe Cassidy, Stanley Sargent, Jack Wood, Bill Cato, Pat Rooney, Charles La Due S: Sophie uses a hatchet to break liquor bottles and beer barrels in Snakeville saloons.

Broncho Billy's Cunning 30 May 1914 Niles D: G. M. Anderson C: G. M.

Anderson (Broncho Billy), Harry Todd (detective), Carl Stockdale (sheriff) S: Billy helps a man hurt in a fall over a cliff and discovers the man is a detective intent on arresting Billy for a train robbery. (remake of *The Outlaw Samaritan*, released 22 July 1911)

Sophie Pulls a Good One 4 June 1914 Niles 00264 D: Roy Clements C: Margaret Joslin (Sophie Clutts), Harry Todd (Mustang Pete), Victor Potel (Slippery Slim), True Boardman (outlaw) S: Sophie sets up shop as a dentist in Snakeville and captures an outlaw that robbed her of some chocolate creams.

Broncho Billy's Duty 6 June 1914 Niles D: G. M. Anderson C: G. M. Anderson (Broncho Billy), Marguerite Clayton, Carl Stockdale (man), True Boardman (cowboy) S: Billy's wife leaves him for another man, but he forgives her a few years later on her deathbed and attempts to kill the man who took, then neglected her.

Anderson made The Good-for-Nothing, *the Niles studio's first and last four-reel feature, in January, 1914. It paved the way for a series of features made at the Chicago studio.*

The Good-for-Nothing 8 June 1914 four reels Niles 00230 D: G. M. Anderson C: G. M. Anderson (Gilbert Sterling), Lee Willard (Ralph Sterling), Elsa Lorimer (Gertrude Chapin), Carl Stockdale (John Sterling), Eveleyn Selbie (Mrs. Sterling), Victor Potel (old clerk), Frank Stockdale, Emory Johnson S: Gilbert Sterling, the wayward son of a businessman, is disowned by the family and goes west to make his fortune.

Meanwhile, his ruthless brother Ralph has forced their father into bankruptcy and put both parents in the poor house. Gilbert returns to the east, rescues his parents and ruins his brother in the stock market. But the family is reunited once more when the father's old business is restored and renamed John Sterling & Sons. (remake of The Black Sheep, released 7 July 1909)

The Snakeville Volunteer 11 June 1914 Niles 00271 D: Roy Clements C: Victor Potel (Slippery Slim), Margaret Joslin (Sophie Clutts), Harry Todd (Mustang Pete), Bud Jerome Anderson, Shorty Martin S: Preparations for The Great War inspire the men of Snakeville to do their duty and volunteer.

Broncho Billy and the Mine Shark 13 June 1914 Niles D: G. M. Anderson C: G. M. Anderson (Broncho Billy), Marguerite Clayton (Mildred Young), Carl Stockdale (William Young), True Boardman (True Boardman), Fritz Wintermeier (assayer), Victor Potel (hotel clerk), Harry Todd S: Billy helps William Young and his daughter Mildred turn a profit off a worthless mine sold to them by True Boardman by using the same scheme Boardman employed on them.

T*he Wooing of Sophie* 18 June 1914 Niles 00257 D: Roy Clements C: Margaret Joslin (Sophie Clutts), Harry Todd (Mustang Pete), Victor Potel (Slippery Slim), Bud Jerome Anderson S: Slim tries to slip past rivals Mustang Pete and Toad Totter at a dance, with the object of marrying Sophie.

Broncho Billy, Outlaw 20 June 1914 Niles D: G. M. Anderson C: G. M. Anderson (Broncho Billy), Harry Todd (sheriff), Evelyn Selbie (sheriff's wife), Carl Stockdale (Mexican), Stanley Sargent, Pat Rooney S: After escaping a sheriff's arrest, Billy unknowingly arrives at the sheriff's house in time to stop a bad man from avenging a recent imprisonment by killing the sheriff's wife.

Sophie Finds a Hero 25 June 1914 Niles 00262 D: Roy Clements C: Margaret Joslin (Sophie Clutts), Harry Todd (Mustang Pete), Victor Potel (Slippery Slim), True Boardman, Carl Stockdale, Bud Jerome Anderson, Stanley Sargent, Pat Rooney, Tom Crizer, Emory Johnson, Bill Cato, Fritz Wintermeier S: Sophie is looking for a hero to marry, and both Pete and Slim aspire to be the man, but a bad man complicates matters.

Broncho Billy's Jealousy 27 June 1914 Niles D: G. M. Anderson C: G. M. Anderson (Broncho Billy), Marguerite Clayton (Marguerite), Emory Johnson (Roy Turner), Carl Stockdale (minister), True Boardman (rancher) S: Marguerite stops a deadly duel between Billy and Roy Turner over her affections by getting a minister and marrying Billy.

Sophie Gets Stung 2 July 1914 Niles 00257 & 00258 D: Roy Clements C: Margaret Joslin (Sophie Clutts), Victor Potel (Slippery Slim), Harry Todd (Mustang Pete), True Boardman, Bud Jerome Anderson, Joe Cassidy S: The rivalry for Sophie is so intense this time that all four major contenders become disheartened and Sophie is left alone.

Broncho Billy's Punishment 4 July 1914 Niles 00263 D: G. M. Anderson C: G. M. Anderson (Broncho Billy), Evelyn Selbie (Billy's wife), True Eames Boardman (Billy's son) S: Billy vows to reform his drunken ways after he wounds a doctor in a barroom fight, preventing the doctor from saving the life of Billy's young daughter, shot in a game of cowboys and Indians by her younger brother.

Slippery Slim — Diplomat 9 July 1914 Niles 00267 D: Roy Clements C: Victor Potel (Slippery Slim), Margaret Joslin (Sophie Clutts), Harry Todd (Mustang Pete), True Boardman, Stanley Sargent, Jack Wood, Bill Cato, Tom Crizer, Bud Jerome Anderson, Frank Pementel S: Slim, the town postmaster, marries Sophie for her 18th (?) birthday by holding back all the invitations, so that he and a minister are the only ones there, then Slim releases the invitations so the whole town can visit the next day.

Broncho Billy and the Sheriff 11 July 1914 Niles 00260 D: G. M. Anderson C: G. M. Anderson (Broncho Billy), Carl Stockdale (sheriff), Marguerite Clayton, True Boardman, Evelyn Selbie, Lee Willard (minister) S: A cowardly sheriff makes a deal with an outlaw to let the outlaw escape later so the sheriff can appear heroic by capturing him, but Billy, the deputy, recaptures the man, who confesses to the trick, and Billy becomes sheriff.

Snakeville's New Waitress 16 July 1914 Niles 00269 D: Roy Clements C: Margaret Joslin (Sophie Clutts), Victor Potel (Slippery Slim), Harry Todd (Mustang Pete), Bud Jerome Anderson, Evelyn Selbie, Tom Crizer, Jack Wood, Jack Roberts, Mervyn Breslauer, Stanley Sargent, Al Herman, Joe Cassidy, Charles La Due S: Sophie gets a job as a waitress at the Snakeville Hotel and takes the mind of the menfolk off food and onto her.

Broncho Billy Puts One Over 18 July 1914 Niles 00265 C: G. M. Anderson (Broncho Billy), Marguerite Clayton, Carl Stockdale, Evelyn Selbie S: Roger Newman, a rancher, sends his daughter Mae away by stagecoach to keep her from Billy, his foreman at the ranch, but Billy kidnaps her from the coach, they marry and settle on Newman's land. Newman finds out Billy has squatted on his land, but doesn't realize Mae is there until he plants Mae's horse in Billy's corral to get Billy arrested for stealing.

Slippery Slim's Inheritance 23 July 1914 Niles 00278 D: Roy Clements C: Victor Potel (Slippery Slim), Margaret Joslin (Sophie Clutts), Harry Todd (Mustang Pete), Shorty Martin S: Informed by Ketchum and Cheatum, attorneys, that he will inherit a fortune, Slim still can't get Sophie to marry him until he pretends to be on his deathbed.

Broncho Billy and the Gambler 25 July 1914 Niles 00268 D: G. M. Anderson C: G. M. Anderson (Broncho Billy), Marguerite Clayton (Stasia), Carl Stockdale (Grant Wynn), Lee Willard (John Mackey) S: Broncho Billy hears gambler John Mackey brag that a beautiful woman gave him a scarf pin, and Billy recognizes it as the pin Billy gave to his wife Stasia. Billy grabs Mackey and takes him home to confront his wife. Her father Grant Wynn confesses he stole the pin and lost it gambling with Mackey.

Snakeville's Home Guard 30 July 1914 Niles 00273 D: Roy Clements C: Victor Potel (Slippery Slim), Harry Todd (Mustang Pete), Margaret Joslin (Sophie Clutts), Josephine Rector, True Boardman, Lee Willard, Jack Wood, Joe Cassidy, Bill Cato, Carl Stockdale, Sam Marshall, Madrona Hicks S: Slim forms a regiment to protect Snakeville against a band of Mexicans, but ends up capturing them singlehanded.

The Squatter's Gal 1 August 1914 Niles D: G. M. Anderson C: G.M. Anderson (Broncho Billy), Carl Stockdale (squatter), Marguerite Clayton (squatter's daughter) S: Billy orders a posse to evict a squatter from his land, but the squatter's daughter pleads with Billy to let them stay and he falls in love with her. He tries to stop the posse but they have already burnt the squatters' house down, so Billy offers them his own home.

Slippery Slim's Dilemma 6 August 1914 Niles 00275 D: Roy Clements C: Victor Potel (Slippery Slim), Margaret Joslin (Sophie Clutts), Harry Todd (Mustang Pete), Bud Jerome Anderson S: Pete tries to get Slim quarantined for small pox so he can get Sophie for himself.

* Broncho Billy's Fatal Joke 8 August 1914 Niles D: G. M. Anderson C: G. M. Anderson (Broncho Billy), Carl Stockdale (Rundell), Marguerite Clayton (Marguerite Rundell), Bill Cato

(store clerk), Victor Potel (doctor), True Boardman, Lee Willard, Fritz Wintermeier S: Billy and his friends plant gold in an old prospector's worthless mine as a joke, but when the miner sees the gold he has a heart attack and dies. Billy, feeling responsible, switches his rich claim for the worthless one and gives it to the dead man's daughter when she arrives in town. [video]

Slippery Slim and His Tombstone 13 August 1914 Niles 00280 D: Roy Clements C: Victor Potel (Slippery Slim), Margaret Joslin (Sophie Clutts), Harry Todd (Mustang Pete), Ernest Van Pelt (minister), True Boardman (sheriff), Fritz Wintermeier, Carl Stockdale, Stanley Sargent, Bill Cato S: Slim leaves town unexpectedly and the people of Snakeville believe he's dead.

Broncho Billy Wins Out 15 August 1914 Niles 00276 D: G. M. Anderson C: G. M. Anderson (Broncho Billy), Marguerite Clayton (school teacher), Harry Todd (hotelkeeper), Victor Potel (school trustee), Lee Willard (coward), Carl Stockdale, True Boardman, Tom Crizer S: A rival tries to shoot Billy and blame his death on Billy's sweetheart.

Slippery Slim and the Claim Agent 20 August 1914 Niles 00277 D: Roy Clements C: Victor Potel (Slippery Slim), Margaret Joslin (Sophie Clutts), Harry Todd (Mustang Pete) S: Slim rigs up a dummy to get hit by a train in order to sue for injuries and collect $50,000, but Pete settles it for $9.00.

Broncho Billy's Wild Ride 22 August 1914 Niles 00279 D: G. M. Anderson C: G. M. Anderson (Broncho Billy),

Marguerite Clayton, True Boardman (sheriff), Carl Stockdale, Victor Potel, Harry Todd, L. Allen Dealey, Joe Cassidy, Tom Crizer, Stanley Sargent S: Billy, an outlaw on trial, escapes from court, but is caught after he saves the judge's daughter on a runaway horse.

Slippery Slim and the Fortune Teller 27 August 1914 Niles 00282 D: Roy Clements C: Victor Potel (Slippery Slim), Margaret Joslin (Sophie Clutts), Harry Todd (Mustang Pete), Evelyn Selbie (fortune teller), True Boardman (sheriff) S: Slim bribes a fortune teller into stating that the biscuits Sophie has made for Pete are poison, which chases Pete away and leaves Slim alone to pursue Sophie.

Broncho Billy's Indian Romance 29 August 1914 Niles 00288 D: G. M. Anderson C: G. M. Anderson (Broncho Billy), Carl Stockdale (chief), Evelyn Selbie (Indian), Lee Willard, Marguerite Clayton S: Billy, jilted by a woman, goes into the mountains to prospect and saves an Indian woman from being sold to a chief she dislikes. She falls in love with Billy, but realizes it's hopeless when she sees Billy's sweetheart. The chief she disliked saves her from suicide, and she goes with him.

When Macbeth Came to Snakeville 3 September 1914 Niles 00284 D: Roy Clements C: Harry Todd (Macbeth), Evelyn Selbie (Lady Macbeth), Victor Potel (Slippery Slim), Margaret Joslin (Sophie Clutts), Ernest Van Pelt (constable), True Eames Boardman, Spider Roach S: Sophie is entranced by the actor playing Macbeth, but that night when she sleepwalks with a butcherknife

in her hand, the actor gets scared and leaves town.

Broncho Billy, the Vagabond 5 September 1914 Niles 00286 D: G. M. Anderson C: G. M. Anderson (Broncho Billy), Eugenia Clinchard, Victor Potel, Bill Cato S: Billy steals money to help a starving family, but is caught and about to be hanged when the little girl returns the money. The posse realizes Billy's motive and releases him, then takes up a collection for the family.

Snakeville's Most Popular Lady 10 September 1914 Niles 00290 D: Roy Clements C: Margaret Joslin (Sophie Clutts), Harry Todd (Mustang Pete), Victor Potel (Slippery Slim), Evelyn Selbie (Senorita Pepper), Virginia Eames (Tuscan Annie), Tom Crizer, Bud Jerome Anderson, Mervyn Breslauer, G. M. Anderson, Darr Wittenmyer, Frank Stockdale, Jack Roberts, Eva Sawyer, Fritz Wintermeier, Ernest Van Pelt, Sam Marshall, Charles La Due S: A popularity contest at the Snakeville church bazaar pits Sophie against Senorita Pepper.

Broncho Billy, a Friend in Need 12 September 1914 Niles 00294 D: G. M. Anderson C: G. M. Anderson (Broncho Billy), Carl Stockdale (storekeeper), Marguerite Clayton (storekeeper's daughter), Victor Potel S: Billy, an outlaw, knocks on the door of a general store looking for food. The daughter of the owner, all alone that night, locks him up at the point of a gun. Bandits who have terrorized the area break in looking for money and Billy holds them off while the woman goes for help. (remake of *Broncho Billy and the Bandits*, released

4 May 1912)

Sophie's Legacy 17 September 1914 Niles 00291 D: Roy Clements C: Margaret Joslin (Sophie Clutts), Victor Potel (Slippery Slim), Harry Todd (Mustang Pete), Evelyn Selbie, Ernest Van Pelt, Eleanor Blevins S: When Sophie becomes heir to an uncle's estate, Pete and Slim both press her for marriage. Slim hires a beautiful woman to pretend to be Pete's wife, and Pete retaliates by sending in an Indian with a baby that's supposed to be Slim's.

Broncho Billy Butts In 19 September 1914 Niles 00281 D: G. M. Anderson C: G. M. Anderson (Broncho Billy), Marguerite Clayton, Carl Stockdale, Fritz Wintermeier S: When a hotel-owner's daughter becomes engaged to a young man he doesn't approve of, the father shoots the young man. Billy, a guest at the hotel, keeps the father from further interfering while a doctor is sent for, then Billy forces the father to consent to the young couple's marriage. (remake of *Broncho Billy's Adventure*, released 30 December 1911)

Slippery Slim and the Green-Eyed Monster 24 September 1914 Niles 00297 D: Roy Clements C: Victor Potel (Slippery Slim), Margaret Joslin (Sophie Clutts), Harry Todd (Mustang Pete), Ernest Van Pelt (Hiram Clutts) S: Sophie's father objects to her having gentleman callers, so she sneaks Pete into the house when her father is asleep, but Slim, jealous of Pete, refuses to be left out alone in the cold and wakes up the old man.

The Strategy of Broncho Billy's Sweetheart 26 September 1914 Niles 00292?

D: G. M. Anderson C: G. M. Anderson (Broncho Billy), Marguerite Clayton (Billy's sweetheart), Carl Stockdale (her father), Lee Willard (outlaw) S: Billy shoots an outlaw for speaking badly about Billy's sweetheart. The rest of the outlaw gang go looking for Billy and get his girl to reveal his hiding place by telling her it was her father he shot. When she realizes the lie she tricks them so Billy can escape.

The Snakeville Sleuth Almost released 1 October 1914 (it opened in England in January, 1915), *Slippery Slim Gets Cured* was released instead. Niles 00293 D: Roy Clements C: Victor Potel (Slippery Slim), Margaret Joslin (Sophie Clutts), Harry Todd (Mustang Pete), Fritz Wintermeier (minister), Ernest Van Pelt (Hiram Clutts) S: Slim becomes a correspondence school detective and breaks up the wedding of Sophie and Pete.

Slippery Slim Gets Cured 1 October 1914 Niles 00295 D: Roy Clements C: Victor Potel (Slippery Slim), Margaret Joslin (Sophie), Harry Todd (Mustang Pete), Ernest Van Pelt (doctor) S: Slim has been drinking heavily and Sophie tries to cure him by making him drink spirits of ammonia. He gets sick.

Broncho Billy Trapped 3 October 1914 Niles 00296 D: G. M. Anderson C: G. M. Anderson (Broncho Billy), Marguerite Clayton (Billy's wife), Lee Willard (moonshiner), Carl Stockdale, Bill Cato S: Billy, employed by a moonshiner, is fingered for arrest because the moonshiner has designs on Billy's wife, but on the way to jail Billy and his captors stop at Billy's home, find the man harrassing Billy's wife and arrest him instead.

When Slippery Slim Met the Champion 8 October 1914 Niles 00299 D: Roy Clements C: Victor Potel (Slippery Slim), Margaret Joslin (Sophie Clutts), Harry Todd (Mustang Pete), Ted Barnes (world champion), Lee Willard, Fritz Wintermeier, Al Herman, Bill Cato, Spider Roach, Mervyn Breslauer, True Boardman, Frank Stockdale S: Anyone who can last three rounds against the world's champion boxer will win $100 and Slim is elected.

* Broncho Billy and the Greaser 10 October 1914 Niles 00298 D: G. M. Anderson C: G. M. Anderson (Broncho Billy), Lee Willard (greaser), Marguerite Clayton, Carl Stockdale, True Boardman, Bill Cato, Joe Cassidy, Danny Kelleher, Tom Crizer, Fritz Wintermeier S: The greaser makes trouble by cutting in front of a girl in line at a post office and Billy kicks him out. Vowing revenge, the greaser goes to Billy's shack, ties him up and taunts him with a knife. The girl sees the situation and brings a posse that rescues Billy in the nick of time. [video]

Snakeville's Peace-Maker 15 October 1914 Niles 00300 D: Roy Clements C: Victor Potel (Slippery Slim), Margaret Joslin (Sophie), Harry Todd (Mustang Pete), Darr Wittenmyer, Ernest Van Pelt S: Ranchmen Pete and Slim fight over a checker game, and Slim vengefully hires away all of Pete's cowboys at double their salaries, but Sophie, Pete's daughter, brings her girlfriends home from boarding school and the cowboys come back to Pete's ranch. Slim is hired too, and

that ends the feud.

Broncho Billy Rewarded 17 October 1914 Niles 00303 D: G. M. Anderson C: G. M. Anderson (Broncho Billy), Carl Stockdale (sheriff), True Boardman (bandit), Tom Crizer, Joe Cassidy, Bill Cato, Stanley Sargent, Darr Wittenmyer, Jack Roberts S: Several shops in town are robbed and Billy, the local good-for-nothing, asks to be hired as a deputy to go after the thief. His offer is rejected. He goes anyway, alone, tricks the bandit into thinking he can collect a reward on Billy and gets the bandit put in jail.

* Slippery Slim, the Mortgage and Sophie 22 October 1914 Niles 00301 D: Roy Clements C: Victor Potel (Slippery Slim), Margaret Joslin (Sophie Clutts), Harry Todd (Mustang Pete), Ernest Van Pelt (Hiram Clutts), Evelyn Selbie, Henry Youngman S: Slim threatens to forclose on Hiram's mortgage unless Sophie marries him, but Sophie elopes with Pete, and, in disguise, they're married by Slim, who is also the local Justice of the Peace. [LOC]

Broncho Billy - Favorite 24 October 1914 Niles 00302 D: G. M. Anderson C: G. M. Anderson (Broncho Billy), Marguerite Clayton, Lee Willard (Billy's pal), Carl Stockdale (mailman) S: A girl's gun is taken away by a suitor she rejected, and he declares her boyfriend can come get it if she wants it back. The boyfriend is afraid to do so, and tells Billy. Billy gets the gun, gives it to the boyfriend and departs, but when the girl finds out who the real hero is she goes after Billy and brings him back. (remake of *The Cowboy Coward*, released 16

December 1911)

Snakeville and the Corset Demonstrator 29 October 1914 Niles 00304 D: Roy Clements C: Margaret Joslin (Sophie Clutts), Victor Potel (Slippery Slim), Harry Todd (Mustang Pete) S: Sophie, who has the most perfect figure in the world, arrives in Snakeville to demonstrate straight-back corsets and attracts the attention of every man in town.

Broncho Billy's Mother 31 October 1914 Niles 00304/5 D: G. M. Anderson C: G. M. Anderson (Broncho Billy), Evelyn Selbie (Billy's mother), Al Herman, Tom Crizer, Carl Stockdale S: Billy is a drunk, raising hell in town. The sheriff arrests him, then Billy's mother arrives, and the sheriff, taking pity upon Billy, trades positions with him, putting handcuffs on himself and giving Billy his badge. Billy sobers up. (remake of *Broncho Bill's Last Spree*, released 9 September 1911)

Slippery Slim and the Impersonator 5 November 1914 Niles 00312 D: Roy Clements C: Victor Potel (Slippery Slim), Margaret Joslin (Sophie Clutts), Harry Todd (Mustang Pete), Ernest Van Pelt (impersonator), Warren Sawyer, Spider Roach, Tom Crizer, Orlando Hicks, Henry Youngman, Fritz Wintermeier, Al Herman, Lee Scott, Earl Esola, Darr Wittenmyer S: Pete swipes a diamond ring Slim wanted to give Sophie, and with it he becomes engaged to Sophie. Slim breaks it up by getting a female impersonator to woo Pete, and when Sophie sees the impersonator with Pete the engagement is off. [LOC]

Broncho Billy's Mission 7 November 1914 Niles 00274 D: G. M. Anderson C: G. M. Anderson (Broncho Billy), Lee Willard (minister), Marguerite Clayton, Ernest Van Pelt (blackmailer), Stanley Sargent S: Billy, an outlaw, is found wounded in a road by a minister and his wife. They take him to their home, and while the minister goes for a doctor, the wife tends Billy. A blackmailer threatens to expose the wife's imperfect past to her husband unless he gets money, but Billy interferes and escorts the man out of the county.

Sophie and the Man of Her Choice 12 November 1914 Niles 00306 D: Roy Clements C: Margaret Joslin (Sophie Clutts), Victor Potel (Slippery Slim), Harry Todd (Mustang Pete), Ernest Van Pelt (Hiram Clutts) S: Pete and Sophie's father Hiram try to stop her from marrying Slim, but Sophie hides Slim in a trunk and has Pete carry it to the preacher.

Broncho Billy's Decision 14 November 1914 Niles 00311 D: G. M. Anderson C: G. M. Anderson (Broncho Billy), Marguerite Clayton, Ernest Van Pelt (her father), True Boardman S: Billy is sent by a railroad company to buy the right of way on some property owned by an old settler, but the owner refuses to sell because his wife is buried on the land. Billy tells the railroad to forget it.

The Tell-Tale Hand 19 November 1914 three reels Niles 00317 D: G. M. Anderson ST: Frank Blighton C: G. M. Anderson (Broncho Billy), Marguerite Clayton (Annie Fango), Lee Willard (Tim Cantle), True Boardman (sheriff), Roy Clements (prosecuting attorney),

Harry Todd (judge), Ernest Van Pelt (Peter Fango), Evelyn Selbie, Victor Potel, Bill Cato, Leo West, Lee Scott, Warren Sawyer, Henry Youngman, Frank Stockdale, Tom Crizer, Darr Wittenmyer, Joe Cassidy, Nathan Anderson, Jack Roberts, Charles La Due, Orlando Hicks S: Annie flees from her abusive father, Peter Fango, and that leaves Tim Cantle free to seek his own personal revenge on Fango by stabbing him to death, then planting evidence that points to Annie's guilt. She is arrested and convicted, but Billy believes Cantle's eagerness to testify against Annie is suspicious, and the bloody imprint of a hand on Peter Fango's shirt gives Billy the idea of getting an impression of Cantle's hand to compare them. When Billy presents Cantle and the handprint to the sheriff, Cantle breaks down and confesses, and Billy sets Annie free.

A Horse on Sophie 19 November 1914 Niles 00287 D: Roy Clements C: Margaret Joslin (Sophie Clutts), Victor Potel (Slippery Slim), Harry Todd (Mustang Pete), Ernest Van Pelt (Deacon) S: Sophie decides to marry the man with the best-looking horse. Slim and Pete find out, go to the deacon (who raises prizewinners) and they buy terrible horses, then the two men get in a fistfight. Meanwhile, the deacon drives to Sophie's house in his buggy (pulled by a prize-winning horse) and picks up Sophie.

Broncho Billy's Scheme 21 November 1914 Niles 00308 D: G. M. Anderson C: G. M. Anderson (Broncho Billy), Marguerite Clayton (Miss Emmett), True Boardman (outlaw),Evelyn Selbie,

Tom Crizer, Joe Cassidy, Bill Cato, Jack Roberts, Darrell Wittenmyer S: An outlaw kidnaps Miss Emmett, intent on forcing her to marry him, but she feigns illness and the outlaw gets Billy, a doctor, first blindfolding him so he doesn't know where she's held. She gives Billy a note explaining the situation and he drops white pills along the trail to mark it so he and the sheriff can find their way back. (remake of *The Marked Trail*, released 12 November 1910)

Snakeville's Reform Wave 26 November 1914 Niles 00318 D: Roy Clements C: Margaret Joslin (Sophie), Victor Potel (Slippery Slim), Harry Todd (Mustang Pete), True Boardman (bartender), Tom Crizer, Bill Cato, Evelyn Selbie, Joe Cassidy, Jack Roberts, Darr Wittenmyer, Fritz Wintermeier, W. Coleman Elam S: Sophie, fed up with Slim's drinking, rallies the women in town to vote for the prohibition of alcohol in Snakeville.

Broncho Billy's Double Escape 28 November 1914 Niles 00315 D: G. M. Anderson C: G. M. Anderson (Broncho Billy), Lee Willard (deputy), True Boardman (sheriff), Harry Todd (sheriff), Al Herman (bartender), Tom Crizer, Stanley Sargent, Darr Wittenmyer, Jack Roberts, Ernest Van Pelt, Fritz Wintermeier S: Billy, an outlaw, crosses the Bear County line, eluding one sheriff, but is captured by another. A deputy arrives to bring him back to Bear County, but they stop en route for the night, and in a card game downstairs the deputy loses the money Billy was caught with. Billy robs the money back and gives it to the deputy, who lets Billy escape. (remake of *A*

Westerner's Way, released 5 November 1910)

Sophie's Fatal Wedding 3 December 1914 Niles 00313 D: Roy Clements C: Margaret Joslin (Sophie Clutts), Victor Potel (Slippery Slim), Harry Todd (Mustang Pete), Lee Willard (justice of the peace), Ernest Van Pelt, Leo West, Bill Cato, Joe Cassidy, Darr Wittenmyer, Fritz Wintermeier, Evelyn Selbie, Madrona Hicks, Virginia Eames, Tom Crizer, Florence Cato, Stanley Sargent S: Slim tries to prevent Pete and Sophie from getting married by hiring a bad man to hold up a minister. Pete retaliates by going for a justice of the peace, but Slim puts a smallpox sign on the door. The guests, tired of waiting, pack up their presents and go home.

Broncho Billy's Judgement 5 December 1914 Niles 00307 D: G. M. Anderson C: G. M. Anderson (Broncho Billy), Lee Willard (Billy's pal), Evelyn Selbie (girl), Al Herman, Darr Wittenmyer, Tom Crizer S: Billy and his pal find out the girl they both love has married a gambler. Ten years later, Billy is a sheriff investigating the gambler's death and he discovers the man was killed by Billy's pal after the gambler beat girl. Billy resigns rather than arrest his pal.

Sophie's Sweetheart 10 December 1914 Niles 00316 D: Roy Clements C: Margaret Joslin (Sophie Clutts), Victor Potel (Slippery Slim), Harry Todd (Mustang Pete), Ernest Van Pelt (Hiram Clutts), Evelyn Selbie (Mrs. Clutts), Fritz Wintermeier (minister), Bill Cato (suitor) S: Sophie doesn't want to marry Pete, whom her father favors, nor Slim, whom her mother has chosen. She mar-

ries a stranger.

Broncho Billy's Dad 12 December 1914 Niles 00328? D: G. M. Anderson C: G. M. Anderson (Broncho Billy), Carl Stockdale (Billy's dad), Evelyn Selbie (Billy's mother) S: Billy, the sheriff, must arrest his dad for shooting a surveyor who trespassed on his property. When the wounded man regains consciousness and makes a confession Billy is relieved to hear his dad shot the man in self-defense.

Snakeville's Blind Pig 17 December 1914 Niles 00319? D: Roy Clements C: Victor Potel (Slippery Slim), Margaret Joslin (Sophie), Harry Todd (Mustang Pete), Evelyn Selbie S: Snakeville's women take over the town and the men are forced to stay home and do housework.

Broncho Billy's Christmas Spirit 19 December 1914 Niles 00324 D: G. M. Anderson C: G. M. Anderson (Broncho Billy), Lee Willard (prospector), Evelyn Selbie (his wife), Eugenia Clinchard (his daughter), True Eames Boardman (his son) S: A poor prospector with two small children steals Billy's horse and sells it to buy presents for Christmas. Billy organizes a posse to hang the prospector. When the posse sees how the money was spent they take up a collection for the family.

Slippery Slim Gets Square 24 December 1914 Niles 00307 & 00310 D: Roy Clements C: Victor Potel (Slippery Slim), Margaret Joslin (Sophie Clutts), Harry Todd (Mustang Pete), Ernest Van Pelt S: Slim takes a bath in the creek in preparation to take Sophie to a dance, but Pete steals his clothes.

Broncho Billy and the Sheriff's Office
26 December 1914 Niles 00314 D: G.
M. Anderson C: G. M. Anderson
(Broncho Billy), Lee Willard, True
Boardman, Victor Potel S: Billy is re-
quested to resign as sheriff so another
man's son can be sworn in. When an
outlaw scares the son and tries to in-
timidate Billy, Billy gets reinstated, captures the outlaw and resigns.

Snakeville's Rising Sons 31 December
1914 Niles 00326 D: Roy Clements C:
Victor Potel (Slippery Slim), Harry
Todd (Mustang Pete), Margaret Joslin
(Sophie), Danny Kelleher (Slim's son),
Sam Marshall (Pete's Son), Evelyn Selbie
(Mrs. Pete), Ernest Van Pelt S: The
friendly relationship between Pete, Slim
and their wives is destroyed when their
sons fight over doughnuts.

On 2 December 1914 Essanay copyrighted
The Slim Princess, *a feature film made
at the Chicago studio. The first Niles film
to be copyrighted was* When Love and
Honor Called, *although* Broncho Billy
and the Escaped Bandit *was released
first. Copyright dates are listed following
the release date.*

1915
Broncho Billy and the Escaped Bandit
2 January 1915 © 14 December 1914
Niles 00320 D: G. M. Anderson C: G.
M. Anderson (Broncho Billy), Marguerite Clayton (Billy's wife), Lee Willard
(bandit), True Boardman (sheriff), Jack
Roberts, Bill Cato, Warren Sawyer, Tom
Crizer, Fritz Wintermeier S: Billy's arms
are paralyzed while working his mining
claim, and his wife brings him home.

An outlaw hiding in their house sees the
situation and tries to force her into giving up their savings, but Billy regains
the use of his arms and knocks the villain down. (remake of *A Story of the West*,
released 26 December 1911)

The Battle of Snakeville 7 January 1915
Niles 00321 D: Roy Clements C: Victor Potel (Slippery Slim), Margaret
Joslin (Sophie Clutts), Harry Todd
(Mustang Pete), Ernest Van Pelt (hotel
owner), Evelyn Selbie, Jack Roberts, Joe
Cassidy S: Slim and Pete quarrel over
Sophie, the new cook at the O. K. Hotel, and are thrown out. They retaliate
against the whole town with potatoes
and tomatoes as weapons, but are no
match for a Snakeville fire hose.

*** * Broncho Billy and the Claim Jumpers***
9 January 1915 © 30 December 1914
Niles 00327 D: G. M. Anderson C: G.
M. Anderson (Broncho Billy), Marguerite Clayton (stagedriver's daughter), Lee
Willard (stagedriver), True Boardman
(bartender), Tom Crizer (clerk), Bill
Cato (claim jumper), Fritz Wintermeier
(claim jumper), Ernest Van Pelt (claim
jumper), Warren Sawyer (assayist) S:
Three claim jumpers try to file a claim
on Billy's gold mine with the help of a
bartender who drugs a stagecoach driver
transporting Billy to the claim office.
The driver's daughter, along for the ride,
takes the reins while Billy holds off the
crooks from the back of the coach. (remake of *The Stage Driver's Daughter*,
released 14 October 1911) [NFTA]

*** * When Slippery Slim Went for the Eggs***
14 January 1915 Niles 00329 D: Roy
Clements C: Victor Potel (Slippery
Slim), Margaret Joslin (Sophie), Harry

Todd (Mustang Pete), Ernest Van Pelt (Hiram Clutts), Bill Cato S: Slim and Sophie can't get their hen to lay eggs, prompting Pete and Hiram to give them an anonymous note with some impractical advice on the care and feeding of their chicken.

Broncho Billy and the Sisters 16 January 1915 © 30 December 1914 Niles 00330 D: G. M. Anderson C: G. M. Anderson (Broncho Billy), Marguerite Clayton (Marguerite), Mae Thorn (Mae), Victor Potel (minister), True Boardman (sheriff), Bill Cato S: Marguerite, a cripple, loves Billy, but he's engaged to her sister Mae. When he gets arrested as a moonshiner, Mae gives him back his ring, but Marguerite pays for his release with the money she's been saving for an operation to help her walk. A romance develops. (remake of *Western Hearts*, released 15 June 1912)

When Love and Honor Called 18 January 1915 © 9 December 1914 three reels Niles 00325 D: G. M. Anderson P: Rollie Totheroh ST: Frank Blighton C: G. M. Anderson (Broncho Billy), Marguerite Clayton (Elizabeth Barton), Lee Willard (Juan Martin), True Boardman (sheriff), Harry Todd (deputy), Warren Sawyer, Mervyn Breslauer, Bill Cato, Tom Crizer, Ernest Van Pelt, Evelyn Selbie, Stanley Sargent, Joe Cassidy, Lee Scott, Victor Potel, Fritz Wintermeier, Leo West, W. Coleman Elam, Darr Wittenmyer, Jack Roberts, Charles La Due S: Billy is assigned to find some cattle rustlers in the area, goes to the Bar-O ranch, and comes up against Juan Martin. Martin is engaged to Elizabeth Barton, but she's bothered by Martin's jealousy, especially after Billy

interferes when Martin wants to force her into marriage. Martin frames Billy for rustling Bar-O cattle and the sheriff locks Billy up, then goes out on his own to discover the truth, leaving a deputy in charge. The townspeople want to lynch Billy, but Elizabeth, Billy and the deputy hold them off until the sheriff returns with the real thieves.

Sentimental Sophie 21 January 1915 Niles 00323 D: Roy Clements C: Margaret Joslin (Sophie Clutts), Victor Potel (Slippery Slim), Harry Todd (Mustang Pete), Ernest Van Pelt, Bill Cato, Tom Crizer, Darr Wittenmyer, W. Coleman Elam, Joe Cassidy, Eddie Fries, Jack Roberts S: Slim tricks Sophie into going for a ride with him instead of with Pete, but Pete discovers the ruse just in time to gather some friends and run Slim out of town.

* *Broncho Billy and the Baby* 23 January 1915 © 8 January 1915 Niles 00334 D: G. M. Anderson C: G. M. Anderson (Broncho Billy), Bernice Sawyer (the baby), Evelyn Selbie (her mother), Lee Willard (her father) S: Billy, an outlaw with a reward posted for his capture, rescues a little girl after she falls over a ledge. The grateful mother offers him a room for the night, but the husband recognizes him and wants to turn him in for the reward. His wife holds off her husband at gunpoint until Billy escapes. (remake of *Broncho Billy and the Sheriff's Kid*, released 22 February 1913) [UCLA, GEH, video]

When Slippery Slim Bought the Cheese 28 January 1915 Niles 00333 D: Roy Clements C: Victor Potel (Slippery Slim), Margaret Joslin (Sophie Clutts),

Ernest Van Pelt (Hiram Clutts) S: A piece of limburger cheese complicates the secret courtship of Slim and Sophie, ending with Sophie's father Hiram chasing Slim and Pete up a telephone pole.

Broncho Billy and the False Note 30 January 1915 © 15 January 1915 Niles 00331 D: G. M. Anderson C: G. M. Anderson (Broncho Billy), Lee Willard, Evelyn Selbie, Fritz Wintermeier, Tom Crizer, Bill Cato, Darr Wittenmyer S: A cruel man tricks Billy's sweetheart into marrying him instead of Billy. Years later, Billy, as sheriff, must protect him from a cowboy mob that wants to hang the man for abusing his wife.

G. M. Anderson signed Chaplin with Essanay in December, 1914. Although Chaplin's first film was not made within Anderson's western division, it is listed here for cast clarification. The Chaplin films were assigned a new still code number series, beginning with 001.

* His New Job 1 February 1915 © 1 February 1915 two reels Chicago 001 D: Charles Chaplin P: Jackson Rose C: Charlie Chaplin, Ben Turpin, Leo White (office manager & actor), Robert Bolder (studio president), Gloria Swanson (office worker), Charlotte Mineau (lead actress), Charles Stine (director), Arthur Bates (carpenter), Jess Robbins (cameraman), Charles Hitchcock? (leading man) S: Charlie gets a job at a movie studio and creates havoc. [video]

Sophie's Home-Coming 4 February 1915 Niles D: Roy Clements C: Margaret Joslin (Sophie Clutts), Harry Todd (Mustang Pete), Victor Potel (Slippery Slim), Ernest Van Pelt (Hiram Clutts) S: Sophie wants Slim to meet her at five in the morning when her stagecoach gets into town, but Pete gets there first. Slim gets even by putting snuff in Pete's handkerchief, causing Pete to have a sneezing fit.

* Broncho Billy's Greaser Deputy 6 February 1915 © 21 Janaury 1915 Niles 00322 D: G. M. Anderson C: G. M. Anderson (Broncho Billy), Marguerite Clayton, Lloyd Bacon, Lee Willard (outlaw), Ernest Van Pelt S: A man who married Billy's sweetheart robs a stagecoach with another outlaw, and Billy, the sheriff, goes after him with a posse. The man's wife persuades Billy to let the man go, but once he gets outside Billy's deputy shoots him. [MOMA]

Slim the Brave and Sophie the Fair 11 February 1915 Niles 00335 D: Roy Clements C: Victor Potel (Slippery Slim), Margaret Joslin (Sophie Clutts), Harry Todd (Mustang Pete), Ernest Van Pelt (Hiram Clutts) S: Pete and Sophie elope by stagecoach, but Slim, in disguise, holds up the coach, chases Pete and the driver away, and claims Sophie.

* Broncho Billy's Sentence 13 February 1915 © 26 January 1915 Niles 00289 D: G. M. Anderson C: G. M. Anderson (Broncho Billy), True Boardman (sheriff), Carl Stockdale (minister), Evelyn Selbie (minister's wife), Harry Todd (warden), Warren Sawyer (jailer), Ernest Van Pelt (old man in cabin), Virginia Eames (old man's daughter), Spider Roach, Fritz Wintermeier, Frank Dolan, Frank Stockdale, Mervyn Breslauer, Tom Crizer, Lee Scott, Frank Rose, Henry Youngman, Earl Esola, Bill

Cato, Jack Roberts, Charles La Due S: Billy, an outlaw on the run, is transformed by the kindness of a minister and his wife, and gives himself up to the sheriff. After a term in prison he's released for good behavior. [video, GEH]

Chaplin, Ben Turpin and Leo White arrived in Niles from the Chicago Essanay studio on 18 January 1915. Harris Ensign served as his cameraman for the rest of Chaplin's Essanay films. Chaplin conceived and directed his films. Tom Crizer edited under Chaplin's supervision.

* A Night Out 15 February 1915 © 10 February 1915 two reels Niles and Oakland 002 D: Charles Chaplin C: Charlie Chaplin, Ben Turpin (Charlie's pal), Bud Jamison (headwaiter), Edna Purviance (the waiter's wife), Charles Allan Dealey (restaurant manager), Leo White (the Count & first hotel desk clerk), Eva Sawyer (the Count's companion), Fritz Wintermeier (cop), Earl Esola (bellboy with cigar boxes), Frank Dolan (waiter), Lee Willard (soup slurper), Madrona Hicks (veiled woman), Danny Kelleher (bellboy carrying suitcases), Eddie Fries, W. Coleman Elam S: Charlie antagonizes a hot-tempered headwaiter at home and at work. [video]

* Snakeville's Beauty Parlor 18 February 1915 © 9 February 1915 Niles 00337 D: Roy Clements C: Victor Potel (Slippery Slim), Margaret Joslin (Sophie Clutts), Harry Todd (The Beauty Doctor), Ernest Van Pelt (Hiram Clutts) S: Slim is hired to assist the beauty doctor and manages to put them both in jail. [LOC]

Broncho Billy and the Vigilante 20 February 1915 © 1 February 1915 Niles 00332 D: G. M. Anderson C: G. M. Anderson (Broncho Billy), Lee Willard (rustler), Harry Todd (cattle owner), Victor Potel (cattle owner), Ernest Van Pelt (hotelkeeper), Tom Crizer, Joe Cassidy S: Billy, a sheriff, captures a cattle rustler, then lets him escape to prevent a lynching party from hanging the man.

Sophie Changes Her Mind 25 February 1915 © 9 Febraury 1915 Niles 00341 D: Roy Clements C: Margaret Joslin (Sophie Clutts), Victor Potel (Slippery Slim), Harry Todd (Mustang Pete), Ernest Van Pelt (Hiram Clutts), Warren Sawyer, Joe Cassidy S: Slim makes a desperate effort to marry Sophie by having her kidnapped, but Pete overhears the plot, dresses up as Sophie and is taken instead. Slim discovers the switch only after a minister marries them.

Broncho Billy's Brother 27 February 1915 © 4 February 1915 Niles 00338 D: G. M. Anderson C: G. M. Anderson (Broncho Billy), Ernest Van Pelt (Billy's brother), Evelyn Selbie (Billy's mother), Lee Willard (Mexican), Lloyd Bacon, Tom Crizer, Warren Sawyer, Joe Cassidy S: Billy's brother, a drunk, argues with a Mexican in a saloon, then comes home and abuses his mother. Billy fights with his brother as a result, and while so engaged, the Mexican shoots and kills the brother. The sheriff goes to arrest Billy on information provided by the Mexican, but Billy escapes and gets the Mexican to confess.

Slippery Slim's Wedding Day 4 March 1915 © 17 February 1915 Niles 00340 D: Roy Clements C: Victor Potel (Slippery Slim), Margaret Joslin (Sophie Clutts), Harry Todd (Mustang Pete), Ernest Van Pelt (Hiram Clutts), Tom Crizer, Joe Cassidy, Bill Cato, Florence Cato, Evelyn Selbie, Darr Wittenmyer S: While Slim is asleep, Pete paints Slim's foot black and convinces a doctor that Slim has the Black Plague, thereby delaying Slim's wedding to Sophie.

Broncho Billy's Vengeance 6 March 1915 © 22 February 1915 Niles 00336 D: G. M. Anderson C: G. M. Anderson (Broncho Billy), Lee Willard (gambler), Fritz Wintermeier (doctor), Evelyn Selbie (girl), Tom Crizer, Joe Cassidy, Mervyn Breslauer, Warren Sawyer S: Hearing of his former wife's death, Billy goes after the gambler that took her away from him, but after he ties the man to a tree and is about to brand him, Billy remembers her last request to forgive the man. Billy sets the man free.

Mustang Pete's Pressing Engagement 11 March 1915 © 27 February 1915 Niles 00344 D: Roy Clements C: Harry Todd (Mustang Pete), Margaret Joslin (Sophie Clutts), Victor Potel (Slippery Slim), Ernest Van Pelt (Hiram Clutts) S: Pete makes a date with Sophie and goes to get his pants pressed at Slim's tailor shop, but Slim has his own designs on Sophie and leaves Pete behind with a hole burned through his pants.

* *The Champion* 11 March 1915 © 5 March 1915 two reels Niles 003 D: Charles Chaplin C: Charlie Chaplin, Edna Purviance (trainer's daughter), Ernest Van Pelt (Spike Dugan), Bill

Cato (first sparring partner & trapeze man in gym), Lloyd Bacon (second sparring partner, exerciser in gym, referee), Frank Dolan (second stretcher bearer), Fritz Wintermeier (cop), Danny Kelleher (second cop), Bud Jamison (Bob Uppercut), Leo White (fight fixer), G. M. Anderson, Jess Robbins, Eddie Fries, Henry Youngman, Leo West, W. Coleman Elam, Ben Turpin (cigar vender) S: Charlie enters the world of boxing as a sparring partner and has enough punch to take on the champion. [video]

Broncho Billy's Teachings 13 March 1915 © 27 February 1915 Niles 00347? D: G. M. Anderson C: G. M. Anderson (Broncho Billy), Carl Stockdale (Billy's partner), Marguerite Clayton (Indian girl), Evelyn Selbie (Indian) S: Billy's mining partner robs him of their claim and leaves him for dead, but an Indian girl finds him and helps restore his health. The partner is captured by the Indians and Billy attempts to kill him, but is reminded by the Indian girl of something he taught her — Thou Shalt Not Kill. (remake of *The Indian Maiden's Lesson*, released 22 April 1911)

A Horse of Another Color 18 March 1915 © 8 March 1915 Niles 00346 D: ? C: Victor Potel (Slippery Slim), Harry Todd (Mustang Pete), Leona Anderson (lady) S: Slim and Pete try to outdo each other when a new lady comes to Snakeville.

* *In the Park* 18 March 1915 © 12 March 1915 San Francisco 004 D: Charles Chaplin C: Charlie Chaplin, Edna Purviance (nursemaid), Leo White (the Count), Leona Anderson (the

Count's girl), Ernest Van Pelt (sausage seller), Sam Marshall? (sausage thief), Lloyd Bacon (pocketbook thief), Bud Jamison (Edna's boyfriend) S: Charlie flirts with a nursemaid and drives her boyfriend to suicide. [video]

The Western Way 20 March 1915 © 6 March 1915 Niles 00345 D: G. M. Anderson C: G. M. Anderson (outlaw), Lee Willard (rancher), Hazel Applegate (rancher's wife), Bernice Sawyer (their daughter) S: A rancher saves an outlaw from a posse, then discovers he himself may be arrested for a crime committed years ago. The outlaw confesses to the crime to protect the rancher and his family. (remake of *The Two Fugitives*, released 29 July 1911)

Two Bold Bad Men 25 March 1915 © 19 March 1915 Niles 00348 C: Victor Potel (constable), Harry Todd (nagged husband), Ben Turpin (bad man), Leo White (bad man), Margaret Joslin S: A husband nagged by his wife hires two bad men to steal everything in the house, but they're foiled by the local constable.

The Outlaw's Awakening 27 March 1915 © 16 March 1915 Niles 00343 D: G. M. Anderson C: G. M. Anderson (outlaw), Neva West (outlaw's wife), Bernice Sawyer (outlaw's daughter) S: An outlaw is about to rob a stagecoach, but when he encounters his wife and young daughter, on their way west to join him, he resolves to end his life of crime. (remake of *The Bandit's Child*, released 16 March 1912, and *The Redemption of Broncho Billy*, released 3 January 1914)

A Coat Tale 1 April 1915 © 22 March 1915 Niles 00350 C: Ben Turpin (husband), Margie Rieger (wife), Lee Willard, Eva Sawyer, Victor Potel, Harry Todd, Hazel Applegate, Harry Pollard, Florence Cato, Eva Heazlett, Bill Cato S: A husband buys a cheap coat to substitute for a $100 coat his wife wants, but this backfires and they both end up in a police station with him facing jail unless he pays a $100 fine.

* *A Jitney Elopement* 1 April 1915 © 23 March 1915 two reels Niles and San Francisco 005 D: Charles Chaplin C: Charlie Chaplin, Edna Purviance (Edna), Ernest Van Pelt (her father), Leo White (Count de Ha Ha), Lloyd Bacon (young butler & cop), Paddy McGuire (old butler & cop), Bud Jamison (cop with baton) S: Edna's father wants her to marry a count, but she and Charlie have other ideas. [video]

Ingomar of the Hills 3 April 1915 © 23 March 1915 Niles 00347 D: G. M. Anderson C: G. M. Anderson (Ingomar), Marguerite Clayton (girl), Lee Willard (her father), Tom Crizer, Victor Potel S: Associates of Ingomar, a bandit, kidnap a girl during a stagecoach holdup and bring her to a cabin where Ingomar is in bed, wounded. She takes pity on him, and he helps her escape.

Sophie's Fighting Spirit 8 April 1915 © 29 March 1915 Niles 00342 D: Roy Clements C: Margaret Joslin (Sophie Clutts), Victor Potel (Slippery Slim), Harry Todd (Mustang Pete), Evelyn Selbie (the other woman) S: Jealousy fuels a misunderstanding between Sophie and the neighbor woman. They fight until they notice their husbands laughing at them from the roof. They throw rocks at their husbands and knock them off the roof.

Andy of the Royal Mounted 10 April 1915 © 31 March 1915 Niles 00349 D: G. M. Anderson C: G. M. Anderson (Andy), Marguerite Clayton (school teacher), Lee Willard (trooper), Harry Todd (Captain) S: Andy must get his man, a former friend and fellow trouper who has shot a gambler in a brawl, but Andy's girlfriend, a school teacher, holds him off at gunpoint to allow the man to escape because he saved her life when her horse ran away with her onboard. Andy forgives her.

* *The Tramp* 12 April 1915 © 7 April 1915 two reels Niles 006 D: Charles Chaplin C: Charlie Chaplin, Edna Purviance (farmer's daughter), Ernest Van Pelt (farmer), Leo White (first thief), Lloyd Bacon (second thief & boyfriend), Bud Jamison (third thief), Paddy McGuire (farmhand), Billy Armstrong (minister) S: Charlie rescues a girl from thieves, gets a job on her father's farm and falls in love. [video]

* *The Face at the Curtain* 16 April 1915 © 6 April 1915 Niles 00351 D: G. M. Anderson C: G. M. Anderson (burglar), Marguerite Clayton (a wife), Lee Willard (her husband), Darr Wittenmyer (cop), Joe Cassidy (cop), Warren Sawyer (club steward), Jess Robbins, Leo West, Tom Crizer, Harry Todd, Eddie Fries S: A burglar hiding in a house interrupts a squabble between a wealthy man and his wife. The man calls the police and the wife threatens to tell them the burglar is her "friend." In the end the burglar walks free and

the couple patch things up. (remake of Gratitude, released 22 September 1909) [on video as *After Midnight* and *His Wife's Secret*]

His Wife's Secret 23 April 1915 © 12 April 1915 Niles C: G. M. Anderson (burglar), Lee Willard (the husband), Marguerite Clayton (the wife) S: A husband's jealousy is fueled by his wife's suspicious uneasiness, but a burglar discovers the secret she's kept from her husband, that she is pregnant, and when the burglar explains this to the husband he begs his wife to forgive him.

The Undertaker's Uncle 29 April 1915 © 17 April 1915 Niles 00351 C: Harry Todd (undertaker), Ben Turpin (uncle), Victor Potel (Slippery Slim), Margaret Joslin, Hazel Applegate S: The undertaker hires a hobo to play his rich uncle and impress the lady he wants to marry, but when the "uncle" plays dead, implying the undertaker will inherit his "wealth," Slim pokes the uncle back to life while the lady is paying her last respects.

The Chaplin Essanay unit left Niles on 7 April 1915 for Los Angeles and set up a temporary studio at the Bradbury mansion on the corner of Court and North Hill streets. Scenes from By the Sea *and* Work *were shot there.*

* *By the Sea* 29 April 1915 © 17 April 1915 Los Angeles and Santa Monica D: Charles Chaplin C: Charlie Chaplin, Billy Armstrong (man in straw hat), Margie Rieger (Billy's wife), Bud Jamison (man in top hat), Edna Purviance (Bud's girlfriend), Harry Pollard (ice cream clerk), Ed Armstrong (tobacco and candy clerk), Paddy McGuire (first cop), Ernest Van Pelt (second cop) S: Charlie stirs up trouble by the sea.

The Tie That Binds 30 April 1915 © 20 April 1915 Niles D: G. M. Anderson C: G. M. Anderson (husband), Marguerite Clayton (wife) S: A married couple contemplate divorce, but find a reason to be together when a baby is left on their doorstep.

How Slippery Slim Saw the Show 6 May 1915 © 26 April 1915 Niles 00357 D: Roy Clements C: Victor Potel (Slippery Slim), Margaret Joslin (Slim's wife), Harry Todd (the villain), Ben Turpin, Harry Pollard, Pat Rooney, Bill Cato, Carrie Turpin, Tom Crizer, Joe Cassidy, Leo West, Roy Clements, Robert McKenzie, Elizabeth Scott, Joe Cassidy, Ida Totheroh, Florence Cato, Belle Mitchell, Eddie Fries, Ralph Richmond, Madrona Hicks, Eva Heazlett S: Slim's wife sees the show and becomes enchanted by the villain, while Slim minds their noisy baby outside.

The film originally scheduled for release on 7 May 1915 as His Regeneration *was actually* Broncho Billy Reforms, *first released 13 September 1913. At the last minute it was replaced by the following film using the new title.*

* *His Regeneration* 7 May 1915 © 3 May 1915 Niles 00362 D: G. M. Anderson C: G. M. Anderson (burglar), Marguerite Clayton (the girl), Lee Willard (burglar's accomplice), Hazel Applegate (maid), Belle Mitchell (saloon girl), Lloyd Bacon (her companion), Robert McKenzie (waiter), Bill Cato (first cop at house), Darr Wittenmyer

(second cop at house), Victor Potel (pawn shop clerk), Florence Cato, Bud Jamison, Ben Turpin, Robert Burroughs, Henry Youngman, Warren Sawyer, Carrie Turpin, Harry Todd, Joe Cassidy, Madrona Hicks, Charlie Chaplin S: A burglar shot in a barroom brawl is shown sympathy by a society woman. Later, the burglar and an accomplice rob a house and he discovers the woman who previously helped him lives there. He attempts to call off the robbery, argues with his partner and the partner is shot and killed in a struggle. The woman claims to the police she killed him in self-defense and the burglar vows to reform.[LOC, video]

The Other Girl 14 May 1915 © 6 May 1915 Niles 00365 D: G. M. Anderson C: G. M. Anderson (artist), Ethel Wallace (girl), Marguerite Clayton (the other girl), Lee Willard (her father) S: An artist breaks off an engagement with a girl, goes to the country to paint and meets the other girl. She falls in love with him, but when he is injured by a falling tree and, in his delirium, he speaks of the first girl, the other girl reunites them. (remake of The Western Girl's Sacrifice, released 2 September 1911) Note: Not to be confused with another Essanay film with the same title starring Francis X. Bushman, released 14 February 1914.

The Revenue Agent 21 May 1915 © 12 May 1915 Niles 00339 D: G. M. Anderson C: G. M. Anderson (Tom), Neva West (girl), Lee Willard (revenue agent), Victor Potel (minister) S: A revenue agent disguised as an artist is found out by Tom, one of the moonshiners the agent is after. Tom's former girl, now in love with the agent, is willing to marry Tom if he lets the agent go, but when they get to the minister's house Tom gives her up to the agent. (remake of *The Moonshiner's Heart*, released 27 July 1912)

A Bunch of Matches 28 May 1915 © 15 May 1915 Niles 00353 D: ? C: Robert McKenzie (Old Daddy), Florence Cato (daughter), Margie Rieger (daughter), Hazel Applegate? (daughter), Victor Potel (clerk), Ben Turpin (justice of the peace), Bill Cato, Harry Pollard, Pat Rooney, Tom Crizer S: Old Daddy keeps the boyfriends of his four unmarried daughters at bay with a buggy whip, but the Merry Widow distracts him long enough for the daughters to marry.

The Bachelor's Burglar 28 May 1915 © 15 May 1915 Niles 00366 D: G. M. Anderson C: G. M. Anderson (bachelor), Marguerite Clayton (burglar), Robert McKenzie, Victor Potel, Lloyd Bacon, Rollie Totheroh, Darr Wittenmyer, Leo West, Bill Cato, Eddie Fries S: A woman newspaper reporter researches a story on a rich bachelor by breaking and entering his house. He discovers her and calls the police. His apparel of cap and coat suggests that of a burglar, so she holds him at gunpoint, turns him over to the police and goes to file her story.

Sophie and the Faker 3 June 1915 © 21 May 1915 Niles 00360 D: Roy Clements C: Margaret Joslin (Sophie), Ben Turpin (Sophie's husband), Harry Todd (faker), Victor Potel (faker's assistant), Joe Cassidy, Ben Murphy S: The faker, an electric belt salesman, flirts with Sophie at her boarding house.

When her husband protests, the faker and his assistant hang him from a barn by a rope. Sophie releases her husband, straps an electric belt on him and he beats up the two salesmen.

Broncho Billy's Word of Honor 4 June 1915 © 28 May 1915 Niles D: G. M. Anderson C: G. M. Anderson (Broncho Billy), Marguerite Clayton, Harry Todd (sheriff), Lee Willard (bad man), Eva Heazlett S: During a stagecoach robbery, Billy finds a letter from his dying mother begging him to come home. Billy is caught by a posse, but he explains the situation to a sympathetic deputy and is released. The deputy loses his job, but all is set right when Billy returns.

The Wealth of the Poor 11 June 1915 © 2 June 1915 Niles D: G. M. Anderson C: G. M. Anderson (husband), Marguerite Clayton (wife) S: A couple with seven children are offered a house, land and money by the husband's wealthy brother to adopt one of their children, but the couple can't bear to part with any child and they resign themselves to be thankful for what they have.

Broncho Billy and the Land Grabber 18 June 1915 © 10 June 1915 Niles D: G. M. Anderson C: G. M. Anderson (Broncho Billy), Marguerite Clayton (girl), Lee Willard (land grabber), Harry Todd (sheriff), Robert McKenzie, Lloyd Bacon, Fritz Wintermeier, Victor Potel S: Billy tries to prevent his fellow employees from hanging a land grabber they work for, but they attempt to hang him too. A girl sees the situation and gets a sheriff who stops the hangings in the nick of time.

Work 21 June 1915 © 7 June 1915 two reels Los Angeles D: Charles Chaplin C: Charlie Chaplin (assistant), Charles Inslee (paperhanger), Edna Purviance (maid), Billy Armstrong (homeowner), Marta Golden (wife), Leo White (secret lover), Paddy McGuire (cart passenger) S: A paperhanger and his assistant make a shambles of a home in the course of their work. [video]

A Hot Finish 24 June 1915 © 12 June 1915 Niles 00359 C: Robert McKenzie (father), Eva Heazlett (mother), Margie Rieger (daughter), Harry Pollard (actor) S: A girl reads a book about how to become an actress, falls asleep, dreams of marrying an actor and becoming famous.

Her Realization 25 June 1915 © 17 June 1915 Niles 00375 D: G. M. Anderson C: G. M. Anderson (sweetheart), Marguerite Clayton (girl), Lee Willard (doctor), Leona Anderson (singer), Eva Heazlett, Robert McKenzie S: A girl refuses to marry her sweetheart, wanting a career instead, but when, as a nurse, she takes care of a singer who has had a breakdown and longs for a family, the girl returns to her sweetheart.

A Countless Count 1 July 1915 © 22 June 1915 Niles 00361 C: Robert McKenzie (father), Margie Rieger (daughter), Eddie Fries (sweetheart), Harry Pollard (count), Ed Armstrong (Irishman), May White S: A girl's father wants her to marry a count that he's never seen and mistakes an Irishman for the count, but the girl's sweetheart takes matters into his own hands and throws both suitors out of the house.

The Little Prospector 2 July 1915 © 24 June 1915 Niles 00378 D: G. M. Anderson C: G. M. Anderson (Broncho Billy), Marguerite Clayton (his wife), Lee Willard (fellow prospector), Ella McKenzie (Billy's son), Ida McKenzie (Billy's daughter) S: Billy and his prospector friend have no luck striking it rich, but Billy's little son and daughter have better success.

Broncho Billy Well Repaid 9 July 1915 © 30 June 1915 Niles 00309 D: G. M. Anderson C: G. M. Anderson (Broncho Billy), Marguerite Clayton, Lee Willard S: Billy gives up his country-girl sweetheart for a woman of the city, but when the woman laughs at him after he visits her in town he goes back to the girl only to find his rival has married her. (remake of *The Puncher's New Love*, released 13 May 1911)

A Woman 12 July 1915 © 7 July 1915 two reels Los Angeles D: Charles Chaplin C: Charlie Chaplin (a woman), Charles Inslee (a father), Marta Golden (a mother), Edna Purviance (their daughter), Margie Rieger (a flirt), Jess Robbins (soft drink stand clerk), Billy Armstrong (tophatted man without cane), Leo White (top-hatted man with cane) S: A father flirts in a park, and his wife and daughter do the same with Charlie. They take Charlie home, and when the father shows up Charlie dresses as a woman to escape, but the daughter encourages Charlie to teach her father a lesson about flirting. [video]

The Bachelor's Baby 16 July 1915 © 7 July 1915 Niles 00380 D: G. M. Anderson C: G. M. Anderson (bachelor), Jack Totheroh (baby), Marguerite Clayton (the baby 19 years later), Lee Willard (butler) S: A baby is abandoned in a bachelor's limousine, and he cares for her as she grows up. When she's nineteen he's about to ask her to marry him, but she introduces him to a young man she wants to marry and he gives them his blessing.

Others Started But Sophie Finished 22 July 1915 © 7 July 1915 Niles 00355 D: Roy Clements C: Margaret Joslin (Sophie), Victor Potel (Slippery Slim), Harry Todd (Mustang Pete), Ben Turpin (the husband), Carrie Turpin (the wife) S: A wife-beating husband gets whipped by Mustang Pete, impersonating the wife's mother, then Sophie, the real mother, arrives and beats the husband and Slim as well.

Broncho Billy and the Posse 23 July 1915 © 15 July 1915 Niles 00385 D: G. M. Anderson C: G. M. Anderson (Broncho Billy), Lee Willard (the father), Ella McKenzie (young daughter), Ida McKenzie (young daughter), Harry Todd, Bill Cato, Joe Cassidy, Lloyd Bacon, Robert McKenzie S: A man is about to be hung as a cattle thief, but Billy brings the man's two young daughters to the mob and they plead for their father's life until he's set free. (remake of *A Child of the West*, released 6 January 1912)

Snakeville's Twins 29 July 1915 © 17 July 1915 Niles 00363 D: Roy Clements C: Ella McKenzie (a twin), Ida McKenzie (the other twin), Margaret Joslin (Sophie Clutts), Victor Potel (Slippery Slim), Harry Todd (Mustang Pete), Ben Turpin (henpecked husband), Eva Heazlett (his wife) S: Sophie sells

hair restorer to Pete, Slim and the henpecked husband. Slim goes bald, Pete gets a head of hair and the husband's twin daughters drink his potion.

Broncho's Surrender 30 July 1915 © 21 July 1915 Niles C: G. M. Anderson (Broncho), Lee Willard (husband), Marguerite Clayton (wife), Ella McKenzie (daughter), Robert McKenzie, Belle Mitchell, Henry Youngman S: A school teacher saves Broncho, an outlaw, from capture by misdirecting a posse. The teacher's estranged husband later kidnaps their daughter, but Broncho recognizes her when he robs a stagecoach they're on and sacrifices his freedom by returning the girl to her mother. (remake of *Broncho Billy's Gratitude*, released 18 June 1912)

Hal Roach was hired to direct the actors in the Los Angeles unit when Chaplin wasn't using them. It's uncertain how many films Roach directed before he resumed work at his own company, but he probably directed at least five of the eight films in the series, beginning with Street Fakers. *Still code numbers began at 101.*

Street Fakers 5 August 1915 © 22 July 1915 Los Angeles 101 D: Hal Roach C: Bud Jamison (faker), James T. Kelly (second faker), Margie Rieger (faker's wife), Ann Ivers (second faker's wife), Jack Pollard (hotel proprietor), C. E. Hopkins (young sport) S: Two rivaling fakers and their wives are unable to con the village folk. Bricks start flying between the two couples, but they narrowly escape arrest.

Broncho Billy's Protege 6 August 1915 © 29 July 1915 Niles 00389 D: G. M.

Anderson C: G. M. Anderson (Broncho Billy), Marguerite Clayton (the girl), Lee Willard (her brother), Lloyd Bacon (her sweetheart), Ella McKenzie S: Billy takes back his engagement ring when his girl eyes a newcomer. She marries the man, but two years later he dies. When she herself dies her young daughter goes to Billy and he takes her in.

The Bank 9 August 1915 © 14 August 1915 two reels Los Angeles D : Charles Chaplin C: Charlie Chaplin (Charlie the janitor), Edna Purviance (stenographer), Carl Stockdale (Charles the cashier), Billy Armstrong (another janitor), Charles Inslee (bank president), Leo White (clerk), Lawrence A. Bowes (bond salesman), Paddy McGuire (cashier in white coat and short robber with mustache), Fred Goodwins (bald cashier and robber with derby), Lee Hill (tall robber with mustache) S: Charlie the janitor fails to receive the love of the bank stenographer and dreams of foiling a bank robbery, disgracing Charles the cashier and getting the girl, but when he wakes up he's kissing a mop. [video]

The Bell Hop 12 August 1915 © 5 August 1915 Niles 00382 D: Roy Clements C: Ben Turpin (the bell hop), Victor Potel (Slippery Slim), Robert McKenzie (desk clerk), Harry Todd (cop), Eva Heazlett, Sam Marshall S: The bell hop can't get a wink of sleep because of the stream of guests signing in at the hotel.

Broncho Billy Steps In 13 August 1915 © 3 August 1915 Niles 00386 D: G. M. Anderson C: G. M. Anderson (Broncho Billy), Marguerite Clayton (teacher), Lee Willard (outlaw), Lloyd Bacon (rancher), Victor Potel, Ben Turpin, Harry Todd, Robert McKenzie, Eva Heazlett, Darr Wittenmyer, Charles Allen Dealey, Leo West, Belle Mitchell, Bill Cato, Joe Cassidy, Warren Sawyer S: A rancher sets up a school for his cowboys and hires a pretty school teacher to boost attendance, but an outlaw tries to break that up by becoming the teacher's only pupil and that's when Billy steps in. (remake of *Circle C Ranch's Wedding Present*, released 3 December 1910) [NFMA]

Tale of a Tire 19 August 1915 © 3 August 1915 Los Angeles 102 D: Hal Roach C: Bud Jamison (hubby), Margie Rieger (the wife), Jack Pollard (knight of the avenue), Harry Pollard (another knight), Peggy Blevins (the girl) S: Hubby and his wife get a flat tire while driving in their new car and hubby goes in search of a mechanic. Two men flirt with the wife, and a girl flirts with hubby, but the three interlopers are all left flat when the car is rolling again.

Broncho Billy's Marriage 20 August 1915 © 14 August 1915 Niles D: G. M. Anderson C: G. M. Anderson (Broncho Billy), Marguerite Clayton (the girl), Lee Willard S: The girl's father tries to force her into marrying a wealthy man, but she elopes with Billy instead. (The reviewer from the New York Dramatic Mirror claimed this was a reissue of *Broncho Billy's Elopement*, released 25 October 1913)

The Drug Clerk 26 August 1915 © 14 August 1915 Los Angeles 104? D: Hal Roach C: Ed Armstrong (drug clerk), Harry Pollard (the husband), Margie

Rieger (the wife), Jack Pollard (the uncle), Jean Jarvis (the maid), Tom Crizer (fruit peddler) S: The drug clerk poses as a baby for the benefit of his boss and winds up in a kidnapping scheme to pump money out of the boss's rich uncle.

Her Return 27 August 1915 © 20 August 1915 Niles 00392 D: G. M. Anderson C: G. M. Anderson (the husband), Marguerite Clayton (the wife), Lee Willard (doctor), Eva Heazlett (nurse), Gilbert Scott (baby) S: A wealthy young man marries a poor girl, but refuses to give up his single life. The wife leaves him after he comes home drunk one night. He discovers her missing, tracks her to a hospital and sees her with their new baby. He promises to give up drinking.

Versus Sledge Hammers 2 September 1915 © 20 August 1915 Niles 00370 D: Roy Clements C: Margaret Joslin (Sophie Clutts), Victor Potel (The Count), Harry Todd (Mustang Pete), Robert McKenzie (hotel proprietor) S: The Count hears that Sophie has inherited a million dollars and comes to Snakeville intent on marrying her, but Pete won't give up without a fight. Being a blacksmith, Pete's weapon of choice is a sledge hammer.

Broncho Billy Begins Life Anew 3 September 1915 © 1 September 1915 Niles D: G. M. Anderson C: G. M. Anderson (Broncho Billy), Lee Willard (deacon), Marguerite Clayton (deacon's daughter), Ella McKenzie (deacon's granddaughter), Lloyd Bacon (sheriff) S: Following a stagecoach accident, Billy, an outlaw, finds a little girl and her

mother wandering through the countryside. He takes them to the mother's parents, and later attends a church service where the mother's father, a deacon, speaks. Impressed by the sermon, Billy surrenders to the sheriff.

A Quiet Little Game 9 September 1915 © 25 August 1915 Niles 00374 D: ? C: Harry Todd (Peter Fuss), Lloyd Bacon (Jack Henry), Ben Turpin (the undertaker), Margaret Joslin (Mrs. Fuss), Eva Heazlett (Mrs. Henry), Robert McKenzie (the constable), Charles Allen Dealey S: Fuss and Henry are invited to a poker game. They keep it quiet from the wives by sending them a telegram claiming they're going out of town on business. The wives hear their husbands were killed in a wreck and pay the undertaker to take care of the bodies.

Broncho Billy and the Lumber King 10 September 1915 © 3 September 1915 Niles 00398 D: G. M. Anderson C: G. M. Anderson (Broncho Billy), Marguerite Clayton (thief's daughter), Lee Willard (thief), Lloyd Bacon (sheriff), Harry Todd, Bill Cato S: Billy, a ranger on the trail of some lumber thieves, comes upon their cabin in the woods, and is greeted by the leader's pretty daughter. The thieves discover Billy's identity and draw lots to decide who will kill him, but the daughter goes for the sheriff and prevents the crime.

Mustaches and Bombs 16 September 1915 © 31 August 1915 Los Angeles 103 D: Hal Roach C: Bud Jamison (hubby), Margie Rieger (wife), Jack Pollard (doctor), Tom Crizer S: A movie crew accidently leaves a sign "Pay over $5,000 or we'll drop a bomb on your doorstep!" in front of hubby's house and hubby thinks some mysterious mustached men are involved with it.

Broncho Billy and the Card Sharp 17 September 1915 © 7 September 1915 Niles 00400 D: G. M. Anderson C: G. M. Anderson (Broncho Billy), Lee Willard (Faro Dan), Lloyd Bacon (cattle thief), Harry Todd (rancher), Florence Cato (his daughter), Victor Potel, Robert McKenzie, Warren Sawyer, Leo West, Mervyn Breslauer, Bill Cato, Ben Turpin, Darr Wittenmyer S: Billy argues with Faro Dan during a card game, shoots him and escapes with the aid of a friend. Years later, Billy is sheriff in another county and must arrest his friend for cattle rustling despite threats from the friend he'll talk about the shooting. Billy jails the man, resigns, goes back to the scene of his old crime and gives himself up.

Snakeville's Hen Medic 23 September 1915 © 7 September 1915 Niles 00367 D: Roy Clements C: Victor Potel (Slippery Slim), Harry Todd (Mustang Pete), Margaret Joslin (Sophie Pain, hen medic), Ben Turpin (Bloggie), Carrie Turpin (Bloggie's wife), Robert McKenzie (constable) S: Sophie Pain, a woman doctor, drives the men in Snakeville wild, especially Bloggie, who ends up in a water trough.

An Unexpected Romance 24 September 1915 © 13 September 1915 Niles 00380 D: G. M. Anderson C: G. M. Anderson (landowner), Lee Willard (agent), Harry Todd (old settler), Marguerite Clayton (his daughter) S: A real estate agent tries to foreclose on a settler who's unable to pay his mortgage

despite the landowner's request to be lenient, but the landowner stops the eviction when he goes to the country for his health and a romance develops with the settler's daughter. (remake of *The Millionaire and the Ranch Girl*, released 3 September 1910)

The Convict's Threat 28 September 1915 © 17 September 1915 two reels Niles 00388 D: G. M. Anderson C: G. M. Anderson (convict), Lee Willard (his cellmate), Marguerite Clayton (convict's wife), Harry Todd (warden), Eva Heazlett (warden's wife), Ella McKenzie (warden's daughter), Victor Potel (guard), Warren Sawyer (guard), Bill Cato (guard) Ben Turpin (prisoner), Joe Cassidy (prisoner), Robert McKenzie (bartender), Mervyn Breslauer, Robert Burroughs, Lloyd Bacon, Darr Wittenmyer, Leo West S: The convict's wife resists her husband's former cellmate when the crook tries to blackmail her for money and favors, but she's pressed further until the convict himself, released on good behavior after saving the warden's little daughter from drowning, comes to his wife's rescue.

Off for a Boat Ride 30 September 1915 © 18 September 1915 Los Angeles 105 D: Hal Roach C: James T. Kelly (father), Ann Ivers (mother), Margie Rieger (daughter), Jack Pollard (fiance), Bud Jamison (crook), Leo White S: The family rides in a boat only after father wanders off to help a lady catch a fish and the family ends up in the water.

Broncho Billy Misled 1 October 1915 © 20 September 1915 Niles 00402 D: G. M. Anderson C: G. M. Anderson (Broncho Billy), Marguerite Clayton (prospector's daughter), Lloyd Bacon (prospector), Lee Willard (neighbor), Robert McKenzie, Charles Allen Dealey, Bill Cato, Lee Scott, Mervyn Breslauer S: An old prospector kills a man in a fight. Billy, the sheriff, goes after him, but the prospector's daughter tricks Billy and locks him in a shed, enabling her father to escape. (remake of *Broncho Billy Outwitted*, released 14 September 1912)

* *Shanghaied* 4 October 1915 © 27 September 1915 two reels Los Angeles D: Charles Chaplin C: Charlie Chaplin, Edna Purviance, Wesley Ruggles (Edna's father), Lawrence A. Bowes (first mate), Billy Armstrong (first shanghaied sailor), Paddy McGuire (second shanghaied sailor), Leo White (third shanghaied sailor), John Rand (cook), Fred Goodwins (sailor in coveralls), Lee Hill (sailor in rain hat) S: Charlie helps the first mate of a ship shanghai a sailing crew by conking each man on the head with a mallet, then Charlie gets shanghaied himself. [video]

Snakeville's Weak Women 7 October 1915 © 24 September 1915 Niles 00390 D: Roy Clements C: Margaret Joslin (Sophie Clutts, copette), Victor Potel (City Chap), Harry Todd (a bad example), Robert McKenzie (the police force), Eva Heazlett, Madrona Hicks, Eva Sawyer, Elizabeth Scott, Carrie Turpin S: Sophie is appointed to the police force and begins arresting lawbreakers (all men), beginning with her fellow officer, whom she sees accepting a free stein of beer. When none of the men arrive home for dinner their wives march to the jailhouse and confront Sophie.

Broncho Billy, Sheepman 8 October 1915 © 2 October 1915 Niles D: G. M. Anderson C: G. M. Anderson (Broncho Billy), Marguerite Clayton (school teacher), Eva Heazlett (Billy's mother), Robert McKenzie (Billy's father), Lee Willard (cattle king) S: The cattle king and his men try to run Billy out of the county because he raises sheep. In a gun battle both Billy and the cattleman are wounded. Billy flees to safety at the home of his school teacher sweetheart, and Billy's parents come to the aid of the cattleman. When the cattleman discovers who has saved his life he begs Billy's forgiveness.

Supressed Evidence 9 October 1915 © 27 September 1915 two reels Niles 00394 & 00395 D: G. M. Anderson C: G. M. Anderson (husband), Leona Anderson (wife), Ella McKenzie (their daughter as a child), Marguerite Clayton (their daughter grown up), Lee Willard (music instructor), Robert McKenzie S: A wife and a music instructor who loves her conspire to kill her husband, but the husband kills the instructor in a struggle. The husband keeps his wife's involvement a secret for the sake of his child. He gets out of jail fifteen years later and their daughter brings them together again.

All Stuck Up 14 October 1915 © 1 October 1915 Los Angeles 106 D: Hal Roach? C: Jack Pollard (storekeeper), Bud Jamison (his assistant), Marta Golden (daughter), Leo White (lover), Billy Armstrong (rival lover) S: A flypaper salesman sells his product to a storekeeper, and everyone who comes to the store gets stuck to the paper.

***Broncho Billy's Parent*s** 15 October 1915 © 9 October 1915 Niles 00406 D: G. M. Anderson C: G. M. Anderson (Broncho Billy), Harry Todd (Billy's father), Eva Heazlett (Billy's mother), Arthur Jasmin (Billy as a boy) S: Billy is sent to reform school for stealing, but escapes and goes west. Years later, Billy tries to steal a stagecoach strongbox at a general store, discovers the store is run by his parents and begs their forgiveness. (remake of *A Western Redemption*, released 21 October 1911)

When Snakeville Struck Oil 21 October 1915 © 8 October 1915 Niles 00396 D: Roy Clements C: Harry Todd (Simon Slick), Victor Potel (Slippery Slim), Robert McKenzie (Simon's accomplice), Margaret Joslin (Snakeville's leading lady), Ben Turpin, Charles Allen Dealey, L. Allen Dealey, Mervyn Breslauer, Lloyd Bacon, Bud Jerome Anderson, Bill Cato, Leo West, Henry Youngman, Eva Heazlett, Belle Mitchell S: Simon Slick and his accomplice quietly buy land in town, then leak word that oil has been discovered, causing a mad rush for real estate.

Broncho Billy Evens Matters 22 October 1915 © 13 October 1915 Niles 00407 D: G. M. Anderson C: G. M. Anderson (Broncho Billy), Marguerite Clayton (Billy's wife), Lee Willard (storekeeper), Robert McKenzie (doctor and real estate agent), Harry Todd (sheriff), Bill Cato, Lee Scott, Mervyn Breslauer, Eva Heazlett, Charles Allen Dealey, Lloyd Bacon S: Billy has no money for a doctor when his wife becomes ill, so he steals from a storekeeper, then flees the county. Years later, the storekeeper is in bankruptcy and the

store is being auctioned off, so Billy, now wealthy, buys it and gives the deed to the storekeeper. (remake of *A Vein of Gold*, released 30 April 1910)

Fun at a Ball Game 28 October 1915 © 14 October 1915 Los Angeles 107 D: Hal Roach? C: Jewel Mendel (storekeeper), Margie Rieger (the girl), C. E. Hopkins (ballplayer), Harris (ballplayer), Carl Stockdale, Dee Lampton, Harry Pollard S: A storekeeper on the way to a ballgame gets his pocket picked by a beautiful woman and resorts to selling peanuts to get inside the park. He sees the woman who stole his money and demands his money back, but she gets two players to beat him up.

Broncho Billy's Cowardly Brother 29 October 1915 © 19 October 1915 Niles 00409 D: G. M. Anderson C: G. M. Anderson (Broncho Billy), Lloyd Bacon (Billy's brother), Marguerite Clayton (Billy's sweetheart), Harry Todd (sheriff), Lee Willard (outlaw) S: Billy loses his girl to his brother, but when an outlaw shoots her father, Billy's brother, the sheriff, is afraid to go after the outlaw. Billy captures the man and allows his cowardly brother to take credit.

The Night That Sophie Graduated 4 November 1915 © 21 October 1915 Niles 00383 D: Roy Clements C: Margaret Joslin (Sophie Clutts), Victor Potel (Slippery Slim), Harry Todd (Mustang Pete), Robert McKenzie (principal of the school), Madrona Hicks, Henry Youngman, Arthur Jasmin, Robert Burroughs, L. Allen Dealey, Bill Cato, Lawrence Abrott, Lloyd Bacon, Elizabeth Scott, Leo West, Eva Swayer, Darr

Wittenmyer, Orlando Hicks, Eddie Fries, Mervyn Breslauer, Frank Dolan, Carrie Turpin, Ida Totheroh, Florence Cato, Eva Heazlett, Belle Mitchell S: Pete is a sore loser, first delaying Slim and Sophie on the way to her graduation exercises, then setting fire to the school.

Broncho Billy's Mexican Wife 5 November 1915 © 26 October 1915 Niles D: G. M. Anderson C: G. M. Anderson (Broncho Billy), Edna Robinson (Billy's wife), Lee Willard (Mexican), Leona Anderson (Mexican's sweetheart) S: Billy's Mexican wife falls in love with a Mexican, and, to get Billy out of the way, stabs herself and blames it on Billy to get him arrested. In the meantime, the Mexican's sweetheart gets revenge by stabbing Billy's wife and her lover. (remake of *Broncho Billy's Mexican Wife*, released 30 November 1912)

Wine, Woman and Song 9 November 1915 © 30 October 1915 two reels Niles 00369? D: G. M. Anderson C: G. M. Anderson (young man), Lee Willard, Harry Todd, Lloyd Bacon S: A young man inherits money, spends it all, forges a check and ends up in prison.

Cupid's Bath 11 November 1915 © 30 October 1915 Los Angeles 108 D: Hal Roach? C; Carl Stockdale (Percy Ogler), Bonnie Leonard (Mrs. Sheeza Bird), Margie Rieger (Margaret), Lee Hill (Jimmie), Leo White (the tramp) S: Percy, a self-professed ladykiller, is ridiculed by a group of ladies. He steals their clothes when they go for a swim and then gets arrested.

The Indian's Narrow Escape 12 November 1915 © 30 October 1915 Niles D: G. M. Anderson C: G. M. Anderson (Indian), Robert McKenzie, Lee Willard, Darr Wittenmyer, Ella McKenzie, Ida McKenzie S: An Indian is accused of kidnapping two little girls after he saves them from a runaway horse and buggy. The girls save him from hanging when they plead his innocence.

* *A Night at the Show* 15 November 1915 © 2 November 1915 two reels Los Angeles D: Charles Chaplin C: Charlie Chaplin (Mr. Pest and Mr. Rowdy), Frank J. Coleman (first in line), Paddy McGuire (feather duster, clarinet player), Lawrence A. Bowes (ticket taker, in balcony next to blackface Leo White), Leo White (first man in front row, blackface man in balcony), Wesley Ruggles (second man in front row), Charles Inslee (tuba player), James T. Kelly (trombone player), John Rand (conductor), May White (pushed into fountain), Edna Purviance (lady with beads), George Cleethorpe (behind bead lady), Bud Jamison (tall singer), Carrie Clark Ward (ostrich plume hat), Dee Lampton (fat boy) S: Mr. Pest disrupts the show from the main floor and Mr. Rowdy finishes things off from the balcony. [video]

Snakeville's Eugenic Marriage 18 November 1915 © 10 November 1915 Niles 00399 D: Roy Clements C: Margaret Joslin (Sophie Clutts), Victor Potel (Slippery Slim), Robert McKenzie (Dr. McSwat), Belle Mitchell (the nurse) S: A new law requires Sophie and Slim to pass a doctor's examination before they can get a marriage certificate.

Too Much Turkey 19 November 1915 © 11 November 1915 Niles 00418 D: G. M. Anderson C: G. M. Anderson (Frank Potter), Ruth Saville (Potter's wife), Ben Turpin (a neighbor), Carrie Turpin (neighbor's wife), Robert McKenzie, Eva Heazlett, Arthur Jasmin, Ella McKenzie, Ida McKenzie, Frank Dolan S: Frank Potter can't afford a turkey for Thanksgiving, but he pawns his dress suit to get one. Meanwhile his wife pawns her ring for one. When they discover their error they each compound it by quietly giving away both turkeys to the needy. As they argue, another turkey arrives from Frank's mother-in-law. (remake of *The Tale of the Thanksgiving Turkey*, released 18 November 1908)

It Happened in Snakeville 25 November 1915 © 13 November 1915 Niles 00408 D: Roy Clements C: Margaret Joslin (Sophie Clutts), Harry Todd (Mustang Pete), Ben Turpin (Bloggie), Bill Cato, Lloyd Bacon, Eddie Fries, Arthur Jasmin, Marguerite Clayton, Robert McKenzie, Charles Allen Dealey, Belle Mitchell, Eva Heazlett, Carrie Turpin S: Sophie dreams she answers a want ad to become a movie star and achieves great success, but misses her two rival boyfriends, Pete and Bloggie.

The Barber never released Niles 00414 D: ? C: Ben Turpin (the barber), Lloyd Bacon, Robert McKenzie, Charles Allen Dealey, Ruth Saville, Carrie Turpin, Belle Mitchell, Eva Heazlett, Mervyn Breslauer, Leo West, Darr Wittenmyer, Harry Todd

Broncho Billy's Love Affair 26 November 1915 © 15 November 1915 Niles 00417 D: G. M. Anderson C: G. M. Anderson (Broncho Billy), Ruth Saville (Billy's sweetheart), Lee Willard (her father), Harry Todd, Ben Turpin, Robert McKenzie, Lloyd Bacon, Eva Heazlett, Charles Allen Dealey, Ida Totheroh, Florence Cato, Bill Cato, Darr Wittenmyer, Eva Sawyer, Belle Mitchell, Fritz Wintermeier S: Billy and his sweetheart break their engagement when her father receives a fortune and moves the family to the city. But the father and daughter long for the west, return to it, and she is reunited with Billy.

Jack Sprat and the Scales of Love 2 December 1915 © 22 November 1915 Niles D: Roy Clements C: Victor Potel (Slippery Slim), Margaret Joslin (Sophie), Harry Todd (Mustang Pete) S: Slim and Sophie, man and wife, buy bottles of Thino to make her thin and Fato to make him fat, but Pete switches the contents and the couple are not satisfied with the results.

The Burglar Godfather 3 December 1915 © 22 November 1915 Niles 00420 D: G. M. Anderson C: G. M. Anderson (crook), Lloyd Bacon (his pal), Lee Willard (businessman) S: Two crooks robbing a house come upon the owner's wife and her baby. They leave their spoils behind and later get jobs in the factory of the homeowner. The businessman finds out the crook is working for him, but instead of firing him, makes him the godfather of his child.

Roy Clements left Niles to direct films at Universal in Los Angeles and Wallace Beery came from the Chicago Essanay studio to direct films in Niles. Although no titles have been confirmed, the abrupt change in the style of the Snakeville Com-

edies suggests Beery began with The Merry Models.

The Merry Models 9 December 1915 © 29 November 1915 Niles 00419 D: Wallace Beery? C: Ben Turpin (Bloggie), Margaret Joslin (Bloggie's wife), Harry Todd (Mustang Pete), Carrie Turpin (Pete's wife), Ruth Saville, Belle Mitchell, Robert McKenzie, Charles Allen Dealey S: The manager of the Brezlah Cafe convinces Pete and Bloggie to stand in for two statues destroyed by fire, and everything goes well until their wives enter the cafe and recognize their husbands. A riot ensues and the place is destroyed.

*** The Escape of Broncho Billy*** 10 December 1915 © 29 November 1915 Niles 00423 D: G. M. Anderson C: G. M. Anderson (Broncho Billy), Rodney Hildebrand (Billy's rival), Lee Willard (ranchman), Eva Heazlett (ranchman's wife), Ruth Saville (ranchman's daughter), Lloyd Bacon (sheriff), Ella McKenzie (sheriff's child), Bill Cato (deputy), Joe Cassidy, Warren Sawyer, Ben Turpin, Darr Wittenmyer, Fritz Wintermeier, Henry Youngman S: A ranchman opposed to Billy marrying his daughter drops dead of a heart attack and a rival frames Billy by shooting the dead body and blaming Billy for the "murder," but the sheriff's little daughter has seen the trick and tells her father. (remake of *A Story of Montana*, released 13 July 1912) [NFTA]

Snakeville's Champion 16 December 1915 © 6 December 1915 Niles 00422 D: Wallace Beery? C: Ben Turpin (Bloggie), Lloyd Bacon (Hotch), Margaret Joslin (Bloggie's wife), Rodney Hildebrand (referee), Harry Todd, Darr Wittenmyer S: Hotch tries to defend his world champion wrestling title against Bloggie. (released as *Bloggie the Champion* in England)

Broncho Billy's Marriage 17 December 1915 © 6 December 1915 Niles 00391 D: G. M. Anderson C: G. M. Anderson (Broncho Billy), Marguerite Clayton (the girl), Lee Willard, Fritz Wintermeier, Harry Todd, Victor Potel, Lloyd Bacon, Robert McKenzie, Eva Heazlett, Belle Mitchell, Joe Cassidy, Madrona Hicks, Leo West, Henry Youngman S: Billy stops a saloon patron from forcing a drink upon a woman piano player, and she loses her job. They meet later, she tells him her life story, they fall in love and marry.

*** A Christmas Revenge*** 18 December 1915 © 6 December 1915 two reels Niles 00413 D: G. M. Anderon ST: based on "A Chaparral Christmas Gift" by O. Henry C: G. M. Anderson (Broncho Billy), Marguerite Clayton (school teacher), Lloyd Bacon (Billy's rival), Ben Turpin (loafer), Robert McKenzie (minister), Harry Todd (deacon), Darr Wittenmyer, Leo West, Lee Willard, Joe Cassidy, Bill Cato, Mervyn Breslauer, Fritz Wintermeier, Henry Youngman, Eva Heazlett, Warren Sawyer, Arthur Jasmin, Madrona Hicks, Belle Mitchell, Eva Sawyer, Charles Allen Dealey, L. Allen Dealey, Ida Totheroh, Elizabeth Scott, Carrie Turpin, Helen Dolan, Lee Scott, Eddie Fries, Frank Dolan S: Billy dresses up as Santa Claus to sneak into a church and kill the man who married the woman Billy loves, but at the last moment Billy relents. (remake of *The*

Badman's Christmas Gift, released 24 December 1910) [NFTA]

1916

Her Lesson 4 January 1916 © 22 December 1915 two reels Niles 00421 D: G. M. Anderson C: G. M. Anderson (capitalist), Ruth Saville (his wife), Rodney Hildebrand (interloper), Lloyd Bacon (butler), Eva Heazlett (maid), Eva Sawyer, Robert McKenzie, Darr Wittenmyer, Charles Allen Dealey, Leo West S: A capitalist's wife receives a lot of attention from another man. The capitalist confronts the man and offers him $25,000 to leave the country for two years. The man takes it. But when the capitalist then suggests to his wife that she should leave too, she asks her husband's forgiveness and he gladly gives it.

The Book Agent's Romance 18 January 1916 © 5 January 1916 two reels Niles D: G. M. Anderson C: G. M. Anderson (book agent), Lee Willard (capitalist), Eva Heazlett (capitalist's wife), Ruth Saville (their daughter), Lloyd Bacon (butler) S: A door-to-door book salesman is mistaken by jewel thieves as a jewelry store messenger delivering a necklace to a rich family's home. The salesman and the capitalist's daughter outwit the thieves.

The Man in Him 8 February 1916 © 7 February 1916 two reels Niles 00427 & 00437 D: G. M. Anderson C: G. M. Anderson (John Stone), Ruth Saville (Margaret Houston), Lee Willard (Harry Gardner), Darr Wittenmyer (policeman), Harry Todd, Robert McKenzie, Eva Heazlett, Bill Cato, Warren Sawyer, Arthur Jasmin, Leo West, Lee Scott, Charles Allen Dealey, Ralph Richmond, Florence Cato, Eddie Fries, Belle Mitchell, Helen Dolan, Fritz Wintermeier S: Harry Gardner gets John Stone jailed for jewelry theft at a party so he can marry Margaret Houston. Stone vows revenge, but when he gets his chance years later the look in Margaret's eyes causes him to back down. (Originally set for release as a one-reeler on 15 October 1915, more scenes were shot on 16 January 1916 to turn it into a two-reeler, the last completed film in Niles to be released.)

Chaplin finished Burlesque on Carmen *as a two-reeler by January 15th. Additional scenes were shot in February and/or March by others to make it a four-reeler.*

* **Charlie Chaplin's Burlesque on Carmen** 10 April 1916 © 3 April 1916 four reels Los Angeles D: Charles Chaplin C: Charlie Chaplin (Don Jose), Edna Purviance (Carmen), Leo White (Morales), Ben Turpin (Le Remendado), John Rand (Escamillo), Jack Henderson (Lillas Pastia), May White (Frasquita), Wesley Ruggles (the tramp), Bud Jamison (soldier) S: Don Jose, ordered to guard a passage into the city, is tricked by Carmen into allowing a band of gypsies to smuggle goods in. Morales, the captain of the guards, orders her arrest, but Don Jose fights to defend her and kills Morales. Now a fugitive, Don Jose escapes, but Carmen goes with Escamillo, the matador. In the end Don Jose apparently kills her, then kills himself, but reveals in the closing moments that the knife blade is retractable.

Chaplin used footage from his unrealized feature film Life *(also called* Nine Lives) *and shot more film in January to finish* Police, *his final Essanay film.*

* **Police** 27 May 1916 © 9 May 1916 two reels Los Angeles D: Charles Chaplin C: Charlie Chaplin (Charlie, Convict 999), Edna Purviance (the girl), Billy Armstrong (crooked preacher, second cop), James T. Kelly (drunk, second flophouse customer), Fred Goodwins (honest preacher, policeman at station with monicle), John Rand (policeman at house), Wesley Ruggles (crook), Leo White (fruit vender, flophouse manager, policeman at station), Harry Pollard (first flophouse customer), Bud Jamison (third flophouse customer), Paddy McGuire (fifth flophouse customer), George Cleethorpe (policeman at station with dark mustache) S: Charlie, released from prison, tries to survive on the streets, but his old cellmate recruits him to rob a house.

The following Niles films, made before The Man in Him, *were released much later, probably to capitalize on Ben Turpin's growing popularity.*

A Safe Proposition 8 November 1916 © 22 October 1916 Niles 00393 D: Roy Clements C: Ben Turpin (burglar), Victor Potel (policeman), Harry Todd, Eva Heazlett, Belle Mitchell S: A burglar and his accomplice try to rob an empty safe that the lady of the house doesn't want.

Some Bravery 22 November 1916 © 11 November 1916 Niles D: Wallace Beery? C: Ben Turpin (bell hop) S: The bell hop keeps busy delivering ice water to the hotel guests, then turns a firehose on them.

A Waiting Game 6 December 1916 © 27 November 1916 Niles 00426-7 D: Wallace Beery? C: Ben Turpin (a tramp), Lloyd Bacon (waiter), Rodney Hildebrand, Belle Mitchell, Charles Allen Dealey, Joe Cassidy, Henry Youngman, Alice Abrott, Mervyn Breslauer, Elizbeth Scott, Eva Sawyer, Florence Cato, Fritz Wintermeier, Arthur Jasmin, Ruth Saville, Carrie Turpin, Robert McKenzie, Harry Todd, Eddie Fries, Lee Willard, Robert Burroughs, Eva Heazlett, L. Allen Dealey S: A tramp orders everything on the menu at a high class restaurant and can't pay the bill. The manager makes a mistake by putting him to work as a waiter.

Taking the Count 20 December 1916 © 13 December 1916 Niles 00410 D: Wallace Beery? C: Ben Turpin (cabin steward), Harry Todd (another cabin steward), Eva Heazlett, Lloyd Bacon, Leo White, Belle Mitchell, Robert McKenzie, Margaret Joslin, Charles Allen Dealey, Darr Wittenmyer, Carrie Turpin S: Two cabin stewards are mistaken by a society crowd as a count and his companion.

Anderson made Humanity *in his last few weeks at Essanay, and held onto the film when he left. It premiered in New Orleans 17 February 1916 in a rough cut of five reels.*

1917

* **Humanity** 19 May 1917 six reels Niles 00432 Released by Select Photoplay Company D: G. M. Anderson C: G. M. Anderson (Broncho Billy Adair), Ruth Saville (Edith Adair), Rodney Hildebrand (Arthur Stanton), Robert

McKenzie, Harry Todd, Lee Willard, Tom Crizer, Bill Cato, Robert McKenzie, Darr Wittenmyer, Henry Youngman, Ella McKenzie, Fritz Wintermeier, Helen Dolan, Belle Mitchell, Eddie Fries S: After a long struggle, Billy strikes gold at his mine, but it's too late for his wife Edith, who runs off with Arthur Stanton to live the good life. Billy, living a wealthy life alone, runs across Stanton at a party, and when Stanton jokes about Edith, Billy swears he'll strangle Stanton with his naked hands if anything befalls Edith. Stanton abandons Edith and Billy visits her on her deathbed. He goes after Stanton to kill him, but Stanton's little daughter begs him not to kill her daddy. Billy stops, composes himself and walks away. (based upon *What a Woman Can Do*, released 28 April 1911, re-released by Renowned Pictures Corporation in five reels as *Naked Hands* in January 1918, a two-reel version of which exists) [video]

The final Niles Essanay releases were put together more than a year after the Niles studio closed as part of the Black Cat series from the Chicago studio.

Two Laughs 21 July 1917 © 26 January 1917 25 minutes (two reels) Niles 00421 & 00379? D: Wallace Beery and Roy Clements? C: Ben Turpin (special delivery boy), Robert McKenzie, Ruth Saville, Darr Wittenmyer, Lloyd Bacon, Florence Cato, Victor Potel, Eva Heazlett, Belle Mitchell S: A special delivery boy tries to deliver flowers to a stage actress. He later goes to the beach and flirts with the local bathing beauties. (This film appears to be two previously unreleased one-reelers edited into a two-reeler.)

Pete's Pants 28 July 1917 © 24 July 1917 26 minutes (two reels) Niles 00352? & ? D: Roy Clements? C: Harry Todd (Pete), Ben Turpin (himself), Margaret Joslin (Sophie Clutts), Victor Potel (Slippery Slim) S: Slim and Ben, two hoboes, steal milk and pies from the farm owned by Pete and his wife Sophie. When Pete tries to catch them they get Pete in a yoke and poke his pants full of holes with a pitchfork. The constable arrests them, but they escape and crash a society function, where they catch a jewel thief and are each rewarded with a debutante. (This film appears to be two one-reelers edited together into a two-reeler.)

Some filmographies list Broncho Billy and the MacGuire Gang, *and* Broncho Billy and the Revenue Agent. *No firm evidence of these films has been found. The* Last Round-Up *seems to be a temporary title for a film once at the Nederlands Filmmuseum.*

Alphabetical Film Listing.

Use the release date to check the main filmography listing for more information. The asterisk (*), as in the main filmography, indicates the film exists in some form.

The Accusation of Broncho Billy 15 April 1913

Across the Broad Pacific 24 September 1912

Across the Great Divide 13 February 1913

*Across the Plains 1 April 1911

Across the Rio Grande 24 June 1913

The Actor's Baby Carriage 13 January 1909

"Alkali" Ike and the Hypnotist 21 June 1913

"Alkali" Ike and the Wildman 18 October 1913

* "Alkali" Ike Bests Broncho Billy 26 March 1912

"Alkali" Ike Plays the Devil 27 August 1912

* "Alkali" Ike's Auto 20 May 1911

"Alkali" Ike's Boarding House 23 April 1912

"Alklai" Ike's Bride 7 May 1912

"Alkali" Ike's Close Shave 16 November 1912

"Alkali" Ike's Gal 15 August 1913

"Alkali" Ike's Homecoming 19 April 1913

"Alkali" Ike's Love Affair 6 February 1912

"Alkali" Ike's Misfortunes 31 May 1913

"Alkali" Ike's Mother-in-Law 10 May 1913

"Alkali" Ike's Motorcycle 14 December 1912

"Alkali" Ike's Pants 21 September 1912

"Alkali" Ike Stung 8 October 1912

All Is Fair In Love and War 4 March 1908

All Stuck Up 14 October 1915

An All Wool Garment 25 November 1908

Andy of the Royal Mounted 10 April 1915

An Arizona Escapade 30 March 1912

The Arm of Vengeance 26 February 1914

The Atonement 26 March 1914

At the Break of Dawn 7 July 1911

At the Lariat's End 5 July 1913

*Aviation at Los Angeles, California 16 February 1910

The Awakening at Snakeville 2 January 1914

Away Out West 4 June 1910

*An Awful Skate; or, the Hobo on Rollers 27 July 1907

Babies Will Play 8 February 1908

The Bachelor's Baby 16 July 1915

The Bachelor's Burglar 28 May 1915

The Bachelor's Wife 12 May 1909

The Backwoodsman's Suspicions 15 July 1911

The Bad Man and the Preacher 16 April 1910

The Bad Man's Christmas Gift 24 December 1910

The Bad Man's Downfall 11 February 1911

The Bad Man's First Prayer 15 April 1911

The Bad Man's Last Deed 2 July 1910

The Bandit's Child 16 March 1912

The Bandit's Wife 18 June 1910

*The Bank 9 August 1915

The Baseball Fan 19 August 1908

A Battle Royal 16 December 1908

The Bearded Bandit 8 October 1910

Beg Pardon 30 September 1908

The Bell Boy's Revenge 28 December 1907

The Belle of the Siskiyou 2 October 1913

The Bell Hop 12 August 1915

The Best Man Wins 20 November 1909

Bill Jones' New Year Resolutions 23 December 1908

A Birthday Affair 6 October 1909

The Biter Bitten 20 February 1912

The Black Sheep 7 July 1909

Bonnie of the Hills 11 September 1913

The Book Agent's Romance 18 January 1916

The Border Ranger 21 January 1911

A Borrowed Identity 16 October 1913

The Boss of the Katy Mine 28 November 1912

Breaking into Society 3 October 1908

Bring Me Some Ice 17 February 1909

The Broken Parole 18 September 1913

Broncho Bill's Last Spree 9 September 1911

Broncho Billy, A Friend in Need 12 September 1914

*Broncho Billy and the Baby 23 January 1915

Broncho Billy and the Bad Man 24 January 1914

*Broncho Billy and the Bandits 4 May 1912

Broncho Billy and the Card Sharp 17 September 1915

*Broncho Billy and the Claim Jumpers 9 January 1915

Broncho Billy and the Escaped Bandit 2 January 1915

Broncho Billy and the Express Rider 24 May 1913

Broncho Billy and the False Note 30 January 1915

Broncho Billy and the Gambler 25 July 1914

Broncho Billy and the Girl 9 April 1912

*Broncho Billy and the Greaser 10 October 1914

Broncho Billy and the Indian Maid 29 June 1912

Broncho Billy and the Land Grabber 18 June 1915

Broncho Billy and the Lumber King 10 September 1915

*Broncho Billy and the Maid 4 January 1913

Broncho Billy and the Mine Shark 13 June 1914

Broncho Billy and the Navajo Maid 9 August 1913

Broncho Billy and the Outlaw's Mother 11 January 1913

Broncho Billy and the Posse 23 July 1915

Broncho Billy and the Rattler 18 April 1914

Broncho Billy and the Red Man 7 February 1914

*Broncho Billy and the Rustler's Child 26 April 1913

Broncho Billy and the Schoolmam's Sweetheart 26 July 1913

Broncho Billy and the Schoolmistress 3 February 1913

Broncho Billy and the Settler's Daughter 31 January 1914

Broncho Billy and the Sheriff 11 July 1914

*Broncho Billy and the Sheriff's Kid 22 February 1913

Broncho Billy and the Sheriff's Office 26 December 1914

Broncho Billy and the Sister 16 January 1915

Broncho Billy and the Squatter's Daughter 9 March 1913

Broncho Billy and the Step-Sisters 15 March 1913

Broncho Billy and the Vigilante 20 February 1915

*Broncho Billy and the Western Girls 12 July 1913

Broncho Billy Begins Life Anew 3 September 1915

Broncho Billy Butts In 19 September 1914

Broncho Billy Evens Matters 22 October 1915

Broncho Billy – Favorite 24 October 1914

Broncho Billy and the Sheriff 31 August 1913

Broncho Billy Gets Square 17 October 1913

Broncho Billy - Guardian 17 January 1914

Broncho Billy – Gun-Man 25 April 1914

Broncho Billy Misled 1 October 1915

Broncho Billy, Outlaw 20 June 1914

Broncho Billy Outwitted 14 September 12

Broncho Billy Puts One Over 18 July 1914

Broncho Billy Reforms 13 September 1913

Broncho Billy Rewarded 17 October 1914

Broncho Billy's Adventure 30 December 1911

Broncho Billy's Bible 1 June 1912

Broncho Billy's Brother 18 January 1913

Broncho Billy's Brother 27 February 1915

Broncho Billy's Capture 7 June 1913

Broncho Billy's Christmas Deed 20 December 1913

* Broncho Billy's Christmas Dinner 23 December 1911

Broncho Billy's Christmas Spirit 19 December 1914

Broncho Billy's Close Call 2 May 1914

Broncho Billy's Conscience 6 September 1913

Broncho Billy's Cowardly Brother 29 October 1915

Broncho Billy's Cunning 30 May 1914

Broncho Billy's Dad 12 December 1914

Broncho Billy's Decision 14 November 1914

Broncho Billy's Double Escape 28 November 1914

Broncho Billy's Duty 6 June 1914

Broncho Billy's Elopement 25 October 1913

Broncho Billy's Escapade 24 August 12

Broncho Billy's Fatal Joke 8 August 1914

Broncho Billy's First Arrest 22 November 1913

Broncho Billy's Gratefulness 29 March 1913

Broncho Billy's Gratitude 18 June 1912

Broncho Billy's Greaser Deputy 6 February 1915

Broncho Billy's Grit 17 May 1913

Broncho Billy's Gun-Play 25 January 1913

* Broncho Billy's Heart 23 November 1912

Broncho Billy, Sheepman 8 October 1915

Broncho Billy's Indian Romance 29 August 1914

Broncho Billy's Jealousy 27 June 1914

Broncho Billy's Judgement 5 December 1914

* Broncho Billy's Last Deed 8 February 1913

Broncho Billy's Last Holdup 13 August 1912

Broncho Billy's Leap 16 May 1914

* Broncho Billy's Love Affair 7 December 1912

Broncho Billy's Marriage 20 August 1915

Broncho Billy's Marriage 17 December 1915

* Broncho Billy's Mexican Wife 30 November 1912

Broncho Billy's Mexican Wife 5 November 1915

Broncho Billy's Mission 7 November 1914

Broncho Billy's Mistake 23 August 1913

Broncho Billy's Mother 31 October 1914

* Broncho Billy's Narrow Escape 6 July 1912

Broncho Billy's Oath 11 October 1913

Broncho Billy's Pal 30 July 1912

Broncho Billy's Parents 15 October 1915

Broncho Billy's Promise 21 December 1912

Broncho Billy's Protege 6 August 1915

Broncho Billy's Punishment 4 July 1914

Broncho Billy's Reason 12 April 1913

Broncho Billy's Redemption 30 July 1910

Broncho Billy's Scheme 21 November 1914

Broncho Billy's Secret 8 November 1913

* Broncho Billy's Sentence 13 February 1915

Broncho Billy's Sermon 9 May 1914

Broncho Billy's Sister 22 March 1913

*Broncho Billy's Squareness 6 December 1913

Broncho Billy's Strategy 28 June 1913

Broncho Billy's Surrender 30 July 1915

Broncho Billy's Teachings 13 March 1915

* Broncho Billy Steps In 13 August 1915

Broncho Billy's True Love 28 March 1914

Broncho Billy's Vengeance 6 March 1915

Broncho Billy's Ward 15 February 1913

Broncho Billy's Way 5 April 1913

Broncho Billy's Wild Ride 22 August 1914

Broncho Billy's Word of Honor 4 June 1915

Broncho Billy, the Vagabond 5 September 1914

Broncho Billy Trapped 3 October 1914

Broncho Billy Well Repaid 9 July 1915

Broncho Billy Wins Out 15 August 1914

* The Brother, the Sister and the Cowpuncher 28 May 1910

The Bully 16 September 1908

A Bunch of Matches 27 May 1915

The Bunco Game at Lizardhead 6 May 1911

The Burglar's Godfather 3 December 1915

* By the Sea 23 April 1915

The Calling of Jim Barton 14 February 1914

The Call of the Plains 29 July 1913

The Canning Industry in California 31 March 1914

Carmenita, the Faithful 4 February 1911

* A Case of Seltzer 28 July 1909

A Case of Tomatoes 15 September 1909

The Cast of the Die 16 January 1914

The Cattle King's Daughter 20 April 1912

The Cattleman's Daughter 18 February 1911

The Cattle Rustler's Father 18 November 1911

* The Champion 5 March 1915

* Charlie Chaplin's Burlesque on Carmen 10 April 1916

Checker Fiends 8 July 1908

A Child of the Purple Sage 8 June 1912

A Child of the West 6 January 1912

Children of the Forest 11 December 1913

China and the Chinese 14 January 1913

* A Christmas Revenge 18 December 1915

Circle C Ranch Wedding Present 3 December 1910

A Close Shave 21 September 1910

A Coat Tale 1 April 1915

The Coming of Sophie's Mamma 4 April 1914

The Conquest of Man 5 March 1914

The Convict's Threat 28 September 1915

* The Corporation and the Ranch Girl 8 July 1911

The Count and the Cowboys 7 January 1911

A Countless Count 1 July 1915

The Cowboy and the Squaw 19 February 1910

* The Cowboy Coward 16 December 1911

The Cowboy Samaritan 20 November 1913

A Cowboy's Mother-In-Law 15 October 1910

The Cowboy's Sweetheart 23 April 1910

A Cowboy's Vindication 10 December 1910

The Cowpuncher's Ward 14 May 1910

The Crazy Barber 10 March 1909

The Crazy Prospector 3 May 1913

Cupid's Bath 11 November 1915

A Cure for Gout 27 January 1909

* Curing a Masher 28 September 1909

Curiosity 20 February 1912

Cutting California Redwoods 14 November 1912

The Dance at Eagle Pass 23 July 1913

The Dance at Silver Gulch 19 November 1912

The Dancing Nig 21 September 1907

Dan Cupid, Assayer 2 April 1914

The Daughter of the Sheriff 8 July 1913

Days of the Pony Express 25 September 1913

* The Dead Man's Claim 11 May 1912

The Deputy and the Girl 10 February 1912

* The Deputy's Love 27 August 1910

The Deputy's Love Affair 23 March 1912

The Desert Claim 25 November 1911

The Desert Sweetheart 25 May 1912

The Deperado 23 July 1910

The Directoire Gown 15 July 1908

A Disastrous Flirtation 22 July 1908

The Doctor's Duty 1 November 1913

The Dog and the Sausage 2 June 1909

The Dog Cop 22 February 1908

A Dog on Business 7 September 1910

Don't Pull My Leg 6 May 1908

The Drug Clerk 26 August 1915

The Dumb Half-Breed's Defense 20 August 1910

The Edge of Things 12 August 1913

Educated Abroad 10 February 1909

The Effect of a Shave 21 October 1908

Electric Insoles 12 January 1910

The End of the Circle 21 November 1913

The Energetic Street Cleaner 24 March 1909

An Enterprising Florist 8 July 1908

* The Episode at Cloudy Canyon 28 August 1913

* The Escape of Broncho Billy 10 December 1915

The Escape of the Ape 5 August 1908

An Expensive Sky Piece 10 March 1909

* The Face at the Curtain 16 April 1915

The Faithful Indian 18 March 1911

* The Fence on "Bar Z" Ranch 12 March 1910

A Flirty Affliction 21 September 1910

* The Flower of the Ranch 2 April 1910

Flower Parade at Pasadena, Cal. 19 January 1910

The Football Craze 4 January 1908

The Foreman's Cousin 22 June 1912

The Forester's Plea 28 October 1911

The Forest Ranger 25 June 1910

* Forgiven in Death 10 June 1911

A Free Lunch 2 November 1907

The Frontier Doctor 9 December 1911

Fun at a Ball Game 28 October 1915

A Gambler of the West 31 December 1911

A Gambler's Way 5 February 1914

The Gentle Sex 10 June 1908

The Girl and the Fugitive 19 March 1910

The Girl Back East 11 November 1911

The Girl of the West 14 January 1911

The Girl on Triple X 13 Aaugust 1910

The Good-for-Nothing 8 June 1914

Greed For Gold 30 October 1913

Hank and Lank – Blind Men 20 December 1910

* Hank and Lank Dude Up Some 28 September 1910

Hank and Lank – Joyriding 17 September 1910

Hank and Lank: Life Savers 8 November 1910

* Hank and Lank: Sandwich Men 22 November 1910

Hank and Lank: They Get Wise to a New Scheme 12 October 1910

Hank and Lank: They Make a Mash 31 January 1911

Hank and Lank: They Take a Rest 26 October 1910

Hank and Lank: Uninvited Guests 19 October 1910

Hard Luck Bill 4 September 1913

* The Haunted Lounge 6 January 1909

The Heart of a Cowboy 25 December 1909

The Heart of a Gambler 17 July 1913

* He Met the Champion 14 September 1910

Her Lesson 4 January 1916

Her Realization 25 June 1915

Her Return 27 August 1915

Hey There! Look Out! 19 October 1907

He Who Laughs Last, Laughs Best 11 November 1908

The Hidden Mine 24 June 1911

High Life Hits Slippery Slim 16 April 1914

The Hills Of Peace 8 January 1914

Hired – Tired – Fired 23 September 1908

His Reformation 4 December 1909

* His Regeneration 7 May 1915

His Wife's Secret 23 April 1915

A Home at Last 18 January 1908

The Hoodoo Lounge 18 November 1908

The Hoosier Fighter 1 February 1908

A Horse of Another Color 18 March 1915

A Horse on Sophie 19 November 1914

A Hot Finish 24 June 1915

A Hot Time in Snakeville 21 March 1914

The Housekeeper of Circle C 18 March 1913

How Slippery Slim Saw the Show 6 May 1915

Hubby's Scheme 14 November 1911

Humanity 19 May 1917

A Hungry Pair 5 July 1911

A Hustling Advertiser 16 June 1909

Hypnotizing Mother-in-Law 18 March 1908

I Can't Read English 20 May 1908

If It Doesn't Concern You, Let It Alone 11 November 1908

The Impersonator's Jokes 21 October 1908

The Indian and the Child 27 April 1912

An Indian Girl's Awakening 10 September 1910

* The Indian Maiden's Lesson 22 April 1911

An Indian's Friendship 9 November 1912

The Indian's Narrow Escape 12 November 1915

An Indian's Sacrifice 23 September 1911

An Indian Sunbeam 28 September 1911

The Indian Trailer 19 May 1909

The Infant at Snakeville 3 June 1911

The Influence on Broncho Billy 1 March 1913

Ingomar of the Hills 3 April 1915

The Installment Collector 16 December 1908

The Interference of Broncho Billy 14 March 1914

* In the Park 18 March 1915

Italian Love 19 February 1914

It Happened in Snakeville 25 November 1915

Jack of All Trades 11 January 1908

Jack Sprat and the Scales of Love 2 December 1915

James Boys in Missouri 8 April 1908

* A Jitney Elopement 1 April 1915

* Judgment 27 November 1909

Juggler Juggles 11 March 1908

Just Like a Woman 20 May 1908

Ker-Choo 6 May 1908

The Kid Sheriff 23 October 1913

The Last Laugh 12 November 1913

The Last Shot 5 June 1913

Life of a Bootblack; or, the Street Urchin 7 September 1907

The Life We Live 3 July 1913

The Little Doctor of the Foothills 21 May 1910

The Little Prospector 19 November 1910

The Little Prospector 2 July 1915

The Little Sheriff 10 August 1912

* The Loafer 20 January 1912

* The Loafer's Mother 3 August 1912

A Lord for a Day 25 March 1908

Louder Please 15 February 1908

Love and the Law 9 October 1913

Love on Tough Luck Ranch 5 October 1912

Love's Lottery (made around March 1914)

The Lucky Card 27 May 1911

The Making of Broncho Billy 1 February 1913

The Man in Him 8 February 1916

The Man in the Cabin 16 August 1913

The Marked Trail 12 November 1910

The Masquerade Cop 8 November 1910

The Merry Models 9 December 1915

* Method in His Madness 16 March 1910

* The Mexican's Faith 26 February 1910

A Mexican's Gratitude 5 May 1909

A Midnight Disturbance 24 March 1909

The Millionaire and the Ranch Girl 3 September 1910

The Millionaire and the Squatter 16 September 1911

The Miner's Request 2 January 1913

The Mistaken Bandit 16 April 1910

A Montana Mix-Up 6 March 1913

A Moonshiner's Heart 27 July 1912

The Mother of the Ranch 2 November 1912

The Mountain Law 2 December 1911

* Mr. Flip 12 May 1909

Mr. Inquisitive 24 August 1907

Mustaches and Bombs 16 September 1915

Mustang Pete's Love Affair 11 July 1911

Mustang Pete's Pressing Engagement 11 March 1915

The Naming of the Rawhide Queen 27 November 1913

* The Neighbors' Kids 6 January 1909

Never Again 23 September 1908

* The New Schoolmarm of Green River 13 November 1913

The New Sheriff 27 May 1913

* A Night at the Show 15 November 1915

A Night on the Road 22 January 1914

* A Night Out 15 Febbruary 1915

The Night That Sophie Graduated 4 November 1915

99 in the Shade 28 September 1907

Novice on Stilts 18 January 1908

The Oath of His Office 27 January 1912

Off for a Boat Ride 30 September 1915

Oh, What an Appetite 2 September 1908

Oh, What Lungs 1 July 1908

* Old Gorman's Gal 13 March 1913

On Another Man's Pass 25 August 1909

* On El Monte Ranch 4 June 1912

On the Cactus Trail 2 July 1912

On the Desert's Edge 4 March 1911

On the Moonlight Trail 17 August 1912

* The Ostrich and the Lady 5 March 1910

The Other Girl 14 May 1915

Others Started But Sophie Finished 22 July 1915

* The Outlaw and the Child 25 February 1911

The Outlaw Deputy 4 November 1911

The Outlaw Samaritan 22 July 1911

The Outlaw's Awakening 27 March 1915

An Outlaw's Sacrifice 19 October 1912

Outwitting Papa 31 October 1911

A Pair of Garters 21 April 1909

A Pal's Oath 19 August 1911

* Pals of the Range 22 October 1910

Patricia of the Plains 1 October 1910

Pete's Pants 28 July 1917

Pie for Sophie 30 April 1914

The Pipe Dream 15 July 1915

* Police 27 May 1916

The Pony Express Rider 17 September 1910

The Power of Good 28 September 1911

President Taft at San Francisco 10 November 1911

Professor's Love Tonic 13 January 1909

The Prospector 12 December 1912

The Prospector's Legacy 17 February 1912

The Puncher's Law 14 September 1911

* The Puncher's New Love 13 May 1911

A Quiet Little Game 9 September 1915

The Ranch Feud 14 June 1913

* The Ranch Girl's Legacy 5 March 1910

* The Ranch Girl's Mistake 2 March 1912

The Ranch Girl's Partner 13 May 1913

The Ranch Girl's Trial 26 October 1912

The Ranchman's Anniversary 7 November 1912

The Ranchman's Blunder 4 February 1913

The Ranchman's Feud 11 June 1910

* The Ranchman's Rival 11 December 1909

The Ranchman's Son 12 August 1911

The Ranchman's Trust 7 September 1912

A Ranchman's Wooing 26 March 1910

The Ranch Widower's Daughters 12 March 1912

* The Ranger's Bride 9 April 1910

The Redeemed Claim 20 September 1913

The Redemption of Broncho Billy 3 January 1914

Red Riding Hood of the Hills 23 May 1914

The Revenue Agent 21 May 1915

The Reward for Broncho Billy 28 December 1912

The Road Agents 17 March 1909

A Road Agent's Love 6 April 1912

A Romance of the Hills 4 December 1913

A Romance of the West 9 March 1912

The Romance on "Bar O" 11 March 1911

The Rubes and the Bunco Men 14 April 1909

The Rustler's Spur 19 June 1913

The Rustler's Step-Daughter 6 November 1913

A Safe Proposition 8 November 1916

Scenes from the World's Largest Pigeon Farm 26 May 1909

Sentimental Sophie 21 January 1915

The Shadowgraph Message 10 June 1913

Shanghaied 3 March 1909

* Shanghaied 4 October 1915

The Sheepman's Escape 13 January 1912

The Sheriff and His Man 18 May 1912

The Sheriff of Cochise 21 August 1913

The Sheriff's Brother 1 July 1911

The Sheriff's Child 22 January 1913

* The Sheriff's Chum 8 April 1911

The Sheriff's Decision 6 October 1911

The Sheriff's Honeymoon 25 March 1913

The Sheriff's Inheritance 24 December 1912

The Sheriff's Luck 19 December 1912

The Sheriff's Sacrifice 7 May 1910

The Sheriff's Son 1 April 1913

The Sheriff's Story 30 January 1913

The Sheriff's Wife 9 April 1913

The Shotgun Ranchman 12 October 1912

The Silent Message 20 October 1910

Single-Handed 19 March 1914

The Slavey 30 June 1909

The Sleeping Tonic 2 June 1909

Sleepy Jim 8 September 1909

Slim the Brave and Sophie the Fair 11 February 1915

Slippery Slim and His Tombstone 13 August 1914

Slippery Slim and the Claim Agent 20 August 1914

Slippery Slim and the Fortune Teller 27 August 1914

Slippery Slim and the Green-Eyed Monster 24 September 1914

* Slippery Slim and the Impersonator 5 November 1914

Slippery Slim and the Stork 23 April 1914

Slippery Slim, Diplomat 9 July 1914

Slippery Slim Gets Square 24 December 1914

Slippery Slim's Dilemma 6 August 1914

Slippery Slim's Inheritance 23 July 1914

Slippery Slim's Strategem 14 May 1914

Slippery Slim's Wedding Day 4 March 1915

* Slippery Slim, the Mortgage and Sophie 22 October 1914

Slow But Sure 10 August 1907

* The Smuggler's Daughter 16 July 1912

Snakeville and the Corset Demonstrator 29 October 1914

A Snakeville Courtship 27 December 1913

A Snakeville Epidemic 7 May 1914

A Snakeville Romance 21 May 1914

Snakeville's Blind Pig 17 December 1914

* Snakeville's Beauty Parlor 18 February 1915

Snakeville's Champion 16 December 1915

Snakeville's Eugenic Marriage 18 November 1915

Snakeville's Fire Brigade 21 February 1914

Snakeville's Hen Medic 23 September 1915

Snakeville's Home Guard 30 July 1914

The Snakeville Sleuth 1 October 1914

Snakeville's Most Popular Lady 10 September 1914

Snakeville's New Doctor 10 January 1914

Snakeville's New Sheriff 9 April 1914

Snakeville's New Waitress 16 July 1914

Snakeville's Peace-Maker 15 October 1914

Snakeville's Reform Wave 26 November 1914

Snakeville's Rising Sons 31 December 1914

Snakeville's Twins 29 July 1915

Snakeville's Weak Women 7 October 1915

A Snakeville Volunteer 11 June 1914

Some Bravery 22 November 1916

Sophie and the Faker 3 June 1915

Sophie and the Man of Her Choice 12 November 1914

Sophie Changes Her Mind 25 February 1915

Sophie Gets Stung 2 July 1914

* Sophie Picks a Dead One 13 February 1914

Sophie Pulls a Good One 4 June 1914

Sophie's Birthday Party 7 March 1914

Sophie's Fatal Wedding 3 December 1914

Sophie's Fighting Spirit 8 April 1915

* Sophie's Hero 29 November 1913

Sophie's Home-Coming 4 February 1915

Sophie's Legacy 17 September 1914

Sophie's New Foreman 13 December 1913

Sophie's Sweetheart 10 December 1914

Sophie Starts Something 28 May 1914

Soul Kiss 30 September 1908

The Spanish Girl 18 December 1909

"Spike" Shannon's Last Fight 26 August 1911

The Squatter's Gal 1 August 1914

The Stage Driver's Daughter 14 October 1911

The Story of the Old Gun 15 January 1914

A Story of Montana 13 July 1912

A Story of the West 26 December 1911

The Story the Desert Told 1 May 1913

The Strategy of Broncho Billy's Sweetheart 26 September 1914

Street Fakers 5 August 1915

The Street Fakir 2 November 1907

The Strike at the "Little Jonny" Mine 30 September 1911

The Struggle 4 October 1913

Stung; or, What Can It Bee? 15 July 1908

Suppressed Evidence 9 October 1915

* Taft in Chicago, and at the Ball Game 20 September 1909

Tag Day 17 February 1909

Take Me Out to the Ball Game 24 August 1910

Taking the Count 20 December 1916

The Tale of a Tire 19 August 1915

* A Tale of the West 7 April 1909

The Tell-Tale Hand 19 November 1914

The Tenderfoot Foreman 11 January 1912

The Tenderfoot Messenger 17 December 1910

The Tenderfoot Sheriff 2 August 1913

That Pair from Thesbia 25 December 1913

Their Promise 6 August 1913

The Three Gamblers 12 December 1913

Three Reasons for Haste 15 September 1909

Through Trackless Sands 1 January 1914

The Tie That Binds 29 November 1910

The Tie That Binds 30 April 1915

* The Tomboy on Bar Z 22 October 1912

Too Much Dog Biscuit 27 January 1909

Too Much Turkey 19 November 1915

The Tout's Rememberance 24 September 1910

Townhall, Tonight 7 October 1911

The Tragedian 17 June 1908

Trailed to the Hills 16 July 1910

The Trail of the Snake Band 18 December 1913

* The Tramp 12 April 1915

The Tramp Story 28 June 1909

The Treachery of Broncho Billy's Pal 11 April 1914

The Tribe's Penalty 17 June 1911

A Thwarted Vengeance 25 March 1911

Two Bold, Bad Men 25 March 1915

The Two Fugitives 29 July 1911

The Two-Gun Man 5 August 1911

Two Laughs 21 July 1917

The Two Ranchmen 19 July 1913

The Two Reformations 28 January 1911

Two Western Paths 8 May 1913

The Unburied Past 22 April 1913

Under Mexican Skies 13 April 1912

The Undertaker's Uncle 29 April 1915

* Under Western Skies 6 August 1910

An Unexpected Romance 24 September 1915

The Unknown Claim 9 July 1910

The Vagabond 26 October 1907

A Vein of Gold 30 April 1910

Versus Sledge Hammers 2 September 1915

A Waiting Game 6 December 1916

The Warning 12 March 1914

The Weaker's Strength 12 February 1914

The Wealth of the Poor 11 June 1915

Well-Thy Water 11 March 1908

* Western Chivalry 12 February 1910

A Westerner's Way 5 November 1910

Western Girls 3 December 1912

A Western Girl's Sacrifice 2 September 1911

Western Hearts 15 June 1912

A Western Kimono 24 February 1912

The Western Law That Failed 25 February 1913

A Western Legacy 21 May 1912

A Western Maid 1 January 1910

A Western Redemption 21 October 1911

A Western Sister's Devotion 20 August 1913

The Western Way 20 March 1915

A Western Woman's Way 26 November 1910

What a Woman Can Do 29 April 1911

What Came to Bar Q 29 January 1914

When Love and Honor Called 18 Janaury 1915

When Macbeth Came to Snakeville 3 September 1914

When Slippery Slim Bought the Cheese 28 Janaury 1915

When Slippery Slim Met the Champion 8 October 1914

* When Slippery Slim Went for the Eggs 14 January 1915

When Snakeville Struck Oil 21 October 1915

Where Is My Hair 14 December 1907

Who Is Smoking That Rope 23 December 1908

* Why Broncho Billy Left Bear County 27 September 1913

The Widow 20 October 1909

Widow Jenkins' Admirers 23 January 1912

A Widow of Nevada 22 May 1913

A Wife of the Hills 20 July 1912

Wine, Women and Song 9 November 1915

A Woman 12 July 1915

* A Woman of Arizona 10 September 1912

Won By a Hold Up 19 January 1910

The Wooing of Sophie 18 June 1914

* Work 21 June 1915

Wouldn't It Tire You? 1 July 1908

Source Notes

Introduction "S" & "A"

1. Anderson's daughter was the informant for his death certificate, but it's inaccurate. Part of the reason for this may be due to Anderson himself, who was often vague or misleading about the year and place of his birth. The correct information is based upon United States Census, 4 June 1880, Arkansas, E.D. 143, sheet 12, line 26, the 1881-82 Little Rock city directory, and his application to the United States Social Security, 1 March 1941. His parents, Henry Aronson (February 1844, Prussia - 18 December 1908, St. Louis, Missouri) and Esther Asch Aronson (September 1847, New York City - 1 January 1925, San Francisco, California), presumably met in New York City, where Anderson's older brothers and sisters, Gertrude, Hattie, Edward and Jerome were born. Nathan was born in Texas, and the youngest, Leona, was born in St. Louis. Although Anderson's mother was the daughter of Rabbi Joseph Asch, his Jewish background was never discussed by him at any time in his movie career, or during his rediscovery late in life. One fact is telling: contrary to Jewish tradition, Anderson was cremated instead of buried. His older sister Gertrude and her family are listed as living at 717 W. Second Avenue in Pine Bluff, Arkansas, according to Pine Bluff city directories from 1903 to 1910. (My thanks to Tony and Brenda Hall for the Pine Bluff information.) St. Louis city directories from 1884 to 1909 document the Aronson family moves within that city, and the various occupations of Aronson family members.
2. "The King of the Movies," *San Francisco Chronicle*, 6 January 1914, p.26.
3. Edward F. O'Day, "Gilbert Anderson - 'Broncho Billy,'" *The Recorder*, 25 September 1945, p. 1.
4. Gilbert M. ("Broncho Billy") Anderson interview, June, 1958, Oral History Research Office of Columbia University, p. 4; John Ince was the father of Ralph, John and Thomas Ince, who would all enter the movies themselves. Thomas in particular became Anderson's fierce competitor beginning in 1911 by directing western movies and giving William S. Hart a chance in 1914.
5. *New York Clipper* ads, October, November 1903.
6. Anderson claimed to have appeared in *The Messenger Boy's Mistake*, but he's clearly not in that film. He also claimed to have directed the film, which may be more likely, and would suggest he began with Edison at some earlier date. He did remake the film at Vitagraph and Essanay.
7. Anderson interview, Columbia University, p. 4.
8. *Ibid.*, p. 5-6.
9. *Ibid.*, p. 6; Broncho Billy Anderson interviewed by William K. Everson, 1958, New York.
10. Albert E. Smith, testimony, 13 November 1913, *United States v. Motion Picture Patents Co.*, p. 1712; Albert E. Smith with Phil A. Koury, *Two Reels and a Crank*,

(Doubleday, New York, 1952)

11. *Views and Film Index*, 2 June 1906, p. 8.

12. Anderson-Everson interview; James S. McQuade, "Essanay's Western Producer: G. M. Anderson," *Views and Film Index*, 30 July 1910, p. 22.

13. Eugene Lemoyne Connelly, "The First Motion Picture Theater," *Western Pennsylvania Historical Magazine*, March 1940, pp. 2-3.

14. "The Nickelodeon," *Moving Picture World*, 4 May 1907, p. 140.

15. "Moving Pictures on Denver Streets," *Denver Republican*, 9 January 1907, p. 1; *Golden Globe*, 26 January 1907, p. 1; "Actors and Actresses Pursue Dude and Are Photographed," *Denver Republican*, 9 February 1907, p. 1; *Moving Picture World*, 21 March 1914, p. 1528.

16. *Views and Film Index*, 4 June 1910, p. 12; *New York Clipper*, 17 February 1912, p. XI.

17. An announcement of the first Kinodrome projector used in Chicago is seen in the *Chicago Tribune*, 17 September 1899, p. 41; Bell and Howell's relationship to Spoor is described in "A Letter from Donald Bell, *International Photographer*, February 1930, pp. 18-21.

18. Anderson describes his meeting with Spoor in the Everson interview and in an interview by Arthur B. Friedman, 1958, Los Angeles; Peerless incorporation notice in Chicago Tribune, 1 May 1907, p. 14; see also: Charles Musser, *The Emergence of Cinema*, University of California Press (Berkeley, Los Angeles, London, 1990), p. 527, note 48.

19. "Announcement," *Moving Picture World*, 27 July 1907, p. 327.

Chapter One Going West

1. Anderson interview, Columbia University, p. 25; Gilbert Hamilton's involvement is described in *Views and Film Index* 9 July 1910, p. 12.

2. Anderson interview, Columbia University, p. 18

3. Harry C. Carr, "Looking Backward with Ben," *Photoplay*, December 1918, p. 61.

4. *Ibid*.

5. The figure of $5,000 is conservatively based on 50 prints selling for $100 dollars each. Albert E. Smith testified in the patents trials (see date above, p. 1727) that it wasn't unusual to sell one hundred prints of a subject in the early days. The cost of a print was based on total footage. Anderson's 1907 Selig film, *The Girl From Montana*, was 900 feet long and sold for $108.00. The Matinee Idol, at 480 feet, was $57.60 according to the Selig catalog. So even a $10,000 profit for a $100 investment was possible.

6. *Moving Picture World*, 9 May 1908, p. 415.

7. *Views and Film Index*, 6 June 1908, p. 6.

8. Jess Robbins interviewed by Jordan Young, 16 September 1972, Los Angeles, courtesy of Jordan Young.

9. Anderson-Friedman interview.

10. Anderson interview, Columbia University p. 19.

11. *Pasadena Star*, 28 December 1908, p. 6.

12. Fred E. Basten, *Santa Monica Bay: The First 100 Years*, (Douglas-West Publishers, Los Angeles, 1974), p. 88.

13. *New York Dramatic Mirror*, 27 March 1909, p. 13.

14. *Moving Picture World*, 15 May 1909, p. 636.

15. For Dwan's Essanay beginnings see: Kevin Brownlow's *The Parade's Gone By...* and

Peter Bogdanovich's *Allan Dwan: the Last Pioneer*; on the new studio: *Moving Picture World*, 5 June 1909, p. 750.

16. Ben Turpin, "Life of a Moving Picture Comedian," *Moving Picture World*, 3 April 1909, p. 405.

17. *Moving Picture World*, 18 September 1909, p. 381.

18. *Golden Globe*, 2 October 1909, p. 8; *Denver Post*, 26 October 1909, p. 4; Pansy Perry's photo is in the *Post*. The Morrison brothers' grandfather, George Morrison, founded the town of Morrison in 1874.

19. Church's death certificate gives his correct birthplace, confirmed by Audrey and Dave Clark (Church's nephew) interviewed by author, Oceanside, California, 1998.

20. D. Wooster Taylor, "The Moving Picture Drama as Played in Wild Marin," *San Francisco Call*, 3 September 1911, magazine section, pt. 1 p. 4. It most likely occurred at this early date and is therefore mentioned here.

21. George Creel, *Rebel At Large* (G. P. Putnam's Sons, 1947), p. 134.

22. *Ibid.*, p. 135.

23. *Ibid.*

24. *Denver Post*, 14 November 1909, section 2 p. 1.

25. Creel, p. 137.

26. *Ibid.*, p. 138.

27. For Anderson's debut as an Essanay actor see "King of the Movies," *San Francisco Chronicle*, 6 January 1914, p. 26.

28. Anderson's move to El Paso is mentioned in *Views and Film Index*, 4 December 1909, p. 22, but not in the two El Paso newspapers; "Hotel Arrivals," *Mexican Herald*, 28 December 1909, p. 11; Fred Church's scrapbook has an envelope addressed to his parents (but no letter) with a 24 December 1909 cancellation stamp.

29. *Moving Picture World*, 17 November 1917, p. 1010.

Chapter Two Santa Barbara

1. "Mascarel Arrivals," *Santa Barbara Independent*, 3 January 1910, p. 8.

2. "Local Setting Chosen for Motion Pictures, *Santa Barbara Morning Press*, 2 January 1910, p. 3.

3. Dora Eckl, "Afield with Moving Picture Actors," *Santa Barbara Independent*, 5 January 1910, p. 2.

4. *Ibid.*

5. *Ibid.*

6. "Interview with George K. Spoor," *Bioscope*, 26 May 1910, p. 8.

7. *Los Angeles Daily Times*, 11 January 1910, pt. 2, p. 1.

8. *Ibid.*, p. 8.

9. *Ibid.*

10. *Ibid.*

11. *Los Angeles Daily Times,* 19 January 1910, pt. 2, p. 1.

12. *Ibid.*, p. 1, 9; the footage was used in Essanay's release, *Aviation at Los Angeles, California*, 16 February 1910, which still exists.

13. Eckl; locations not mentioned in the Eckl article are taken from notations on photos in the Fred Ilenstine collection, courtesy of the Ilenstine family.

14. "Pictures Please So Do Actors," *Santa Barbara Morning Press*, 3 February 1910, p. 5.

15. "Play Acting Becomes a Realistic Scene," *Santa Barbara Independent*, 24 January 1910, p. 8; "Picture Scene Proves Realistic," *Santa Barbara Morning Press*, 5 February 1910,

p. 3.

16. *Santa Barbara Morning Press*, 6 February 1910, p. 8.

17. "Moving Picture Troup to Leave for Denver," *Santa Barbara Independent,* 15 March 1910, p. 4.

18. "Essanay in Colorado," *Moving Picture World*, 9 April 1910, p. 555.

Chapter Three Riding the Range

1. "Interview with George K. Spoor," *Bioscope*, 26 May 1910, p. 8.

2. *Moving Picture World*, 13 August 1910, p. 350.

3. H. Tipton Steck, "Doing My Bit," *Moving Picture World*, 21 July 1917, p. 408.

4. Edward Arnold with Francis Fisher Dubuc, *Lorenzo Goes to Hollywood,* (Liveright, New York, 1940), pp. 163-4.

5. Mabel Condon, "Sans Grease Paint and Wig," *Motography*, 5 April 1913, p. 229.

6. *The Baseball Fan* was released 19 August 1908. For World Series games see: "Essanay to Film the Philadelphia-Chicago Baseball Games," *Moving Picture World,* 22 October 1910, p. 925. Essanay filmed the 1911 series between the Athletics and the Giants but Spoor decided not to bother with the 1912 games, saying: "There is nothing new to take in the baseball game, and each season's picture is more or less a repetition of the season before, and there is doubt in my mind that the pictures would be profitable to the exhibitors. They certainly would not be to the manufacturer for the cost necessary to their making." "Essanay Will Not Make Baseball Pictures This Year," *Moving Picture World*, 5 October 1912, p. 28.

7. James S. McQuade, "Hank and Lank in Breezy Essanay Filmlets," *Views and Film Index*, 27 August 1910, pp. 12-3.

8. George K. Spoor, testimony, 10 March 1914, *United States v. Motion Picture Patents Co.*, p. 2991; see also American Film ad, *New York Dramatic Mirror,* 5 October 1910, p. 31.

9. "Partners Disagree," *Variety*, 12 September 1910, p. 12.

10. "Essanay Company in Flourishing Condition: A Malicious Rumor Denied," *Moving Picture World*, 1 October 1910, p. 742.

11. "$100 for New Name," *New York Dramatic Mirror*, 23 July 1910, p. 28; "Photoplay," *Moving Picture World*, 15 October 1910, p. 858. The judges were George Kleine (Kleine Optical Co.), Fred Aiken (at that time manager of the General Film Company Chicago branch office) and Aaron Jones (a Chicago theater owner).

12. *Views and Film Index*, 24 September 1910, p. 7.

13. Information on Orrin Denny: *United States Census for 1900*, Indiana, Washington County, Jackson Township, E. D. 131, sheet 7, line 53; *United States Census for 1910*, Colorado, Denver, E.D.117, sheet 8A, line 15; *Motion Picture News*, 12 May 1917, p. 3010.

14 . "Pioneer movie producer recalls LG film making," *Los Gatos Times Observer*, 29 July 1958, p. 9.

15. "Moving Picture Film Troupe Leave Los Gatos," *Los Gatos Mail*, 9 February 1911, p. 1; "Moving Picture Company Here," *Redlands Daily Review*, 7 February 1911, p. 5; "Moving Pictures True to Life," *Redlands Daily Facts*, 8 February 1911, p. 3; "Moving Picture Studio Building," *Redlands Daily Facts*, 10 February 1911, p. 5.

16. "Thrilling Story of Border Life Told for Motion Films," *Redlands Daily Facts*, 23 February 1911, p. 8.

17. *New York Dramatic Mirror,* 3 May 1911, p. 31.

18. "Margaret Joslin Tells Her Secret 'Just Be Serious,' She Advises," *Essanay News*?, n. d.

19. "Moving Picture Co. Rents Cottages," *Venice Daily Vanguard*, 10 April 1911, p. 4; "Picture People are to Depart," *Venice Daily Vanguard*, 25 May 1911, p. 1. The houses were at 1347 and 1437 Ocean Avenue.

20. "Pictures from the Santa Monica Canyon," *The Daily Outlook* (Santa Monica), 27 May 1911, p. 1.

21. *Views and Film Index*, 6 May 1911, p. 8.

Chapter Four San Rafael

1. "Essenay[sic] Pictures Co. to Operate Here," *Marin Journal*, 1 June 1911, p. 1. While the total rainfall at Los Gatos had climbed to 48 inches, San Rafael received under 6 inches.

2. "House Rentals," *Marin Journal*, 1 June 1911, p. 4. The three houses mentioned were at 75 and 85 Palm Avenue, and 148 Grand Avenue. A fourth house was at 801 Second Street. San Rafael changed house numbers by the next decade; the Palm addresses are now probably 168 and 130. Grand Avenue is now 448. The last house is now 1301 Second Street.

3. Timothy J. Lyons, ed., "Roland H. Totheroh Interviewed: Chaplin films," *Film Culture*, Spring 1972, p. 231.

4. "Fairfax Holdup Pictures at Victory Tonight," *Marin County Tocsin*, 22 July 1911, p. 4.

5. "Wild West Show and Ball Realizes $250 for Fairfax Fire Department," *San Rafael Independent*, 5 September 1911, p. 1.

6. D. Wooster Taylor, "The Moving Picture Drama as Played in Wild Marin," *San Francisco Call*, 3 September 1911, magazine section part 1 p. 4.

7. *Ibid.*

8. *Ibid.*; Mabel Condon, "Sans Grease Paint and Wig," *Motography*, 1 February 1913, p.92.

9. "Elder Comer," *San Diego Sun*, 15 January 1912, p. 15.

10. "Big Crowd Sees Four Round Bout," *Marin Journal*, 22 June 1911, p. 6.

11. "Picture Company to Prolong its Stay," *Marin County Tocsin*, 29 July 1911, p. 8; Jack O'Brien letter to Fred Church, 26 September 1911, courtesy of Dave and Audrey Clark. O'Brien wrote: "I have just finished a 5,000 foot feature film of the life of Colonel Cody and from all reports received from New York, it has made a hit with Broadway. I told you I could do it old man and I have made good."

12. "Over 800 Witness Baseball Show," *Marin County Tocsin*, 25 November 1911, p. 1.

13. "Taft Topical by Essanay Company," *Moving Picture World*, 11 November 1911, p.478.

14. Philip H. Kinsley, "Silver Spade for Golden Future," *San Francisco Examiner*, 15 October 1911, p. 52.

15. "Motion Picture Men Arrive," *Santa Rosa Republican*, 31 October 1911, p. 4; "Photoplay Has Plot Laid Here," *Santa Rosa Press Democrat*, 1 November 1911, p. 8; "Big Laugh Went with the Show," *Press Democrat*, 1 November 1911, p. 5; "'The Man from Mexico' Is Decidedly Pleasing," *Republican*, 1 November 1911, p. 3.

16. "Moving Picture Robbers Hold Up Bank and Do Other Exciting Things," *Petaluma Argus*, 11 December 1911, p. 4; "Moving Picture 'Hero' Seriously Wounded in 'Capture' of Bandits," *San Diego Union*, 13 December 1911, p. 9.

17. George Blaisdell, "At the Sign of the Flaming Arcs," *Moving Picture World*, 30 August 1913, p. 963.

18. "Essanay Coach Upsets," *Marin County Tocsin*, 25 November 1911, p. 1; "Moving Picture Proved Too Real," *San Rafael Independent*, 28 November 1911, p. 7; "Stage

Hold-Up and Runaway," *Marin Journal*, 30 November 1911, p. 3; "Moving Picture Stunt Was Too Realistic at San Rafael," *Petaluma Argus*, 25 November 1911, p. 5; "Accident Not in the Play," *Petaluma Daily Courier*, 27 November 1911, p. 3; "Miss Edna Fisher Was Badly Hurt," *Santa Rosa Press Democrat*, 26 November 1911, p. 2; "Serious Mishap of Picture Actress," *Moving Picture World*, 9 December 1911, p. 823; "Essanay Leading Woman a Real Heroine," *Moving Picture World*, 16 December 1911, p. 894; "Heroic Edna Fisher," *New York Dramtic Mirror*, 20 December 1911, p. 29.

19. "Motion Picture Firm to Establish Company of Actors at La Mesa," *San Diego Union*, 21 December 1911, p. 10.

20. "Essanay Company Tendered Banquet," *San Rafael Independent*, 5 December 1911, p.1.

21. *Photoplay*, March 1915, p. 56.

22. Mabel Condon, "Sans Grease Paint and Wig," *Motography*, 5 April 1913, p. 229.

23. "Coming Essanay Westerns," *Motography*, January 1912, p. 25.

24. Brian Wiersema, "The Not-So-Good Old Movie Making Days," *Hayward Daily Review*, 14 March 1971, p. 2.

25. "Claims Elder Can Beat 'White Hopes'," *San Diego Sun*, 11 January 1911, p. 11.

26. *Moving Picture World*, 12 April 1913, p. 166; *Motion Picture News Studio Directory*, 29 January 1916, p. 23.

27. "Fight Marvel in Preliminaries," *Los Angeles Times*, 22 February 1912, pt. 3 p. 3.

28. "Elder, White Hope, Injured in Auto Crash; Essanay Party Plunges Off a Steep Bank," *San Diego Sun*, 24 February 1912, p. 12; "Leave Agnew," *San Diego Sun*, 26 February 1912, p. 11

29. *Moving Picture World*, 8 June 1912, p. 934.

30. G. M. Anderson letter to Josephine Rector, 7 February 1912, courtesy of Milly Rubiolo.

31. "Lakeside Hotel Being Improved," *San Diego Evening Tribune*, 1 April 1912, p. 13.

32. I'm in agreement with William Sagar of the Fairfax Historical Society that a possible reason Essanay didn't return to San Rafael was because of an impending lawsuit by Tupper Malone, the owner of the two Palm Avenue houses which Essanay rented. Curtains, furniture, glass and silverware dissappeared from the houses when Essanay left. (Perhaps they were used as props.) The suit was rejected the first time, but on appeal Malone won a judgement of $200. See: *San Rafael Independent*, 18 June 1912, p. 1; *Marin Journal* 13 June 1912, p. 1; *Marin County Tocsin*, 15 June 1912, p. 1; *Marin Journal*, 29 May 1913, p. 5.

Chapter Five Niles and the Canyon

1. Alameda County deeds, book T, p. 407, recorded 7 March 1866.

2. Early Niles history can be traced in various newspapers. See "Niles Station," *Oakland Tribune*, 26 May 1875, p. 1; "Interior Towns," *San Francisco Call*, 19 October 1890, p. 3; "Niles and Vicinity," *San Francisco Call*, 24 December 1891, p. 7; "Thriving Towns," *Oakland Tribune*, 23 December 1896, p. 2.

3. No specific day was mentioned in the newspapers. This April 1st date is based upon references in both papers to the company arriving that week, that it was a school day according to Marie Bishop and that, since they left Lakeside on a Saturday, it would have taken them two days at most to arrive in Niles.

4. *Township Register*, 6 April 1912, p. 1; *Washington Press*, 5 April 1912, p. 4.

5. *Press*.

6. *Register*.

7. Tape recorded conversation with Hal Angus and Marie Sharpe Bishop, 1973, courtesy of Fremont Main Library and Barbara Baxter.
8. Stuart Nixon, "How the Movies Came to Niles," *Township Register*, 6 March 1953, p.4.
9. Alameda County deeds: book 2146 p. 254, 8 April 1912, recorded 31 March 1913; book 2160 p. 218, 10 April 1912, recorded 19 March 1913; book 2134 p. 359, 11 April 1912, recorded 19 March 1913; book 2134 p. 360, 26 April 1912, recorded 19 March 1913; *Washington Press*, 12 April 1912, p. 1,; *Hayward Review*, 16 April 1912, p. 6.
10. Angus and Bishop, 1973; *Washington Press*, 26 April 1912, p. 1; *New York Dramatic Mirror*, 11 September 1912, p. 25.
11. Edwin Schallert, "Boom Towns of Filmland," *Picture Play*, October 1921, p. 46.
12. Angus and Bishop, 1973.
13. For an account of Anderson's working method in Niles see Walter Anthony, "Starring Where Nature Sets the Stage," *San Francisco Call*, 21 April 1912, p. 54-5. People can be seen reflected in windows during some shots for *Method in His Madness* in Santa Barbara.
14. Brian Wiersema, "The Not-So-Good Old Movie Making Days," *Hayward Daily Review*, 14 March 1971, p. 2.
15. Angus and Bishop, 1973. Sets were still being taken to the canyon in 1915. Confirmation of this comes from Charles Barton, a teenage actor at the time (as an adult he directed films), who recalled his introduction to the movies: "It was a completely open stage. They had gauze on strings that cut off the shadows from the sharp sunlight. The sets were painted canvas with the windows open so that you could see right out into Niles Canyon. That gave an exterior, too.... There was another set on the other side of the stage. At the same time that we were doing a scene with Broncho Billy, Ben Turpin was doing a comedy scene. At the same time!" Frank Thompson, *Between Action and Cut*, (Scarecrow Press, New Jersey, 1985), p. 188.
16. *New York Dramatic Mirror*, 5 March 1913, p. 27; *Washington Press*, 7 February 1914, p. 2; *New York Dramatic Mirror*, 11 March 1914, p. 32.
17. "Mr.. G.M. Anderson at San Francisco," *Moving Picture World*, 24 August 1912, p.775.
18. Lyons, p. 231-2.
19. Bill Strobel, "Niles Days as Film Capital Recalled by Oakland Woman," *Oakland Tribune*, 21 May 1958, p. 8-S.
20. "Evelyn Selbie, of the Western Essanay Company," *Motion Picture*, February 1914, p.150.
21. "Leading Lady Reveals Identity," *Washington Press*, 26 July 1912, p. 8; "Pretty Boston Society Girl is Motion Picture Heroine," *San Francisco Call*, 25 July 1912, p. 4; "Photoplay Star Dies at Merritt Hospital," *Oakland Enquirer*, 27 August 1912, p. 1; "Actress' Death Reveals History: 'Vedah Bertram' Adele Buck," *San Francisco Call*, 27 August 1912, p. 3; certificate of death, County of Alameda, death date is 26 August 1912, cause of death is listed as embolus of medulla, secondary cause as endocarditis, laparotomy.
22. She was born and raised in Brooklyn, was not a Wellesley College graduate; her brother, Jerome Buck Jr. (18 years old) was not an attorney; her father was the editor of a Brooklyn newspaper.
23. Angus and Bishop, 1973; Anderson-Everson interview; *Los Gatos Times Observer*, 29 July 1958, p. 9.
24. Stuart Nixon, "Essanay Made Him," *Township Register*, 2 April 1953, p. 8.
25. Angus and Bishop, 1973.

26. *Washington Press*, 4 October 1912, p. 1.

27. *New York Dramatic Mirror*, 9 October 1912, p. 27.

28. *Washington Press*, 11 October 1912, p. 1.

Chapter Six A Western Town

1. G. M. Anderson interviewed by Lawrence Lipton, 1958, Los Angeles.

2. Bill Cato interviewed by Ray Hubbard for the documentary *When the Movies Came from Niles*, 1964.

3. Gilbert M. Anderson interviewed by Ray Hubbard for the documentary *When the Movies Came from Niles*, 1964. Anderson put his own riding abilities in perspective: "I could ride fairly well, but I couldn't do these stunts or falling off the horse. In fact I did fall off a horse— an accident— and it stayed with me for years. But I never was an expert rider." Anderson-Friedman interview.

4. "Cowboy Thrills Conclude Rodeo," *Oakland Tribune*, 4 August 1913, p. 7.

5. "Moose 'Frontier Days' Show Opens," *Oakland Enquirer,* 16 May 1912, p. 3.

6. Padgett letter of recommendation, 2 April 1911; letter to Padgett, 26 July 1912, courtesy of Beverly Padgett.

7. Diana Serra Cary in *The Hollywood Posse* (Houghton Mifflin, Boston, 1975, reprinted by University of Oklahoma Press, Norman & London, 1996) describes how casual it could be. Her father Jack Montgomery, a cowboy in Northern California during the fading days of the Chowchilla Ranch, was out of work, wandering in the hills near Niles with some fellow cowboys when they stumbled upon a startling sight, Broncho Billy at work on a western movie.

8. A group photograph of the Kalem company shows Texas George in the background; Louis Morisette is also there; Moving Picture World, 12 June 1911, p. 1382.

9. "Soldier Elder, Stabbed, Forced to Cancel Bout with Chas. Horn," *San Francisco News*, 11 July 1912, p. 3; "Elder Stabed [sic] by Parks," *Washington Press*, 12 July 1912, p. 1; "Moving Picture Employee in Trouble," *Marin County Tocsin*, 13 July 1912, p. 5.

10. Stuart Nixon, "Essanay in Niles: III," *Township Register,* 19 March 1953, p. 8.

11. "Daze of Studio Days Back in Niles," *Hayward Daily Review*, 1 June 1953, p. 14.

12. Lyons, p. 234.

13. Cato-Hubbard interview, *When the Movies*.

14. A drunken man (not an Essanay employee) with a rifle was captured and disarmed by Rose after several people were fired upon during a rampage; "Goes on the Warpath," *Washington Press*, 30 May 1914, p. 1; "Niles Shot Up by 'Bad Man' with Big Gun," *San Francisco Bulletin*, 25 May 1914, p. 11; "Holds Road by Rifle Fire," *Oakland Tribune*, 25 May 1914, p. 1.

15. "Essanay at Los Angeles," *Moving Picture World*, 30 November 1912, p. 871.

16. *Moving Picture World*, 11 January 1913, p. 142.

17. "Mr. Mackley Experimenting on Mr. Static," *Moving Picture World*, 15 March 1913, p. 1090; "Camera Men's Static Club a Flourishing Body," *Motion Picture News*, 3 April 1915, p. 172.

18. *Moving Picture World*, 14 December 1912, p. 1080.

19. "Studio Gossip," *New York Dramatic Mirror*, 19 February 1913, p. 34.

20. "How I Became a Photoplayer," *Motion Picture*, December 1914, p. 108.

21. Martha Groves McKelvie, "Everything's Lovely," *Motion Picture Classic,* May 1918, p. 29.

22. *Moving Picture World*, 30 August 1913, p. 963.

23. "New Theatre on O'Farrell St. to Rise on Old Alcazar Site," *San Francisco Examiner,*

23 March 1913, p. 59; *San Francisco Real Estate Circular,* 6 March 1913, p. 1; "Geo. M. Anderson's Latest," *New York Clipper,* 19 April 1913, p. 5.

24. Opening night program booklet for the Gaiety Theatre, 18 October 1913, at the California Historical Society.

25. Spoor made a veiled reference to Anderson's $150 a day in his *Bioscope* interview, 26 May 1910; Ezra Goodman, "The Movies' First Chaps and Spurs Hero," *New York Times,* 10 October 1948, pt. II p. 5.

26. S. L. A. Marshall, *Bringing Up the Rear,* manuscript (1970s), p. 35, courtesy of The S. L. A. Marshall Military History Collection, University of Texas at El Paso and Thomas Burdett, Curator. (My thanks to Sam Gill for locating it.)

27. Anderson-Lipton interview.

28. George K. Spoor, testimony, 10 March 1914, *United States v. Motion Picture Patents Co.,* p. 2993.

29. "Film Company Buys Residence Property in Niles," *Hayward Review,* 16 April 1912, p. 6; "Niles Factories and Rich Fruits," *Oakland Enquirer,* 3 January 1914, p. 6.

Chapter Seven The Studio

1. *The Rounder,* 15 July 1911, p. 22.

2. "The 'Essanay' $50,000 Plant," *Washington Press,* 24 May 1913, p. 1; Alameda County deeds, book 2163, p. 128, recorded 31 March 1913; O'Day, p. 6.

3. *Washington Press,* 28 March 1913, p. 4.

4. *Washington Press,* 5 April 1913, p. 3; Memo from G. M. Anderson, 8 April 1913, Jess Robbins collection, USC Cinema-Television Library.

5. Lyons, p. 234.

6. *Ibid.,* p. 235.

7. School and work information supplied by Robert D. Stone, Ira Morgan's nephew.

8. *Sunnyvale Sun,* 9 May 1913, p. 8; *Sunnyvale Sun,* 16 May 1913, p. 4; *Sunnyvale Standard,* 5 September 1913, p. 4.

9. *Washington Press,* 5 April 1913, p. 5; *Washington Press,* 12 April 1913, p. 8.

10. *Washington Press,* 26 April 1913, p. 3.

11. *Moving Picture World,* 28 June 1913, p. 1341.

12. Strobel, p. 8-S; Lyons, p. 230.

13. Lloyd Ingraham Paramount publicity release, 1930, p. 3.

14. Anderson interview, Columbia University, p. 20.

15. *Township Register,* 13 March 1953, p. 4.

16. *Ibid.*

17. For details about the film see: "The Fall of Montazuma: Essanay's Splendid Historical Pageant," *Motography,* 20 July 1912, pp. 41-7.

18. "Want an 'Alkali' Ike Doll?" *Moving Picture World,* 31 May 1913, p. 926; *Billboard,* 7 June 1913, p. 17; *Motography,* 23 August 1913, p. 127; *New York Dramatic Mirror,* 26 November 1913, p. 27; *Motography,* 29 November 1913, p. 394.

19. *Township Register,* 27 September 1913, p. 1.

20. Kalton C. Lahue and Samuel Gill, *Clown Princes and Court Jesters,* (A. S. Barnes, New Jersey, 1970), p. 78.

21. "Carney to be 'Universal Ike,'" *Motion Picture News,* 14 February 1914, p. 20.

22. *Moving Picture World,* 30 May 1914, p. 1248; *New York Dramatic Mirror,* 11 August 1915, p. 29; *New York Dramatic Mirror,* 19 May 1917, p. 35.

23. *New York Dramatic Mirror,* 9 September 1914, p. 35.

24. *New York Dramatic Mirror*, 23 September 1914, p. 35.

25. *New York Dramatic Mirror*, 10 December 1913, p. 31; *Washington Press*, 6 December 1913, p. 1.

26. *Washington Press*, 24 May 1913, p. 1; floor plan drawing in Geoffrey Bell papers, Bancroft Library, Berkeley; "Essanay Western Plant," *Moving Picture World,* 10 July 1915, p. 237-8.

27. For Ensign: "Doings of the Essanay People,' *Township Register,* 20 September 1913, p. 1; for Johnson: *Oakland Tribune*, 8 February 1914, p. 22; for Breslauer: *Marin County Tocsin*, 6 September 1913, p. 5; "Essanay People Go to Beach," *Township Register,* 6 September 1913, p. 1; for Mayer: *San Francisco News,* 25 October 1941, p. 7; "At the Studio," *Washington Press*, 26 December 1914, p. 1. Cantwell is announced in an undated, unidentified clipping, possibly from *Essanay News*. Not everyone who worked at Essanay was announced on arrival, some were mentioned only on leaving, others are only identified by scene stills. For Sudderth: "Funeral Tomorrow for Robert Earl Sudderth, 65," *Oakland Tribune,* 13 June 1957, p. 38.

28. *San Francisco Call*, 13 August 1913, p. 6.

29. *Sacramento Bee*, 6 September 1913, p. 20.

30. "Essanay Notes," *Township Register,* 4 October 1913, p. 1; "Motography's Gallery of Picture Players," *Motography*, 17 October 1914, p. 535.

31. *Township Register,* 20 September, p. 1; "Reina Valdez made an Ideal Director," *Motion Picture News*, 5 June 1915, p. 56.

32. San Francisco Crocker-Langley directories, 1898 to 1918; "Essanay Notes," *Washington Press*, 10 January 1914, p. 4; Washington Press, 28 November 1914, p. 3; "Building Will Be Erected on Chosen Site Near Future," *Hayward Daily Review*, 9 February 1925, p. 1; Allen Dealey's presence indicated by photos and his notations in the Dealey family photo albums.

33. Lyons, p. 242-3.

34. Francis X. Bushman interviewed by Kevin Brownlow, courtesy of Kevin Brownlow.

35. Ray Hubbard, film narration, *When the Movies Came from Niles*, 1964.

36. *Township Register,* 27 September 1913, p.1.

37. Cato-Hubbard interview, *When the Movies*; See also: *New York Dramatic Mirror,* 4 February 1914, p. 39.

38. *Washington Press*, 30 August 1913, p. 3.

39. "Gaiety Theatre Doors Opened," *San Francisco Examiner*, 19 October 1913, p. 72.

40. *San Francisco Chronicle*, 16 October 1913, p. 8.

41. "'The Candy Shop' Wins Skeptical," *San Francisco Call*, 20 October 1913, p. 4.

42. "New Niles Theatre," *Washington Press*, 1 November 1913, p. 1.

43. "Moves Among the Movies," *Washington Press,* 6 December 1913, p. 1.

Chapter Eight Everyone Gets into the Act

1. "The King of the Movies," *San Francisco Chronicle*, 6 January 1914, p. 26.

2. The 'Acting' Member of Essanay," *Moving Picture World*, 6 January 1912, p. 28.

3. Advertisement for The Squaw Man: *Billboard*, 17 January 1914, p. 61.

4. The federal government brought suit against the Patents Company members and its distribution arm, General Film Company, in 1912. Testimony was gathered in 1913-14 and a United States district court decided against the Patents Company in the fall of 1915. By then the upstart independent companies — Warner, Universal, Fox and Paramount — were taking the lead in filmmaking.

5. "Essanay's New Studios," *Moving Picture World*, 11 July 1914, p. 266.

6. *Love's Lottery* was never released, and, based upon still code numbers, it's likely there were as many as eight films that met the same fate.

7. "Broncho Billy To Make Permanent Headquarters in Niles, Cal." *Essanay News*, 11 March 1914, p. 1.

8. George K. Spoor letter to Jess Robbins, 2 April 1914, Robbins collection, USC.

9. Robbins Photo Plays incorporation papers, 15 April 1914, Robbins collection, USC; *Edwards Abstracts*, San Francisco, incorporation filed 6 May 1914 (the company was capitalized for $10,000); "Essanay Notes," *Washington Press*, 11 April 1914, p. 1; "Gone to Form New Movie Co.," *Washington Press*, 18 April 1914, p. 2; *When a Woman Loves* was released 2 August 1914.

10. *Moving Picture World*, 23 May 1914, p. 1092.

11. *Motion Picture News*, 20 June 1914, p. 67.

12. *New York Dramatic Mirror*, 17 June 1914, p. 32.

13. *Variety*, 12 June 1914, p. 21.

14. The additional movie each week came from Chicago, a new series starring Wallace Beery as a Swedish servant girl called Sweedie. The first release was *Sweedie the Swatter*.

15. *Washington Press*, 14 November 1914, p. 1.

16. For early evidence of the problem see: "Saloons in Niles Canyon Closed," *San Francisco Call*, 6 November 1906, p. 12; For Scott's employment see: Alameda County, *Great Register of Voters*, Niles Precinct, 1914.

17. Paul Donovan, "Highlights in the News," *Napa Journal*, 20 August 1943, p. 1.

18. Kathleen McKinley, "Movie extras recall era of Broncho Billy and the Little Tramp," *Fremont Argus*, 5 June 1998, p. NEWS-1, 15.

19. Dennis Rockstroh, "Boyhood memories of a film star," *San Jose Mercury News*, 26 October 1983, p. 3.

20. Barbara Wyman, "Chaplin recalled as 'snob,'" *Hayward Daily Review*, 6 June 1986, p.11.

21. Georgia Chalmers Wagner interviewed by author, 17 January 1999, Fremont.

22. Anita Garcia Stubinger interviewed by author, 14 August 1999, San Lorenzo.

23. Kitty Kelly, "Flickerings from Film Land," *Chicago Tribune*, 5 April 1915, p. 14; "Margaret Joslin, of the Essanay Co." *Motion Picture*, April 1914, pp. 113-4.

24. True Boardman, "When Hollywood and I Were Young," *Wonderful Inventions* (Library of Congress, Washington D. C.., 1985), p. 48.

25. Marshall, p. 34.

26. *Ibid.*, p. 36.

27. Alice Phillips, "An Unforgettable Four Years with Bronco [sic] Billy And His Buddies," *Redwood City Tribune*, Peninsula Living, 1 May 1971, p. 8.

28. Among several newsclippings, n.d., from 1913-15, *San Francisco Chronicle*, *San Francisco Call*, *Oakland Tribune*, courtesy of Susan Brandon, Eugenia's granddaughter.

29. *New York Dramatic Mirror*, 10 December 1913, p. 31.

30. Susan Brandon interviewed by author, September 2001, Burbank.

31. *New York Dramatic Mirror*, 20 November 1912, p. 38; Walter Anthony, "Eltinge Spurns Films: $100,000 Bid Refused," *San Francisco Call*, 7 November 1912, p. 4; Walter Anthony, "Julian and not Julia, Eltinge Speaks," *San Francisco Call*, 10 November 1912, p. 29.

32. Belvoir Hotel register, courtesy Susan Richardson; "Star Assails Gaiety Managers: Marie Dressler to Bring Suit," *San Francisco Chronicle*, 27 January 1914, p. 1; "Gai-

ety Theater Scrap Now Storm in Teacup," *San Francisco Chronicle*, 29 January 1914, p. 2; "Gay and Merry Gambol Done at Gaiety: Marie Dressler Is Whooping Success," *San Francisco Examiner*, 3 February 1914, p. 6; "Dressler and Rosenthal Fall Out," *Billboard*, 7 February 1914, p. 6; "Marie Gambols at Gaiety and Wins an Ovation," *San Francisco Daily News,* 20 February 1914, p. 8; "Another Climax in Gaiety Scrap," *San Francisco Chronicle*, 10 March 1914, p. 9; "U. S. Probes Dressler's 'Marriage' to Dalton," *San Francisco Examiner*, 11 March 1914, p. 1; "Broncho Billy Sues Marie Dressler," *Billboard*, 21 March 1914, p. 48.

33. "Forget War; Jolson Is Here," *Oakland Tribune*, 27 April 1914, p.5; "Deputy Sheriff Al Jolson Is Caught Speeding," *Oakland Tribune*, 28 April 1914, p. 2; *Sacramento Bee*, 13 June 1914, p. 28.

34. Stuart Nixon, "'Everything Died': Essanay Goes," *Township Register,* 9 April 1953, p. 2; *Washington Press*, 1 August 1914, p. 6; "Musical Comedy Staged as Benefit," *Washington Press*, 8 August 1914, p. 4; Mr. & Mrs. William Rock signatures in Belvoir register, 17 July 1914, p. 74, courtesy of Susan Richardson.

35. "'Candy Shop' Benefit Was Big Success," *Washington Press*, 15 August 1914, p. 5.

36. *Moving Picture World*, 6 January 1912, p. 28.

37. "Mrs. Harry Todd Hurt While Acting in Canyon," *Township Register*, 10 September 1915, p.1; *Washington Press*, 10 January 1914, p. 4;"Motion Picture Actor Sends Shot Into Hand," *Oakland Tribune*, 21 August 1912, p. 2; *Township Register,* 6 September 1913, p. 1.

38. "Three Women Injured in Wild Movie Ride," *Oakland Tribune*, 3 November 1914, p. 9; "Movie Actress and Companies in Crash," *Oakland Enquirer*, 4 November 1914, p. 3; *Washington Press*, 3 December 1914, p. 6.

39. The family story recalled was of someone being killed in the accident, but this wasn't true. Nellie Bogdon would return to the movies in the late 1920s as Sally Phipps.

40. "San Francisco Looms as Producing Center," *Motion Picture News*, 30 May 1914, p. 29.

41. *Washington Press*, 27 June 1914, p. 4.

Chapter Nine Chaplin

1. *Moving Picture World*, 5 December 1914, p. 1366.

2. "Slippery Slim of Snakeville Weds Charmer," *San Francisco Bulletin*, 23 November 1914, p. 1.

3. "Cupid Slams Slippery Slim," *Washington Press*, 28 November 1914, p. 1. Victor and Mildred remained married for 33 years, until his death in 1947.

4. *Motion picture News*, 21 March 1914, p. 37.

5. Louis M. Starr, "How Chicago Spawned an Industry - and a Lot of Great Names," *Chicago Sun*, 26 January 1947, p. 21.

6. Charles Chaplin, *My Autobiography*, (Simon & Shuster, New York, 1964), p. 160.

7. Anderson-Friedman interview.

8. *Ibid*.

9. Millie Robbins, "Remembering Bronco Billy," *San Francisco Chronicle*, 14 July 1966, p. 25; Herbert Choynski was a San Franciscan who dared to take on the city's corrupt mayor, Abe Roef, and his administration in the early 1900s, and brought about the graft prosecutions a few years later.

10. "New Comedian for S. & A.," *Washington Press*, 19 December 1914, p. 1.

11. *Washington Press*, 14 November 1914, p. 4; "Marguerite Clayton Leaves Essanay," *Motion Picture News*, 2 January 1915, p. 30; *Motion Picture News*, 3 April 1915, pp.

190-1.

12. Chaplin, p. 162; "Charles Chaplin," *Moving Picture World*, 9 January 1915, p. 197, indicates he was working in Niles before Christmas, 1914. There was a lag of 2-3 weeks between actual events and publication.

13. Chaplin, p. 169.

14. "Gone to Chicago," *Washington Press*, 26 December 1914, p. 1.

15. *United States Census of 1900*, St. Cloud, Minnesota, Mollie Schabbleman, ED 170, Sheet 7, Line 47; Chicago city directory, 1915.

16. William P. Grisham, "Those Marvelous Men and Their Movie Machines," *Chicago Tribune Magazine*, 7 December 1969, p. 43. Chaplin states he and Anderson were met by the Chicago studio manager.

17. Grisham.

18. Clarence J. Caine, "Charles Chaplin in a Serious Mood," *Motography*, 16 January 1915, p. 95.

19. Mae Tinee, "Charles Chaplin, a Modest Violet, Scared to Death of Publicity," *Chicago Tribune*, 10 January 1915, VIII p. 7. Mae Tinee, a play on the theatrical "matinee," was the pseudonym of Frances Smith.

20. Tinee.

21. *Ibid.*

22. *Ibid.*

23. Caine.

24. Grisham.

25. Victor Eubank, "The Funniest Man on the Screen," *Motion Picture*, March 1915, p. 75.

26. "Broncho Billy in Town," *Variety*, 9 January 1915, p. 21; "Gilbert M. Anderson in Town," *Moving Picture World*, 23 January 1915, p. 490.

27. Chaplin, *My Autobiography*, p. 166.

28. Charles J. McGuirk, "Chaplinitis," *Motion Picture*, August 1915, p. 85.

29. The stage, about 90 ft. by 50 ft., happens to be the one part of the studio that still gives some idea of what the silent-era building interior must have looked like in the old days. These days it's called the Chaplin Stage.

30. Jackson Rose, ASC (American Society of Cinematographers), was also the cameraman for famed-comedian Max Linder during Linder's Essanay comedies. When Essanay bought Bell & Howell's first all-metal camera, the remarkable 2709 model, it was assigned to Rose. Rose filmed hundreds of movies, was an inventor, and compiled and edited the first *American Cinematographer Manual*.

31. McGuirk, pp. 85-6.

32. Arnold, p. 167.

33. Anderson-Hubbard interview, *When the Movies*.

34. "Chaplin Returns to California," *Motography*, 30 January 1915, p. 166.

Chapter Ten The Tramp Out West

1. On Leo White's death certificate his second wife Maxine lists his birthplace as Graudenz, Germany, and his German-born parents as Julius and Ida Berg White. Graudenz is now Grudziadz, Poland.

2. Chaplin, *My Autobiography*, p. 170.

3. *San Francisco Chronicle*, 19 January 1915, p. 10.

4. Belvoir Hotel register, 21 January 1915, p. 111, courtesy of Susan Richardson.

5. Purviance was mentioned in "That Mustache is Going to Big Ball," *San Francisco Call*

& *Post*, 30 January 1915, p. 3; Carr is mentioned in "Gilbert M. Anderson Back at Niles Studio," *Motion Picture News*, 13 February 1915, p. 28; Rieger is mentioned in Henri Armand De Masi, *Who's Who in Motion Pictures*, (Henri Armand De Masi, Chicago, 1915), p. 142. My thanks to Sam Gill and Morris Everett for access to the De Masi book.

6. "Officer Arrests 'Movie' Actors, Then Apologizes," *Oakland Tribune*, 22 January 1915, p. 2.
7. Chaplin, p. 170
8. *Oakland Tribune*, 26 May 1963, p. FL-7. The Tait Cafe had just gone through an extensive remodel, so it's possible Edna had just been hired. See: "Other San Francisco Items," *Moving Picture World*, 16 January 1915, p. 406.
9. Bud Jaimison's name has been spelled several ways. It more or less settled into Jamison, but the family spelled it Jaimison, based on his Vallejo Obituary in the *News-Chronicle*, October 2, 1944, p. 6 and the 1900 Census.
10. "That Mustache..."
11. "Two Chaplin Prints Ordered for Los Angeles," *Motion Picture News*, 13 February 1915, p. 30.
12. Lyons, p. 237.
13. Carr, p. 61.
14. *New York Dramatic Mirror*, 5 May 1915, p. 31.
15. "Anderson Gone South," *Washington Press*, 11 February 1915, p. 6; "Shows in Los Angeles," *Variety*, 20 February 1915, p. 11.
16. "Gay Musical Comedy to Open Season at Gaiety," *San Francisco Chronicle*, 9 March 1915, p. 7; "Gaiety House is Leased for Long Term," *San Francisco Chronicle*, 11 April 1915, p. 58; *San Francisco Examiner*, 2 May 1915, p. 27.
17. According to a 1945 publicity release from 20th Century-Fox, Lloyd Bacon's father said, "If you go into that deaf and dumb racket don't ever tell anyone you're Frank Bacon's son." If this is true, Frank Bacon soon saw the wisdom of his son's choice; Frank made his movie debut later that year in *The Silent Voice*, a Quality Pictures Metro release starring Francis X. Bushman.
18. *Township Register*, 18 March 1915, p. 1; "Charles Chaplin Visits the Success," *Oakland Enquirer*, 8 March 1915, p. 8; "Movie Comedian Visits Exposition Joy Zone," *San Francisco Chronicle*, 10 March 1915, p. 5.
19. Kitty Kelly, "Flickering in Film Land," *Chicago Tribune*, 1 April 1915, p. 14. Kelly's real name was Audrie Alspaugh.
20. Lyons, p. 236.
21. Angus and Bishop taped conversation.
22. Kitty Kelly, "Flickerings from Film Land," *Chicago Tribune*, 2 April 1915, p. 23.
23. Phillips, p. 22.
24. Bill Strobel, "Magic Wove Spell Over Niles in 1913," *Oakland Tribune*, 21 December 1962, p. DA-17.
25. Wiersema, p. 2.
26. Stuart Nixon, "Top Stars in Niles," *Township Register*, 26 March 1953, p. 11.
27. Marshall, p. 41.
28. *Ibid*
29. *Ibid*
30. *Ibid.*
31. Grisham, p. 44.

32. "Chaplin Takes Portland, Ore., by Storm," *Motion Picture News*, 17 April 1915, p.60.

33. "Chaplin Crowds Detroit Houses," *Motion Picture News,* 17 April 1915, p. 38.

34. "Chaplin Releases Short," *Variety,* 16 April 1915, p. 17.

35. "Chaplin Co. Goes South," *Township Register,* 8 April 1915, p. 1.

36. Nixon, "Top Stars," p. 11.

37. Nixon, "Essanay Made Him," *Township Register,* 2 April 1953, p. 8.

38. "Chaplin Co. Goes South."

39. "Screen Club Elects," *Moving Picture World*, 1 May 1915, p. 759; *Moving Picture World*, 15 May 1915, p. 1057. The headliner at the Empress Theater that week was Oscar Lorraine, a Hungarian violinist. A *San Francisco Chronicle* article (7 April 1915, p. 18) gave an interesting description of Lorraine: "His eccentric violin playing is unique in vaudeville. He discloses the genius of a great player and the shrewdness of a showman. The result is great applause."

40. Chaplin, *My Autobiography*, p. 162.

41. Anderson interview, Columbia University, p 26.

Chapter Eleven The Final Year

1. "Niles State Bank Visited By Robber," *Washington Press*, 11 March 1915, p. 1; "Bank Holdup Gets Six Years' Term," *Oakland Tribune*, 11 May 1915, p. 18; "Four Niles Men Receive Rewards," *Washington Press*, 24 July 1915, p. 1.

2. "Landmark Torn Down," *Washington Press*, 14 March 1914, p. 1.

3. "One Reelers Going," *Variety*, 21 May 1915, p. 15.

4. "Four Large Licensed Manufacturers Merge," *Billboard*, 3 April 1915, p. 54.

5. Kitty Kelly, "Tells How Name of Selig Grew Famous," *Chicago Tribune*, 30 April 1915, p.16.

6. Harold Lloyd and Wesley W. Stout, *An American Comedy*, (Longman, Greens & Co., New York, 1928), p. 82-3.

7. The Hal Roach Essanay films began with Street Fakers, still code number 101. A total of eight films were made, but it's uncertain if Roach directed them all before he left to restart his own company. *Moving Picture World*, 10 July 1915, p. 238; *Motion Picture News,* 22 May 1915, p. 53; *Motion Picture News*, 12 June 1915, p. 53.

8. "Now Talking of Faces: Cost of Countenances," *Oakland Tribune*, 16 May 1915, p. 13; "Chaplin Not Coming to New York," *Moving Picture World*, 29 May 1915, p. 1414.

9. *Moving Picture World*, 26 June 1915, p. 2081.

10. "Chaplin Barkers Prove Drawing Cards," *Motion Picture News*, 10 July 1915, p. 47.

11. Anderson interview, Columbia University, p. 33.

12. *New York Dramatic Mirror,* 18 August 1915, p. 32.

13. *Motion Picture News*, 30 October 1915, p. 99.

14. *Township Register,* 10 July 1915, p. 1.

15. Official Program for *The Man From Mexico*, 24 November 1915, courtesy of Kely McKeown and Steve Pool.

16. Anderson held onto *Humanity* and premiered it in rough cut form at the Tudor Theater in New Orleans. He tried to release it in May 1917 on a states rights basis through the Select Photoplay Company. It was released again through Renowned Pictures Corporation in January 1918, but this time as *Naked Hands*. Only a two-reel version of *Naked Hands* still exists.

17. Gloria Swanson, *Swanson on Swanson*, (Random House, New York, 1980), p. 37-8.

18. *Ibid.*, p. 46.

19. *Ibid.*

20. Phillips, p. 22.

21. *Township Register,* 8 October 1915, p. 1.

22. Phillips.

23. *Moving Picture World*, 11 September 1915, p. 1817.

24. Anderson interview, Columbia University, p. 33.

25. "Big Shake-up in Local Essanay Co.," *Township Register,* 21 January 1916, p. 1.

26. "Film Plant to Have New Head," *Oakland Tribune*, 23 January 1916, p. 19.

27. Kitty Kelly, "Flickerings from Film Land," *Chicago Tribune*, 17 January 1916, p. 16.

28. "Chaplin's Enormous Offers; Turns Down $500,00 Yearly," *Variety*, 21 January 1916, p.1.

29. "Broncho Billy Breaks Range," *New York Dramatic Mirror,* 5 February 1916, p. 27.

30. *Ibid.*

31. Anderson-Friedman interview.

32. *Ibid.*

33. Anderson interview, Columbia University, p. 35.

34. Kitty Kelly, Flickers from Film Land," *Chicago Tribune*, 18 February 1916, p. 14.

35. Nixon, "Everything Died," p. 2.

36. *Ibid.*

Epilogue The Aftermath.

1. The Culver City Essanay studio was being used by Max Linder, the pioneering French comedian, for a series of two-reelers that George Spoor hoped would rival Chaplin. Linder was signed for $5,000, half Chaplin's rate, and scheduled to produce twelve films in a year. Only three were made when Linder, according to press reports, suffered a breakdown and the series was cancelled.

2. "Miscellaneous," *Inter-City Express*, 6 July 1918. p. 6; "Essanay Film Plant Figures in Lawsuit," *San Francisco Chronicle*, 16 September 1919, p. 5.

3. "Early Home of Movies Passes into Hands of Prominent Niles Man," *Township Register,* 2 July 1931, p. 1, 7; "Interest in Essanay Studio Spread in Picture Industry," *Township Register,* 23 July 1931, p. 1; "Results Promised in Attempt to Revive Niles Movie Studio," *Township Register,* 30 July 1931, p. 1, 3.

4. "Niles' Last Hope for World Movie Fame Dies as Old Essanay Studio Is Torn Down," *San Francisco News*, 22 July 1933, p. 3.

5. "Old Essanay Studio, First Film Center, is Being Dismantled," *Township Register,* 22 June 1933, p. 1; "Last Vestiges of Essanay Studio Removed," *Township Register,* 27 July 1933, p.5.

6. "Former Essanay Cowboy Regrets Studio Passing," *Township Register,* 29 June 1933, p.2.

7. "That's show biz," *Fremont Argus*, 24 April 1980, p. 14.

8. Silva's cottage is at 37189 2nd St.; Essanay bungalow #1 is 153 G St.; #2 is 37218 2nd St.; #3 is 37374 2nd St.; #4 is 37354 2nd St.; #5 is 309 School St.; #6 is 37340 2nd St.; #7 is 37324 2nd St.; #8 is 249 School St.; #9 is 37308 2nd St.; #10 is 37268 2nd St.

9. "When the Movie Stars Began," *Chicago Daily News*, 9 January 1929.

10. "'Triple Trouble' Genuine Says Spoor," *Moving Picture World*, 17 August 1918, p. 974.

11. "The George Spoor Collection," *Image*, September 1956, p. 185.

12. "Buy Longacre Theatre," *New York Times*, 14 April 1916, p. 6; "Another San Francisco Theater," *Architect and Engineer*, January 1916, p. 108; "Biggest Air Plane Built in S. F. Suburb," *San Francisco Examiner*, 8 March 1916, p. 1; *New York Times*, 2 November 1916, p. 14; "Nothing But the Truth to London," *New York Clipper*, 13

December 1916, p. 1; "Gray Taxi Head Gone; $18,000 is Missing," *San Francisco Examiner*, 17 May 1916, p. 1; "Anderson in Again," *New York Clipper,* 2 September 1916, p.13.30; *Motion Picture News*, 19 May 1917, p. 3104.

13. Anderson-Everson interview.
14. "'Bronco [sic] Billy' Recalls Films of 1911," *Los Angeles Enquirer,* 28 June 1943, p. ?.
15. Smith and Koury, *Two Reels*, p. 285.
16. Bob Thomas telephone interview by author, 1997.
17. Robert Osborne, *60 Years of the Oscar,* 1989, p. 146.
18. Kevin Brownlow, *The War, the West and the Wilderness,* (Alfred A. Knopf, New York, 1979), p. 252.
19. Information provided by David Totheroh.

References

Bell, Geoffrey. *The Golden Gate and the Silver Screen*, Fairleigh Dickinson University Press, Cornwall Books, Rutherford, 1984.

Bogdanovich, Peter. *Allan Dwan: the last pioneer*, Praeger, New York, 1971.

Bordwell, David, Janet Staiger and Kristin Thompson. *The Classical Hollywood Cinema*, Columbia University Press, New York, 1985.

Bowser, Eileen. *The Transformation of Cinema: 1907 - 1915*, University of California Press, Berkeley, Los Angeles, London, 1990.

Brownlow, Kevin. *The Parade's Gone By...*, Alfred A. Knopf, New York, 1969.

Country Club of Washington Township, *History of Washington Township*, Centerville, 1904.

Dardis, Tom. *Harold Lloyd: The Man on the Clock*, Penguin Books, New York, 1983.

Holmes, Philip. *Two Centuries at Mission San Jose, 1797 - 1997*, Museum of Local History, Fremont, 1997.

Koszarski, Richard. *An Evening's Entertainment: The Age of the Silent Feature Picture, 1915-1928*, University of California Press, Berkeley, 1990.

Lahue, Kalton C. *Mack Sennett's Keystone*, A. S. Barnes, New Jersey, 1971.

Lahue, Kalton C. *Motion Picture Pioneer: The Selig Polyscope Company*, A. S. Barnes, New Jersey, 1973.

Lahue, Kalton C. and Sam Gill. *Clown Princes and Court Jesters,* A. S. Barnes, New Jersey, 1970.

Mitchell, Glenn. *The Chaplin Encyclopedia*, B. T. Batsford, London, 1997.

Musser, Charles. *Before the Nickelodeon: Edwin S. Porter and the Edison Manufacturing Company*, University of California Press, Berkeley, 1991.

Musser, Charles. *The Emergence of Cinema: The American Screen to 1907*, University of California Press, Berkeley, 1990.

Robinson, David. *Chaplin: His Life and Art*, McGraw-Hill, New York, 1985.

For help with the Essanay personnel and selected filmographies:

Bushnell, Brooks. *Directors and Their Films: A Comprehensive Reference, 1895-1900*, McFarland & Company, Jefferson, North Carolina and London, 1993.

Connelly, Robert. *The Motion Picture Guide: Silent Film 1910-1936*, Cinebooks, Chicago, 1986.

Doyle, Billy H. *The Ultimate Directory of Silent Screen Peformers*, The Scarecrow Press, Metuchen New Jersey and London, 1995.

Halliwell, Leslie. *The Filmgoer's Companion*, sixth edition, Hill and Wang, New York, 1977.

Hanson, Patricia K, ed. *The American Film Institute Catalogue of Motion Pictures Produced in the United States: Feature Films, 1911-1920*, University of California Press, Berkeley, 1988.

Hanson, Patricia K., ed. *The American Film Institute Catalog of Motion Pictures Produced in the United States: Feature Films, 1931-1940*, University of California Press, Berkeley, 1993.

Hanson, Patricia K., ed. *The American Film Institute Catalog of Motion Pictures Produced in the United States: Feature Films, 1940-1949*, University of California Press, Berkeley, 1999.

Katchmer, George A., filmographies by Richard E. Braff,, *Eighty Silent Film Stars*, McFarland & Company, Jefferson, North Carolina and London, 1991.

Katz, Ephraim, revised by Fred Klein and Donald Dean Nolen. *The Film Encyclopedia, fourth edition,* Harper Resource, New York, 2001.

Maltin, Leonard. *The Great Movie Shorts; Those Wonderful One- and Two-reelers of the Thirties and Forties*, Crown Publishers, New York, 1972.

Moore, Joe, with Rob Farr & Richard Roberts, *Hal Roach Filmography, A Work in Progress,* 2000.

Munden, Kenneth W., ed. *The American Film Institute Catalog of Motion Pictures Produced in the United States: Feature Films, 1921-1930,* Bowker, New York, 1971.

Nash, Jay Robert, and Stanley Ralph Ross, *The Motion Picture Guide,* Cinebooks, Inc. Chicago, 1987.

Ragan, David. *Who's Who in Hollywood: The Largest Cast of International Personalities Ever Assembled,* Facts on File, New York, 1992.

Ramsaye, Terry. *A Million and One Nights*, Simon and Schuster, New York, 1926.

Spehr, Paul, with Gunnar Lundquist, *American Film Personnel and Company Credits, 1908-1920*, McFarland & Company, Jefferson North Carolina and London, 1996.

Stone, Rob. *Laurel or Hardy*, Split Reel, Temecula, 1996.

Truitt, Evelyn Mack. *Who Was Who on the Screen,* R. R. Bowker, New York, 1983, 3rd Ed.

Yallop, David A., with filmography by Samuel A. Gill, *The Day the Laughter Stopped: The True Story of Fatty Arbuckle,* St. Martin's Press, New York, 1976.

Index

Italic numerals signify illustrations.